Nature & History
in the Potomac Country

Nature & History
in the Potomac Country

From Hunter-Gatherers to the Age of Jefferson

JAMES D. RICE

The Johns Hopkins University Press

Baltimore

The Johns Hopkins University Press
2715 North Charles Street
Baltimore, Maryland 21218-4363
www.press.jhu.edu

Library of Congress Cataloging-in-Publication Data
Rice, James D., 1963–
Nature and history in the Potomac country : from Hunter-Gatherers to the age of
Jefferson / James D. Rice.
p.   cm.
Includes bibliographical references and index.
ISBN-13: 978-0-8018-9032-1 (hardcover : alk. paper)
ISBN-10: 0-8018-9032-2 (hardcover : alk. paper)
1. Potomac River—Environmental conditions. 2. Potomac River Valley—
Environmental conditions. 3. Potomac River—History. 4. Potomac River Valley—
History. 5. Indians of North America—Potomac River Valley—History. 6. Potomac
River Valley—Colonization. 7. Nature—Effect of human beings on—Potomac River
Valley—History. 8. Landscape changes—Potomac River Valley—History.
9. Human ecology—Potomac River Valley—History. I. Title.
GE55.P68R53 2009
975.2—dc22   2008011844

A catalog record for this book is available from the British Library.

*Special discounts are available for bulk purchases of this book. For more information,
please contact Special Sales at 410-516-6936 or specialsales@press.jhu.edu.*

The Johns Hopkins University Press uses environmentally friendly
book materials, including recycled text paper that is composed of at least
30 percent post-consumer waste, whenever possible. All of our book papers are
acid-free, and our jackets and covers are printed on paper with recycled content.

To the memory of
Walter B. Rice, 1937–2002

CONTENTS

The Hole in the Map

This book began with a mystery.

Much of the 14,670 square miles drained by the Potomac River offers fertile soil, good fishing, and excellent hunting. Yet early seventeenth-century maps and archaeological evidence alike show that much of the Potomac basin—a region encompassing vast swaths of modern-day Virginia, Maryland, West Virginia, and Pennsylvania—was uninhabited on the eve of European colonization. Although the lower Potomac was thickly settled, virtually no one lived along the Potomac above modern-day Washington, D.C., or along major tributaries such as the Shenandoah River.

I wondered why.

I also wondered how the existence of this no-man's-land affected nearby Native American and (later) colonial societies. Did it function as a commons, perhaps, as a place where all could hunt and fish? Or as a demilitarized zone? Was it perceived as a strange and hostile wilderness or as familiar terrain?

In exploring these questions I came to an unexpected realization: that one cannot fully understand American history without first coming to terms with the long, preconquest histories of Native American societies. I also came to appreciate the centrality of nature in the lives of the peoples inhabiting the region—of all of them, whether English or Algonquian, German or Iroquoian. The further I pursued this inquiry, the more it seemed that environmental concerns moved to the center of the story.

Gradually, the story broadened into an exploration of the connections between environment and human history in the Potomac basin over the course of a millennium. It turns out that deep-time environmental forces, and human responses to them, profoundly shaped both Native American and colonial life along the river. Among other things, the region's ecology supported the rise of powerful Indian nations. Consequently, English newcomers could not simply overwhelm Natives. Instead, imaginative Native American adaptations to environmental changes created a complex cultural and diplomatic landscape to which European newcomers were in turn forced to adapt. Thus nature, Native Americans, and colonists *all* had a hand in governing the timing, extent, and character of colonization in Virginia and Maryland.

By the time of the American Revolution, Indians exercised no direct political or military power along the Potomac, but their ancestors' presence could still be discerned in the appearance of the land, as well as in the cultural, political, social, and economic lives of the region's newer inhabitants. The ancient Indian influence could be felt even beyond the Potomac basin, for the interior served as a cultural hearth for southern Appalachia, while the coastal plain spawned the plantation South. We would do well to remember that these remarkably influential cultural hearths were the products of a world created by Native Americans in the millennium before the American Revolution, because we live with the consequences to this day.

Over the years it took to write this book, I have often looked forward to the opportunity to thank the many, many people who helped along the way. It is no exaggeration to say that the final result is as much the product of their contributions as it is of my labor.

This project was very much shaped in its formative stages by conversations with Warren Hofstra and Cynthia Van Zandt. If not for them this book would have been finished years ago, but it also would have been much narrower in scope. Robert J. Brugger of the Johns Hopkins University Press also took an early interest in the book, and his advice has very much influenced its style and organization.

Much of this book was tried out first in conversations and correspondence with Dennis Blanton, Lois Green Carr, Roberta Culbertson, Gary Cummisk, Catherine Desbarats, Keith Egloff, Stuart Fiedel, Allan Greer, John Hart, David Hsiung, Richard Johnson, Laura Kamoie, Alice Kehoe, Lisa Loria, Paul Mapp, Joseph Miller, Alice Nash, Helen Rountree, Gabrielle Tayac, and Margaret Holmes Williamson. My old friends Kevin Hardwick, Larry Peskin, and Stephen Whitman were, as always, wonderful sounding boards, and they also provided comfortable places to stay during numerous research trips to Virginia, Maryland, and Pennsylvania.

Several colleagues shared their unpublished research and data. Stephen Potter provided mountains of data from new excavations above the Great Falls of the Potomac, and he always stood ready to answer questions about Potomac basin archaeology. Lois Green Carr and Jean Elliot Russo made available masses of data on colonial Maryland's social history, and Wayne Clark, Martin Gallivan, and Justine McKnight allowed me to cite some of their unpublished research.

Kathleen Bragdon, Vincent Carey, Colin Duncan, J. Frederick Fausz, James Horn, Gary Kroll, Joshua Piker, Stephen Potter, Timothy Shannon, Larry Soroka, Mark David Spence, Gabrielle Tayac, and Lorena Walsh read and commented on sections or chapters of the manuscript, offering reams of helpful advice. Two intrepid souls, Tom Wellock and Peter Welsh, read the entire manuscript just before the last major rewrite, and the two anonymous referees for the Johns Hopkins University Press suggested revisions that have made this a better (and shorter) book.

Participants in seminars at the University of Maryland, the University of Toronto, and the Omohundro Institute of Early American History and Culture read and critiqued drafts of chapters 1 through 3. Presentations at the Virginia Historical Society and at the annual meetings of the American Historical Association, the Organization of American Historians, and the American Society for Ethnohistory also put my ideas to the test. So, too, did presentations to diverse audiences at the Virginia Foundation for the Humanities, at the Potomac River Forum, at a two-day forum called "The Potomac: America's River, 1491–1789," sponsored by the National Park Service and the Potomac River Valley Consortium, and at a 2004 conference entitled "The Atlantic World and Virginia," held at Colonial Williamsburg and sponsored by the Omohundro Institute of Early American History and Culture.

I am also deeply grateful to the librarians and archivists at the Handley Regional Library in Winchester, Virginia, the George Peabody and Milton Eisenhower Libraries at the Johns Hopkins University, the Library of Virginia, the Maryland Historical Society, the Maryland State Archives, the University of Virginia, and the Virginia Historical Society, and above all to the staff of the Interlibrary Loan Office at SUNY Plattsburgh's Feinberg Library.

This project involved a fair amount of travel. The Dean of Arts and Sciences, the Department of History, the United University Professions, and the Center for the Study of Canada at SUNY Plattsburgh funded research trips and travel to conferences. A Presidential Research Award and additional support from the Office of Sponsored Research at Plattsburgh made it possible to spend a semester in Charlottesville, Virginia. Fellowships from the Virginia Historical Society and the Huntington Library in San Marino, California, supported research in the collections of these remarkable institutions.

This book took a long time to write, but it would have taken longer still if not for a semester in residence at the Virginia Foundation for the Humanities, a wonderful experience that provided a much-needed opportunity to get up to full speed on this project. To Roberta Culbertson, Robert Vaughn, and my fellow fellows at the VFH: many, many thanks. A term at the Institute for Ethics and Public Life at SUNY Plattsburgh provided a reduced course load and a quiet office midway through, while the final push to complete this book came during a semester-long sabbatical from Plattsburgh.

My colleagues in SUNY Plattsburgh's History Department, Dean Kathy Lavoie and her staff, and Provost Robert Golden were completely supportive throughout. In this, as in so many other ways, they have made Plattsburgh a hidden gem of a college where the teacher-scholar model is not only held up as an ideal but also actively promoted.

Some debts go especially deep, beginning with several teachers who have not read this book in manuscript but who have nevertheless shaped it in fundamental ways: the late T. K. Barton, who loved the English language and books and who never hesitated to identify stylistic "barbarisms" when they crept into my prose; James Henretta, who has always encouraged, and modeled, bold and ambitious scholarship; and Lois Green Carr, who has inspired so many scholars with her razor-sharp mind, her prodigious appetite for archival research, her passion for getting things right, and her ability to make a pencil last an unbelievably long time.

The greatest debts are to my family: to Nancy Rice and Walter Rice for raising me in a house with no television but lots of books and conversation; to Ian Rice and Megan Rice Faiello for joining those conversations over the years; and to William Cox, Janet Cox, Pamela Forst, and George Forst, the best in-laws one could ask for. The Forsts provided a place to stay during numerous research trips to Virginia, welcoming me into their family on more evenings than I can count, and their children (Blake, Caitlin, Allison, and Kevin) kept me from dwelling too much on the day's work by always demanding one more shoulder ride or game of "circle." Finally, words cannot convey how grateful I am to Laura Rice for sharing her life with me and to Emily Rice for lighting up our household. I mention them last because, in the end, all of my thoughts lead back to them.

This book is primarily an environmental history, but it is largely peopled by Native Americans. Any attempt at writing about Indians raises certain questions about language, which ought to be addressed at the outset. For example, should one speak of "Native Americans"? "Indians"? "First Nations"? "Indigenous People"? Wherever possible I have avoided all of those terms, preferring to highlight specific individuals, communities, or nations. When necessary I refer to "the Potomac nations" or to "Algonquians" (by which I mean the people living around the Potomac and its tributaries rather than the larger linguistic family that spreads across much of North America). If called upon to generalize even more broadly, I use "Indians," "Native Americans," and "Natives" interchangeably. All are inadequate terms to capture the variety of experiences they are supposed to cover, but they nevertheless are common usage.[1]

Native names and terms can be difficult to pronounce and to remember, but, to quote the poet Robert Bringhurst, using them is "an essential gesture of respect and recognition—one I hope most readers of this book will want to make." The many Indian nations, individuals, and place names used in this book can be confusing, not because of any inherent difficulty lying in those names, waiting to trip us up, but rather because we don't often hear or read them. That the Native American material is less familiar, however, is simply another indication of how important it is to redress the balance.[2]

Another "essential gesture of respect and recognition" is using the plural form when referring to Native groups. Although it has long been conventional to write of "the Powhatan" rather than "the Powhatans," using the singular form when referring to whole groups of Native people strikes me as ungrammatical and misleading; it implies a homogeneity and timelessness to Native communities and cultures that have never existed. As historian Daniel K. Richter notes, if we are going to use the singular form for Native groups, we should do the same for non-Natives, as in "the *German* were reunited in 1990."[3]

I have retained the original spelling and punctuation of all sources, partly to avoid tampering with the authors' observations, partly to invoke the very foreign nature of the world they inhabited, and partly to serve as a reminder that we are often seeing that world through the distorting lens of their necessarily imperfect understandings. I have, however, silently modernized capitalization and have omitted italics except where the author clearly meant to use them for emphasis. I have also filled out abbreviations and converted archaic characters to their modern equivalents, so that, for example, "ye" is rendered as "the," and "condiçon" as "condition." I have also partially modernized dates. The British stuck with the "Old Style" Julian calendar until 1752, which meant that the new year began on 25 March rather than 1 January. I have converted dates falling between 1 January and 25 March so that the Powhatan uprising of 22 March 1621 (Old Style) is recorded here as having taken place on 22 March 1622. When the British switched to the Gregorian calendar, they also skipped eleven days to make up for the distortions created by the Julian year, which was slightly longer than the lunar year, but I have made no effort to correct for those eleven days: 22 March remains 22 March.

*Nature & History
in the Potomac Country*

Ahone's Gift

In the beginning, a great Hare known as Ahone created the waters and the land, the fishes and deer—and the humans.

Ahone made the world with the help of four other gods, who came as winds from the corners of the earth. After shaping the earth, the Hare paused to contemplate his creation. He pondered what kinds of creatures he should make and how he should go about introducing them into the world. Eventually he decided to begin by creating women and men. But after he had already made the first humans, the Hare had second thoughts about releasing them into the wild. The problem lay not with Man or Woman but with the world. It still seemed too dangerous a place for humans. There was no food to sustain them; nor could the humans protect themselves against the variety of spirits that roamed the newly created earth. So the great Hare decided to shelter his humans, feeding them and keeping them safe in a great bag at his dwelling place near the rising sun until he had better prepared the way for them.

Other beings soon learned of the humans. Giant cannibal spirits came to the Hare's dwelling, hoping to devour the new creatures, but the Hare would have none of this. He chastised the cannibal spirits and chased them away. Having fended off that threat, the Hare turned to the task of providing for the humans' diet and clothing. He made the water and stocked it with fish. He created the land, placed upon it a Great Deer, and provided the deer with food to browse. But the humans were still endangered, for other troublesome spirits lurked about. The gods of the four winds, who had earlier helped the Hare to make the world, now grew jealous of his new creation. Coming from the east and west, north and south, they converged upon the Great Deer, killing him with hunting poles. They feasted upon him and dressed his skin, leaving behind neither meat to feed nor deerskin to clothe the newborn humans. Again they returned to the four corners of the earth.

Once more the Hare defended his humans against malevolent spirits. The gods of the winds may have destroyed the Great Deer's skin and meat, but in dressing him they had left his short, stiff hairs scattered about. The Hare gathered these hairs and spread them over the earth. Then the Hare spoke deeply powerful words and performed equally powerful rituals over the hairs, causing each of them to grow into a new deer. The four winds could never chase down and kill so many deer; nor could they destroy the fish in the waters.

At last, decided the Hare, the earth was safe for women and men. He opened the great bag and removed the humans, peopling the land by placing a man and a woman in each country. And so the Hare created the world.[1]

This regrettably brief account of the creation, related in 1610 by Iopassus, an important figure at the Potomac River village of Patawomeck, does not focus on the importance of forming a right relationship with a single, all-powerful God. Instead it places humans in relationship with nature. The story puts deer on the land, creates plants as forage for the Great Deer, conjures into being fish and gives them a place to swim, and then, when all is ready, places humans in the midst of this bounty. We can see in Iopassus's account of the creation the foundations of his peoples' lives together: fishing, hunting, and harvesting.

My story takes its cue from his. It, too, roots humans in nature, focusing on the interplay of climate, people, plants, animals, and other forces of nature. In Iopassus's account the creator takes the form of an animal, and the four winds are characters; in this story, too, animals and weather play active roles in the affairs of humans (and humans in the affairs of the rest of nature). The story focuses on that which most concerned eighth-century Indians and eighteenth-century colonists alike: how to live on the land, subject to the bounty, constraints, and caprice of nature. It follows that over the long haul—in this case from 700 to 1800—the histories of culture and environment cannot be understood separately. Each new society in the Potomac basin entered into its own peculiar sort of relationship with the environment. The result was not always a healthy relationship, but there can be no divorce between nature and culture.

Where we live shapes *how* we live, and Iopassus's people lived at one of the most important crossroads on the Atlantic seaboard. The Potomac's size and reach alone made it an important place. The Potomac is 383 miles long and up to 11 miles wide. Draining a total of 14,670 square miles, an area nearly the size of Massachusetts and Connecticut combined, the Potomac and major tributaries such as the Shenandoah River (itself 223 miles long) encompass much of modern-day

Virginia, Maryland, and West Virginia and even a goodly chunk of Pennsylvania. The basin extends as far north and almost as far west as Pittsburgh and nearly as far south as Richmond, Virginia. It delivers an average of seven billion gallons per day into the Chesapeake Bay, a total volume of water greater than any eastern river except the Susquehanna or the St. Lawrence.

This far-reaching riverine system connected north and south, east and west, forming a crossroads akin to the juncture of the Mohawk and Hudson rivers at modern-day Albany, or the meeting of the Ottawa and St. Lawrence rivers at Montréal. The west-to-east orientation of the Potomac linked the Chesapeake Bay to the Ohio and Mississippi valleys via a portage in modern-day western Maryland. Cutting across the eastward-flowing Potomac River, numerous north-south tributaries formed wide-open valleys conducive to canoe and overland travel. The Shenandoah connected the Potomac to the southeastern quadrant of the continent, and the Cumberland and Monocacy valleys linked the Potomac to a long series of valleys extending through central Pennsylvania, New York, and into Canada. Before railroads and asphalt, these waterways and valleys constituted the superhighways of the day. The Potomac and its tributaries provided by far the best routes for anyone traversing the region by canoe or on foot; the alternatives were the Chesapeake Bay, which many travelers found less convenient and more hazardous, and the James River, which had less extensive and convenient connections to the west and north.

The Potomac and its tributaries assumed still greater importance because of their proximity to a climatic and topographic fault line. A northbound traveler from the Potomac could enter the Susquehanna River drainage by crossing a short portage in the broad, fertile Cumberland Valley. Just to the north of these portages, however, the Susquehanna and its tributaries disappear into a series of narrow valleys cutting through the Appalachian Mountains. Here the average annual temperature dropped markedly, as did the length of the growing season—often to less than 120 frost-free days, the minimum required for maize. Level, fertile, and well-drained soils could be found to the north of the juncture between the Potomac and the lower Susquehanna drainage, but they were significantly more plentiful to the south of that divide. Moreover, the fast-flowing rivers through the mountains created few freshwater marshes, a critical source of food, medicine, and building materials in the less rugged terrain of the Potomac basin and points south.

This climatic and topographic fault line corresponded to a major cultural and diplomatic fault line between southern Algonquians and northern Iroquoians. The seven thousand people who occupied the Potomac in 1608—the very first moment for which we have clear evidence of ethnicity—were Algonquians. Like other Algonquians scattered throughout the eastern woodlands, they spoke languages that were about as closely related to each other as Portuguese is to French, Spanish, and Italian. Algonquians also shared broadly similar (but by no means uniform) cultural practices and beliefs. Algonquians occupied most of the rivers feeding the Chesapeake Bay, although Siouan-speakers lived on the upper reaches of the rivers below the Potomac. The Potomac nations frequently interacted with Algonquians on the nearby James, York, Rappahannock, and Patuxent rivers, yet also maintained distinctive cultural traditions, social systems, and polities. Even within the Potomac Valley, Patawomecks saw themselves as distinct from Chicacoans, who in turn maintained an identity separate from the Yaocomacos, Piscataways, Nacotchtanks, and others. The rivers and valleys to the north of the Potomac connected the largely Algonquian and Siouan peoples of the upper South to the largely Iroquoian peoples of modern-day Pennsylvania, New York, Ohio, and Ontario. Like the Algonquian peoples of the South, northern Iroquoians were divided into many distinct nations, only a minority of which joined the famous Five Nations. But also like the southern Algonquians, northern Iroquoians shared a broadly similar set of environmental conditions, adopted similar subsistence strategies, spoke closely related languages, and had in common several key cultural practices and beliefs.

In short, the divide between the Susquehanna and the Potomac basin constituted a transitional zone between two different cultural traditions, each occupying and adapting itself to a significantly different landscape and climate. Under the right circumstances this might have fostered a lively cross-cultural trade and correspondingly amicable relationships between northern Iroquoians and the Algonquian peoples of the Potomac—but here it did not. Indeed, the troubled relationship between the two groups, rooted in culture and nature alike, became one of the central facts of life along the Potomac. Long after the advent of European colonization, the peoples of the Potomac continued to worry as much about their ancient northern foes as they did about the English newcomers.

To be sure, the influx of Europeans in the seventeenth century greatly complicated matters. The English invaders slowly absorbed the Potomac into their own colonial system, and their descendants eventually assimilated the very memory of Native peoples into the founding myths of the United States. Yet the continuation of stories begun long before the arrival of white people fundamentally shaped life along the Potomac throughout the colonial period. The river continued to function as a critically important intercultural arena. It still served as a strategic crossroads for dozens of contending Native polities, now joined by a diverse array of colonists and enslaved Africans. And even colonists were subject to the same north-south fault line that had for centuries divided northerners from the peoples of the Potomac.

Clearly, the geography of the Potomac basin exposed its inhabitants to a unique combination of powerful outside forces. Each of the four winds in Iopassus's account of the creation had a historical counterpart. On the Potomac, the strongest winds usually come from the north, and generations of Iroquoian raiders coming from that direction sculpted Potomac societies into shapes that enabled them to withstand all but the strongest gales. Breezes from the south commonly blow warm, moist air to the Potomac, bringing both nourishing rains and terrifying thunderstorms; in human terms, the rains had their counterpart in the steady flow of trade goods and cultural practices from the Algonquians who lived between Albemarle Sound and the Potomac, while the rapid late sixteenth-century expansion of the famous Powhatan chiefdom from its original nucleus on the James River all the way to the south bank of the Potomac resembled a severe thunderstorm: brief in duration but powerful. And hurricanes approach from the south and the east—much like the successive waves of colonists from England, the British borderlands, and central Europe that broke over the Potomac in the seventeenth and eighteenth centuries. Westerly breezes are less common than southerly or northerly winds and are relatively mild; nevertheless Shawnee, Delaware, and even French influences from that direction also shaped life in the Potomac basin at strategically important moments.

Telling a coherent story about a millennium of human habitation in such a large region presents something of a challenge. Part of the problem lies in the nature of the evidence. Before about 1600 we have archaeological remains supplemented by a few precious snippets of oral traditions, whereas after 1600 we have mainly written documents. Archaeology and archives tell us about very different things: documents reveal more about specific events, individuals' choices, and abstract thoughts, while archaeological remains provide insight into the workings of everyday life, material culture, settlement patterns, and subsistence strategies. The difficulty, then, is to find the common ground between archaeological and documentary evidence.

The solution adopted here is to write about that which every inhabitant of the region had in common, both before and after the advent of written sources: a relationship to the land itself. This is not exactly a new idea, for environmental historians have already fundamentally altered our understanding of early America. In a series of now-classic works, writers such as Alfred Crosby and William Cronon offered several great insights that no responsible student of early America can now ignore: first, that Indians played an active role "in reshaping and manipulating the ecosystem" by farming, fishing, hunting, and burning the woods; second, that in "the inherent conflict between the land uses of the colonists and those of the Indians," Indian ways were swept away by "the expansion of European capitalism"; and third, that Indian people themselves were swept away by European diseases to which they often had only limited immunity.[2]

Yet beyond these fundamental insights we know surprisingly little about early American environmental history, for in recent decades environmental historians have collectively turned their attention to the nineteenth and twentieth centuries. We know too little about specific places within the eastern woodlands, or about how particular events might have been rooted in the endless interplay of nature and culture. Historians know virtually nothing of precolonial environmental history, even though archaeologists and scientists have generated ample information to support such an inquiry. Nor has the environmental history of colonial-era Native Americans been sufficiently explored, except in their capacity as victims. We don't know much about the ecological imaginations of colonial farmers beyond their increasingly strong penchant for exclusive definitions of property and their ever-tightening engagement with global capitalism. But how, in their own minds, did they conceive of themselves in relation to the rest of nature? Were there ethnic variations? Competing visions within ethnic groups? And there are deeper questions to be addressed as well: what kind of interplay was there between environmental changes, social structures, land use, political cultures, economies, and diplomatic relations? How did large-scale processes shape specific events? Or, to turn the question around, how did individual people and discrete events feed into (and perhaps even redirect) broader processes such as colonial conquest and the commodification of nature?[3]

Such questions point to the need to make early American environmental history more historical, to make it more attentive to distinctions of time and place. Those who write about early American and Native American history have all too often contented themselves with generalizations—with deducing from general principles, for example, that epidemic diseases *must* have laid waste to villages throughout the Chesapeake region starting with the very first contact with Europeans in the sixteenth century.[4] But in fact there is no evidence of this; instead, different communities were afflicted with different diseases at different times, in a pattern that was contingent upon everything from the etiologies of specific disease organisms to the stresses caused by warfare, dispossession, and droughts.

Generalizations about virgin soil epidemics will no longer suffice, however, for the timing and character of individual epidemics are more than petty details; such particulars are, rather, the very stuff of which history is made.[5]

Geographical details are also critical; to counter the homogenizing tendencies of environmental histories focusing on the entire "South," or on "New England" as a whole, or even on the entire eastern seaboard, we need (in historian Mart Stewart's words) "to understand the intricate and complex relationship between humans and nature *on the local level* if we are to understand it at all."[6] The Potomac basin—a place much larger than a single field, pond, or stand of timber, yet considerably smaller than "the South" or "New England"—fits the experiences of the people who lived *there,* exactly, and not in a generic "America," "West," or other vast region. The larger swath of territory of which the Potomac was a part (whether defined as the "Chesapeake," the "South," or the "eastern woodlands") was neither monolithic nor everywhere identical. If we are to understand the lives of the people who lived there, we must better understand the particular places in which they made their homes. (And yet for all of the Potomac's uniqueness and particularity, it is still a part of colonial Virginia and Maryland, a part of the world to which Americans still look for their founding myths; thus it is a strategically important place in which to argue for the importance of environmental history.)[7]

Thinking on this modest geographical scale makes it possible to explore the precise ways in which nature and culture played out over the long term. It even makes possible a narrative, in which we can see fire, ice, drought, and the river itself changing the course of history along the Potomac. We can also see, through narrative, grand cultural forces at work in the particular lives of specific people, and simultaneously acting upon nature: we can see the rise of agriculture, revolutionary political changes, the commodification of nature, and more, always being produced and perpetuated through the actions of individual people. We can see the links between humans working and nature's work and discern the connections between work, power, consumption, and social organization. We can even make out the connections between environmental history and specific events, including wars, alliances, and everyday encounters between people on the land.[8]

In practice this means that the story told in this book is comprised of three intertwining narratives. The first narrative line traces the ever-changing relationships between shifting environmental conditions and humans' cultural, economic, and political adaptations to their natural environment. As anthropologist Julian Steward has noted, each society has a "core . . . constellation of features which are most closely related to subsistence activities and economic arrangements." Although Steward would never have countenanced a simple environmental determinism in which there is a direct and invariable connection between environment and culture, neither could he imagine a society that was not in *some* way adapted to its natural surroundings. Each society must dream up a workable relationship with nature or suffer the consequences.[9] To cite but one example, many Potomac basin groups that had previously made their living by foraging, fishing, and hunting responded to a phase of relatively long and warm growing seasons between 900 and 1300 by adding farming to the mix. They could have exercised their imagination to make other choices, yet the choice they did make was consistent with the changed climate of that four-century period.

This first narrative thread is neither simple nor linear, and it is further complicated by the fact that different people tried to mold the same environment into very different landscapes. English tobacco planters and English fur traders, for example, found the differences in their ecological imaginations irreconcilable, as did Algonquians and English tobacco farmers. It would have been possible for two such people, endowed with two very different sets of ideas about their proper relationship with nature, to walk shoulder to shoulder over the same ground and still be moving through radically different landscapes. Moreover, each of these two hypothetical individuals might well change her understanding of the landscape at any time.[10]

The second narrative strand begins with the proposition that how people chose to live within nature also has something to do with how they chose to live with one another. Thus it is possible to trace the ways in which "different groups of humans have gained or lost power" as a result of new ways of living upon the land. C. S. Lewis said it best: "what we call Man's power over Nature," he wrote in *The Abolition of Man*, "turns out to be a power exercised by some men over other men with Nature as its instrument."[11]

This is a recurring theme in the Potomac's history: it can be seen in the colonization of the Potomac by outsiders during the tenth century and again in the fifteenth and sixteenth centuries; in the rise of hierarchical societies and of hereditary chiefdoms; and in patterns of war, diplomacy, and trade between the dozens of Native American polities that lived or had strategic interests along the Potomac. The truth of Lewis's observation can also be seen in the gradual, century-long English conquest of the Potomac. Here the "[English]man's power over nature," and thus over other people, started with the domestication of cattle, horses, and swine. English hogs and cattle were the entering wedge, for they bred rapidly and ran wild in the woods—and in Indian fields. The resulting conflicts raised the issue of who had the right to adjudicate differences between Natives and newcomers. The English gradually won the argument over the place of hogs in nature, and in the process they established English sovereignty over Algonquian communities. And, notoriously, they also established a system of racial slavery in the tobacco fields, an especially thorough melding of power over nature and power over people.

The third narrative strand builds upon the first two: just as humans must reckon with their natural environment, so, too, they must adapt to the landscapes created by their predecessors. Again, C. S. Lewis put it best: "all long-term exercises of power," he writes, "must mean the power of earlier generations over later ones . . . Each generation exercises power over its successors: and each, in so far as it modifies the environment bequeathed to it and rebels against tradition, resists and limits the power of its predecessors." The very last generation of humans, "far from being the heirs of power, will be of all men most subject to the dead hand of the great planners and conditioners." If we take this long view, Lewis asserts, it is obvious that the most innovative generations have the most power over their successors. Along the Potomac that included not only market-oriented tobacco planters but also the fourteenth-century villagers who decided to make agriculture the centerpiece of their economy and society, or the sixteenth-century communities that decided to place power in the hands of powerful hereditary chiefs, or the warriors who decided that their most inveterate enemies were their Iroquoian neighbors to the north.[12]

This third narrative reveals a dimension of colonial American history that has been almost entirely ignored. Writers commonly emphasize the transformative effects of "newcomers" upon "Natives," but have largely missed the point that "changes in the land" predating colonization had an equally fundamental effect in shaping colonial societies. Equally fundamental but less obvious: we've missed seeing it because the effects were less direct. Whereas colonists made changes in the land that acted directly on Indians (by introducing devastating epidemics, for example, or by allowing their livestock to destroy Indian crops), Native Americans' changes in the land acted upon colonists at one remove, mediated by politics and diplomacy. In other words, large ecological forces were inextricably bound up with human adaptations such as the rise of chiefdoms, which in turn profoundly shaped the course of postcontact history. Fledgling colonies had to respect their most powerful Native neighbors, whose cultures and politics were rooted in ways of living upon the land that had been developed in preceding centuries. The Virginians and Marylanders who eventually took over the Potomac had to adapt to both their natural environment and to the political, economic, and diplomatic configurations it had nurtured, for they were confronted at every step with a diverse array of Indian nations and individuals, each of whom had a different set of ideas about how they might exploit, survive, or revenge themselves against the newcomers.

Although this is intended mainly as an environmental history of a single river and its tributaries, it is also a story about the Native American people who lived in that network of waterways and about their enduring influence on life within its bounds.[13] It is not solely about Indians (British and German colonists, and to some extent enslaved Africans, also figure in), but nevertheless Native ways of living upon this land are central to this story. Thus it inevitably touches upon certain cherished American understandings about Indians, colonists, and nature—*misunderstandings* that have come to seem like part of the natural order but are not. I aim to complicate some of these notions, especially those seemingly natural understandings that are rooted in the persistent human habit of organizing the world into a series of paired opposites: humans versus nature, natural Indians versus artificial Europeans, and prehistory versus history.

Consider the first distinction, between humans and nature. One of the most common understandings about nature in modern America is that humans are not properly a part of it. A few writers have argued against this point of view, reminding us that "*wild*ness (as opposed to wilderness) can be found anywhere: in the seemingly tame fields and woodlots of Massachusetts, in the cracks of a Manhattan sidewalk, even in the cells of our own bodies," and that "there is no easy way to disentangle the natural and cultural."[14] But such arguments have not yet carried the day. A sense of nature as something apart from humans still suffuses the language of influential environmental writers. "Wilderness" comes to stand for all of nature, and it is by definition "pristine"—free, that is, of corruption by the presence of humans.[15]

The second understanding builds upon the first: in contemporary America, Indians are regarded as having been more deeply connected to nature than are Europeans. Here the distinction is between natural Indians versus artificial Europeans. This is an old idea. London-based executives of the Virginia Company called Indians "naturals," and the idea runs through American culture from the Boston Tea Party to recent films such as *Pocahontas*. Indians knew "the secret of how to live in harmony with Mother Earth," but not artificial Europeans: "*the white destroyed his land.*"[16] Unfortunately, this simple division confuses the present with the past. Surely we moderns are too nearly alienated from nature, but seventeenth- and eighteenth-century colonists' experiences were very different from ours; they understood their surroundings intimately, for they spent their entire lives working in nature with their bare hands, and their lives were hitched to the seasonal rhythms of plants, animals, and weather. This simple division also projects the concerns of modern-day environmentalism onto Indian people, without regard to the ecological and cultural diversity of America's Native peoples and places or to changing practices over time (which becomes a source of bitter conflict when environmentalists question the authenticity of Indians whose practices do not conform to their expectations).[17]

Thinking as if there were only two kinds of people in early America—natural Indians and artificial Europeans (joined later by Africans)—also impedes our attempts to understand the complex relationships between various Indians and colonists in the seventeenth and eighteenth centuries. Indians, if a single entity, ought not to have fought among themselves. Nor should colonists. Indians and colonists, of course, should have found no common ground. Yet Indians waged war against other Indians and worked closely with colonists. English colonists fought each other, not to mention the Dutch and the French. Such behavior begins to make sense only when we honor the ways in which people chose to identify themselves: as individuals, as kinfolk, by occupation, by village, by allegiance to a paramount chief or a patron, as men or women, as elders or youths; as Germans, Virginians, Swedes, French, Marylanders, or Dutch—and when we conceive of all people, including Indians, as the product of complex cultures rather than as uncomplicated children of nature.

The contrast between natural Indians and artificial Europeans contains within itself yet another profoundly misleading, yet seemingly natural, understanding. Writers commonly draw an implicit contrast between a timeless "prehistory" in which Native American life changed much from season to season but varied little from year to year and an almost instantaneous transformation of Indians' lives upon the arrival of Europeans. The distinction is more frequently implied than stated: it can be discerned in the common practice of beginning with a chapter describing an Indian society on the eve of colonization, then moving on to the real history in chapter 2. Although few people would consciously defend this prehistory-versus-history distinction, it meshes all too well with the habit of imagining Indians as straddling the (presumed) divide between nature and humanity: nature has (Indians had) seasons, while humans (Europeans) have history.[18]

Each of these seemingly natural distinctions—between humans and nature, natural Indians and artificial Europeans, and prehistory and history—describes two fundamentally different ways of being, two enduring essences that simply *exist*, independent of history. But the peoples of the Potomac lived in specific times and places, rooted in specific environmental settings and historical contexts; and their particular stories, in all their details, reveal the futility of drawing such distinctions. In a historical narrative, the stereotypes of natural, timeless Indians and artificial, historical Europeans explain nothing. They are exposed as simplistic, shallow, and contrived and as insufficient to support the cultural and political weight that is placed upon them.

So what difference does it make if we consider the Potomac basin as a distinctive place, rather than as a variation on the more familiar loci of early American history such as "Virginia," or "the South"? What difference does it make if we think of the peoples of the Potomac as having been bound together by their common environment, notwithstanding their separate cultural and political identities? What happens if the generalizations offered in seminal works of early American environmental history are subjected to the discipline of a narrative? And finally, what if that narrative transgresses the implicit boundaries between people and nature, Indians and colonists, prehistory and history?

To begin with, the pages that follow highlight some major turning points, some critical and defining moments in the region's history, that do not fit the standard periodization of early American history. Some of the most important turning points happened centuries before European colonization, which dramatizes the importance of Native American people as actors, as creators of their world, rather than as people who simply reacted, however courageously, to Europeans' attempts to destroy their world. Chapters 1 through 3, for example, show how the "medieval optimum," a centuries-long warm spell between the ninth and fourteenth centuries, fostered the northward spread of maize cultivation from Mexico. This, combined with a phase of accelerated population growth, led the peoples of the Potomac and their neighbors to rely increasingly on maize and other cultivated crops to feed themselves. Most crossed the point of no return by about 1300, which surely must be accounted one of the major turning points in the region's history. So must the onset of the "Little Ice Age." This cold, wet phase, lasting from the fourteenth through the nineteenth centuries, significantly shortened growing seasons, with dire consequences for agricultural communities; in response, the peoples of the Potomac abandoned their relatively egalitarian social and political orders in favor of powerful hereditary chieftaincies supported by a priestly caste.

These precolonial transformations profoundly shaped the lives not only of those who lived through them but also of seventeenth- and eighteenth-century colonists. Imaginative Native American adaptations to environmental changes between 700 and 1600 created a complex cultural and diplomatic landscape to which European newcomers were forced to adapt. These adaptations firmly established the Potomac basin as a complex transitional zone between northeastern and southeastern societies and laid down patterns of land use, diplomatic relations, and culture that profoundly shaped Indians' responses to the European presence. Those responses in turn shaped the lives of colonists, who had no way of seeing the chain of cause and effect that linked their lives to events that had transpired centuries before their ancestors even knew of America's existence. A farmer living in the Shenandoah Valley in 1800 might well have been aware that his particular form of rural life, dominated by independent small farmers, was much celebrated in the age of Jefferson, but he would have had no reason to consider how Native people in centuries past had shaped the society in which he lived.

With the advantage of hindsight we can see the connections between the long-term trajectory of Native American history in Potomac country and the long-delayed English conquest of the region: the conquest of the Native peoples of the Potomac did not begin in earnest until after 1650, after two full generations of English colonialism, while the region's first postcontact ecological revolution got underway only after 1740. Even today, centuries after the destruction of the last Indian polity along the Potomac, Native Americans' dynamic adaptations and adjustments to their ever-changing environment after 700 CE have left their mark on the human geography of Potomac country. If we want to know why colonists failed to resettle the interior for over a generation after they had destroyed the original Potomac nations or why German Lutherans were thick on the ground in the eighteenth-century backcountry while English Anglicans and Catholics predominated nearer the coast, then we must look back to those pivotal moments that gave shape to the region long before the advent of colonization.

Ahone was not alone before he made humans; even in the creation story, the Great Hare shared the pantheon with numerous other spirits. Afterward Ahone stood back from his creation, delegating another spirit, Okeus, to deal directly with humans. Okeus was frequently meddling and disruptive, but he looked after the humans' interests and taught them how to live in the world Ahone had created; from Okeus they learned how to cultivate plants, how to dress, and otherwise adapt to their surroundings. Nature and culture were always in flux, so Okeus continued to teach new lessons to his people even as Europeans arrived and began the grinding conquest that in time nearly scrubbed the original peoples of the Potomac from the face of the earth. It was under his tutelage that the region's several landscapes first took shape. And although very few people today recognize the names of these Algonquian spirits, millions of modern Americans still enjoy the blessings of Ahone's gift and live with the consequences of Okeus's lessons.

CHAPTER ONE

Ahone's Waters

The Great Hare created a dynamic, ever-changing world. Successive generations of humans accumulated knowledge about the world in which they had been placed, and they passed on their wisdom to their descendants. Plants and animals came and went over the millennia, sometimes preferring one part of the world, then another. The very rivers, coastlines, and valleys shifted shapes. Yet change came slowly. For hundreds of generations, human societies along the Potomac altered their ways by increments. People survived dramatic environmental changes and the vicissitudes of human history by adopting a highly flexible regime of hunting, fishing, and gathering wild plants that yielded a secure livelihood with a minimum of labor. In short, they were foragers—people who lived off of what they found growing, swimming, running, and flying around them—rather than domesticators of animals and plants.

Five thousand years ago nearly all of the foods that would become dietary staples for the Native peoples of the Potomac were already widely available: plants and animals, fish and fowl, deer and oyster. Groups spent much of their time on the move, carrying lightweight tool kits (atlatls, axes, pestles, awls, and the like) suitable for a wide variety of purposes. Archaeological sites dating to this era show no indications of year-round, long-term occupations, which strengthens the impression of people who were mobile generalists, few in number and thus with room to range widely in search of a highly diverse variety of foods and other supplies. And in the broadest sense, developments from 5,000 years ago to about 700 CE were simply variations on increasingly well-established themes. The human population grew very, very slowly. As the population inched upward, communities increasingly spent a part of each year at a permanent base camp, and they likely developed ever more elaborate annual subsistence cycles, social organizations, and ceremonial lives. The basic logic of subsistence and settlement patterns, however, still revolved around a diversified diet of fish, wild plants, shell-fish, and game.[1]

Ahone's World

The Chesapeake Bay was still under construction when the first humans appeared on the scene some eleven thousand years ago. The glaciers left over from the last Ice Age had locked up so much water that sea levels had yet to rebound from a low point of a hundred meters below current levels (consider that a mere ten-meter drop today would expose 75 percent of the floor of the Bay). The Susquehanna River flowed where the northern Chesapeake Bay stands today, and the mouth of the Susquehanna was located dozens of miles to the east of the modern Atlantic coastline. The Potomac River was a tributary of the Susquehanna. The Bay itself emerged very slowly, only gradually spreading over the drowning Susquehanna River as global temperatures warmed, glaciers melted, sea levels rose, and salt water pushed back freshwater streams and rivers.[2]

Ten thousand years ago, July temperatures averaged about five degrees cooler than today, and the region received much less precipitation. Tundra lay just to the north and west of the Potomac Valley, which was itself covered with vegetation more often found these days in Canada. Spruce and pine dominated, with the occasional deciduous birch and alder breaking the near-monopoly of coniferous trees. Ferns, mosses, and sedges sheltered under their needles. Perhaps ten thousand years ago gaps began to open in the forest; pines became more common while spruce became less so. Oaks made an occasional appearance, but there were not so many that people could count on gathering nuts for food (although that would later become a critical part of the forager's diet). The prevalence of spruce and pine over hardwoods providing mast and browse meant that deer could live, but not really flourish, in these forests. Nor had oysters or anadromous fish (salt-water fish that spawn in fresh water) such as shad and herrings established them-selves in the pre–Chesapeake Bay ecosystem.

By five thousand years ago rising temperatures and sea levels caused the Poto-mac River to empty into the expanding Chesapeake Bay rather than merging with the Susquehanna River. The still-dry but increasingly warm climate caused more lightning strikes and more fires, which opened up spaces for herbs and shrubs, such as blueberry, elderberry, and goldenrod. New food sources that eventually provided critical parts of the foragers' diets began to emerge. Oaks now dom-inated the forests, along with hickory, beech, chestnut, pine, and walnut. The improved mast and browse supported burgeoning populations of white-tailed deer. Wetlands spread, harboring useful plants, fish, and fowl. Clams, crabs, and oysters took root in the new Chesapeake Bay, and migratory fish runs were establishing themselves. The woods teemed with deer, and turkeys, bears, and over a hundred other mammal species roamed the landscape. More than thirty species of fowl flew overhead.

By three thousand years ago the topography and watercourses of the Potomac basin broadly resembled those of today. Then as now, the tides pushed salt water up to sixty miles upriver from the Potomac's mouth. These lower sixty miles of the river, called the "outer coastal plain," are bordered by low, slightly rolling hills punctuated by the mouths of numerous creeks and rivers. Some of these are quite wide, more like small bays than rushing creeks. The shoreline and the water often bleed together into extensive marshes and wetlands. Saltwater marshes predominate near the river's mouth, but even there the upper reaches of the wide, slow-moving streams include freshwater marshes filled with marine life, lilies, wild rice, tuckahoe, sedges, and cattails. Much of the surrounding soil is sandy and infertile, supporting mainly pines, but there are also fertile floodplains along the tributaries; the soil contains few rocks, for the bedrock is buried beneath millions of years of sedimentary deposits from higher elevations. Two rivers roughly parallel the Potomac: the Rappahannock to the south and the Patuxent to the north. Together the three rivers form two long peninsulas: in Maryland, a wedge of territory running all the way up to modern-day Washington, D.C., and in Virginia the "Northern Neck," a finger of land extending even farther inland.

The inner coastal plain, a tidal yet freshwater zone, begins sixty miles upriver from the Bay and extends to the impressive cascades at the upstream end of Washington, D.C. The hills along this thirty-mile stretch of the Potomac are somewhat higher than on the outer coastal plain, often forming low bluffs such as the one now occupied by George Washington's home at Mount Vernon. The Potomac's tributaries run more swiftly here, and their mouths are generally narrower than the bay-like openings on the outer coastal plain. The narrowed channels frequently overflow, depositing a fair amount of fertile soil on floodplains and river terraces. A diverse array of deciduous trees thrive on the inner coastal plain's varied topography and soils. Yet the rivers' flows are not so swift as to prevent freshwater marshes and swamps from forming nor spawning fish from traveling far up the tributaries each spring. Altogether, about 10 percent of the 14,670 square miles in the Potomac basin is in the coastal plain.[3]

Above Washington, D.C., the river runs shallow (often no more than two to four feet deep during droughts), with several rapids. The first set of rapids, just west of the modern Washington, D.C., line, is known as the Little Falls, to dis-

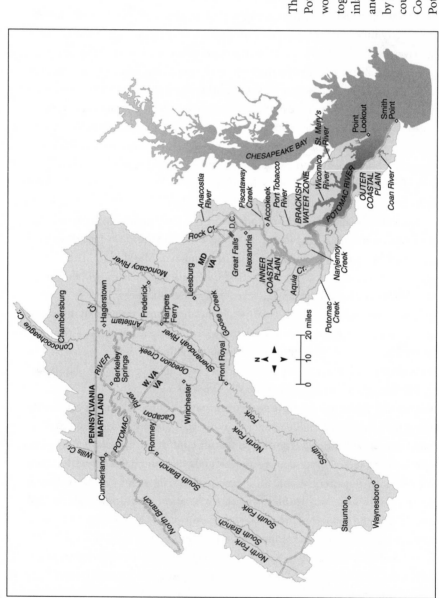

The Potomac basin. The Potomac country was a world of waterways, knitting together western mountains, inland valleys, the Piedmont, and the coastal plain. Drawn by J. Willoughby. Base map courtesy of the Interstate Commission on the Potomac River Basin.

tinguish it from the Great Falls. At the Great Falls the river suddenly drops more than two hundred feet over a series of rocky shelves. This is a heady drop for such a large river; a white-water kayakers' guide notes that this "ridiculously danger-ous-looking" stretch "has only been run by deranged experts."[4] At some places the river cuts through sheer rock walls up to two hundred feet high.

Above the falls lies the Piedmont, a belt of substantial, rolling hills between the Great Falls and the eastern front of the Appalachian Mountains that accounts for about 30 percent of the land drained by the Potomac and its tributaries.[5] Here the Potomac narrows considerably. Carving narrow channels around a number of low-lying, fertile islands, the river bends and twists around the hills. There are more rapids at Seneca Falls, some ten miles above the Great Falls. Many of the tributaries here are small, amounting to no more than steep ravines with rapid, seasonal flows. Even the largest of them, the Monocacy River, moves too quickly to widen much at its juncture with the Potomac. The Monocacy, working with the grain of the mostly north-south ridges of the Piedmont, carves out a notably fertile valley of its own, as do several smaller tributaries such as Goose Creek and Catoctin Creek.

The western edge of the Piedmont is bordered by the easternmost ridges of the hundred-million-year-old Appalachian Mountains, a patchwork of volcanic and granite rocks known locally as Catoctin Mountain, South Mountain, and the Blue Ridge. The utterly charming Middletown Valley separates Catoctin Moun-tain and South Mountain on the north side of the Potomac, while the south bank is more uniformly rugged. The Potomac blasts right through these moun-tains, cutting a thousand-foot notch in the mountains near modern-day Harpers Ferry, West Virginia. The Potomac is still working on the mountain here, trying to deepen the shallow channel running over the bedrock.

The horizon opens up rather suddenly at the west end of the notch, where the Shenandoah River merges with the Potomac at Harpers Ferry. Here the moun-tains give way to the wide-open Shenandoah Valley (to the south) and Cumber-land Valley (to the north). The two valleys, each of which is up to twenty miles wide, are rimmed by mountains rising one to two thousand feet above the valley floor. The various branches of the Shenandoah extend over a hundred miles to the south and west, where their headwaters compete for rainfall with streams that drain into the Ohio and Mississippi rivers. To the north of the Potomac, a series of tributaries such as Conococheague Creek and Antietam Creek water the wide Cumberland Valley, which extends well into modern-day Pennsylvania. To-gether, the Shenandoah and Cumberland valleys form the Potomac basin's share of a great inland trough running from far southwestern Virginia to Canada's St.

Lawrence River. These valleys are more nearly level than any other part of the Potomac basin, though the terrain is somewhat rolling in the southern reaches of the Shenandoah Valley and the western reaches of both valleys. The valley floors are laced with long, steep ridges in some places, and limestone and shale outcroppings stud the soil, which is quite rich and well drained. Before they were cleared by farmers, the valleys' fertile soils were covered with a mixed deciduous forest similar to that found in the Piedmont.

The ridges and valleys above the Piedmont cover about 7,500 square miles, over half of the entire Potomac basin. They continue beyond the western edge of the Cumberland Valley, where the river punches through another high ridge before opening onto a series of smaller north-south valleys. Beyond the last of these valleys lies the extensive Appalachian Plateau, of which less than a thousand square miles contribute to the Potomac. The river has its source here at an elevation of about three thousand feet, at a place marked by the "Fairfax stone," a 1746 marker that now forms the western boundary of modern-day Maryland with West Virginia. Long since vandalized and replaced, the stone originally stood in a dense wood; now it is the center of a small state park with well-tended lawns shaded by oaks and pines.

The Peoples of the Potomac at 700

By 700 CE people already lived throughout the Potomac basin, from the upper reaches of the Shenandoah River to the Chesapeake Bay. Each group had developed an intricate annual round of gathering, fishing, and hunting that enabled its members to enjoy a diverse diet and to avoid an overreliance on any one source of food. Community members regularly split apart to pursue their varied seasonal tasks, but they returned repeatedly to a central base camp. They preferred to locate these semipermanent settlements at ecological transition zones, typically along a navigable stream that was both close to the Potomac and adjacent to a freshwater marsh.[6] Although the details varied, the peoples of the Potomac broadly resembled each other in their subsistence strategies and thus shared strikingly common life experiences and relationships with the natural world.

The prominent anthropologist Marshall Sahlins once wrote that "if economics is the dismal science, then the study of hunting and gathering economics must be its most advanced branch." Even piecing together the annual round of a single community's movements from one source of food or other necessities to the next can be frustratingly difficult for archaeologists. At a certain basic level, it is a matter of connecting the dots on a map representing a scattered array of sites that may or may not have been in use at the same time or by the same groups. Connecting those dots is not completely impossible, however, thanks to the insights gleaned from modern studies of mobile bands of hunters, gatherers, and fishers. Foragers worldwide, it has been noted, tend to share certain common characteristics: most notably, a band organization in which groups united by some degree of kinship come together and disperse at intervals throughout the year in order to exploit seasonal natural resources, for rituals, to fulfill social obligations, and to mingle or fight with other bands. They tend to prefer "exogamous" marriages (outside the band), which requires (and promotes) alliances with neighboring groups; group members have equal access to all natural resources; and economic and social relations are based on reciprocity rather than competitive accumulation (though competitive *gifting,* in which sharing creates obligations, is not uncommon). Hunter-gatherers do not simply wander about; instead they think carefully and talk through each decision. Given the dire consequences of a failed experiment, they are fairly conservative about sticking to familiar places rather than experimenting with new spots for gathering, fishing, and hunting.[7]

Such generalizations, however, do not tell us about the rhythm and texture of lives lived along the Potomac. For that we need to turn to the work of archaeologists, whose reconstructions of ancient settlement patterns begin with one essential truth: people need to eat just about every day. Thus connecting the dots between different archaeological sites is a matter of noting the presence of shells, bones, and other food remnants at each site; or, in the absence of food remains, identifying the food and other key resources that were available or the types of tools found there. Since most foods are readily available only part of the year, it is possible to make educated guesses about the seasonal rounds of local bands: deer-hunting in the Potomac basin, for example, is best done in the fall through midwinter; oystering when the water is tolerably warm (oysters were gathered by divers); fishing during the annual runs of migratory shad, herrings, and the like, and to a lesser extent throughout the summer; and gathering wild plants between spring and fall.

In combination, modern ethnographic observations and archaeological surveys suggest that Potomac residents generally came together for a good part of the year at a single base camp near the mouth of a tributary of the main river, where they could take advantage of large oyster beds or prime fishing locations. (This may account for the increasing use of relatively heavy and easily broken ceramics to supplement other vessels such as baskets and sacks: the "container revolution" in this region had begun around 1100 BCE, and was still in progress in 700 CE.) From their base camps people could also go out on forays to hunt, fish, or oyster at secondary sites and to gather plants (the lower reaches of these tributaries tend to have a rich mixture of marshes, swamps, and uplands, which together contain a wide variety of useful plants). When the most bountiful season at the base camp was over, the community broke into small groups that mostly headed into the interior, following the streams to upland locations where the hunting was good.[8]

Local ecological regimes gave birth to variations on the base camp/outlier settlement model. The most common permutations of the system grew out of varying degrees of access to shellfish, fish, and deer. People on the lower Potomac devoted considerable effort to harvesting shellfish, while groups closer to the fall line enjoyed superior access to anadromous fish runs. Deer assumed proportionately greater importance for those living above the fall line.[9] Consequently the Potomac basin encompassed three zones—the inner coastal plain, the outer coastal plain, and the interior valleys above the fall line—distinguished by their inhabitants' means of subsistence, settlement patterns, and social organization.

Recognizing this general pattern of social fusion at a base camp alternating with fissioning off into outlying procurement areas, however, does not mean that we have recovered the experiences of the people who followed it. That requires imagination, which in turn requires the willingness to speculate and even to be wrong. But that is a risk worth taking, because sticking to a purely analytical approach to recovering the past, without considering how individuals felt, smelled, and saw the world they moved through, disregards their humanity; and consistently disregarding their humanity amounts to denying it altogether. Better, then, to indulge in some informed speculation, at least to the point of formulating questions.

The extensive research of archaeologist Stephen Potter on the lower Potomac provides ample fodder for such speculations. Potter's excavations on the Coan River and in adjoining portions of the lower Northern Neck suggest how varied and complex the merging and splitting of local groups could be, and they hint at the flavor of life in this outpost on the lower Potomac River. The center of life here was in one of several base camps, the most prominent of which was at Boathouse Pond, a small bay some two miles above the mouth of the Coan River. Photographed from above the site shows up only as a large swath of dark soil in a cleared field, but below the surface are ample indications of what went on there thirteen centuries ago. Mostly there are oyster shells—mountains of them, spreading over many acres—marking "a village site where a local or regional band gathered as a complete unit for several months during a particular season." Smaller sites scattered along the Coan River within a mile of Boathouse Pond contain mostly shell middens, while several very small upland sites a few miles away "seem to have been specialized procurement sites or temporary camps designed primarily to exploit the resources of the interior uplands."[10]

It is well worth imagining Boathouse Pond on a bright day in early summer in 700 CE. The scene might begin with a boy and a girl taking turns plunging beneath the surface of the pond and bursting to the surface with clusters of oysters in hand, then splashing ashore to hand them over to several women who are alternately opening and drying the oysters on racks above a small fire, or weaving reeds into a basket, or filling a basket with crushed oyster shells for the potter's use. A five-year-old child is gathering kindling for the fire, while an infant crawls about discovering interesting pieces of driftwood and digging in the sand with a mussel shell. But where are the men? Perhaps the boy resting from his last dive wishes he were out at the Coan River with them, trying to capture a prize sturgeon, or at a nearby marsh hunting beaver or fowl. Looking forward to the cool autumn as he baked in the sun, the boy might imagine the hustle-and-bustle of the preparations for the now-familiar move into the interior, then packing mats, baskets, and tools several miles to the upper reaches of a creek feeding the Coan River. Perhaps by now he could summon from his memory the sharp scent of the autumn camp near the creek's headwaters, mingling autumn leaves with woodsmoke and the smell of drying venison. In previous years he has stayed with the women to set up shelters, gather nuts, and process the venison and hides brought home by his elders or to practice hunting by snaring small game in his traps, but maybe this time he will join the men for the hunt. If he did go, would his sister and mother be relieved to have him gone? Would they relax in the absence of his increasingly masculine presence in what they thought of as a woman's place? Or would they miss his help as they scraped hides and ground acorns? Or would his sister even be around by then? Bands often come together in the autumn for ceremonies, diplomacy, and society—perhaps she will go home with a new husband.

Such speculations about how people at Boathouse Pond experienced even a single afternoon in July inevitably raise questions about their social lives with each other and with outsiders. For example, could they travel freely beyond their usual bounds? Were people from the nearby Nomini River allowed to pass through the Coan River? The best evidence suggests that in 700, the peoples of the Potomac probably did not divide the world into distinct territories from which they systematically excluded outsiders. If they were territorial, we would expect to find fortified villages (to defend their territory), distinctive local ceramic styles and mortuary practices (due to lack of interaction with outsiders or to conscious expressions of local identities), and other material signs of exclusivity.

Archaeological evidence, however, shows just the opposite: there were no fortifications, but broadly similar ceramic types and mortuary practices could be found across thousands of square miles of territory. Albemarle ware, a coil-constructed, rimless, rounded or semiconical shaped, cord-marked style, was ubiquitous in the ten-thousand-square-mile interior from about 300 CE to 1300. On the coastal plain, Mockley ware vessels, largish, thick-walled, coil-constructed jars with direct rims, rounded or semiconical bottoms, wide mouths, and minimal decorations, spread throughout the coastal plain from the James River to the Severn River and on the Delmarva Peninsula.[11]

Perhaps the most striking evidence that the peoples of the Potomac did not exclude each other from carefully bounded territories comes from the widespread access they had to rhyolite deposits in western Maryland. Remarkably, parties from all points of the compass traveled to the quarries, lingered at unfortified processing stations in the foothills, and packed rhyolite (an excellent material for making all manner of stone points) back to their homes. Thus a large swath of territory between Conococheague Creek and the Monocacy River formed an exceptionally open domain in which people could freely travel and exploit common resources.[12]

The social and political structures erected by the peoples of the Potomac appear to have been just as fluid as the relationships between the different societies. There are no signs of public works projects, military buildups, or of a priestly caste. It is possible that a hierarchy developed at prime fishing and oystering locations or that charismatic individuals established temporary dominance over their groups. But if so, that hierarchy was not deeply embedded in culture, for there is little evidence of it in burial practices or any material remains.[13]

Fluid and egalitarian societies, however, still have complex social organizations. Consider again the complex logistics of the annual round of gathering, hunting, and harvesting undertaken by Potomac Valley societies. This annual subsistence cycle required a detailed and intimate knowledge of botany, animal behavior, and weather and a wide variety of skills ranging from building traps and snares to making ceramics, weaving mats and baskets, constructing fishing weirs, navigating rivers, applying herbal remedies, and diving for oysters. No single person could absorb all of this knowledge, and each generation had to learn it anew.

Consequently, individual members of a small society in the Potomac basin *had* to differ from each other but in such complementary ways that together they made up a functioning society capable of sustaining itself in a highly complex relationship with a diverse and ever-changing natural world. They also had to continually pass on their knowledge of how to function in that world. If other gatherer-hunter societies from around the world are any indication of how this might have worked on the Potomac River, individuals passed on their knowledge to people like themselves or to whom they had some special connection: women to girls, men to boys, kin to kin. Each dimension of a person's identity—hide-tanner, herb-gatherer, woman, aunt, old woman, representative of a lineage or clan—multiplied the complexities of social life even in a small, relatively nonhierarchical society.[14]

Most of the complexities of social life in these small societies would have originated from or found expression in the group's carefully scripted subsistence activities, and for centuries those activities changed but incrementally. But what would happen if something forced people to reconsider how they organized their intricate subsistence systems? The Potomac basin in 700 supported only a modest population; more people lived on the coastal plain than in the interior, possibly because the lack of anadromous fish runs and shellfish above the fall line made it difficult to feed a large population during the lean times of early spring.[15] But what would happen if population growth accelerated? Would communities modify their settlement patterns? Would they become more territorial? Would they alter their political and social orders? The small gatherer-hunter societies of the Potomac would soon face this test, for by 800 agriculture, one of the most transformative forces in human history, was already working its way toward the valley.

CHAPTER TWO

Foragers into Farmers

The foragers of the Potomac adapted to their environment in careful increments, altering their habits but little from one generation to the next. Yet the foragers' incremental adaptations to their environment before 900 CE contained the seeds of more radical changes that would come after that date, when climate change, population growth, a deepening commitment to farming, and competition for prime village locations caused Potomac societies to transform their relationships with nature, their landscape, and their social and political organizations. These far-reaching changes were rooted in an increasing dependence on the fruits of agriculture, a slow-motion revolution that unfolded bit by bit over the course of several centuries as individual people and small groups chose to more efficiently harness solar power by selecting, storing, planting, and carefully cultivating starchy, calorie-packed seeds such as maize, beans, and squash. The energy from these plants fueled an unprecedented increase in the region's population as well as major changes in community life, social and political organization, warfare, and diplomacy, the cumulative effect of which was to profoundly reshape power relations among the peoples of the Potomac. Ultimately farming altered nature itself, modifying both the ecology of the Potomac basin and the ways in which Potomac peoples imagined and organized their landscapes.

Flirting with Farming, 900–1300

Maize, the centerpiece of Native agriculture in the eastern woodlands, emerged as a major crop in the middle Mississippi Valley with the onset of several centuries of consistently warm weather after about 750. This warming trend coincided with the introduction of a new variety of maize by way of Mexico, the American Southwest, and the Mississippi Valley: northern flint, a variety that had larger kernels and required a shorter growing season than its predecessors. The combination led to increased reliance on maize to the north, east, and west of the middle Mississippi Valley: maize appeared in the momentarily well-watered Great Plains and as far north as the Canadian Shield—almost anywhere, in fact, where the frost-free growing season exceeded the 120 days required by northern flint maize. It moved quickly into the northeast, appearing on the upper Susquehanna River and on the far upper reaches of the Potomac River in the late eighth century.[1]

Archaeologists working in Potomac country have uncovered less than a handful of seeds and kernels from 900 to 1300, but they have found plenty of other signs that people were experimenting with domesticated plants.[2] The paucity of seeds is not all that surprising: boiling and digestion destroyed most of the evidence, and some important sites were excavated without separating out and identifying floral remains (a rueful archaeologist writes of one excavation that "unless a large portion of charred corncob had popped up on the end of a shovel blade, the untrained laborers hired to do most of the digging . . . would not have noticed or recognized plant remains").[3]

The supporting evidence of widespread experiments with maize, squash, and beans is compelling, however. After 900, for instance, people increasingly developed tooth decay and other disorders associated with a high-carbohydrate diet.[4] In addition, potters gradually altered the shape and materials of their ceramics to make them more suitable for boiling starchy cultigens. Pre-900 ceramics normally had thick walls, conical or spherical shapes, wide mouths, were often coil-constructed, and used large-caliber quartz and sand tempering. Such vessels were fine for storage but cracked when heated and cooked poorly and thus were unsuitable for cooking foods such as beans and maize. To create vessels that could more efficiently conduct and hold heat without cracking, potters began making thinner-walled, globular-shaped vessels with smaller mouths, reduced the amount of tempering materials used to bind the clay, used fine-grained limestone and shell tempering instead of quartz and sand, and moved away from coil construction.[5] And in still another indication of farming's increasing importance, communities modified their settlement patterns along more agrarian lines, gradually consolidating their extensive networks of numerous small camps into more compact and simplified networks that also encompassed land suitable for agriculture.[6]

Notwithstanding these experiments, the peoples of the Potomac had good reason to stick with proven ways of hunting and gathering. If any one food became scarce, the tremendous diversity of their diet made it easy to adjust. Also, people in hunter-gatherer societies spend far less time working than do people in agricultural societies—as little as fifteen hours per week. Any community that decided to abandon foraging and hunting in order to concentrate more heavily on cultivated plants would be letting itself in for more work while actually undermining its economic security by putting all of its eggs in one basket. Moreover, the peoples of the Potomac began using the bow and arrow at about the same time that they commenced experimenting with agriculture. With this new weapon they could hunt more effectively, thus improving their diet without having to alter their former subsistence practices. Finally, the climate during these centuries was often droughty, a phenomenon that is recorded in charcoal-laden sediments on the bottoms of the Chesapeake region's waterways; under these circumstances one could not always count on getting in a good harvest.[7]

Consequently, the peoples of the Potomac did not simply leap into farming and leave their foraging ways behind at the first opportunity. Instead they integrated domesticated plants into their time-tested annual subsistence cycles while still spending much of the year collecting wild plants, fishing, hunting, and oystering. Potters accommodated this diverse diet by continuing to make older-style vessels appropriate for storing gathered foods even as they also produced state-of-the-art vessels suitable for cooking the new cultivated plants. The teeth of people living in the Potomac Valley after 900 also graphically illustrated the in-between nature of their diets, for they suffered in equal measures from tooth decay (from eating soft, starchy cultivated plants) and rapid tooth wear (from eating meat and uncooked plants).[8]

Despite these disincentives, Potomac societies did slowly and hesitantly alter their ways to accommodate the demands of cultivating domesticated plants, possibly because those calorie-rich plants fueled accelerating population growth that made it increasingly difficult to survive by fishing, gathering, and hunting alone. The peoples of the Potomac became noticeably more sedentary, village-based, insular, and territorial after 900, and they showed signs of creating increasingly distinctive and localized cultures. Long-distance treks to the rhyolite quarries and processing stations at South and Catoctin mountains, for example, petered out after 900—a clear sign of declining interaction among the peoples of the Potomac.[9]

Local societies also adopted distinctive settlement patterns, mortuary practices, and ceramic traditions. By 1150, for instance, the northern-influenced "Montgomery complex" appeared along the Monocacy River and on the Potomac River above the fall line. The people of the Montgomery complex stood apart from their neighbors. They made an earlier and more significant commitment to agriculture and to village life than did people living on the coastal plain, and they developed very different ceramic techniques. Their mortuary practices (shallow graves in which single individuals were buried in flexed positions, and normally without grave goods) contrasted sharply with those of upper Shenandoah Valley residents, some of whom constructed accretional mounds in which the deceased were layered in an upward-growing cemetery. The size and spacing of the Shenandoah mounds suggests that some kind of political organization bound together groups of hamlets there, unlike the Montgomery complex villages. Moreover, Montgomery complex houses were much smaller than dwellings in the southern Shenandoah, perhaps indicating different ways of reckoning kinship.[10]

That experiments with agriculture were linked to sharper divisions between increasingly localized societies seems clear enough, but it is much harder to say who gained or lost power as a result. Did some people reject agricultural production, preferring to maintain a more mobile existence? If so, did they live separate lives, or did they struggle against more sedentary types over their community's direction? Did they continue to enjoy certain advantages over farmers? And what of the women, who appear to have taken primary responsibility for farming? Did this give women more freedom in choosing their marriage partners or help them to exercise more power within their marriages? Were there clans, moieties, or special societies that gained or lost power as a consequence of the transition to agriculture? Unfortunately, we lack even such rudimentary information about social organization in this period; we can make only partially informed guesses about the ways in which experiments with agriculture shaped life within each community along the Potomac.

What *is* clear is that for several centuries after 900 the peoples of the Potomac gradually integrated domesticated plants into their diets, and thus added the work of clearing, planting, cultivating, and harvesting fields to their annual round of subsistence activities. Although this altered relationship with nature went hand in hand with modified settlement patterns, social relations, and culture, the Natives' reluctance to fully commit themselves to farming muted the extent of social and cultural changes. The thirteenth-century peoples of the Potomac remained *societies with agriculture* rather than *agricultural societies*. Yet by 1300, cultivated plants had already altered their very imaginations. They had absorbed the notion that one could select and preserve seeds from the most productive plants, wait until spring to plant those seeds in carefully selected and prepared soil, and protect the emerging plants from competitors and predators. The peoples of the Potomac could now at least conceive the possibility of depending more heavily on agriculture. And if they did come to rely on agriculture, what could be more natural than to take the subtle modifications to social relations and cultural life that had accompanied early experiments with agriculture and use them as templates for the creation of new societies?

Climate, Plants, and Conflict, 1300–1500

In the fourteenth century, the warm "Medieval Optimum" gave way to a centuries-long cold spell known as the "Little Ice Age." In combination with the disruptive effects of population increase and a deepening dependence upon agriculture, the new weather pattern forced major adjustments upon people living throughout the eastern woodlands. As each society modified its economy or political order to meet these new challenges, the changes rippled outward from their places of origin, setting in motion additional changes well beyond their source. The resulting tempest set off a vast reshuffling of peoples, led to increased warfare and territorialism, created new patterns of trade and alliance, and necessitated a new set of relations between the peoples of the Potomac and their natural environment.

Temperatures between the fourteenth and eighteenth centuries averaged several degrees cooler than in the preceding centuries. This may seem like a minor difference, but even a modest decrease in average temperatures translates into significantly shorter growing seasons and thus greatly increases the chance of a catastrophic crop failure. The Little Ice Age brought more late spring and early autumn frosts and more cool and rainy summers, all of which could curtail or even ruin a harvest. Such events were potentially deadly, for population sizes are limited not by periods of maximum or even average food resources but rather by the minimum resources available during periodic food shortages: it's not enough to have good harvests in some or even most years, because people need to be able to feed themselves *every* year.[11] Without extensive long-distance trade networks in food to get them through the bad years, communities that depended upon farming were hard-pressed to make it through poor harvests. To the north of the Potomac and in higher elevations within the basin, the growing season often dropped below the minimum 120 days required for maize, making such places particularly susceptible to crop failures and lowered yields.[12]

Potomac societies also had to reckon with accelerating population growth. A slowly tightening circle of population growth (albeit at a very slow, almost imperceptible rate of increase) and increasingly year-round residency had been at work for centuries before 900 CE, long before any significant experiments with cultivated plants. Potomac societies had gradually found ways to limit the travel

necessary for the group's subsistence through increasingly efficient use of local resources. The partial commitment to agriculture after 900 promoted even
greater sedentism, for the crops required at least some attention for much of
the year, and seeds needed to be securely stored over the winter, both for consumption and for the next year's planting. The conversion of base camps into
year-round hamlets stimulated still more population growth—much more rapid
than the painfully slow growth of earlier centuries—partly because of the addition of calorie-rich corn and other starchy plants to peoples' diets and partly
because year-round settlements made it possible to have more children.[13] One by
one Potomac communities reached the point of no return: each, at some point,
grew large enough that they could no longer feed themselves without calorie-rich
maize, beans, and squash. Though domesticated plants still provided only a minority of the calories consumed in any community, it was a substantial minority;
without those calories (as during a drought) people would have gone hungry.[14]

The peoples of the Potomac might well have adapted to climatic change and
population growth without making sudden, revolutionary changes, but many of
their neighbors in colder locales to the north found it more difficult to adjust.
Groups in central New York and on the upper Susquehanna River had made earlier and more significant commitments to agriculture than had people in most
of the Potomac basin, and their populations had grown accordingly. Unfortunately, these were also the people most directly affected by the changing climate,
for many of them lived in upland areas where, during the Little Ice Age, growing seasons frequently dropped below the minimum number of days needed
to get a crop in. Some people gravitated to fertile, low-altitude bottomlands in
the northern valleys where the winters were comparatively short, consolidating themselves into larger villages more fully dedicated to farming. Such villages
formed the foundation for the Five Nations Iroquois, the Susquehannocks, and
related groups. Other people, however, migrated longer distances to reach lower
latitudes and elevations—often finding their way into the Potomac basin.[15]

These migrations transformed life along the Potomac. They forced a major
reshuffling of peoples in the region, and in the process foragers who farmed gave
way to farmers who foraged, thus significantly altering the relations between Potomac societies and the land. And since humans' relationships with their natural
environment can never be separated from their relationships with each other,
warfare and territorialism increased and new trading and alliance networks
emerged.

It is difficult to say exactly who migrated where, for archaeological evidence is
notoriously unhelpful on this score; it is easier to spot an intrusive culture than

to identify its source and easier to note a peoples' disappearance than to pinpoint their destination.[16] The general trend of migrations, though, was clearly down the latitudes and downward in altitude, sloping along toward warmer weather and more fertile soils. Take, for example, the emergence of the "Potomac Creek complex," whose defining features include distinctive ceramics, ossuary burials (collective secondary reburials), and palisaded villages; the complex spread over most of the Potomac below the fall line beginning in approximately 1300. Archaeologists generally agree that this was an intrusive culture, and though there is no consensus on precisely where it came from, the evidence points to the north. One school of thought has it that proto-Iroquoian groups came directly from the upper Susquehanna River and central New York, from roughly the same population that would eventually coalesce into the Five Nations and the Susquehannock nation; as evidence, they cite close affinities between ceramic motifs and technology, comparable settlement patterns and subsistence practices, and similar configurations to the fortifications surrounding villages in the two areas. Another interpretation has the Potomac Creek complex originating on the Eastern Shore, as part of a chain reaction of northern groups bumping their southern neighbors still farther to the south; the last stage in this chain reaction, adherents say, brought the Potomac Creek complex to the lower Potomac. (The best evidence for this scenario is oral tradition, supported by a close linguistic affinity and enduring trade and diplomatic relations between the two areas.) Finally, there are those who note that the Montgomery complex disappeared from the Piedmont just as the Potomac Creek complex emerged below the fall line; this coincidence, together with some affinities between the ceramics and the subsistence practices of the Montgomery and Potomac Creek complexes, also suggests a chain reaction begun by northern migrants and completed by the relocation of Montgomery complex villagers to the coastal plain.[17]

Migrants from the north and west, now more than ever dependent upon agriculture, gravitated toward a few vital enclaves of rich, well-drained soils along the Potomac and its major tributaries. Eighth-century foragers could have established their base camps at any location that had fresh water and easy access to outlying procurement camps, but their farming-dependent descendants required all of that *plus* good agricultural soils and thus had far fewer village sites to choose from. Most such locations were already claimed, but planting at a less-than-ideal village site would have increased the chances of disastrous crop failures. And the harvest-time stakes were higher than ever, because calorie-rich cultigens had fueled additional population growth. The combination of natural increase and migrations considerably boosted the Potomac basin's population, thus promoting a still greater commitment to agriculture. Residents' numbers on the outer coastal plain sharply increased, and whole new villages sprang up on the inner coastal plain and in the interior.[18]

One such village appeared in about 1300 near the mouth of Potomac Creek, a site that had been little used in the preceding ten thousand years. Its founders, who have been aptly characterized as "uncomfortable immigrants" who were anxious to defend their cultural distinctiveness and their newly claimed territory from their new neighbors in the region, set about building a compact and well-fortified village. Not one but several palisades encircled the village, and the outer fortifications included bastions that permitted defenders to fire upon the flanks of enemies who came too close to the walls. These palisades encompassed nearly 5,700 square meters, enough to shelter a population of perhaps 250–300 people.[19]

Like the residents of a second, and culturally very similar, new village at the mouth of Accokeek Creek (some twenty miles upriver and across the Potomac), the people at Potomac Creek chose to establish their new colony at a site adjacent to good soils, excellent fisheries, upland hunting areas, marshes and swamps, and mast-rich forests, giving them access to foods and building materials that could sustain them year-round without the necessity of long treks to distant procurement stations. Their location, taken together with the contents of trash pits within the walls, points to the very sort of annual subsistence cycle that one would expect in this place after 1300. Plant remains are dominated by wood (for housing and for fires), and the food remains that were unearthed in just one season of archaeological research included nearly ten thousand bone fragments and a wide variety of edible plants. The bone fragments included fish, turtle, turkey, and other birds but were dominated by deer, which accounted for most of the meat consumed at Potomac Creek, while the edible plants included squash and beans but were dominated by nuts and maize. Fish, a critical food resource during the otherwise lean late winter and early spring, were apparently caught, processed, and consumed mostly at satellite fishing stations away from the main village.[20]

Paradoxically, population growth at year-round agricultural settlements such as Potomac Creek turned out to be a partial solution to the problems created by . . . population growth. Farmers everywhere greatly simplify the ecosystem. They replace a variety of plants, only a few of which can be eaten by humans, with a less diverse array of plants that they *can* eat. In a natural clearing very little of the biomass can support the human population, while in a cultivated field most of the biomass goes to sustaining humans; as a result, the farmer's field can feed many more people than a gatherer's clearing. A community that controlled good farmland in addition to fishing places, uplands for hunting, and wetlands for gathering could feed a growing population, and thus field more warriors, and so could better defend its privileged location. An increasing number and complexity of fortifications around Potomac villages after 1300 reflected the strategic importance of prime village locations. Like the new fourteenth-century villages of the inner coastal plain—Potomac Creek and Accokeek—by the late fifteenth century many villages in the interior also had fortifications.[21]

Increasing warfare went hand in hand with trade and diplomacy. Some people on the outer coastal plain sharply increased their oyster harvest and began drying the surplus for trade. Ceramics from the inner coastal plain and the Piedmont found their way to southern Delaware, and ceramics and clay pipes moved between the inner coastal plain and the Shenandoah Valley. People in the Great Valley could even get their hands on shell beads from the distant shores of the Chesapeake Bay. Copper, rare in the Chesapeake, was also a favored trade good. If their ideas about trade were anything like those of their seventeenth-century descendants, they regarded the exchange of such goods as creating a sense of reciprocity that made peaceable relations possible—and they especially needed alliances in this period of increased conflict.[22]

It is a pity that the archaeological record has so little to say about the details of these wars and alliances or even about the key moments in a community's transition to living in year-round agricultural villages. How did people feel about spending more time at a fixed abode? Were women relieved at not having to carry their young children such long distances? Did they mind hoeing and planting? Did men chafe at having to hack clearings out of the woods so that women could plant their crops, or did they do so with grace and good cheer? Did women and men squabble over how to divide the labor of constructing their homes or over the design of those homes? And what was it like when newcomers arrived? Did they always fight over village sites, or were there some peaceful mergers? Either way, what was it like? How did the newcomers fit in, or how did they wage war? How did they wage peace—how would an onlooker have described a diplomatic exchange? The list of unanswerable questions is long, and frustrating to contemplate.

And yet the archaeological record, if supplemented with other sources, *can* tell us about *some* of the ways in which villagers experienced climate change, agricultural life, and the attendant social and political changes. We can catch a glimpse of these experiences by following the seasonal rounds of work and social life in a typical community.

The Five Seasons of Algonquian Life

The individual decisions made by thousands of different people over the centuries added up to grand historical developments on the Potomac, including the transition to agriculture, the emergence of year-round villages, and the colonization of portions of the Potomac by outsiders. Yet individuals' lives did not simply follow the trajectory of major historical trends. Instead their lives revolved around short and very nearly cyclical narratives. The annual round of the seasons, when fully integrated with the work of fishing, gathering, planting, and hunting, formed the central narrative of community life. By 1500 the annual cycle had been transformed by the rise of agriculture, so much so that, as far as it is possible to tell from the archaeological record, it closely resembled the rhythm of the seasons witnessed by English colonists in the early seventeenth century. (Thus in the description that follows I have drawn upon colonists' accounts wherever they are consistent with the archaeological record of the fifteenth century.) Their subsistence cycle reflected cultural notions about the proper relationship between humans and the rest of nature and about the proper relationships between different kinds of people—women and men, old and young, insiders and outsiders. The annual subsistence cycle that had emerged by 1500 also gave the peoples of the Potomac plentiful opportunities to reflect on the limits of human control over nature.

In springtime it is still possible to stand along a small tributary of the Potomac and *hear* the herrings coming upstream, churning the water as they race to their spawning grounds. A few months later, in midsummer, one can stand on a dock in the salty lower reaches of the river and watch crabs scuttling in the shallows, while in the freshwater zone one can find wild rice and lingering perch, summering in the shallows before returning to deeper and saltier water for the winter.[23] Acorns and other nuts still litter the ground in the autumn, and deer scramble to fatten up on the plentiful autumn mast. With the onset of winter, however, the fish and crabs huddle deep in the river channels or return to salt water. White-tailed deer become thinner and weaker after the new year as the forest's carpet of nuts and tender plant shoots grows threadbare. Ever-dependent on the immediate availability of food, the very bodies of deer wax and wane with the seasons.

In an earlier age, one could also read the changing seasons in the bodies and movements of the peoples of the Potomac. Dependent for their livelihoods on season-specific plants and animals, Algonquians patiently endured occasional hunger. John Smith marveled that "it is strange to see how their bodies alter with their diet, even as the deare . . . they seeme fat and leane, strong and weak." Unlike the deer, however, people can draw upon cultural memory and human imagination to adjust to environmental changes. Smith recognized this as well, noting that "by their continually ranging, and travel, they know all the advantages and places most frequented with deare, beasts, fish, foule, rootes, and berries" at each season. Thus work routines and social life shifted with the seasons, following a well-established annual cycle developed over the course of many generations.[24]

Time itself was reckoned by the comings and goings of plants and animals. Divided into five seasons, the year began with Cohonks, named for the sound made by the migrating geese that arrived with the onset of cold weather. Then came Cattapeuk, the "budding or blossoming of the spring"; followed by Cohattayough, "the summer or highest sun"; Nepinough, the "earing of their corne"; and Taquitock, "the harvest and fall of leafe." The moons were also named for the food of the moment: the "Moon of Stags," the "Corn Moon," and the "second moon of cohonks."[25]

Many Potomac Algonquians began the new year by leaving their villages. As Cohonks set in, fish and edible plants went dormant. Not so the game. Deer, elk, turkeys, and bears grew fat from binging on autumn mast. Rutting bucks, distracted by comely does, paid less attention to approaching hunters, and bears grew sluggish as they gradually moved into hibernation. Animals' coats thickened, making for superior clothing and bedding. Game was most plentiful several days' journey from the villages, partly because fall-line and Piedmont oak-hickory forests provided the best browse for deer, and partly because similar upland habitats near home were hunted year-round. Women bundled up mats, children, corn, acorns, nuts, and tools and moved in large groups to "the most desert [uninhabited] places." There they built mobile hamlets, using the mats to make temporary houses resembling arbors. There the women dressed carcasses, gathered nuts and acorns, cooked, and prepared for the winter. The men hunted, not only for food and clothing, but also to impress women with their prowess.[26]

Men often hunted in groups, taking as many as fifteen deer at a time. Early each morning the "principall" men on the hunt gathered in a circle away from the camp to decide where to hunt that day. They sought guidance from the deity Okeus, who would "by some knowne signe manifest himselfe, and direct them to game: they all with alacritie acknowledging that signe, and following." Arranging themselves in a great ring several miles around, the men set afire the dry winter underbrush and fallen leaves. The frightened deer fled from the fire, but the men moved slowly inward to the center of the circle, spreading the flames until the animals were trapped "in a narrow roome" and cut down by the hunters' arrows. Hunters also herded game onto narrow points of land, killing them as they crowded onto the tip of a peninsula or floundered in the water. Other game, such as turkeys and bears, had to be hunted one at a time, thus giving individual hunters greater opportunities to display their skill.[27]

Some people stayed behind at the village even during the early winter hunt, and by the late winter most people had returned from the woods. Men continued to hunt, but other tasks and food sources pulled people toward home. That "home" looked and felt "like an oven." Called a *yeahawkan,* a Chesapeake house was framed with bowed saplings lashed together to frame oval buildings with rounded roofs, then covered with layered bark or with mats sewn from reeds. Small openings let smoke out at the top and people in on the sides. The entrances were covered with mats, and houses were often sited under trees for additional shelter. Between a half-dozen and twenty people shared houses that were normally ten to sixteen feet wide, twenty to thirty feet long, and ten feet high. People slept on built-in cots around the perimeter of the room, covered with mats or skins and snuggled "heads and points one by the other against the fire." The women kept a fire burning at all times, considering it an "evil signe" if it went out. Not surprisingly, yeahawkans were "as warme as stooves" in all weather.[28]

Snug in their yeahawkans, those who remained at home worked at dressing game, making tools, spinning and weaving, making clay or woven vessels, sewing reed mats, making rope and twine, processing skins and pelts, and making canoes. They ate high-calorie acorns and nuts gathered in the autumn and early winter, used maize and beans stored after the late harvest to make succotash, cakes, and parched corn, and rationed out smoked fish, oysters, and meat. Men continued to bring home meat, including venison, turkeys, hares, squirrels, and fowl.[29] Vast winter flocks of Canada geese, ducks, snow geese, herons, and pigeons drew men closer to home after the early winter deer hunt. Potomac villages were invariably close to marshes, where great concentrations of fowl could be found. The first English colonists saw their neighbors "kill fowle [in] aboundance." Robert Beverley witnessed Indians "taking their water or land fowl but by the help of bows and arrows; yet so great was their plenty . . . they killed what numbers they pleased." Then, too, winters were much colder than they are today. Even with the aid of bear's grease, deerskin leggings, and heavy fur mantles, comfort and safety alike suggested a return to the relative warmth of village life after the great deer hunts ended.[30]

Potomac Algonquians were at their leanest in late winter and early spring, when Cohonks gave way to Cattapeuk, "the budding or blossoming of the spring." Each thaw held out the tantalizing promise of plenty in the near future, but the nuts and maize gathered in the autumn ran low in February and early March, just as the deer and other game were at their least appetizing and nutritious. Fish remained in their deepwater refuges. Villagers had to make do with deer, fowl, small game, groundnuts, and tuckahoe and other starchy roots. Men likely spent time repairing fishing weirs and otherwise preparing for the spring fish runs. Most of the season's foods could be found close to the villages, so residents spent considerable time at home.[31]

Relief finally came when the migrating fish returned to spawn. Herring, shad, perch, and striped bass began filtering into the rivers in March, and by April they swarmed the shallows and tributaries near the villages. Their numbers astounded early English visitors, who marveled at the "multitudes" of fish. Robert Beverley wrote of herring runs "in such abundance . . . that it is almost impossible to ride through without treading on them." John Smith and his men saw "better fish more plenty or variety than any of us had ever seen." The water was so crowded with fish lying "thicke with their heads above the water" that they tried to catch them with a frying pan; that failing, they leaned over and speared fish with their swords, "taking more in an houre then we all could eat." So many spawning adults crowded into freshwater creeks and rivers that the waterways "reeked" of fish.[32]

Throughout March and April men lived "much upon their fishing weares." Taking advantage of the prevailing river currents and the rising and falling tides, fishermen built mazes and traps from which they harvested fish by the basketful. The particular form of the weir or trap depended upon the current, the shape of the river bottom, and the extent of the tidal flow, all of which dictated where the fish traveled and spawned.[33] Successful fishermen knew intimately their craft, their prey, and their waterway. Such knowledge came from oral tradition and from a deep familiarity with the locale. Fishermen stayed close to home, maximizing their take and minimizing their labor (and risk) by sticking to the rivers and creeks that they knew best. They took their catches directly to their homes, where they could be eaten fresh or smoked for later. Women prepared fish in a variety of ways: broiled or barbequed, without scaling or gutting them first (that was the eater's responsibility); boiled into a broth; or in hominy.[34]

Potomac villagers so valued these timely fish runs that they wove them into their culture. At the creation the Great Hare made two kinds of animals to provide food for the humans: fish and deer. Perhaps the person who carved a stylized fish on a rock near the Great Falls of the Potomac commemorated this event; so, too, possibly, did the "great men" along the Potomac who wore on their foreheads "the forme of a fish" in copper, a high prestige material with considerable ritual significance.[35]

The full promise of spring was finally realized in May. Fish runs peaked, the

Fishing was a critical part of the Potomac nations' diets, especially during late
winter and early spring when other food sources were scarce. Theodore de
Bry, from a watercolor by John White, "Their Manner of Fishing in Virginia."
From Thomas Hariot, *A brief and true report of the new found land of Virginia:
of the commodities and of the nature and manners of the naturall inhabitants . . .*
(Frankfurt: Theodore de Bry, 1590). Courtesy of the Library of Congress, Prints and
Photographs Division, Washington, D.C.

game was fattening up, and blue crabs moved into the more accessible shallows
of saltwater and brackish areas. Warmer water temperatures made oystering and
mussel harvesting more appealing. Berries abounded in the clearings, and water
lilies leafed out in freshwater marshes. One visitor who arrived in Virginia in May
remarked that villagers "eate often and that liberally."[36]

Above all, May was for planting. The men continued fishing and hunting while
the women went into the fields at the end of April. (Although men did the initial

backbreaking work of clearing the woods, women and children planted, culti-vated, and harvested.) The fields, though only one to two hundred feet square, took weeks to plant. Working around the tree stumps left to rot in the field, each woman used a curved wooden stick to dig a series of small holes at four-foot intervals. In each hole she planted several grains of corn and beans together. Next the women turned to the spaces in between the cornstalks, which they filled with melons, gourds, maracocks (passion vines), and pumpkins. (This provided more dietary diversity, greater security against crop failures, and more calories, while also reducing the need for hoeing weeds—spreading vines suppressed their growth—and extending the life of fields, as peas and beans helped to fix nitrogen in the soil.)[37] The planting continued until mid-June. By then each field looked like a miniature forest of tree stumps and cornstalks, with a crowded understory of peas, vines, and melons. Still, the fields required regular cultivation. Women and children hilled the maize when it reached knee-high, supporting each stalk and burying weeds by mounding up the earth around its base. They hoed con-tinuously throughout the summer.[38]

No matter how carefully women tended their fields, they were always at the mercy of the weather. An unseasonable frost or a bad hailstorm could destroy much of their crop, while droughts left crops withering in the fields. Villagers ensured against bad harvests by staggering their plantings and by maintaining a diverse diet even in the best of times. "What they plant in Aprill they reape in August, for May in September, for June in October," noted John Smith. Thus a late April frost that killed tender seedlings had no effect on May plantings, and an August hurricane could not touch the corn that had been harvested in July.[39]

Planting occupied much of the women's attention in late spring, but with the approach of Cohattayough ("the summer or highest sun") tasty oysters, turtles, tortoises, and crabs lured small work parties away from the fields. Women and children gathered strawberries, mulberries, raspberries, May apples, wild plums, and cherries, which thrived in May and June. Berrying meshed well with plant-ing, for the early-ripening fruits and berries were plentiful in nearby abandoned fields. Some people even placed their houses amongst mulberry trees. Most vil-lages on the outer coastal plain were also close to oyster beds, so small groups sometimes moved into temporary camps near prime beds. Adolescents dived for the oysters, while women cooked and smoked them. Some oysters were boiled together with mussels and eaten immediately. The broth they thickened with cornmeal. Other oysters they shucked, hung on strings, dried over a slow fire, and saved for later.[40]

By mid-June the crops were all planted. Women and children, no longer tied so closely to their fields, began to "disperse themselves in small companies and live upon fish, beasts, crabs, oysters, land tortoyses, strawberries, mulberries, and such." Although women and children had to spend at least some time tending to the crops, they could venture out more frequently on gathering expeditions. Oystering continued throughout the summer, and many wild berries and fruits reached their peak in late June and early July. Swamps and freshwater marshes also beckoned, for there one could find wild rice and other foods, in addition to reeds and grasses for making mats, baskets, and twine. Then there was arrow arum, or tuckahoe. Arrow arum provided small edible berries in the spring, but their real value lay in their starchy, potato-like roots. Since arrow arum grows in clumps or rafts where the water is too deep for cattails, mallows, and sedges, the women canoed out to the tuckahoe beds. Waiting until midtide, the women muscled the roots up from under a foot of mud. A work party could uproot a week's supply of the heavy, filament-coved tubers in a single day. After they had sun-dried or baked their haul for a full day to eliminate the oxalic acid that made raw tuckahoe "no better than poisen," women baked or boiled it into loaves.[41]

Men also became more mobile after the fish runs petered out in mid-June. Fish remained an important part of the diet throughout the summer, but now the fishermen used canoes, bone hooks, netting, arrows, and gigs. They also caught sturgeon, some growing to six feet, by looping a noose about the tail and wrestling it ashore. The big, muscular fish floundered, and would "often pull him under water, and then that man was counted a . . . brave fellow, that would not let go." Each of these techniques allowed frequent moves in search of the best fishing, making men more mobile than they were during the springtime fish runs.[42]

Men remained free to follow the fish and game throughout the summer and even to go on long-distance treks to wage war, diplomacy, or trade, but after mid-July women returned to the fields for the beginning of the harvest. Melons and gourds ripened first, followed closely by the earliest-planted maize and beans, then peas and maracocks. The harvest began so early in part because Algonquians preferred to eat green corn and partly because the staggered plantings allowed a more continuous harvest. The unripe cornstalks yielded a sweet juice that could be sucked out right away. Harvesters stripped the ears, piling them into baskets to be carried to mats. There they lay drying in the sun during the day; at night the corn was heaped up and covered with mats to protect it from the dew. Once it had dried, women poured the kernels into storage baskets, which occupied much of the available space in their houses by the time the harvest ended in October.[43]

One observer called corn "the thing most necessary to sustaine man." Another called it "the staff of food upon which the Indians did ever depend; for when sickness, bad weather, war, or any other ill accident kept them from hunting, fishing, and fowling, this, with the addition of some peas, beans, and such other fruits as were then in season, was the family's dependence and the support of their women and children." Harvested just as the fishing season ended, maize provided more calories than any other single food in the Algonquian diet. Barring a bad harvest, maize and other cultivated plants paid tremendous dividends on the women's labor-minimizing horticultural practices. Horticulture made possible the autumn season of plenty that fortified villagers for the lean times to come, and a good harvest could last them deep into the winter. Maize could be prepared in many different ways. Fresh corn was boiled or roasted in the ears. After the harvest, women boiled dried corn together with beans to make a kind of succotash or slowly boiled it to make hominy. Baked in ashes or boiled, cornmeal became bread (modern-day "pone"). Men on long journeys staved off hunger by swallowing a spoonful of parched corn powder, then drinking water to make the corn expand in their stomachs.[44]

Autumn (Taquitock, "the harvest and fall of leafe") brought villagers together once again as men returned from the woods to join in end-of-the-year feasting and to prepare for the coming deer hunts. In addition to the bounty of the harvest, there were turkeys, deer, and other local game, migrating fowl, late season berries and fruits such as chokeberries and persimmons, and wild rice. As in the spring, these pursuits kept many people within the orbit of the village, only this time the autumn feasts provided rare occasions for everyone to come together at once. Together the villagers partook of the season's bounty and made sacrifices to the spirits whose favor and guidance had made it possible to eat so well.

Work and Power

The annual round of planting, gathering, hunting, and fishing molded human relationships along the Potomac in fundamental ways. The fissioning and fusion of family and community as people came and went, the sharp division between men's and women's work, and the lack of occupational specialization within each gender all established the parameters within which people developed relationships with their spouses, fellow women or fellow men, neighbors, and people from other communities and nations. At the same time, relying on farming in a time of shrinking growing seasons, expanding populations, and great migrations led the peoples of the Potomac to gravitate toward more hierarchical forms of social organization.

Families and villages scattered and came together throughout the year as people sought the plants and animals that sustained them. The opportunities for close-knit family life peaked in early winter, late spring, and autumn, while the opportunities for communal activities including most of the people in the village peaked in the autumn. The sharp division between men's and women's work also shaped social relationships. Women took charge of plants and children, while men hunted, fished, waged war, and cleared new fields. Each sex had its own tool kit: men made canoes and projectile points, while women made baskets, mats, pots, and utensils. When villagers fissioned off into small working groups, men and women generally went their separate ways (the great exception being the early winter deer hunts). Gender-specific tasks created a patchwork of feminine and masculine spaces in the village and beyond. The fields were very much a part of the female world, and the woods of the masculine world. Women gathered reeds and tubers from the marshes, while men trapped and hunted there, making the marshes masculine *or* feminine, depending upon the season. The village, of course, was home to all, but women's responsibility for domestic life probably translated into female control of this domestic space.

Given their separate work routines and spaces, it seems unlikely that adult Algonquian men and women knew each other as intimately as modern Americans do in their companionate marriages. In contrast to this rigid division of labor between men and women, a marked lack of occupational specialization *within* each gender meant that people shared with others of the same sex a common set of skills and experiences. Algonquians were not walled off into the many segregated occupation-based spheres that so often divide modern Americans. One woman could not feel superior because she grew maize while other women raised children, for most women did both. A hunter could not lord it over another man who only fished. To acquire prestige he would have to do the things that most men did, only better.

Despite this lack of specialized occupations, the archaeological record suggests that farming and village life promoted increasingly hierarchical social structures. Perhaps the best indication of this can be found in the largest of the new towns on the inner coastal plain. In the fourteenth century extensive palisades sheltered most of the populations at Accokeek and Patawomeck. Erecting, maintaining, and defending palisades and other fortifications amounted to public works projects. Did elites command the labor and resources necessary to complete such projects? The dimensions of the palisades at these inner coastal plain villages also tell a tale. After 1400 the enclosed areas shrank in size; the diminished fortifications protected a smaller number of larger buildings, and the majority of the population lived outside the protective embrace of the palisades. A colonial-era description may explain this trend: Virginian Robert Beverley observed that palisades normally encompassed "only their King's houses, and as many others as they judge sufficient to harbor all their people, when an enemy comes against them. They never fail to secure within their palisado, all their religious reliques and remains of their Princes."[45]

The revival of long-distance trade after 1300, reflected in innovative mortuary practices dating to the fifteenth century, also points to an increasingly hierarchical social order. Commoners and elites were given different burials after 1400. In the Shenandoah Valley, for example, only about a third of the fifteenth-century burials included nonutilitarian prestige items such as copper beads, and a few burials contained a disproportionately large share of such items. A renaissance of long-distance trade in copper and shell beads in the fifteenth century suggests that some people displayed these items as signs of their rank; and unless sixteenth- and seventeenth-century Algonquians who testified to the use of copper and beads to tap into the power of the spiritual world were describing a very recent practice, these goods were also used to create and sustain the power of fifteenth-century elites. Even apart from the spiritual uses of copper, whoever controlled access to trade goods controlled an important source of power, for a person who could give possessions away gained influence over the recipients by creating an undefined but very real obligation that would have to be fulfilled at some later date. The timing of copper's entry into the archaeological record is also suggestive, for it coincided with the spread of palisades.[46]

Some fifteenth-century elites may have even gained the power to exact tribute in maize and other crops. Underground food storage pits were common before 1400 but seem to have been replaced by aboveground storage after that date. Aboveground storage, notes one student of chiefly societies, was "associated with the political economy in contrast to the hidden household stores of the subsistence economy." Aboveground storage made it easier for chiefs to exact tribute and, having transferred that wealth to their own storehouses, to display this visual reminder of chiefly power.[47]

At least some of the new elites of the fifteenth century were religious specialists. That the enclosed village at Patawomeck morphed into a ceremonial center suggests the rise of a priestly caste, which likely gained influence with the advent of their peoples' high-stakes commitment to agriculture. Algonquians fought against bad harvests by enlisting the lesser gods in efforts to control the weather. In time of "great distresse of want," observed one early colonist, "the whole country[,] men women and children, come togither to their solemnityes," dancing and singing under the priests' leadership for hours. Priests combated violent storms by casting tobacco, copper, and other spiritually powerful objects into the water, and they called up rain by praying. At Patawomeck priests offered beads and copper to images of lesser deities "if at any time they want rayne or have to[o] much." Ordinary people began and ended each day with prayers and small sacrifices, and prayed as they sacrificed the first fruits of each plant or animal as it came into season.[48]

Though the archaeological record contains numerous indications that hierarchical societies were emerging along the Potomac and its tributaries in the fourteenth and fifteenth centuries, we are left to wonder how popular such changes were. Did such hierarchies emerge out of a broad consensus about who deserved to be at the top (and the bottom)? Were such distinctions regarded as somewhat arbitrary but necessary if the community was to deal with the challenges of increasing migration, warfare, and climate change? Or were elites simply the winners of naked struggles for power? Did these hierarchies tend to favor men or women? Was status hereditary or a matter of individuals surfacing as "Big Men"? The evidence, unfortunately, does not adequately speak to these questions. We should not, however, assume that everyone approved of these changes or that they were uncontested.

Already by 1500 several dozen generations of people had made fundamental decisions that were fairly binding on the people who lived there in 1500: they had determined the size of the population, for example, how it would be fed, and where people would live. All of these decisions could be undone, of course, but only at a great price, and in fact there are no signs that people in the fourteenth century gave serious consideration to abandoning their commitment to agriculture and other central facts of their collective lives; people seldom do, except under the most extreme conditions.

Yet the peoples of the Potomac had to make some major adjustments in order to maintain even some semblance of the status quo, for the world was changing around them. Their biggest problem was that their location exposed them to the repercussions of developments to their north, where shortened Little Ice Age growing seasons froze out farmers, who moved to the south. These migrations brought profound changes to the Potomac basin—so profound, in fact, that the fourteenth and fifteenth centuries were just as much a critical passage in the region's history as the colonial period of the seventeenth and eighteenth centuries. Pressure from the north heightened the competition for prime village sites in the Potomac basin. The choicest village sites were generally to be found on the inner coastal plain, which had the best combination of good farmland, freshwater marshes, and critically important springtime fisheries. By 1500 numerous villages and hamlets clustered along the inner coastal plain's creeks and rivers, far more than could be found on the outer coastal plain. There, on the inner coastal plain, the population grew most rapidly. There we can begin to see hints of new ways of organizing society, politics, and religion. We can see glimmerings, even, of the centralized chiefdoms that would come to dominate the region in the sixteenth century.

CHAPTER THREE

"Kings" of the Potomac

Fourteenth- and fifteenth-century migrants from the north were almost certainly preceded by small advance parties sent out to reconnoiter the situation along the Potomac and its tributaries. It requires no great leap of imagination to envision a dozen men, well armed but also prepared to engage in a little bit of trade and diplomacy, working their way down rivers and streams during the summer months in search of a new place to which their people might lay claim and colonize. Subsisting on dried cornmeal and carrying their bows at the ready in case they encountered a deer or an enemy, the men would have entered the Potomac first through one of its northern Piedmont or valley tributaries: like the Monocacy River, with its rolling hills and narrow strip of fertile bottomlands, or Conococheague Creek, watering the wide Cumberland Valley from its northern extremities to the Potomac itself. From there, some would have turned to the southeast to travel down the Potomac, while others would have followed other tributaries farther southward, such as Opequon Creek into the Shenandoah Valley, or Goose Creek over the Piedmont portion of the Northern Neck.

Such parties would have found a territory well matched to their existing ways of living upon the land: coming from communities with subsistence patterns very much like those of the villagers already living along the Potomac, they would have noted the success of the resident Algonquians at integrating the production of corn, beans, and squash into a regular annual round of fishing, gathering, and hunting, and they would surely have appreciated the fertility of the soil, the abundance of deer and other game, and the good fishing in the interior.

Thus it is all the more remarkable that by the end of the sixteenth century the interior above the fall line was almost completely uninhabited. We have here quite a mystery: why would farmers across ten thousand square miles of territory collectively abandon their fields? The answers to this question go to the heart of this region's history. They are to be found at the places where nature and culture meet: at the intersection between the rise of agriculture and the advent of the Little Ice Age; in the Potomac's location along the cultural, topographic, and climatic transition between the northeast and the southeast; and in the close fit between the distinctive environmental conditions of the inner coastal plain and the particular blend of subsistence practices adopted by the people who lived there.

The interplay of environment, culture, and events in the sixteenth century explains not only the mystery of the lost villages of the interior but also the creation of powerful, hereditary chiefdoms, the rise of a priestly caste, and the formation of a culture that sustained the increasingly hierarchical societies along the lower Potomac. By the end of the sixteenth century the new order was inscribed on nature itself: the fields in the woods, the weirs in the rivers, and the spatial organization of villages and hamlets all bespoke the transformation of formerly egalitarian communities into hierarchical societies organized for survival on the edge of the expanding interior wilderness.

Histories

Despite the depopulation of the interior, over thirty thousand Native people lived in the Chesapeake region at the end of the sixteenth century, some five to seven thousand of them along the Potomac below the Great Falls. Most of these people were broadly Algonquian in culture, though the Susquehannocks (based on the Susquehanna River) were Iroquoian, and the Monacans and Manahoacs (who lived in the Piedmont between the Rappahannock and James rivers) were likely Siouan.[1] The majority lived within *chiefdoms,* a type of hierarchical political order in which hereditary rulers commanded tribute, coordinated foreign policy, and served as vital intermediaries between humans and the spiritual world. Moreover, by the late sixteenth century an increasing number of people found themselves living within *paramount* chiefdoms, which were comprised of multiple chiefdoms owing tribute (and varying degrees of obedience) to a chief-of-chiefs such as Powhatan. At least five fundamental and thoroughly interrelated forces led the inhabitants of Chesapeake in this direction, all of which we've already seen at work even before 1500 but which came to a head in the sixteenth century: accelerating population growth, an increasing dependence on agriculture, the onset of the Little Ice Age, intensifying competition for prime village locations, and a marked increase in both warfare and long-distance trade.

To solve the strange case of the missing villages, to understand the rise of chiefdoms and paramount chiefdoms, and to see the creation of the Potomac's distinctive diplomatic configuration at the end of the sixteenth century, we must look to the north. Throughout the sixteenth century, the Five Nations Iroquois, the Susquehannocks, and relatively little-known Iroquoian groups such as the Massawomecks and Eries regularly sent warriors to the Potomac, where they created such havoc in the interior that the villages were gradually abandoned over the course of the century, and the surviving villages below the fall line were forced to reorganize their social and political systems along more hierarchical lines in order to survive the assaults.

The northerners' conduct was very much the product of troubles at home. The Little Ice Age had forced the proto-Iroquoian peoples who remained in modern-day New York into increasingly compact and populous agricultural settlements situated on relatively warm bottomlands, where they gradually consolidated into fewer ever-larger and better-defended villages. The transition did not go smoothly: the Iroquois Great League of Peace (the "Five Nations") was intended to bring an end to a maelstrom of fifteenth- and early sixteenth-century warfare between these northern villages, in which (according to oral tradition) "feuds with brother nations, feuds of sister towns and feuds of families and clans made [e]very warrior a stealthy man who liked to kill."[2] The Great League resolved many of these feuds, establishing peace between the Five Nations and fusing them into a loose polity by the middle of the sixteenth century, but the cultural imperatives that inspired Iroquois men to go to war each summer continued unabated. Iroquois culture fostered regular "mourning wars," which were intended to assuage the grief of the relatives of recently deceased people by replacing the dead with captives from other nations. The goal was to ceremonially "requicken" the spirit of the person whose death had inspired the raid. Given this motive for warfare, and since people are prone to die, Iroquois men were called to go to war almost every year.[3]

Because members of the newly formed league constituted a single community, sixteenth-century Senecas, Oneidas, Cayugas, Onondagas, and Mohawks could no more war against each other than they could against members of their own village. Therefore as the Great League coalesced, Five Nations warriors increasingly redirected their efforts outward, placing neighboring peoples not included in the league under tremendous pressure. If the captives taken in these mourning wars were themselves Iroquoian (Susquehannocks, say, or Eries) then their relatives might also demand a mourning war, perpetuating a cycle of violence that was, ironically, rooted in a strong ethic of peace and harmony *within* each community.[4]

The Susquehannocks were especially hard-hit, so much so that after about 1525 they moved from their homeland on the upper Susquehanna River to the

lower Susquehanna, with some continuing southward in the late sixteenth century to establish a half-dozen palisaded villages on the upper Potomac. The
Susquehannocks' presence made the Chesapeake interior a very dangerous place
indeed. Susquehannock warriors harassed their neighbors; and what was worse,
those who were unfortunate enough to live in the Shenandoah Valley or western
Maryland were caught in a deadly crossfire between Susquehannocks and the
Five Nations, who pursued their enemies to their new southern homes. Most of
the Susquehannocks' neighbors in the Potomac basin abandoned their villages.
Those who remained in the Shenandoah Valley built palisades and otherwise
mobilized for war. Even after the Potomac River Susquehannocks relocated to the
lower Susquehanna River in the early seventeenth century, Iroquoian raiders—
Five Nations, Susquehannocks, and a people known to Chesapeake Algonquians
as the "Massawomecks"—continued to harass the northern and western Chesapeake. By 1608 the Potomac basin above the fall line had been almost entirely
abandoned.[5]

The archaeological record can only hint at the experiences of the sixteenth-
century villagers who suffered through this long series of raids from the north.
The remnants of their homes tell us more about settlement patterns and ceramic
techniques than they do about the trepidation women must have felt as they ventured out into their fields during the summertime or that men might have felt
when they went out to hunt. They would go hungry if they did not go forth to
cultivate their crops, but they surely knew that they risked capture and death at
the hands of the northern warriors, who were most likely to be about during the
summer and fall. Many in the village would have known someone who had been
captured by raiders from the north, and most people likely had a fairly detailed
understanding of what would happen to that person in Iroquoia: a ritual adoption, followed by either a thorough integration into a new family, clan, village,
and culture, or else by prolonged torture at the hands of the entire community,
starting with sawing off fingers and ending in a slow fire that could take many
hours to kill the victim.[6] It requires only a little bit of imagination to guess that
villagers from the interior saw chilling reminders of their vulnerability whenever their travels took them through an abandoned village, its buildings rapidly
crumbling, its old fields filling with low shrubs and saplings, and the surrounding
woods choked with underbrush that would, in happier times, have been picked
clean of kindling and burned back by controlled fires.

Nor does the archaeological record have much to say about what it was like to
do battle with the northern raiders. We might begin to get some sense of what it
was like, however, from the account of Henry Spelman, a young English boy who

was living among the Patawomecks, a powerful chiefdom centered on Potomac Creek, when a Massawomeck war party attacked in 1609. The Patawomecks had advance notice of the raid, so they waited in hiding as the Massawomecks paddled their canoes into a reedy marsh. The Massawomecks, sensing the trap, scattered and took positions "sum little distant" from the Patawomecks. Men on both sides readied their bows and hung bark shields over their lead shoulders to protect that side when they stood to shoot. Keeping additional arrows and a war club or tomahawk at hand, the warriors softly crept forward, using the vegetation as cover as they stole ever closer to their enemies. Frequently "squattinge doune and priinge [prying] if they can spie any to shoot at," they avoided open-field confrontations. Instead they awaited a clear shot, with which a bowman could easily put an arrow "quite through the body" of a careless enemy. Whenever a man went down with an injury, opposing warriors took greater risks, rushing forward "to knock him on the heade." The battlefield was noisy, even in the absence of guns, for the Algonquians were noted for their attempts at terrifying opponents with loud rattles, drums, and shouts. Yet Spelman, conditioned by European conventions of war, was struck by the lack of bloodshed: "Ther was no great slawter" on either side, he recalled. The Massawomecks seemed "glad to retier" after a while, for they had grown hungry and "shott away most of ther arrows."[7]

Though a fine description of battlefield tactics, even Spelman's account does not convey the terror that an Indian lad in an exposed village above the fall line would have felt during a fight with a sixteenth-century Massawomeck war party. In part this was because Spelman had relatively little to worry about. By 1609 the numerous and powerful Patawomecks had proven that they could hold their own against raiders from the north; unlike the residents of a typical village above the fall line in the previous century, the Patawomecks had no reason to believe that their very existence as a people was seriously threatened by a single Massawomeck war party.

Nor was Spelman fully aware of what was at stake in the skirmish he witnessed. In European warfare the greatest horrors took place on the battlefield itself. At Patawomeck, however, battlefield carnage was kept to a minimum and the greatest horrors took place after the battle, when captives were put to the test. The Iroquois were not alone in this, for the Algonquians also tortured prisoners. A man taken by Algonquians in 1608, for instance, was "stripped naked, and bound to two stakes, with his backe against a great fire: then did they rippe him and burne his bowels, and dried his flesh to the bones." As he burned, his limbs were severed piecemeal and the skin sliced from his head and face with shells and reeds. Yet such ordeals, if faced with courage, ennobled the sufferer. One Virginian observed that warriors under torture "disdain so much as to groan, sigh, or show the least sign of dismay or concern, so much as in their looks; on the contrary, they make it a point of honor . . . to soften their features, and look as pleased as if they were in the actual enjoyment of some delight." The ideal warrior died with a song on his lips and defiance in his heart. The victors benefited whether the captive broke down under torture or died well: a warrior who broke under torture conceded his captor's mastery over him, but a man who endured torture without flinching demonstrated his captor's prowess in taking such a worthy adversary; thus the torturers would "distribute a collop [a slice of meat] to all that had a share in stealing the victory" over a particularly brave warrior.[8]

Most villages below the fall line survived the sixteenth-century onslaught from the north, but in order to withstand the migrations and warfare of the fourteenth, fifteenth, and sixteenth centuries, they had to transform their social and political systems. Such communities acquiesced in the consolidation of authority in the hands of hereditary chiefs who could exact tribute, send men to war, discipline their subjects, and coordinate the resistance against northern raiders and rival claimants to their homelands.[9] Over the course of the sixteenth century, then, a more elaborate hierarchy of places and rulers emerged around the rim of the Chesapeake Bay. On the lowest level were hamlets without hereditary rulers. Such hamlets paid tribute to a nearby village whose chief, or *werowance*, appointed a "lesser king" to each dependent settlement. Increasingly during the sixteenth century, the werowance was in turn subject to a paramount chief who ruled several village/hamlet clusters.[10]

Of course, the Susquehannock and Massawomeck attacks alone do not explain why people accustomed to a relatively egalitarian social, political, and religious order submitted themselves to the power of village and paramount chiefs, for external threats do not invariably cause people to form chiefdoms; the Susquehannocks, for instance, endured similar pressures without resorting to rule by chiefs. The difference between the Susquehannocks' and Potomac nations' responses lies in their divergent histories: as we have already seen, Potomac River chiefdoms emerged in communities that were already developing more hierarchical societies in the fourteenth and fifteenth centuries. Thus chiefdoms represented an elaboration on a well-established trend rather than a complete break from tradition.

The distinctive environmental conditions of the inner coastal plain made it an especially fertile ground for the growth of chiefdoms. It was no coincidence that the most powerful paramount chiefdoms emerged in the freshwater zone below the fall line, for such locations conferred significant advantages on whomever controlled them. The largest Native populations gathered on the inner coastal plain, for there they could find the best combination of good agricultural soils and other necessities of life. The inner coastal plain provided better fishing and a greater diversity of wild plant life than the outer coastal plain did and thus afforded a greater degree of security when staple foods such as maize and venison were scarce. Their proximity to the increasingly depopulated interior was also an advantage; though it exposed them to raids from the north, it also gave them easy access to a zone where deer and other game could multiply in the absence of year-round residents. Successful chiefs helped villagers on the inner coastal plain to maintain and extend their control over key natural resources. These natural resources supported populations large enough to fend off northern raiders while also keeping potential interlopers out of uncleared fields that might be needed in the future. A chief knit together multiple communities, coordinating their diplomacy and allowing them to combine their forces to field more warriors. In short, chiefdoms located on the inner coastal plain commanded natural resources that gave them the wherewithal to survive and even initiate wars by harnessing the power of their growing populations to the needs of the polity as a whole.[11]

At least a dozen different nations lined the banks of the Potomac and its tributaries, all of which were by the end of the sixteenth century ruled directly by a werowance and indirectly by a paramount chief. On the south bank lived Tauxenents, Patawomecks, Onawmanients, Chicacoans, and Wicocomocos, while across the river lived Wicomicos, Portobaccos, Nanjemoys, Piscataways, and Nacotchtanks. Of the five to seven thousand people who lived along the Potomac, a slight majority were on the north bank. The Patawomecks, with perhaps 850 people, outnumbered all other nations, followed by the Wicocomocos (550), Piscataways, Onawmanients (425 each), and Nacotchtanks (340). Another half-dozen chiefdoms lined the north bank of the nearby Rappahannock River, separated from the Potomac villages by a ten- to twenty-mile neck of land. Three more Patuxent River chiefdoms bordered the north-bank Potomac nations.[12]

According to Piscataway oral tradition, the first paramount chief in the Chesapeake region emerged on the Potomac River some thirteen generations before 1634 (probably somewhere between 1440 and 1530), when "there came a King from the Easterne Shoare" to establish a paramount chiefdom on Piscataway Creek, a choice location on the inner coastal plain. Called the *tayac,* he and his successors expanded Piscataway influence all along the Potomac.[13] The Tauxenents fell into the Piscataway tayac's orbit, as did the peoples of the inner coastal plain on the north bank: the Portobaccos, Nanjemoys, Mattawomans, Pamunkys, and Nacotchtanks. On the outer coastal plain the Wicomicos were likely part of

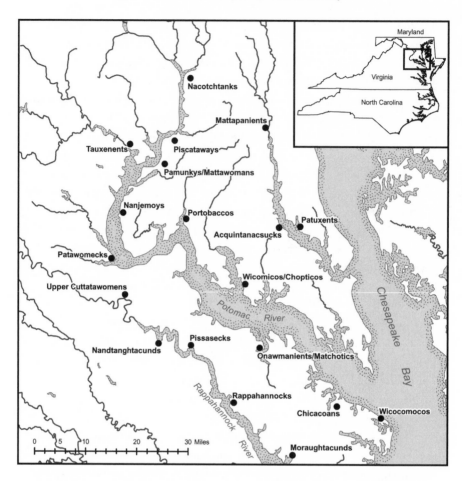

Principal towns of Algonquian communities, ca. 1608. Additional villages and hamlets associated with the main towns dotted the Potomac and its tributaries. Drawn by Susan Winchell-Sweeney. Adapted from Christian Feest, "Nanticoke and Neighboring Tribes," *Handbook of North American Indians*, vol. 15, *Northeast*, ed. William Sturtevant and Bruce Trigger (Washington, D.C.: Smithsonian Institution, 1978).

his chiefdom and were certainly heavily influenced by the tayac. These align-ments shifted frequently, and local werowances varied considerably in the depth of their obedience and loyalty toward their paramount chief. The Patawomecks were part of the Piscataway chiefdom in the late sixteenth century but later broke away, while the three nations of the nearby Patuxent River (the Patuxents, Mat-tapanients, and Aquintanacsucks) avoided being absorbed into the tayac's world altogether, partly by forming their own defensive alliance without a paramount chief.[14]

Already in the mid-sixteenth century, however, an even more powerful chief was consolidating his hold over a half-dozen subordinate werowances near the falls of the James and Pamunky rivers. The man commonly known today as Powhatan inherited these chiefdoms sometime in the 1560s or 1570s; over the next few decades, according to Indian accounts, another two dozen Algonquian nations had "bene either by force subdued unto him, or through feare yeilded" to this charismatic leader. By 1607 Powhatan collected tribute from nearly all of the Algonquian nations in Virginia below the fall line, and he was still adding to Tsenacommacah, the territory encompassed by Powhatan's paramount chiefdom, when the Jamestown colonists arrived. The Kecoughtans, a prosperous nation of about a thousand souls, fell to Powhatan in the late 1590s, while the Chesapeakes were destroyed and their territory colonized by Powhatan loyalists within a year or two of 1607. And in the fall of 1608, Powhatan showed Jamestown colonists a string of two dozen fresh Piankatank scalps, bragging that he had scattered the survivors and replaced them with the "remayne" of the recently conquered Kecoughtans. Powhatan had even begun to extend his influence to the lower Eastern Shore, though he had not yet incorporated the nations there into Tsenacommacah.[15]

All but one of the south-bank nations on the Potomac also gave in to Powhatan, albeit with some reservations. The Patawomecks were among the most numerous and powerful people in the Chesapeake region, and the Northern Neck was the most densely populated part of Virginia, but the south-bank nations' location left them exposed to attacks from all directions. The expansionist Piscataway tayac controlled the north bank of the river, and the Susquehannocks and the Massawomecks regularly swept down the Potomac River to attack villagers there.[16] Clearly it was in the best interests of the Potomac River nations to coordinate their war and diplomacy against these multiple threats. One possibility was to join the tayac's paramount chiefdom, but the Piscataways and Patawomecks were roughly equal in resources and power and had long been competitors; could one truly accept subjugation at the hands of the other? Powhatan offered another option.

Shortly before the arrival of the English, all but one of the nations on the south bank of the Potomac began paying tribute to Powhatan. Powhatan paid regular visits to collect tribute and reinforce his authority. He directed the overall diplomatic policy of the nations on the south bank of the Potomac, and he served as a counterweight against the Piscataway tayac. At the same time, the eighty miles between the Potomac and Powhatan's home village prevented Powhatan from meddling in their everyday affairs. Thus Powhatan offered protection but at a price that the south-bank nations were willing, for the moment, to pay. Indeed, the price was lower than it was for people living closer to the Powhatan heartland: Powhatan's inability to maintain close surveillance, the Patawomecks' military power, and Powhatan's need to cultivate goodwill among the Potomac nations so as to maintain them as a buffer on his northern frontier all conspired to make Powhatan's hold over the Patawomecks very tenuous indeed.[17]

Both the tayac's and Powhatan's paramount chiefdoms, then, were still works-in-progress at the end of the sixteenth century. Most people were well aware that the tayac's and Powhatan's chiefdoms were not the only two games in town; they knew of the independent Chickahominies, living in the heart of Tsenacommacah without being part of it, or of the Patuxent alliance just over a narrow neck of land from the tayac's villages, or of the Piedmont confederation of Monacans and Manahoacs. In nearly every village on the Potomac there were people who could remember when they had become a part of a paramount chiefdom and why. Thus those who had voluntarily joined to avoid some greater threat knew that they could always recalculate their chances of surviving outside of Powhatan's Tsenacommacah or without the protection of the tayac. Those who heeded the tayac, or who had "through feare yeilded," to Powhatan, could recall a time when they neither paid tribute to a paramount chief nor did his bidding; they, too, had every reason to seek opportunities to regain their independence. And of course those who lived uncomfortably close to the edges of Tsenacommacah, such as the Piscataways, were anxious to retain their sovereignty. In short, many Algonquian werowances along the Potomac wished to diminish the power and influence of the paramount chiefs.

Structures

One might reasonably ask what it means to call these polities "chiefdoms" and why it matters. What difference did it make that Chesapeake Algonquians had organized themselves into chiefdoms rather than fashioning themselves into bands, tribes, or states? And what did the specific features of Algonquian chiefdoms have to do with diplomacy and trade? In fact, the particulars of Algonquian political culture as it developed in the sixteenth century did much to determine the course of events during the seventeenth century and beyond. If we are to appreciate the logic that later guided the Potomac nations' varied responses to the English presence, it is critical that we first understand the spiritual sources of *all* power in the Algonquians' world as well as the cosmological vision that explained and sustained chiefly authority—and above all, that we grasp the utter inseparability of spiritual power, trade, diplomacy, and chiefly authority.

We might begin by contrasting chiefdoms with other forms of political organization. Tribal societies, for example, are generally egalitarian. Age and sex place some limits on a person's power, but otherwise anyone with sufficient personal charisma and achievements can exercise leadership. Whoever can lead may lead, for there is no fixed limit on the number of people who can serve a given function. Shamans, for instance, thrive if they seem to do good work, not because they've been initiated into an exclusive priestly caste. In contrast, chiefdoms limit how many people may exercise authority, and they vest some key leadership positions with an authority independent of the charisma and achievements of the officeholder. A priest, for example, possesses authority because he's been consecrated, and not simply because he attracts a following. Although a little charisma never hurts, a chief has authority by virtue of his birth.[18] Chiefly authority is based on commoners' acceptance of their legitimate sovereignty, not just on the chief's ability to persuade and inspire his people. Chiefs in the Chesapeake region used their authority to exact tribute, compel men to go to war, and order executions—all of which marked a real departure from tribal politics, in which tribute was virtually unknown, waging policy-driven wars required an almost impossible degree of consensus, and no one person could order an execution. Yet chiefdoms were also fundamentally unlike a modern nation-state: they lacked bureaucracies, centralized record keeping, police, courts, standing armies, and other trappings of modern nation-states.[19]

All power, authority, and legitimacy had their origins in the world of the spirits. The creator Ahone was "the good and peceable" god, the ultimate source of *manit* (spiritual power) and "the giver of al the good things." Ahone was too awesome for humans to really know. He took a hands-off approach, leaving humans "to make the most of their free will and to secure as many as they can of the good things that flow from him." Therefore, "it was to no purpose either to fear or worship him." Instead Ahone had another spirit, Okeus, to deal directly with humans; Okeus was "always busying himself with our affairs and frequently visiting us, being present in the air, in the thunder, and in the storms." A morally neutral spirit with whom Algonquians needed to maintain a right relationship, Okeus "expected adoration and sacrifice." On the whole, though, he served as a guardian who spoke directly to priests and taught humans how to live: how to dress, how to wear their hair, how to cultivate plants, and otherwise "fashion themselves" according to his will.[20]

On a day-to-day basis, however, Algonquians had less to do with Okeus than they did with *quiyoughcosughs*, a broad term encompassing a veritable host of lesser gods—a host that included their werowances and priests. As embodiments of quiyoughcosughs, chiefs and priests straddled the already indistinct, porous frontier connecting humans and spirits. Only they could enter the sacred precincts of the *quioccasan,* or temple. Only they went on to the lair of the Great Hare after they died, lived a full life there, then returned to this world. While on this earth, quiyoughcosughs maintained contact with their fellow spirits; and while away from earth they served as intercessors on behalf of their living relatives.[21] But priests and chiefs were only part of this pantheon; according to one Algonquian, "there are many of them of the same nature" and "there are tutelar deities in every town." Manit was incarnate in many things, as Smith observed: "All things that were able to do them hurt beyond their prevention, they adore with their kinde of divine worship; as the fire, water, lightning, thunder, our ordinance, peeces, horses, etc." Animals might also have manit or even be incarnations of quiyoughcosughs. Indians frightened by an aggressive hog took him for "the God of the Swine, which was offended with them."[22]

Relations between flesh-and-blood quiyoughcosugh-chiefs mirrored those between the greater gods. Ahone created order and stability, whereas Okeus, assigned to deal with humans, held out the threat of war and famine. Like Ahone, werowances and paramount chiefs served as sources of order and stability within their communities. Primarily concerned with mediating between more powerful spiritual beings and their own people, each hereditary chief delegated Okeus-like external relations such as war and diplomacy to an external chief, normally a relative who was a lesser chief in his own right. The Patawomeck werowance, for example, deputized his brother Iopassus (chief of a Patawomeck hamlet) to deal with outsiders, while Opechancanough, not his elder brother Powhatan, normally came forward to negotiate with the Virginia colonists.[23]

Chiefly lineages emphasized their foreign origins in order to demonstrate that they were part of a universal spiritual order rather than local parvenus. The brother of the Piscataway tayac recalled that their line of chiefs began with "a King from the Easterne Shoare." Similarly, Powhatan was born an outsider to all but a half-dozen of the thirty-plus chiefdoms he acquired during his lifetime, and oral tradition consistently maintained that his predecessor came from the West Indies or the Southwest.[24] Yet without a continuing stream of evidence that they possessed unusual spiritual power, exogamous chiefly lineages would have been little more than pushy outsiders. Priests, bound in a deeply symbiotic relationship with chiefs, provided that evidence. Through rituals, images, architecture, clothing, and bodily markings, priests constantly reminded people of the hereditary and personal spiritual power of chiefs. Priests also tended temples containing sacred images, the bodies of deceased chiefs, and the stored wealth of the current chief.[25]

Although ordinary people could not match the spiritual potency of chiefs and priests, almost anyone could forge some connection with the spirits through rituals, sacrifices, smoking, and dreaming. Indeed, such connections were critical to success in life. Ordinary people constantly tended to their relations with the spirits who inhabited their world. They routinely sacrificed the "first fruits of their corne, and of that which they get by hunting and fishing." Tobacco and other sacred objects opened paths of communication at such moments. Ordinary people also offered tobacco and other goods "when they return from the warrs, from hunting, and upon many other occasions" and after their customary morning bath. Dreams also connected humans and spirits.[26]

For young men, however, there was no substitute for a successful *huskanaw*, a rigorous coming-of-age ritual reserved for the "choicest and briskest . . . and such only as have acquired some treasure by their travels and hunting." A young man who successfully completed the huskanaw established a personal relationship with a spirit who would henceforth serve as a source of power and wisdom, not to mention help him to fight, hunt, and fish better. Having emerged from the ceremony fortified with the power of their tutelary spirit, these young men had much to offer their werowance and their community. A few became priests or conjurors. Others, having ritually "died" to their families in the course of the huskanaw, were "qualified . . . equally and impartially to administer justice, without having respect either to friend or relation." The werowance selected his "best trusted councellors and freindes" from this class of men, consulting them before making important decisions.[27]

People could improve their access to spiritual power if they possessed copper, shell beads, or other potent objects. Such items permitted spiritually gifted users to more readily invoke and more fully employ the power of spiritual beings. These things were literally otherworldly: in Native traditions throughout the eastern woodlands, they were represented as gifts from guiding spirits. As such they formed connecting links through which spiritual power and guidance could flow, allowing their users to boost their own power and well-being. The specific uses to which they were put depended upon their color (the reddest copper was particularly prized, as were particularly white or dark beads) and upon the ceremonies in which they were used. In very concrete ways, copper and beads were the keys to power.[28]

In fact, one can trace the flow and exercise of power by following the transit of beads and copper through networks of trade, tribute, and gifting. Each of these networks tended to funnel spiritually potent items through the hands of the region's werowances and paramount chiefs. Like chiefly lineages, the most spiritually potent trade goods came from the outside: Patawomeck antimony found its way to the James River, copper came from the Great Lakes region, Western Shore puccoon (a sought-after red dye) found its way to the Eastern Shore, and the best shell beads came from the Eastern Shore. Such goods tended to accumulate in the hands of chiefs, who were already presumed to possess spiritual power and thus had the authority to regulate long-distance trade. Chiefs traded directly with outsiders for these goods and attempted (with partial success) to monopolize the trade.[29] But even trade goods acquired by ordinary people were subject to regular demands for tribute, which also channeled them into chiefs' hands. Consequently, werowances and paramount chiefs accumulated tremendous stores of valued goods, some of which was conspicuously displayed as a reminder of chiefly legitimacy.[30]

Smart chiefs, however, also gave away much of their wealth. Gifts conjured up a general sense of indebtedness on the part of recipients, and such obligations could be called in at important moments to gain support for the chiefs' decisions. Yet gift-giving was not necessarily coercive or even a calculated act; it could just as easily be conceived of as a way of maintaining a sense of reciprocity and balance within a relationship. Indeed, a werowance who gratefully accepted a gift of copper from Powhatan might soon afterward turn around and offer another gift to Powhatan—an act more consistent with the cultivation of reciprocity than with the cold calculation of debts owed. Moreover, when a chief distributed copper to his clients, the reddish metal identified its recipients with the spiritual sources of authority, power, and influence. Thus copper was not used to "wage" hireling werowances and war leaders, as the English thought, but rather to enhance the spiritual power they needed if they were to command respect at home and to succeed in war abroad.[31]

Long-distance trade, tribute, and the ethic of gifting merged almost seamlessly into diplomacy. The exchange of goods between chiefs was expected to take the form of mutual generosity rather than competitive bargaining, especially when the diplomatic stakes were high. More than mere goods were exchanged in such encounters. When John Smith's men reconnoitered the Bay in 1608, each nation they came upon wanted to exchange presents "to express their loves." The English party, for example, gave the Massawomecks two bells in order to establish peaceable relations, while the Tockwoghs and Susquehannocks gave gifts to Smith to pave the way for an attempt at enlisting the English as allies *against* the Massawomecks. Gifting in a diplomatic setting created a sense of reciprocity that made peaceable relations possible. The fact that the goods exchanged normally included copper and beads should serve as a reminder that diplomacy constituted an encounter not just between humans but also between the spiritual beings from which the participants derived their power.[32]

In sum, chiefs were generalists: unlike more specialized priests, outer chiefs, warriors, or political advisors, chiefs took the lead in religious, military, political, economic, and diplomatic affairs. Because they combined spiritual, military, and economic power, chiefs could hold their own against fellow elites whose sources of power were more narrowly defined. By 1607 virtually every Algonquian nation in the Chesapeake region had institutionalized the position of werowance. A hereditary chief's authority and power were now as much ascribed as achieved, rooted as much in his *right* to command as in his personal characteristics. Chiefly power and authority were now of a piece with the very structure of the universe: the werowance, Ahone, the outer chief, Okeus, the priest, the shaman, the quiyoughcosugh, the warrior, and the commoner all had their place within the cosmos and in society. Yet each source of chiefly power—spiritual, military, and economic—could cut both ways, either working to consolidate the chief's rule or to undermine it. An individual werowance had access to spiritual power independent of his paramount chief's connections to the spirit world; the warriors who deferred to a chief could also turn on him; and the inherently decentralized nature of exchange networks made them impossible to fully control. Since no werowance or paramount chief could monopolize power, there remained a real tension between the way things were supposed to work (from a chief's perspective) and the way things actually did work. This tension helps to explain why politics, war, and diplomacy along the Potomac were so complicated, fluid, and diverse.[33]

Reading Potomac Landscapes

Both Algonquian ecological imaginations and the tumultuous events of the sixteenth century found expression in the very landscape of the Potomac. Quite sensibly, given the subsistence and settlement systems they had developed in the preceding three centuries, the peoples of the Potomac placed their hamlets and villages very close to their major sources of food and other supplies. The Algonquians' choice of hamlet and village sites reflected the importance of dietary diversity, the difficulty of getting through the late winter and early spring without good fisheries, the importance of women's work, and the need for shelter against raging storms and enemy warriors. Settlements were invariably located near freshwater marshes where women could gather critically important plants such tuckahoe and reeds, and no village was far from the shallows of a freshwater creek or river where men could waylay some of the millions of spawning fish that passed up the Potomac each spring. Women tended corn that they had planted in fertile soil close to their houses. Nearby, recently abandoned fields attracted deer and sprouted edible greens and medicinal plants. With each passing year abandoned fields grew denser with berries and thickets, while the deer continued to feast along the boundary between forest and clearing. The mixed deciduous forests beyond the fields offered nuts, game, saplings and bark, and fuel for the perpetual fires kept in each household. Villagers on the outer coastal plain settlements also lived near oyster beds, mussel shoals, and saltwater marshes where blue crabs could be found in the summer months. Upstream locations on tributaries also provided shelter against Atlantic storms and concealment from Susquehannock and Massawomeck warriors.[34] It was not difficult to find a place with good fishing, or level riverfront soils, or freshwater marshes, or mixed deciduous forests, but few places had *all* of these necessities of life. Where all of these features came together, one could find an Algonquian settlement.

But by the end of the sixteenth century, the Potomac landscape had also come to reflect the transformation of the region's social, political, and diplomatic order; now, superimposed on an older landscape reflecting mainly the subsistence needs of the populace, one could see the lineaments of power in societies led by chiefs, priests, and elites. Thus a meaningful map of a Potomac hamlet would chart the relationships between women and plants, men and women, commoners and chiefs, and spirits, nature, and humans.

A perceptive visitor could discern some of the ways in which these relationships had been written into the landscape simply by touring a single Potomac nation. Imagine, for instance, that it is May 1608 and that you are on your way to the seven Patawomeck hamlets clustered along Aquia Creek. The Potomac River near the mouth of the creek is very wide, so you will want to stay near the shoreline lest the water turns choppy and swamps your dugout canoe. If you canoe downstream and stick to the outside (south) of the river bend, the current will carry you directly to the mouth of Aquia Creek. Normally the water here is fresh, but 1608 is the third consecutive year of a very serious drought, so the reduced flow of the river may have allowed the tides to push water from the Chesapeake Bay farther upriver than usual, making the water taste slightly salty.[35]

Although you won't see any hamlets near the mouth of the creek, the confluence of Aquia Creek and the Potomac is much used. You wave to men fishing for striped bass at their spawning grounds on the main stem of the Potomac and shout a greeting to boys clamming in the brackish shallows at the mouth of the creek. You might well see signs of regular fires in the woods—not only from natural causes but also from fire hunting and from campfires spread out of control. Where the woods have burned, the forest has a park-like feel to it, with mature trees predominating and little underbrush and few saplings or downed limbs in sight. Natural grasses thrive in the small clearings kept open by fire.[36]

After a mile or so you encounter men skimming fish from weirs built on the midstream shelf. For the next two miles you traverse the favored spawning grounds of perch and shad and follow the route of spawning alewives and herrings headed for the far upper reaches of the creek. Three miles upstream from the Potomac, Aquia Creek narrows to less than a quarter-mile wide. On the left Chopawamsic Creek comes tumbling out of low, close-set rolling hills; after this point Aquia Creek widens out again, spreading to nearly a mile in some places. Freshwater marshes line much of the shore, especially on your left. Yet still there are no dwellings or fields, as women will generally use marshes closer to home.[37]

In another mile (now nearly five miles from the Potomac) the landscape changes significantly. You navigate a narrow passage of open water between the tuckahoe, lilies, cattails, and sedges crowding outward from the shoreline. Here you are very likely to encounter women at work, for the first Patawomeck hamlet, Quiyough, lies just ahead. Suddenly the creek narrows to a stream. The marshes recede. The air fills with the sharp scent of woodsmoke. The continuous fires maintained in each house consume a tremendous amount of firewood, so the forest floor has been picked clean of downed branches, trees, and kindling. It may also have been burned recently to discourage insects and other pests or to make it more difficult for enemy warriors to slip up on the hamlet. Thus you can see quite some distance through the trees, where scattered mat-covered houses begin to appear. Elderly men and women work in the shade, minding small children while also tending cookpots and sewing reeds. The dispersed houses stand close to small fields where women and older children hoe, dig, and bend to plant seeds. Some corn has already sprouted. If any adult men are in sight, they are probably resting, for their workplaces—the fisheries, the hunting grounds, the warpaths, and the trading places—lie beyond the edge of the fields. The hamlet spreads out on both sides of the creek, with no more than fifty houses strung along the water for up to a mile.[38]

The hamlet has no discernable center, and most of the buildings are of roughly the same size and design. Chiefs and priests, who need larger buildings, do not live here—only common folks of varying degrees of wealth. An insider could pick out a few structures with specialized functions: a sweathouse, the women's menstrual hut, and possibly the home of the local headman appointed by the werowance or of a shaman or healer. Otherwise, the sameness of the architecture reflects the fact that mostly commoners live in hamlets. Their houses are spread out because everyone wants to live close to their fields and their fresh drinking water.[39] Prevailing agricultural practices also encourage dispersed settlements. Although planting beans and melons between the cornstalks helps to fix nitrogen in the soil and return other nutrients as they return to the soil during the winter, crop yields decline quickly in the absence of fertilizers. Moreover, weeds prosper in Virginia. With every year the labor required to cultivate these fields increases while production goes down. Thus new fields are constantly being cleared, a two-year-long job in which men first girdle the trees near the root, then scorch the roots with fire; the following spring they return to fell the dead trees, uproot the smaller stumps, and work some of the remaining organic matter into the soil. A complex patchwork of fertile and infertile soils borders Aquia Creek, so it is often impossible for the members of a household to clear a new field that is contiguous to the old one. Consequently, hamlets constantly morph into new shapes as people leapfrog over old fields and inferior soils to build new houses next to freshly cleared fields.[40]

You might well encounter several parties of women traveling on the river near the hamlet. (If you see any men on the river, they are probably tending fish traps or carrying baskets full of herrings and alewives back to their houses.) Most women are busy planting at this time of year, but the people crave fruits and starchy foods to supplement their fish-dominated May diet. Thus some of the women are headed for recently abandoned fields in search of blackberries, strawberries, dewberries, and wild plums, while others are taking a day away from planting to go to the extensive marsh immediately upstream from the village, where they can gather reeds and grasses for making mats, baskets, and twine, in addition to arrow arum, or tuckahoe, valued for its starchy roots. Since arrow arum grows in clumps or rafts where the water is too deep for cattails, mallows, and sedges, women waited until midtide and then wrestled the roots up from under a foot of mud, then carried them home to be sun-dried or baked for a day, and then baked or boiled the tuckahoe in loaves.[41]

As you continue upstream beyond the hamlet of Quiyough, the creek widens into the marsh. You press on, passing through five more hamlets in the next dozen miles before reaching a mine. People there are digging away with shells and hatchets, then sifting the ore in a nearby brook, and bagging the remainder to trade with other nations. This is *matchqueon* (antimony), a rare "glistering metal" used to add a silver sparkle to one's facial paint.[42]

The seven hamlets closely resemble each other, for the Patawomecks have inscribed their vision of the world into the very earth in a manner that is consistent not only with their natural surroundings but also perpetuated by their culture. The dispersed settlements, the nearly uniform architecture, the patchwork of gender- and age-specific spaces, the medley of fields, forest, and old fields in varying states of recovery, the park-like woods cleared of brush and fallen timber, and the strategic placement of hamlets comprise a distinctive landscape—a landscape that makes incarnate an Algonquian vision of the proper relationships among humans, the land, and the waters, plants, fish, and animals.

A visit to the nearby werowance's village of Patawomeck would reveal additional dimensions to the Algonquians' worldview. If you drifted with the current down Aquia Creek, then followed the Potomac River downstream a short distance to the next south-bank tributary, you might be surprised to find a substantial village to your right, perched near the end of a narrow peninsula just a half-mile within the mouth of Potomac Creek. You might wonder about the village's placement, as the village of Patawomeck seems more exposed to attack (and to storms) than the hamlets clustered on the upper reaches of Aquia Creek. You might wonder about the food supply as well. There is a small marsh where the creek and the river meet, and a good freshwater spring at the village, but there is very little first-class soil to be found within a mile's radius. People do live here, but clearly the people who selected this village site had something other than subsistence in mind.[43]

Even from the water you can tell that Patawomeck serves different functions than the hamlets along Aquia Creek. The buildings cluster together, many of them within a protective ring of palisades. Whereas the buildings in the hamlets were fairly homogenous, at Patawomeck you can see a variety of buildings ranging up to a hundred feet long. As one might expect, this varied architecture reflects the diversity of people within the village.[44] Just ahead of you a party of men in strange clothing, outlanders by the looks of it, approaches the town. The townspeople are waiting for them, singing, shouting, and clearly joyful about the arrival of these foreign guests. The visitors pass through two parallel rows of townspeople and disappear behind the palisade. Following the townspeople as they file back into the village, you see the werowance of Patawomeck sitting on a mat opposite the strangers. One of his councilors has launched into a formal welcoming oratory. Nearby, townspeople are assembling a feast. Even though it is May and most people have long since used the last of their autumn harvest, it looks as though the guests will eat corn and beans today, in addition to venison, fish, and other delicacies.[45]

While the other guests feast, you can tour the village. On closer examination you learn that some of the larger buildings are the houses of the werowance, his councilors, and other high-status people. Such people need more space for their larger families and also to store their corn and other belongings. This is not a society in which amassing wealth is the primary measure of success. Nevertheless, accomplishments in hunting or war, service as a counselor or priest, good marriages, and emblems of wealth such as food surpluses, numerous children, and large dwellings—all go hand in hand. (Such things, of course, flow from having established a close relationship with a tutelary spirit in the huskanaw.)

The chief's house, extending up to a hundred feet long, is three to five times the size of ordinary houses. The door to an ordinary dwelling opens into a single, general-purpose room, but a person entering a werowance's house passes through "many darke windinges and turnings" before encountering the chief. Here, in one of several rooms partitioned off by woven mats, the werowance receives guests whom he wishes to impress. The werowance also needs extra room to accommodate his multiple wives and their children. Any man may take multiple wives if he can woo them and provide for them, but the werowance's wealth and power give him the right to "send for . . . the fayrest and cumliest mayds" to marry. Multiple wives remind onlookers of the chief's power, and he exercises more control over his wives than is usual in Algonquian marriages.[46]

Priests also occupy a clearly defined space within this werowance's village, maintaining at least some of their temples there. The werowance has actively recruited some of the most gifted priests and built for them temples up to a hundred feet long. Wooden posts carved with the faces of "sentinells . . . to defend, and protect the howse" also distinguish the temples at Patawomeck from other buildings. The temple, considered "so holie, as that none but the Priestes and kings dare come therein," houses spiritually powerful objects that enable priests to "call up spiritts" for consultations. Priests spend much time in the company of these objects and spirits, treating their temples "as solitary asceteria . . . to exercise themselves in contemplacion." They emerge from such retreats with counsel that common folks and chiefs alike must take most seriously.[47]

Somewhere around Patawomeck—where, exactly, you as an outsider will probably never know—is a temple containing sacred images, the bodies of deceased chiefs, and the stored wealth of the current chief. But just knowing that it is around somewhere is sufficient: affiliating the bodies of the chiefs with the images of powerful spiritual beings makes a fairly obvious statement, and associating the fruits of tribute with such potent objects suggests the legitimacy of chiefly demands.[48]

The very existence of this temple points to the contrast between the afterlives of commoners and chiefs. Here on the inner coastal plain, most people go to their rest in mass graves, or "ossuaries," some of which contain the remains of hundreds of people. Except for children, the people buried in ossuaries are not buried with grave goods. In contrast, the bodies of chiefs are placed "upon a little scaffold (as upon a tomb) laying by the dead bodyes feet all his ritches in severall baskets." The chiefs' "inwards" are stuffed with "perle, copper, beades," and other precious items sewed into skin pouches. Such goods are necessary for the road ahead, for after death priests and chiefs go "beyound the mountaines towardes the setting of the sun, and ever remaine there in forme of their Oke." You, on the other hand, need not worry about provisions for that journey, for "the common people they suppose shall not live after death."[49] The holiest of all temples at Patawomeck, then, supports the notion that the werowance's lineage can produce generations of divine, spiritually potent leaders worthy of chiefly power.

A separate building, not in use just now, is reserved for *matchcomico*, or council meetings. The werowance selected his "best trusted councellors and freindes" from among those who had excelled at their huskanaw and had subsequently earned the right to be consulted through some combination of notable bravery, advanced age, manifest wisdom, and family connections. War leaders, often called *cockarouses*, had a voice in council, but so did *wisos*, notable for their age and influence rather than for their recent exploits in the woods.[50] At each meeting, noted an English observer, the junior councilor "begins first and delivers his sentiment without interruption, the second forbearing to speake till a good time after his sessation . . . and after that he speakes not a second time to the same thing, thus orderly they every one declare their judgements, and advice, and after all the King tells them what is his pleasure."[51] Advice from priests carried particular weight, for their direct access to powerful spirits (including the great Okeus) enabled them to foresee the results of decisions, read the minds of distant people, change the weather, and find lost objects. The werowance, of course, had the last word, for none could rival his spiritual power, which was so palpable that his aura of majesty struck "awe and sufficient wonder" into onlookers and inspired their "reverence."[52]

As you continue your exploration, you notice that cues inscribed on the body reveal much about the status of each person you see. Hair clearly distinguishes "maids" from married women, elites from commoners, and accomplished warriors from the rest of the pack. The unmarried women have shaved most of their heads, leaving "the hinder part very long, which they tie in a plate hanging downe to their hips," noted William Strachey, whereas married women let their thick, oiled, black hair grow out all the way around, with their tresses either loose or pinned up in a single knot bound with shells or beads (which marked their wealth, status, and spiritual power). Okeus had long ago taught men how to wear their hair very long on the left side, but plucked clean on the right side of the head so "that it might not hinder them by flappinge about ther bow stringe, when they draw it to shoott." Their long hair on the left side is oiled and kept tied up in a single knot decorated with items reflecting their wealth, status, and accomplishments: "the hand of their enemy dryed, croisetts of bright and shyning copper . . . the whole skyn of a hawke stuffed, with the winges abroad, and buzzardes or other fowles whole wings." Some wear bits of bones, teeth, rattles, and shells in the knot, which when shaken made "a certayne murmering or whistling noyse by gathering wynd . . . and hold that a kynd of bravery."[53]

The adults who are in a position to do so are wearing clothing trimmed or embroidered with beads and copper. Some of them might wish for one last cool day in May, for in cool weather they are able to display their wealth on a broader canvas: on a long deerskin fastened over one shoulder and falling below the thigh, called a "mantle," or on a fur cloak called a matchcoat. The most sumptuous mantles and matchcoats owned by the elites in this village incorporate enormous quantities of turkey feathers, copper, shells, and other prestige items. But in this weather they must content themselves with wearing their beads and copper in necklaces and earrings; other jewelry is festooned with hawks' bills, eagles' talons, pearls, and bone. Even adults' skin announces their place in the community: the married women have tattooed their arms, legs, chests, shoulders, and faces with flowers, snakes, fruits, fish, and birds, while men and women alike have painted their faces and bodies with reddening puccoon, bloodroot mixes, black, yellow, red, and blue dyes; some have embedded down and feathers in the paint.

On the whole, the typical resident of Patawomeck on this day is dressed somewhat like ordinary people in the hamlets but much more richly. The men display more ornaments in their hair, and the women wear more beads and pearls. Many have elaborately painted themselves for the feast, perhaps even using some of the silvery, "glistering" matchqueon dust from the mine on Aquia Creek. A few of the men at Patawomeck, however, wear clothing and hairstyles rarely seen in the hamlets. They wear their hair close-shaven except for "a thin crest like a cockscomb which stands bristling up and runs in a semi-circle from the forehead up along the crown to the nape of the neck." Another strip of hair along the forehead is stiffened with grease and paint; it stands out "like the peak of a bonnet." A striking cloak slung over one shoulder hides one arm altogether; it hangs down to midthigh, and tufts of fur on the partially dressed skin look "very shaggy and frightful." These strangely dressed men, you learn, are priests. Chiefs, priests, and elites stand out all the more when their hair and dress is contrasted with the common folks who have come to the village to wait upon their betters at feasts, to work in the werowance's fields, and to gather for trading, hunting, or war parties. Conspicuous by their lack of rich furs and copper, shell beads, or other ornaments, the commoners are clearly marked as the subjects over whom power is exercised.[54]

By early evening the feast is winding down. The leaders of both parties smoke tobacco together, and the evening ends with a dance in which the welcoming party takes turns rising to join a growing circle until the entire group wheels around the guests. The principal men among the visitors carry away far more food than they alone could eat; they distribute it to other members of the party. The hosts then escort the leaders to their sleeping quarters, where a "bedfellow" awaits, "fresh painted red" with poccune dye and oil. When they leave, the visitors will carry with them small bags of matchqueon dust, having left copper, shell beads, or some other exotic good in exchange.[55]

The people at Patawomeck have created a landscape reflecting their sense of social, political, and spiritual order. Here is a hierarchy of buildings, with the size and external markings of each indicating that it is used by priests, by leading warriors and councilors, or by the werowance himself. Here are people and things that must be prominently displayed yet defended at all costs—hence the exposed location on a peninsula near the mouth of Potomac Creek, the compact settlement, and the palisades. Clearly, this is a place of power.

The landscape of werowances' villages such as Patawomeck embodied fundamental elements of Algonquian spirituality. At the deepest level, the landscape bore the marks of the inherently spiritual power that flowed through a series of paired entities stretching from Ahone the creator to the chiefs and priests who created the peculiar diplomatic configuration of the Potomac on the eve of permanent English colonization. Ahone created order and security, whereas Okeus, assigned to deal with humans, held out the threat of war and famine. Like Ahone, werowances and paramount chiefs served as sources of order and stability within the nation. Primarily concerned with mediating between more powerful spiritual beings and their own people, hereditary chiefs deputed external relations such as war and diplomacy to external chiefs such as Iopassus. Between them, the spirits and their human clients sculpted the landscape into a distinctively Algonquian arrangement of villages, hamlets, fields, forests, and national territories.

On another level, the landscape of a werowance's villages such as Patawomeck clearly demonstrated the wisdom of C. S. Lewis's observation that the most innovative generations have the most power over their successors, that "all long-term exercises of power" over nature "must mean the power of earlier generations over later ones."[56] By 1600 the legacy of those earlier generations included a hierarchical social and political order, which was also written into the landscape and organization of space within Potomac villages. In the village's location, in its specialized dwellings, and in the dress and other trappings adopted by its people, observers could read the political, social, and diplomatic relations that bound together common folks, councilors, priests, and chiefs. Patawomeck, like other werowances' villages, literally put commoners, councilors, priests, and chiefs in their places—in relationship to nature, to each other, and to the spirits who animated the world.

In short, by the end of the sixteenth century the choices people had made about how to live upon the land and with one another had hardened into a system, the contours of which would do much to determine the course of events when Englishmen attempted to establish a colony at Jamestown, eighty miles to the south of the Potomac in the heart of Powhatan's Tsenacommacah.

Yet the colonists had a history, too. They were the products of a specific environment, and they had developed their own peculiar ways of living upon the land and with each other. What is more, they had already developed some ideas about how to justify and carry out the conquest and colonization of indigenous people who lived in chiefdoms. At exactly the same time that the Piscataway tayac and Powhatan's lineage were establishing the paramount chiefdoms that would eventually encompass the Potomac Valley, English adventurers were trying out one strategy after another for establishing and legitimizing English rule in Ireland, learning lessons there that would soon be applied to American colonization. The ideology of colonization they developed in Ireland, the technology of war they employed, and the organization of the colonial societies they established were all firmly rooted in a distinctively English ecological imagination. Thus, while it may seem at first like a digression, we must turn our attention to the diverse landscapes of Tudor England.

CHAPTER FOUR

The Nature of Colonization

The arrival of English colonists at Jamestown in 1607, and the regular contact they initiated with the peoples of the Potomac the following year, marked the intersection of two previously separate historical trajectories and the meeting of two significantly different environmental sensibilities. Contrary to stereotype, however, regular contact between the Potomac nations and English colonists did not immediately transform life along the river. Quite the opposite: compared to the tumultuous fourteenth, fifteenth, and sixteenth centuries, the first half of the seventeenth century brought relatively few major changes to the Native peoples of the Potomac. They were spared for the moment the epidemics that laid waste to other Native American populations in this same period, and they mostly kept their ancestral lands: as late as 1650 all but two of the river's Native groups remained rooted in the same soil that had sustained them in 1607. Nor did the fundamentals of the Potomac nations' subsistence practices, social structure, cosmology, and political culture undergo any major changes. Some nations were even able to exploit the English presence for conservative purposes, to roll back the clock by using the newcomers to regain their independence from Powhatan or the tayac.[1]

In fact, life was harder and more tumultuous for *colonists* in the first half of the seventeenth century than it was for the Native peoples of the Potomac. Far from destroying the environment and laying waste to indigenous populations, the English struggled to survive in their new environment. Few in number and wracked by disease and internal conflicts, colonists along the Potomac were forced to find their niche within Native American networks of trade and diplomacy that had been established well before their arrival. No less than the Algonquians, English colonists sought a place within these indigenous diplomatic and exchange networks in order to survive in a world of expansionist paramount chiefs and northern Iroquoian raiders.

The English ecological imagination also meshed surprisingly well with that of the Potomac Algonquians, even though the English brought to the Potomac very different ideas about the proper relationships between humans and nature. One could read some of these differences in the landscapes they had created. On the one hand, Potomac villagers aimed at dietary diversification within each village or hamlet and traded outside the immediate vicinity mainly for culturally significant goods such as shell beads and copper; thus each local landscape roughly resembled that of every other settlement in the region. On the other hand, the English tended toward distinctive local specializations, producing surpluses of whatever could be best produced and marketed in each specific place, and thus they created a wide variety of landscapes that were linked together by a long-distance trade in virtually everything under the sun. This made it possible for Englishmen to imagine such wildly different places as London, rural Ulster, and the lower Potomac as part of the landscape of greater Britain. Other distinctive features of the English ecological imagination were worked out during the sixteenth-century reconquest of Ireland: many of the men involved in the colonization of Virginia had fought in the savage campaigns of the Nine Years War (1594–1603), in which English officers developed a comprehensive form of ecological warfare specifically intended for people regarded as "natural" or "wild" and thus lacking cultivation and civility.

Surprisingly, it was the very differences between the ecological imaginations and historical trajectories of Natives and newcomers that fostered a half-century of coexistence between the Potomac nations and English colonists at Jamestown and (after 1634) in the new colony of Maryland. Although one prominent historian has asserted that colonial encounters in early America demanded a "choice ... between two different ways of living, two ways of belonging to an ecosystem," on the Potomac circumstances did not immediately force that choice.[2] There were more than two ways of living here, because the region's long-term environmental history had produced a complex economic and diplomatic configuration in which the arrival of the English meant something different to each werowance and his people. No two nations' interests, geographies, or histories were alike; consequently, their responses to the English presence were strikingly varied and fluid. Thus some Native groups were willing to trade with and ally themselves with the English, while others were not (or were willing but on different terms). Nor were Europeans a monolithic, single-minded group. Those with an interest in the Potomac were divided between Virginians and Marylanders; between English, Dutch, and Swedes; and into different factions within each political grouping. These factions often allied themselves with Native American groups, even when doing so put them in opposition to other Europeans—or even fellow countrymen. Moreover, the English ecological vision allowed for a comparable diversity of local landscapes and economic specializations, which led them to establish correspondingly varied relationships with the Chesapeake region's Native Americans.

In short, the historical trajectories and ecological imaginations of English colonists and the peoples of the Potomac were profoundly different but momentarily complementary. Jamestown colonists and officials in the 1610s and 1620s made no effort to conquer the Potomac Valley. Instead the English allied themselves with the Patawomecks and other south-bank nations in order to defeat and declare their material independence from the Powhatans, in whose midst the English had settled. In keeping with Algonquian norms, these alliances were based as much on exchange as they were on military assistance; thus the Potomac served as a breadbasket to the Virginia colony, while the English provided copper, metal tools, and other useful goods that strengthened the positions of their Algonquian recipients.

The Nature of Englishmen

It has become a commonplace that English colonists' relationships with nature were essentially exploitative, driven by the quest for profits and supported by their notions about exclusive property rights. This grossly oversimplifies English realities. Most English people lived in intimate and complex relationships with nature—so intimate, in fact, that their ideas about plants, animals, and the land could not be disentangled from their ideas about human nature, society, and civility. Colonists came from an England that was very much shaped by its significant ecological diversity, by a plethora of locally specific subsistence practices, by a land ethic emphasizing sustainability, and by its inhabitants' sense that the most civilized people were those who created the most highly cultivated landscapes. They projected human characteristics onto some animals and animal traits onto some humans, especially onto humans who failed to meet their standards of cultivation and civility.

England's environmental diversity forced its people to adapt to a wide variety of local ecological regimes, ranging from the fertile and relatively warm lowlands of the south and east to the rugged highlands of the north and west. Even within these broad divisions there was considerable variety. The north and west included a few wide, fertile, and much-cultivated valleys (especially in the west country), as well as heaths, forests, and mountains, while the south and east encompassed forests, fields, and extensive fens.[3] Observers of England found its society to be even more diverse than its landscape. Perplexed travelers struggled to understand local dialects and exclaimed over distinctive local vernacular architectures. Barristers and attorneys had to keep track of a seemingly infinite variety of land tenures, of which fee simple ownership (today's norm) was but one. Manorial law and custom differed radically from one place to the next. Travelers could not even depend on the weight of a pound, the size of an acre, or the length of a yard remaining constant from one place to the next.[4]

Many of these cultural and environmental variations found expression in the landscape. Within the space of a few dozen miles a traveler might traverse a fenced-in and unpopulated forest; a substantial village surrounded by several large, unfenced fields; a densely populated woods with an open, park-like forest floor and dispersed settlements; an area of scattered dairy farms surrounded by extensive pastures; and tiny hamlets adjacent to fields and pastures that were fenced in by hedgerows. Knowledgeable observers could treat each of these landscapes as a text, reading in it a variety of political, social, and economic relations. The fenced-in forest, for example, might well be a deer park reserved for the king and his favorites. In contrast, the large fields surrounding the nucleated village were probably held in common; although individuals owned specific strips or plots within each field, they submitted to communal regulation of their farming practices, worked the fields together, and enjoyed (or endured) common use rights such as pasturage and gleaning. The inhabitants of small hamlets, however, typically enjoyed more nearly exclusive rights over their separate, enclosed fields than did residents of the nucleated village. They had little need to coordinate their farming activities with those of their neighbors, or even to live near their neighbors. Thus each small community entered into its own relationship to the land, compounding England's natural diversity and creating an astonishingly complex patchwork of soil types, field systems, crops, marketplaces, animals, and settlement patterns. These locally specific agricultural practices were carefully tailored to local ecological conditions, but grazing, woodcutting, and farming also altered the environment; culture adapted to nature, and nature to culture.[5]

Two examples, highlands pasture and mixed arable husbandry, illustrate how landscapes reflected both local ecology and local culture. The highlands stretched from Cornwall in the southwest to Northumberland on the Scottish border. Cattle and sheep-rearing predominated at both of these extremes. In the northern highlands, dispersed hamlets and single farms roughly conformed to the distribution of arable soils. (Arable farming is characterized by an annual regimen of plowing, seeding, and cultivating each field.) Most households owned or leased less than ten acres of enclosed arable land. Barley and oats predominated, probably because of their flexibility: they could be used for bread, beer, or fodder. Most farmers worked beans and peas into the crop rotation as well, both for food and to fix nitrogen in the soil. But highland farmers typically devoted as much of their limited acreage to meadow and pasture as they did to arable crops, for they mainly raised cattle and sheep. Thus the moors and heaths rising above the valleys, while largely uninhabited, were absolutely critical to the local economy. Each summer, neighbors and kin combined their herds, driving them into the hills to browse on common pasture until fall. After the harvest the livestock returned to the valleys, where they fed on the stubble in the fields and on fodder stored for the winter and early spring.[6]

To southerners accustomed to fertile, rolling lowlands, the mountains, moors, and heaths of northern Britain looked like "a deformed chaos." Lowlanders preferred a highly cultivated landscape, marked especially by arable farming. They expected to see hedges, fences, and plowed fields. They expected these things because they believed that purposeful, moral human labor could undo the degeneration of nature that had begun with the fall of man: cultivated lands signaled a movement back to the prelapsarian Garden of Eden. "Uncultivated land meant uncultivated men," writes historian Keith Thomas. Civilized people improved the land, displaying their cultivation through their well-tended fields and livestock. Fine, straight furrows and orderly rows of crops took on a moral as well as an economic dimension.[7] Yet while arable farming became the standard of cultivation by which other types of farming were judged, the impulse to reduce the lowlands to cultivation did not translate into a uniform landscape. Varying degrees of access to urban places, market towns, and transportation networks led farmers in some areas to lean toward dairy farming, while those in other locales, with similar soils and climate, emphasized fruit or market-gardening, wheat production, or fishing.[8]

Paradoxically, the very diversity of English landscapes fostered a distinctive English ecological imagination incorporating a shared set of land-use practices, undergirded by generally agreed-upon principles that went to the heart of their relationships with the natural world. This common ground was formed out of concrete experiences, for about 70 percent of the English citizenry engaged directly in agriculture in 1600, and many of the remaining 30 percent had considerable experience with rural life (even those who gave their occupation as "blacksmith" or "clergy" often spent as much time farming as they did smithing or tending their spiritual flocks). Moreover, virtually every parish in the realm included pasture, meadow, woods, and arable fields, albeit in highly variable proportions, and many English people traveled regularly or migrated in pursuit of work, love, or commerce, thus exposing them to a wider array of land-use practices. Consequently, each of the stock elements of English land use was present in the collective consciousness of prospective colonists.[9]

Several underlying principles of land use informed agricultural practices throughout England, beginning with an impulse to "improve" the land. Draining fens, marling soils, upgrading seed stocks, planting hedgerows with useful fruit trees, and a myriad of other "improvements" increased yields and converted "waste" lands that would otherwise have been left to nature alone. English farmers also valued sustainability. They avoided agricultural practices that permanently reduced crop yields or the carrying capacity of pastures, preferring instead technologies that made it possible to cultivate the same lands for generations. Communities with common grazing rights limited the number of cattle and sheep each individual could pasture, while woodsmen coppiced or pollarded trees (a severe pruning to stimulate the growth of young branches, which can be repeatedly harvested from the same tree) rather than clear-cutting. Farmers "folded" their livestock, herding them at night onto fields in need of manuring, and they rotated crops (and left land fallow) to maintain fertility in the long term. The English also preferred domesticated to wild animals, depending upon them for power, fertilizer, meat, dairy, clothing, and transport. Except for game preserves, domesticated animals largely replaced wild game in the realm's forests and fields. Finally, the English carefully subdivided their landscapes into separate spaces. Everything had its place: one crop per field and one type of animal per pen. Thus a typical farm replicated on a small scale the overall pattern of local specializations within a context of national (and later imperial) diversity.[10]

This marked penchant for local specialization, and the resulting diversity of landscapes in England, was made possible by a market economy. The market economy effectively reconciled what at first glance appear to be two incompatible stances toward the natural world. On the one hand, English commercial relations allowed each farmer to decide what to emphasize (wheat, say, or dairy, or sheep, or woodcutting) based on the nuances of local environmental conditions and access to markets. On the other hand, this meant that English people were accustomed to meeting a substantial minority of their needs through extralocal trade and thus did not need to sustain a truly diverse local economy. Aided by a geography in which no part of the realm was more than seventy-five miles from the coast and most of the interior was within striking distance of a navigable river, merchants moved cattle from Ireland to England, conveyed wool from the northwest of England to the southeast, and transported grain from eastern ports to the northern counties. Long-distance trade in turn fostered the commodification of nature, in which *anything*—apples or wool, pork or labor—could be reduced to a uniform and abstract monetary value that made such exchanges possible over such great distances.[11]

On a still deeper level, certain generally agreed-upon philosophical principles undergirded English ideas about the proper relationships between plants, animals, and human societies. First and foremost, the English equated arable farming with proper civility, and civility with full humanity. This equation was firmly embedded in the language. The intertwined meanings of "culture," "cultured," "cultivation," "cultivated," and "agriculture" created a hopelessly tangled knot of words that ensured the association between the plow and personhood: all five words could mean "the tilling of land; tillage, husbandry," but all except "agriculture" equally denoted the nurturing, improvement, and refinement of human minds, faculties, and manners through education and training. In contrast, "barbarians" were part of untended, unimproved nature. Somewhat ominously for such "naturals," English commentators asserted that God had made nature for the use of humanity.[12]

Popular practices blurred the lines between humans and other animals. Ordinary people in the sixteenth and seventeenth centuries knew animals as individuals with unique personalities. Farmers gave personal names to cows, horses, and dogs and occasionally dressed them up with ribbons and bells, while more privileged families were increasingly prone to keep pets. Whether working animals or pets, individual animals were expected to understand English phrases and to be of good character. Human characteristics were projected onto bees, dogs, horses, and even plants, all of whom were implicitly ranked according to their degree of civility. Rewards and punishments were attached to their moral successes and failures. Such familiarity was part and parcel of rural life. Indeed, medieval homes had commonly housed both humans and animals, and in the late sixteenth century people had yet to complete the project of segregating cows' and humans' living quarters.[13]

It was no great leap to go from projecting human traits onto animals to projecting animal traits onto humans who did not seem fully civilized. The poor, for example, were often characterized as "bestial" or "brutish" and frequently compared to slow-witted beasts of burden. In *The Fraternitie of Vacabondes,* for instance, John Awdelay described a type of shiftless, thieving servant who skulked about like a "masterless dog," looking at "every toy" before pilfering some small item. Such characterizations meshed well with elites' interest in maintaining social distinctions, and the analogy between servants and livestock seemed obvious enough. Women, too, were compared to livestock, particularly when burdened with pregnancy, nursing, and child-rearing. The analogy extended to children: an infant was "but a brute beast in the shape of a man," and youths needed to be tamed and bridled like horses. Foreigners could also be characterized as brutes, which paved the way to assertions of natural dominion over people thought to be near the margins of humanity.[14]

The Irish in particular struck many Elizabethans as more animal than human. When English observers scanned the Irish landscape for clues that would help them to gauge the extent of civilization there, they found little that satisfied them. Ireland was sparsely populated, and much of it, particularly the regions under Gaelic control, was boggy or mountainous, and better suited to pasture than to the plow. The combination of a small population and the availability of extensive upland grazing areas promoted a system of "transhumance" similar to that used in England's northern highlands. English observers failed to appreciate the logic of transhumance, though: Irish herders, they argued, left the land "desolate and desert [unused]." By trimming away ill-fitting facts such as the critical importance of cultivated fields and pastures to Irish farmers and by ignoring the folly of arable farming in bogs and on mountainsides, Englishmen managed to fit the Irish into their conception of the uncultivating and uncultivated barbarian. From there it was but a short step to characterizing the Irish as animals. Fynes Moryson minced no words: "these wild Irish are not much unlike the wild beasts."[15]

Casting the Irish as half-beasts brought into play a different set of rules of engagement than those governing relationships between human beings. It opened up the possibility, for example, of using military strategies against the Irish that would ordinarily have been regarded as unethical, including the slaughter of noncombatants and the entrapment of opponents under the pretense of parley and truce. John Derricke, an associate of Henry Sidney, Elizabeth I's lord deputy of Ireland, used analogies from nature to suggest that ordinary restraints did not apply. All "kern" (Irish soldiers) were animals, incapable of civility; even if raised in the Queen's Court, they would return to savagery "as the sow returns to the mire, and the dog to his vomit again." Such "vipers" must be exterminated. Derricke's solution: Sidney, "falling upon" the kern, would show "no mercy or compassion" in hunting down a "wolfish" chieftain.[16]

Elizabeth I made the pacification of Ireland a high priority beginning in the 1570s, and in their efforts to carry out this mission English commanders developed a comprehensive form of ecological warfare—one specifically reserved for attacks against a people regarded as wild, natural, and uncultivated. The strategy that emerged fully integrated their ecological imaginations with their justifications for conquest, as well as with more traditional military strategies.

This integrated strategy was perfected at the conclusion of the Nine Years War (1594–1603), under the direction of Charles Blount, Lord Mountjoy. Mountjoy assumed command of the English forces in Ireland in January 1600. Under Mountjoy's command soldiers timed their raids according to the harvest and "spoyled all the rebels corne" only after taking enough to feed English soldiers and their horses. Mountjoy even planned for the summer's end, when the Irish would have to bring their cattle down from their summer pastures, thus delivering their meat to the English soldiers.[17] In the summer of 1602 Mountjoy sent his armies on a south-to-north sweep of Ireland along several different paths. Along the way, each army left behind small garrisons to harvest and stockpile food taken in local plundering expeditions and to destroy the rest. These garrisons were also supposed to discourage new uprisings and prevent small parties of "kern" from "feeding or stirring upon the Plaine." The strategy worked.[18] By September, thousands of emaciated corpses lay unburied by the roadsides, some of them with their mouths torn and stained green from eating nettles. Scattered pockets of resistance remained on into 1603, but the war was effectively over, won not so much on the battlefield as in the fields and pastures laid waste by English soldiers. Thousands of noncombatants died as the English waged war against the species that sustained entire Irish communities.[19]

On the eve of the founding of Jamestown, it was Ireland, not America, that had most fully captured the imagination of would-be English colonizers. Leading public figures invested heavily in its conquest and colonization, and intellectuals hoping to seize this opportunity to establish themselves in government service or as landed gentlemen used their talent and connections to publicize Irish affairs and to shape English ideas about colonization.[20] Those who actually fought and lived in Ireland learned valuable lessons about *how* to conquer and colonize, and as they did so they routinely drew upon English conceptions of nature. The result was a colonialist ideology, firmly rooted in the English ecological imagination, that inspired a highly integrated and devastating form of environmental warfare and profoundly shaped English colonists' relations with indigenous peoples. This kind of warfare transferred all too readily to America, where it was freely employed against the Powhatans, with important consequences for the Potomac nations.

On the whole, the English had more thoroughly transformed their landscape than had the Algonquians of the Potomac. Whereas Potomac Algonquians aimed at dietary diversification within each village or hamlet, making each local landscape resemble that of every other Chesapeake settlement, the English tended toward distinctive local specializations and thus created a wide variety of landscapes. Algonquians maximized economic diversity within the *village,* while the English sought diversity within the *nation.* The Algonquians cleared small fields and frequently set fire to the woods, but the English largely deforested their landscape, then planted selected species in hedgerows and orchards; and whereas Algonquian hunters merely thinned out the deer population near their villages and hamlets, the English went several steps further by replacing most large game with livestock. Yet the English, like the peoples of the Potomac, had a keen, practical interest in the natural world. They knew their surroundings intimately, for most people spent their entire lives working in nature with their bare hands. They experienced time as a cyclical, as well as a linear, phenomenon, for their working and social lives were inextricably tied to the seasonal rhythms of plants, animals, and weather, none of which they fully controlled. English relationships with their natural surroundings were no less intimate and complex, and no less tailored to local environmental circumstances, than those of the Native peoples of the Potomac basin.

It remained to be seen how English ideas about their place in nature would mesh with the realities of America. The English equation of arable farming with civility (and civility with full humanity) had served to legitimize the brutal conquest and colonization of Ireland. But how would this ideology play out along the Potomac? How would the long-term environmental histories of the Potomac and of its newest arrivals influence a werowance's calculations of the best way to exploit the colonists' presence, or a fur trader's relationships with his Native American partners, or a tobacco planter's encounters with his Indian neighbors? How would those histories translate into specific events, into specific choices made by specific people?

Fitting In

Most American schoolchildren know that Captain John Smith was captured by Powhatan's men in 1607, then "saved" by Powhatan's favored daughter, Pocahontas. What is less well known is that when placed in the context of a series of events staged over the course of his entire four-week captivity, Smith's deliverance from a club-wielding Powhatan executioner appears to have been a key moment in an elaborate ceremony designed to adopt the Jamestown colony as a new tributary nation within Tsenacommacah, with Smith as its werowance. In staying the execution, Powhatan said that he would spare Smith, in exchange for which the

English would "make him hatchets ... bells, beads, and copper," all of which were common items of tribute given by a dependent werowance to his paramount chief. At the ceremony's conclusion, wrote Smith, Powhatan "proclaimed me a werowanes of Powhatan" and directed that "all his subjects should so esteeme" the Jamestown colonists as "Powhatans."[21] Powhatan gave Smith a new territory and a new name to mark his new status: "he would give him [Smith] the country of Capahowasick, and forever esteem him as his son Nantaquoud." He directed the English werowance to abandon Jamestown.[22]

The English, however, refused to move from Jamestown to Capahowasick. Worse still, the wayward werowance Smith took it upon himself to explore the Chesapeake Bay in the summer of 1608, carrying on a trade and diplomacy independent of his paramount chief's.[23] Smith reconnoitered the Chesapeake Bay in two separate voyages that summer, sailing in a small vessel tended by about a dozen men. Smith's party traveled far up each of the major rivers in the area, sometimes leaving their vessel behind and striking out overland. What he couldn't see for himself, he filled in "by information of the Savages," often interviewing several different people for corroboration. Seeking better information on the geography of the region, Smith inventoried the number of "bowmen" each nation could muster, assessed the potential value of the natural resources each nation controlled, and attempted to sort out the cultural and political situation.[24]

One of Smith's chief findings was that fear of the Massawomecks ran very deep. When he encountered "7. or 8. Canowes-full of Massawomecks" at the northern end of the Chesapeake Bay, the Massawomecks communicated by signs that "they had been at warres with the Tockwoghs [an upper Eastern Shore people] the which they confirmed by showing us their green wounds." Smith's men next visited the Tockwoghs. Although initially wary of the Englishmen because they bore Massawomeck trade goods, the Tockwoghs introduced Smith to a party of Susquehannocks. These "mortall enimies with the Massawomecks" showered gifts upon Smith in particular, giving him "a great painted beares skin," an enormous chain of beads, eighteen mantles of various skins, which "with many other toyes, they laid at his feet." They pledged "what they had to bee his, if he would stay with them to defend and revenge them of the Massawomecks." Smith, however, made no promises, leaving the Susquehannocks "much sorrowing for our departure." Smith encountered no more Massawomecks, but everywhere he went he heard about this people who "made warre with all the world."[25]

Smith also discovered the limits of Powhatan's power. Powhatan's emissaries warned the Potomac nations of Smith's impending arrival on the river and directed them to drive the English away. As Smith worked his way up the south bank of the river he first encountered people at Onawmanient, where "strangely painted, grimed, and disguised" warriors attacked the English. The Chicacoans, Patawomecks, "and divers other" nations gave them a similar reception, "showting, yelling and crying" to add to the terror of their attacks. Then, in a series of abrupt turnarounds, each skirmish ended in diplomacy; Smith and his men were "kindly used" by the very people who had just ambushed them. The Onawmanients took James Watkins "6. myles up the woods, to their kings habitation," and the werowance at Patawomeck provided guides to escort the English up Aquia Creek to view the antimony mines. At Patawomeck, Smith struck up a relationship with Iopassus, brother and outer chief to the werowance. And the Tauxenents, Nacotchtanks, and Piscataways, recalled a member of Smith's party, "did their best to content us" without even the formality of a preliminary skirmish.[26]

Smith's *entrada* forced the issue of how the English might fit into the Potomac world. The answer, it soon emerged, was surprisingly well. Although mutual trust and respect were conspicuously lacking between Powhatans, colonists, and the Potomac nations, and while the Patawomecks, Piscataways, and Nacotchtanks suffered at the hands of Virginians on several occasions, early Anglo-Indian relations along the Potomac were on the whole mutually beneficial. The English ecological imagination embraced a diversity of landscapes within an encompassing market economy and thus did not require that the Potomac Valley should be remade into a Little England. On the contrary, to Virginians of the 1610s and 1620s the Potomac appeared best suited as a granary (and possibly a fur-trading reserve), peopled with intact and autonomous Indian communities capable of providing those goods to the small, struggling colony at Jamestown.

This fit well with Algonquian notions about the interconnectedness of spiritual power, trade, and diplomacy. The werowances' tribute system put surplus corn—of which the English were often desperately in need—into the hands of chiefs, while the English could lay their hands on vast quantities of copper and glass beads. The resulting trade made the English major players in the region's diplomacy, despite their small numbers and military weakness. An influx of spiritually potent goods from this new source could be used to strengthen a werowance's hand, both within his nation and in diplomatic affairs. English traders bearing copper and beads seemed to offer access to power that could liberate south-bank nations from the Powhatan yoke, protect the entire Potomac River from the depredations of Iroquoian warriors, and strengthen the hand of any chief who could tap into the English trade. In Algonquian eyes the English trade created a sense of reciprocity that would ensure the newcomers' friendship. English copper and beads, as well as more mundane items such as metal tools, also made the new-comers sufficiently useful that they need not be killed or left to starve.

Smith's expeditions in 1608 laid the groundwork for a new strategy of embracing Powhatan's enemies, particularly those along the Potomac. Although Smith frankly admired the Spanish way of subjugating Indians and thought the Patawomecks "generally perfidious," he nevertheless recognized that the Patawomecks' and Jamestown colonists' mutual antipathy to Powhatan constrained both parties to "a kinde of constancy." This policy was codified in Deputy Governor Thomas Gates's 1609 instructions from the Virginia Company, which advised that he "make freindship" with the nations "that are farthest from you and enemies unto those amonge whom you dwell." Such people, not having had much contact with the English, would be particularly impressed with the newcomers' copper and beads; "with those you may hold trade and freindship good cheape." With Powhatan under attack from the enemies who "environed" him, the English could then liberate "all his other weroances . . . from the tirrany of Powhataon." The secretary of the colony, William Strachey, wholeheartedly endorsed the policy, for people who had but recently been absorbed into Powhatan's chiefdom "maie peradventure be drawne from him for some rownd rewardes and a plentifull promise of copper."[27]

Thus the Patawomeck werowance fairly leapt to cultivate the English as allies when war broke out between the Powhatans and the English in the fall of 1609. Part of Powhatan's strategy was to cut off Jamestown's food supplies, and he soon had the colonists, who relied on corn acquired from their neighbors, teetering on the brink of starvation. The Patawomecks, however, defied Powhatan's trade embargo by selling the captain of an English ship as much corn as he could carry, despite an ugly incident in which the English cut off "towe of the Salvages heads." (The ship sailed directly to England without delivering the food, consigning many of the colonists to death in the famous "Starving Time," but that was hardly the Patawomecks' fault.) A few months later the Patawomeck werowance again defied Powhatan, this time by helping a young man named Henry Spelman to escape from Powhatan's household. Later in 1610 the Patawomeck outer chief, Iopassus, handed Spelman over to Captain Samuel Argall and again traded a boatload of corn to the English. Iopassus filled Argall's ships with another 1,100 bushels of corn in 1612 and then delivered Powhatan's daughter Pocahontas into Argall's hands in 1613 (an act that eventually brought the war to an end).[28]

The Patawomecks and English had relatively little contact during the peace that followed Pocahontas's 1614 marriage to John Rolfe, but Iopassus was poised to renew the alliance when Anglo-Powhatan relations worsened at the end of the

Anglo-Powhatan relations, 1613–14, according to Georg Keller. By Johann Theodore de Bry after Georg Keller. Courtesy of the Virginia Historical Society, Richmond.

decade. In September 1619 Iopassus surprised the English by appearing unannounced in Jamestown, ostensibly to ask that "2 shipps might be speedyly to Patawamack where they should trade for great stoore of corne." Iopassus also surprised the governor by insisting that he dispatch an Englishman to accompany him back to Patawomeck by an overland route, a troublesome and inefficient way of traveling in the watery Tidewater region. Still another surprise awaited the two English ships that arrived at Patawomeck in October: there was no corn to be had! Angered, the two English captains acquired their corn mainly "by force from Jupasons [Iopassus's] Country who deceyved them." Then, despite the fact that Iopassus had clearly duped the English in some way, and although the English had just taken the Patawomecks' corn, Iopassus "made a firme peace againe" just before the English ships departed in late November.[29]

Iopassus's strange behavior makes better sense when understood in the context of 1619—a year, according to English leaders, of increasingly "doubtful times between us and the [Powhatan] Indians." The Governor's Council noted in October that Opechancanough had "stood aloofe upon termes of dout and Jealousy" ever since Governor George Yeardley's arrival and that he "would not be drawne to any treaty at all."[30] The Patawomeck outer chief may also have sensed that the time was right for a challenge to the paramount chief, for Pocahontas had died in 1617 (severing the main diplomatic link between the English and Powhatans), and Powhatan himself had died in 1618 (leaving his untested brother Itoyatan at the helm). Amidst all of this uncertainty, Iopassus's 1619 mission to Jamestown stands out as a dashing and rather daring declaration of independence. By traveling overland through the heart of Itoyatan's paramount chiefdom, with English emissaries in tow, Iopassus clearly signaled that the Patawomecks could make their own deals with the English. Yet Iopassus's initiative amounted to more than a change of masters; he also made fools of the English in order to make a point to Opechancanough, thus indicating the Patawomecks' independence of both of the powers to his south.[31]

Iopassus's journey to Jamestown coincided with renewed English interest in the northern Chesapeake. Virginians along the James River had discovered five years earlier that tobacco was a marketable crop, and by 1619 so many people were planting it that the weed was already well on its way to becoming the dominant staple crop that would shape life in Virginia for nearly two centuries. Virginia Company officials who were concerned with this trend or who sought fortunes from something other than tobacco looked to the northern Chesapeake to diversify the colony's economy. They continued to regard the Potomac as a reserve granary and attempted to reestablish an old saltworks and fishing settlement on

Smith Island (northwest of the mouth of the Potomac). They also tried some-thing new: opening a fur trade on the northern Chesapeake Bay.

Impressed by the profits garnered in the 1610s by Dutchmen on the Hudson River and by Frenchmen on the St. Lawrence and in Acadia, English adventur-ers sought their own source of furs in Virginia.[32] In 1620 John Pory, the colony's secretary, sent company officials a list of current prices for furs and pelts in Vir-ginia. Beaver pelts were clearly the main prize: "bever skins that are full growne, in season" brought seven shillings, and old beaver pelts that had been softened by use brought even better prices. Pory struck out on his own in 1621, making "a dis-coverie into the great Bay northward." Soon the northern Bay had nearly a hun-dred English settlers, mostly on the Eastern Shore and on nearby islands. There they lived "very happily, with hope of a good trade of furres there to bee had."[33] Virginia Company investors in London scrambled to claim their share of the fur trade. The company's leaders took up a subscription to finance a fur-trading ven-ture and immediately raised more than enough capital to begin operations. They selected an agent, recruited translators, and rushed to dispatch a ship before the end of 1621. By early 1622 company officials were writing of "the furr and glasse buissines" as an integrated program, in which beads manufactured at Jamestown could be exchanged for pelts on the northern Bay.[34]

All such plans were set aside after the events of 22 March 1622, when Powhatan warriors struck almost simultaneously against the English settlements scattered up and down the James River. Seizing the colonists' own weapons and tools, the Powhatans cut, bludgeoned, and speared the woefully unprepared settlers to death. They killed over a quarter of the English population in the space of a few hours, "not sparing eyther age or sexe, man, woman or childe." At least 347 colonists died, and survivors reported that the attackers mutilated English corpses: "not being content with taking away life alone, they fell after againe upon the dead, making as well as they could, a fresh murder, defacing, dragging, and mangling the dead carkasses into many pieces, and carrying some parts away in derision."[35] The Powhatans apparently expected the English to accept the attack as a corrective blow, one designed to force them back into their proper territory on the lower James, to end conflicts over natural resources, and to cease mission-izing efforts. The attackers made no attempt to expel the English from Tsenacom-macah, and they spared Jamestown altogether. They did not attack the English again until September 1622, and even then they resumed skirmishes rather than launching another full-scale assault.[36]

News of the attack reached London in July, triggering a stream of words redo-lent of the rhetoric surrounding the Elizabethan conquest of Ireland. Edward

Waterhouse had never been to Virginia, but he already knew plenty about uncivil "savages" because his uncle had served as secretary to the Earl of Essex during the bloody campaigns of the Nine Years War. Thus his *Declaration of the State of the Colony in Virginia,* published just weeks after news of the "massacre" arrived in England, could have passed for an analysis of the Irish situation circa 1600. "You should know," he informed readers, "that these wyld naked Natives live not in great numbers together, but dispersed." Their largely uncultivated lands reflected their largely uncultivated humanity. The colonists, he asserted, had tried to domesticate their "rude, barbarous, and naked" neighbors, but "savageness needs more cultivation then the ground it selfe." Virginia's fertile soils bore ample fruit, "the land being tilled and used well by us," but attempts at cultivating civility amongst "the *Savages* . . . have in stead of that *harvest* which our paines merited, returned nothing but bryers and thornes, pricking even to death many of their benefactors."[37]

Henry Spelman learned of the attacks while trading at Chicacoan, on the south bank of the Potomac near the river's mouth. One of Spelman's acquaintances there told him that Opechancanough had tried and failed to enlist the Chicacoans in the 22 March attack but that the Wicocomocos, who lived at the end of the Northern Neck, had agreed to support Opechancanough's plans. Spelman, accompanied by another ship captained by Raleigh Croshaw, sailed directly to Wicocomoco. The Wicocomocos denied any complicity with Opechancanough and agreed to provide enough corn to fill Spelman's pinnace. Spelman returned to Jamestown, while Croshaw went on to Patawomeck.[38]

Croshaw arrived in Patawomeck at a delicate moment. The Patawomeck werowance had not yet committed himself to either side in the new Anglo-Powhatan War. Now he "earnestly entreated" Croshaw "to be his friend, his countenancer, his Captaine and director against the Pazaticans [on the Rappahannock River], the Nacotchtanks, and Moyaons [Piscataways] his mortall enemies." In exchange, he implied, the Patawomecks might serve the English cause "as an opposite to Opechancanough." Croshaw sent his ship back to Jamestown after finishing his trading, but he stayed behind at Patawomeck to keep an eye on the situation.[39] Shortly after Croshaw's ship left, messengers from Opechancanough appeared at Patawomeck. They bore two baskets of beads and bragged of the Powhatans' successful exploits of 22 March. The Patawomeck werowance, they suggested, should kill his English guests. The werowance demurred, insisting on his neutrality. He refused to accept the beads.[40]

When Captain Ralph Hamor sailed to the Potomac in May 1622, he joined Croshaw in trying to persuade the Patawomecks to commit to an English alliance. The werowance, however, held out for direct military assistance from the English in the Patawomecks' own conflicts along the Potomac River. He told Croshaw and Hamor that he had no corn to spare but that "the Nacotchtanks and their confederats had, which were enemies both to him and them." If the English wished to "fetch" the corn at Nacotchtank, he would provide "40. or 50 choise Bow-men to conduct and assist them." Hamor agreed to the scheme. The Patawomecks and English sailed upriver and laid waste to the Nacotchtanks, killing numerous villagers and driving the rest into the woods. Taking as much corn and loot as they could carry and "spoiling the rest," they returned in triumph to Patawomeck. Hamor went on to Jamestown, but Croshaw decided to stay at least through the coming harvest, when he would procure much-needed corn for Jamestown.[41]

The arrival of another English ship in late July or early August 1622, however, set in motion a chain of events that threatened to destroy the renewed Patawomeck-Virginia alliance. Captain Isaac Madison had been commissioned to assist the Patawomeck werowance against "our enemies, and to defend them *and theire Corne* to his uttmost power." Just as Madison's ship arrived at Patawomeck, Croshaw received an urgent letter from his wife, a prisoner of Opechancanough's on the Pamunky River. Croshaw hastily departed for Jamestown to help arrange her release, leaving Madison in charge of trade and diplomacy on the Potomac.[42] Madison relied heavily upon Robert Poole, an often troublesome interpreter who quickly made himself unpopular with the Patawomecks. The inexperienced and ill-advised Madison almost immediately committed the blunder of trading with the Piscataways, enemies to the Patawomecks; given the close association between Algonquian trade and Algonquian diplomacy, this must have made the Patawomeck werowance very apprehensive.[43]

Amidst all of this uncertainty a fugitive werowance who had recently been "beat out of his Country" by the Nacotchtanks took refuge at Patawomeck. The chief, most likely from a Tauxenent town near the falls of the Potomac, "professed much love to the Patawomeks" but in fact he bore a grudge against them for not coming to his aid against their mutual Nacotchtank enemy. Shortly after arriving at Patawomeck, the "expulsed King" told Poole that the Patawomeck werowance and his "great Conjurer" were plotting with Opechancanough to kill the Englishmen.[44] The day after this rumor reached Madison's ears, the English locked the werowance, his son, and four other Patawomeck men inside an English strong-house, and "setting upon the towne with the rest of his men, slew thirty or forty men, women and children." The survivors took refuge in the woods. After the killing, Poole and Madison accused the werowance of plotting with Opechancanough, abandoned Patawomeck, and carried his hostages back to Jamestown.[45] Experienced Potomac River hands such as Spelman, Hamor, and Croshaw were all in Jamestown when Madison arrived with his prisoners, and they quickly convinced Governor Francis Wyatt that Madison had blundered. Wyatt hastily commissioned Hamor to return the prisoners to their home on the Potomac, but the damage was already done.[46]

Although the future of the Patawomeck alliance seemed doubtful in the fall of 1622, the summer's trade and diplomacy on the Potomac (and parallel initiatives on the Eastern Shore) had at least bought the English time to develop a strategy for repaying the Powhatans. The strategy that emerged was cold, calculating, and devastatingly effective. At first the colonists held back: "to lull them the better in securitie," they deliberately "sought no revenge till thier corne was ripe." Then, throughout the fall and early winter of 1622–23, Englishmen sacked villages from the Rappahannock to the Nansemond River, timing their raids to "surprize their corne." Governor Wyatt's instructions to his officers and his reports to the Virginia Company emphasized corn over conquest, and when he reckoned up his military assets he counted men who were "serviceable for caryinge of corne" as well as fighters.[47] Even diplomacy pointed toward ecological warfare: the English agreed to a truce in the spring of 1623 in order to let Powhatans and English alike plant their crops, all the while planning to resume their attacks after the corn ripened.[48]

The announcement of the spring 1623 Anglo-Powhatan truce coincided with an attempt at making amends with the Patawomecks. Spelman arrived on the Potomac in March and immediately set to trading. On 27 March he went ashore at Nacotchtank, the same town that the Patawomecks and English had sacked in 1622. Suddenly a flotilla of canoes appeared, so swiftly overtaking and overwhelming Spelman's party that the English managed to fire only a single shot. Some of the canoes raced for the larger English ship, whose skeleton crew frantically raised the sails just in time to outpace their pursuers. As they sped away, the survivors "heard a great brute amongst the Salvages a shore, and saw a mans head throwne downe the banke," then retrieved and displayed on a pole. All told, the victorious warriors killed twenty men, captured guns, armor, and swords, and took prisoner a boy named Henry Fleet.[49]

A Patawomeck-English rapprochement followed quickly on the heels of Spelman's death. Opechancanough agreed to meet Captain William Tucker at Patawomeck in May 1623, apparently confident that Madison's rampage there in the summer of 1622 had rendered the Patawomecks neutral or hostile to the English. The Patawomecks, however, had lured Opechancanough into a trap: after the negotiations Captain Tucker provided poisoned drinks to toast the accord then fired on the deathly ill Powhatan delegates. Some of the English took scalps, and Tucker bragged (mistakenly) of killing Opechancanough.[50]

Although the Patawomecks' willingness to conspire against Opechancanough was encouraging to the English, the Virginians had yet to make full reparations for Madison's murders and kidnappings of the previous summer. Indeed, the plot to poison Opechancanough had simply put the English further in debt to the Patawomecks. Making amends would require a grand gesture, which Governor Wyatt performed in the fall of 1623. As soon as the English harvest had been secured, Wyatt personally led a ninety-man force to the Potomac River. Wyatt still did not know who had killed Spelman, but for diplomacy's sake he accepted the Patawomecks' manifestly false assertion that the Piscataways had done the deed. Together, bragged Wyatt, the English and Patawomecks attacked the Piscataways, "putt many to the swoorde," and took "a marvelous quantetie of corne."[51]

Now reconciled with the English, the Patawomecks finally agreed to support an attack against the Pamunkys, the core nation in Itoyatan's paramount chiefdom, "not only to asiste us in that revenge, but to accompeny us and bee our guides in a warr against the Pomunkeys." Defeating the Pamunkys would guarantee the Patawomecks' recently won independence from Itoyatan and make it harder for Opechancanough to retaliate against them for their role in his poisoning in the spring of 1623. It is not clear what role the Patawomecks actually played, but in a decisive battle in the summer of 1624 an English force confronted the Pamunky warriors while an equal number of Virginians took advantage of the diversion to burn the Pamunkys' fields. When the Pamunky warriors finally realized how much damage the English had done, they "gave over fightinge and dismayedly, stood most ruthfully lookinge one while theire corne was cutt downe." For the first time, the English clearly had the upper hand in Tsenacommacah.[52]

Yet Virginia's leaders deliberately prolonged the war for another *eight years* after the climactic victory of 1624. Year after year the Virginians inflicted light casualties and took large quantities of grain, always taking care to leave just enough people (and hope) behind to allow their victims to plant another crop before the next visitation of plundering militiamen. Periodic truces and aborted peace treaties encouraged the Powhatans to plant more food, which the English took as booty when the peace invariably failed.[53] Virtually all of the men who led expeditions against the Indians served on the Governor's Council. They decided when to raid Powhatan fields, and in their capacity as military commanders they kept much of the plunder for themselves, which they then sold at inflated wartime prices or fed to their servants so that they could produce more tobacco rather than wasting time on food crops.[54]

These chieftain-councilors assumed power during a decade when tobacco prices were high, tobacco exports increased dramatically, and indentured servitude (working under an exploitative contract that required workers to serve a master for years in exchange for transport to Virginia, food, lodging, and extremely modest "freedom dues") took firm root in the colony. Tobacco prices gradually declined during the decade but nevertheless remained high enough to ensure tremendous profits until a sharp downward adjustment in 1629. Not coincidentally, every councilor who led a military expedition between 1622 and 1625 ranked among the fifteen colonists controlling the greatest number of servants (including five of the top eight).[55]

The Patawomecks, however, took no part in these raids, for as far as they were concerned the English alliance had already served its purpose. Under the cover of the war, the Patawomecks and other south-bank nations had fully detached themselves from Tsenacommacah. Though buffeted by the Anglo-Patawomeck raids, the tayac's paramount chiefdom also remained largely intact. And while the details of diplomatic alignments had changed, the now-ancient divide between northern Iroquoians and the peoples of the Potomac remained a central fact of life along the river. Above all, the fundamental rhythms of everyday life on the river remained unchanged: villages followed the same annual round of seasonal work and social life as they had before the war, and they followed the same steps through the life cycle. The old rules still governed the workings of political systems, intercultural trade, and warfare. The English posed no immediate threat, for the nearest tobacco plantation in 1629 was still nearly a hundred miles to the south.

CHAPTER FIVE

Peltries and "Papists"

In the course of 1621, while Opitchipam, Opechancanough, and their allies were still planning the massive uprising of 1622, three previously unrelated Englishmen embarked on American adventures that would eventually, through a series of coincidences, hasten and profoundly shape the integration of the Potomac into the English provincial world. Two of these men traveled to Jamestown aboard the same ship: young Henry Fleet, a second cousin of Virginia governor Francis Wyatt, and William Claiborne, Virginia's new surveyor general. The third man, George Calvert, England's secretary of state, had long dabbled in colonial affairs. Now, in 1621, he dispatched a small colony to Newfoundland, where the settlers established a saltworks and took up commercial fishing. Calvert had little time to devote to the colony's affairs at first, but in 1625 he revealed himself as a Catholic. This meant that he could no longer hold public office in Protestant England, so he turned his attention to his much-neglected colonial projects instead. The king helped by elevating him to the Irish peerage (Calvert became the Baron of Baltimore) and settling five thousand acres of Irish land upon him. By the end of the 1620s Calvert had accumulated sufficient wealth and colonial experience to consider an attempt at establishing another colony, this time on the Chesapeake.[1]

In time Claiborne, Fleet, and Calvert became bitter rivals for control of the fur trade in the northern Chesapeake, with important consequences for both Natives and newcomers along the Potomac. By the 1640s, however, the dream of vast profits from the fur trade had been dashed and replaced by dreams of wealth from tobacco production. Yet even that dream turned out to be elusive, for in the 1640s a confluence of disease and civil war nearly destroyed the tiny English settlements along the lower Potomac. Although the Algonquian peoples of the Potomac also suffered reversals during the 1630s and 1640s, the English colonists were not the primary source of their problems. The fur trade required the preservation of existing Indian communities and exchange networks rather than their destruction, and the fewer than two hundred English residents along the Potomac in 1646 posed no immediate threat to the thousands of Algonquians still living there.

Peltries

Henry Fleet led the way to the Potomac. A member of Henry Spelman's crew, Fleet survived the March 1623 Nacotchtank ambush that killed Spelman and most of his men. He remained a captive at Nacotchtank for nearly five years, becoming so fluent in his captors' language that he considered himself "better proficient in the Indian language than mine own." Ransomed in 1627, Fleet returned to London. There he quickly won over a prominent merchant, William Cloberry, with tales of the mountains of furs to be had along the Potomac. Cloberry made Fleet the factor (officer in charge of trading) of the *Warwick,* a hundred-ton vessel bound for America. Fleet settled into a three-way trade in which he carried English-made "trucking stuff" (such as axes, cloth, and beads) to Algonquians throughout the Chesapeake Bay, corn from the Chesapeake to New England, and tobacco to England.[2]

Calvert's route also carried him closer to the Potomac fur trade in June 1627, when he visited Newfoundland for the first time in order to lay the groundwork for the removal of his personal household from Ireland to America. A year later he was back in Newfoundland, where he intended to stay. The move went so poorly, however, that he almost immediately began thinking about leaving. His colonists were chronically ill, and they clashed with the French over access to the Newfoundland fisheries. Their trade in fish plummeted to about one-third of its early 1620s peak. Calvert briefly considered abandoning his American adventures altogether, but instead he traveled to Virginia in 1629 to reconnoiter possibilities in the Chesapeake region. Calvert was much taken with the countryside, and he hastened to London to press his application for a new colony to be carved out of Virginia.[3]

Calvert's 1629 reconnaissance of Virginia met with considerable resistance from Virginians, who knew perfectly well what he was up to. Calvert's visit particularly threatened the interests of William Claiborne, who was by now among Virginia's elite: in 1625 he had won an appointment to the council, and he became the colony's secretary of state in 1626. Claiborne also displayed a real knack for cross-cultural trade, quickly establishing a relationship with the Susquehannocks. In January 1629 the council granted Claiborne a monopoly over the Susquehannock trade, and Claiborne threw himself into the work of securing financing, supplies, and personnel. Claiborne's fellow councilors, a tight-knit group forged in the course of seven years of war against the Powhatans, were not about to let an interloper such as Calvert threaten the success of this venture.[4]

Broader forces at work in 1629 also worked to promote the fur trade on the northern Chesapeake. The invention of a new process for felting beaver pelts had just inspired a burst of investment in fur-trading ventures. English merchants led by David Kirke conquered Québec in 1629 and immediately began reaping tremendous profits. Kirke acquired 6,253 pelts in 1629, and 30,000 more in 1630—and this at a time when a single pelt might bring £1 sterling (compared to but a few pence for a pound of tobacco). At the same moment, plummeting tobacco prices forced people already involved in the American trade to think about diversifying into furs. It was a propitious time for Claiborne to seek investors: Cloberry (Fleet's backer) and four other London merchants provided Claiborne with very substantial backing.[5]

By 1631 Claiborne had established an ambitious, well-capitalized operation on Kent Island, located astride a narrowing of the Bay to the north of the mouth of the Potomac. Claiborne brought in twenty servants, hired experienced traders and translators from the Eastern Shore, stocked nearby islands with hogs and cattle, and maintained several trading vessels. Settlers erected houses and a palisaded fort and cleared fields for tobacco, grain, and gardens. Kent Island quickly became a thriving colony-within-a-colony, sending a representative to the Virginia House of Burgesses and supporting its own Anglican parish. It also did a brisk business with the Susquehannocks, acquiring thousands of bushels of corn and grossing £4,000 sterling from pelts in the first several years.[6]

Whereas Claiborne carefully planned his entry into the beaver trade, Fleet drifted into it. While visiting Wicomico to purchase grain in 1630, Fleet solicited beaver pelts to be picked up when he returned to the river, but by the time he returned in October 1631 the Wicomicos had "by reason of my absence . . . not preserved their beaver." Fleet nevertheless looked forward to expanding his beaver trade in 1632. He persuaded the Wicomicos to stockpile furs over the winter and promised to return by 1 April. Fleet also made note of a tantalizing rumor of "a strange populous" Iroquoian nation, the Massawomecks, that had recently relocated from near Niagara Falls to the Appalachian hinterland of the Chesapeake Bay. In 1627 they staged a massive assault against the Piscataways, then formed an alliance with the Nacotchtanks, who used this new connection to gain a greater degree of independence from the tayac (who was "fearful to punish them, because they are protected by the Massomacks"). In return, the

Nacotchtanks agreed to "convey all such English truck as cometh into the river to the Massomacks." The Englishman who could capture the Massawomeck trade might become even richer than William Claiborne. But Fleet had already pledged to deliver corn to New England, so he reluctantly hastened to fulfill that obligation before the winter set in.[7]

Fleet was delayed in returning to the Potomac in the spring of 1632, which opened the door for Virginian Charles Harmon to nip into the river first and buy up 1,500 pounds of beaver pelts from fourteen hamlets on the lower Potomac. Fortunately for Fleet, however, the very best fur-trading opportunities in 1632 were to be had on the inner coastal plain: the Patawomeck werowance, for example, gave Fleet 114 pelts along with a shipload of corn, "yet that was nothing," wrote Fleet, compared to the 800 pounds of beaver he found waiting at Nacotchtank. There he also met the Massawomecks for the first time. They spun a dazzling tale for Fleet, telling of enormous palisaded villages containing 30,000 people, and "of the infinite store of beaver" there. Brushing aside the objections of the Piscataways (who had so recently been victimized by the Massawomecks) and of the Nacotchtanks (who feared that Fleet would cut them out of the trade), Fleet decided on the spot to "prosecute my trade" with the newcomers.[8] His brother traveled to the Massawomecks' towns, returning "laden with beaver, which could not be less than 4000 weight." Most of the Massawomecks halted above the falls, while a smaller party continued on downriver. Meeting with Fleet, the Massawomeck emissaries traded for what skins they had carried, drew Fleet a map of their homeland, and promised "to get great store of canoes to come down with one thousand Indians that should trade" with Fleet.[9]

Fleet had "stumbled upon the pelt-man's Eldorado" (as one historian has put it). Fur-trade riches, however, proved nearly as elusive as El Dorado's gold. Fleet had blundered at the outset by refusing to include the Nacotchtanks in the trade. They had offered to form an alliance with Fleet, to be sealed by a present for their werowance, but Fleet demurred. He soon realized that "the refusal of this offer was the greatest folly that I have ever committed," but this recognition came too late. Instead of promoting the trade between Fleet and the Massawomecks, the Nacotchtanks prevented the larger body of Massawomecks from descending to the Great Falls and raised questions in the Massawomecks' minds about Fleet's true intentions. The resulting delays forced Fleet to trade much of his truck for "victuals." Soon his stock was so depleted that he could not even pay for the furs already en route to the Great Falls.[10]

By mid-July, two months after entering the river, Fleet decided that only the Piscataway tayac could help him. Fleet apologized "for trading with those that were enemies" and convinced sixteen Piscataways to serve as middlemen in the Massawomeck trade. The new Piscataway recruits succeeded in keeping the Massawomecks interested, returning from a trip above the falls with a gift of eighty additional pelts and persuading the Massawomecks to bring Fleet more furs in the fall. Fleet left in late August after treating three Massawomeck envoys to a final "entertainment" on Piscataway Creek.[11]

"Divers envious people" in Jamestown had been talking since the previous winter of cutting off Fleet's Potomac trade, and his dealings with the Massawomecks only inflamed such sentiment. As Fleet began to work his way down the Potomac, a small pinnace carrying Charles Harmon and council member John Utie intercepted him. In Jamestown Fleet was hauled before a council packed with hard-bitten 1620s-era chieftain-planters, each of whom secretly proposed that Fleet form a partnership with him. Governor John Harvey, however, scooped his councilors: in September he ordered Fleet released and gave him permission to keep the *Warwick* (in effect stealing it from Fleet's London backers). Fleet, in a tidy quid pro quo, gave an unnamed "partner" (surely Governor Harvey) a half-interest in his vessel, kept the profits from the *Warwick*'s 1632 voyages, loaded up with trade goods, and sailed for the Potomac the following spring. Fleet eluded prosecution by his London backers and their creditors by purchasing his trade goods in Canada instead of England and sending his foodstuffs and wood products to the Madeiras instead of to New England. Within Virginia, he hedged his bets by sticking close to Governor Harvey while also cultivating a working relationship with Claiborne.[12]

Fleet and Claiborne were hardly typical Englishmen, yet in opening a northern Chesapeake fur trade they acted entirely within the confines of the English ecological imagination. Like dairymen in Kent, woodsmen in Suffolk, or Yorkshire herdsmen, Fleet and Claiborne carefully tailored their activities to local environmental conditions. They envisioned the north as a fur-trading preserve, which would help, in a modest way, to make England as a whole more self-sufficient. If all went according to plan, of course, it would also make Claiborne and Fleet very wealthy men. The northern Chesapeake remained a rather peculiar part of greater Britain, however, because fur traders could prosper only in the absence of actual British people. Fleet and Claiborne needed Indians, not Europeans. They needed men in the north to hunt down beaver in the depths of winter, when the animals' coats thickened to ward off the bone-chilling cold. They needed Indians to sustain the diplomacy that made it possible to deliver the pelts to Kent Island or to the Potomac. They did not need land-hungry English tobacco planters to disrupt the key intercultural relationships that made the fur trade possible.

"Such a Lucrative Trade with the Indians"

Even as Claiborne and Fleet were embarking upon their first full season in the fur trade, Lord Baltimore was successfully lobbying for a new colony that encompassed both Claiborne's outpost at Kent Island and Fleet's key trading partners on the north bank of the Potomac. Although George Calvert died in April 1632, the new charter nevertheless went into effect in June. The new Lord Baltimore, Cecilius Calvert, initially had in mind a settler colony whose lands would yield a steady income. He wished to distribute much of the land to English elites, who would preside over traditional English manors complete with manorial courts. Maryland would also provide a refuge for English Catholics. Fleet's and Claiborne's successes, however, inspired Calvert to modify his vision of Maryland as a traditional English country society.

During the two years between the granting of the Maryland charter and the arrival of the first shiploads of colonists in Maryland, rumors of the riches to be had in the fur trade convinced Calvert to adopt, at least in part, the Virginians' vision of the northern Chesapeake's place in the English landscape. In 1633 Calvert's prospective colonists heard that on the Potomac alone "there is such a lucrative trade with the Indians, that a certain merchant in the last year exported beaver skins to the value of 40,000 gold crowns, and the profit of the traffic is estimated at thirty fold."[13] Calvert quickly came to see the fur trade as the key to attracting support for the new colony. Land was a long-term investment, especially since it remained mostly uncleared, contested by angry Virginians, and inhabited by thousands of Indians. The fur trade, in contrast, promised quick profits; in the colony's first years, it was hoped, "furres alone" would "largely requite" the "adventure." Calvert organized a joint-stock fur-trading company and promised a free share to those who actually settled in Maryland. His promotional literature touted the fur trade, and Calvert persuaded some of his friends and relatives to invest in the company.[14]

Promoting the fur trade was one thing, but to make it work the Calverts had to overcome several major obstacles. They had to find someone with the personal contacts, linguistic skills, and local knowledge necessary to the fur trade. They had to convince the Susquehannocks or the Massawomecks to trade with their agents. And not least, they had to overcome the hostility of Claiborne, Fleet, and their allies. Claiborne was understandably upset to find his operation on Kent Island included within the Maryland charter. Virginians, he felt, had earned the right to use and occupy the entire Chesapeake region because lack of support from home had left Virginia "weltering in her own blood" during the Anglo-

Powhatan wars, in which "the burthen and charge thereof was onely undergone by the remaining Planters." It seemed patently offensive that Kent Island should become part of a "Papist" colony controlled by a rival fur trader.[15]

Two ships, the *Ark* and the *Dove,* arrived on the Chesapeake in the spring of 1634 with a cargo of about 130 Maryland colonists. Claiborne promptly vowed that he would drive away the interlopers. His agents urged the Susquehannocks to attack them and (according to Maryland's governor) they circulated rumors along the Potomac that "raysed all the nations . . . against us." As the *Ark* and the *Dove* passed up the river to meet the tayac they spotted numerous bonfires, which seemed an ominous sign. At some places "all the Indians fled from their houses," and when the tayac granted a meeting with the Marylanders he had 500 bowmen standing guard.[16]

Among those suspected of having "raysed all the nations" against the Maryland colonists was Henry Fleet, who found himself in a promising yet delicate position. Should he ally himself with Calvert, against Claiborne and his powerful supporters in Virginia? If he did, then perhaps Calvert's joint-stock company would provide Fleet with the trade goods he needed in order to regularize his still-tenuous trade with the Massawomecks. On the other hand, the Marylanders might try to cut Fleet out of the Potomac trade altogether or make a bargain with Claiborne. And what would become of Fleet if he threw in his lot with Maryland only to see the colony fail?

Fleet, it turned out, fit nicely into the Calverts' plans. Impressed by Fleet's excellent "language, love, and experience with the Indians," Governor Leonard Calvert (Lord Baltimore's brother) offered him a share of the beaver trade in exchange for his allegiance and assistance. Fleet agreed to the deal and went right to work. In a matter of weeks he had dissuaded the nations on the lower Potomac from attacking the Marylanders and had deftly guided the tayac and Calvert to an agreement that strengthened both Natives and newcomers against the threats posed by the Massawomecks and the Susquehannock-Claiborne alliance.[17]

Together the tayac and Fleet steered the Marylanders toward the outer coastal plain, where they could best serve the tayac's diplomatic purposes and Fleet's trading ambitions. On the inner coastal plain colonists might have competed for access to the prime resource areas that supported the powerful chiefdoms there, and the ensuing strife would have ruined the fur trade. On the outer coastal plain, however, the colonists provided the tayac with a line of defense against Susquehannock raids while occupying a village location that was, from an Algonquian standpoint, less than perfect. Thus Fleet escorted the Marylanders to a location "more towards the mouth of the said river," where they found "a most convenient harbour, and pleasant countrey lyinge on each side of it, with many large fields of excellent land, cleared from all wood." There, at Yaocomaco, an outlying hamlet of the Wicomico nation and a tributary of the tayac, the Marylanders established St. Mary's City. The Wicomicos agreed to cede half of the hamlet to the colonists in 1634 and the remainder in 1635. The colonists quickly set about planting corn and gardens on fields already cleared by their hosts. The Wicomicos also proved exceptionally willing to teach their guests how to hunt, fish, plant, and build canoes.[18]

The Wicomicos' generosity had a practical side. Father Andrew White, a Jesuit missionary, regarded the hatchets and other trade goods the Marylanders gave to the Wicomicos as "a trifle" compared to their hosts' gifts of "houses, land, and liveings," but he underestimated the significance of the Marylanders' outstanding debt. The Wicomicos had decided even before the Marylanders' arrival to abandon their village, but by welcoming the Marylanders they created a hefty obligation that the colonists would have, according to Algonquian values, to reciprocate. Because of their exposed position near the mouth of the Potomac, the Wicomicos were in sore need of a counterweight to the Susquehannock-Claiborne alliance. Father White acknowledged that "it made them more willing to enterteine us, for that they had warres with the Susquehannockes, who come sometimes upon them, and waste and spoile them and their country, for thus they hope by our meanes to be safe."[19]

The Maryland newcomers were willing to join in this reciprocity, at least to the extent that it promoted the fur trade and allowed them to avoid the bloody precedent of Virginia's Indian wars. While the new colonists built palisades and planted their first crop, Calvert dispatched a pinnace upriver to trade for beaver pelts. He pinned his hopes on the Massawomecks. "Wee understande for certaine, by Indians lately come from the said nation," anticipated Calvert, "that they have brought with them upwards of 2000 skins."[20]

And on that promising note, the Massawomecks abruptly and permanently disappeared from the Potomac scene. French documents and maps ceased to mention the Massawomecks (or "Antouhonorons," as they were known in the north) except to label them a "nation destroyed." Their disappearance coincided with the opening year of the "Beaver Wars," a bitter series of Iroquois mourning wars exacerbated by the introduction of European diseases and by the entry of French and Dutch fur traders into the Great Lakes region. From 1634 to the 1650s, Five Nations warriors scattered, displaced, or destroyed powerful nations such as the Hurons, Neutrals, Eries, Tobaccos, and Petuns. The effects were felt as far west as the Mississippi River. Individual Massawomecks may have survived this conflagration, but as a people they were no more.[21]

Unaware of the Massawomecks' tribulations, Marylanders stockpiled trade goods over the winter. Fleet struck a bargain with Calvert whereby Calvert supplied the trade goods, Fleet provided the expertise, and they shared the profits.[22] Claiborne, meanwhile, fiercely resisted the Calverts' attempts at bringing him to heel. He stayed away from a major parley in June 1634 that brought several key werowances together with the governors of Virginia and Maryland to discuss the Kent Island problem. The following spring Claiborne's ships twice clashed with ships captained by Maryland's Thomas Cornwallis, and Fleet seized another Claiborne ship while it was trading on the Patuxent; he confiscated the ship and its contents and hauled the crew before Governor Calvert at St. Mary's City, who held them for several days and then forced them to walk all the way back to Jamestown—unarmed and with no food. Soon afterward Claiborne joined his fellow members of the Virginia Council in forcibly expelling Governor Harvey from the colony. Harvey had never been part of the faction that dominated the council, and he had frequently angered them: by ending the profitable Anglo-Powhatan War in 1632, for instance, and by promoting the peace parley of June 1634. When Harvey refused to condemn the Marylanders' confiscation of Claiborne's ship the councilors arrested him and shipped him to England. The council appointed a more malleable governor, John West, who fully supported Kent Island's independence from Maryland. It even took steps to shut down Fleet's Potomac River trade, ordering Lieutenant Richard Poppely to "set sail . . . in pursuit and enquiry of Captain Henry Fleet and to apprehend him and bring him prisoner to the governor."[23]

Not surprisingly, Claiborne's resistance against Lord Baltimore and Governor Harvey got him into trouble at home. Charles I flatly rejected the notion that Virginia's councilors could make and unmake governors in a crown colony, and he sent Harvey back to Virginia in 1637. Harvey promptly arrested several councilors, replaced two of them with Lord Baltimore's supporters, and stripped Claiborne of all his offices. Meanwhile, Claiborne's financial backers in London fired him and replaced him with Robert Evelyn, Jr., a Maryland supporter on the reorganized Virginia Council. (Evelyn was not an entirely reliable ally for the Calverts, however; he appropriated large quantities of goods from Kent Island to set up his own Indian trade along the Potomac and stationed one of his men at Patawomeck to learn the language and conduct the trade.) Not satisfied with this political victory, Maryland's Governor Calvert invaded Kent Island in 1638 on the pretext that Claiborne's agent on Kent was encouraging the Susquehannocks to attack St. Mary's City. Two months later the Commission for Foreign Plantations ruled that Kent Island belonged to Maryland. The Susquehannocks countered by giving Claiborne a new trading base on Palmer's Island at the mouth of the Susquehanna River, even going so far as to clear fields for him. But the Marylanders soon completed their rout of Claiborne, passing a bill of attainder against him and seizing his assets on Kent and Palmer's islands. Claiborne, who estimated his losses at a massive £6,000, returned to England to press his case there.[24]

With Claiborne gone, Governor Calvert tried to engross more of the fur trade for himself. He urged Lord Baltimore not to "interest to[o] many sharers" in the windfall he anticipated after taking over Claiborne's operations. He blamed the competitive fur trade for "over bidding the prise [price] of beaver" and thus having "spoyled the trade," but if the company would only "let it out to us [Calvert and his partner Thomas Cornwallis] two or three yeares, rent free," they would whip the concern into shape. Lord Baltimore, the governor expected, would provide the trade goods and shipping necessary to revive the company's fortunes.[25]

This initiative nearly killed the fur trade. It alienated Fleet and failed to impress the Susquehannocks. Fleet realized that the Massawomeck trade would never materialize and that he could carry on a perfectly good local trade in corn and furs without the Calverts' interference. He left Maryland altogether in 1638, moving to a bay on the southeastern end of the Northern Neck. The Susquehannocks proved just as uncooperative. Remarkably loyal to Claiborne and unwilling to ally themselves to the Maryland friends of their Algonquian enemies along the Potomac, the Susquehannocks turned instead to the new Swedish colony on the Delaware River.[26] Thus the Calverts had defeated all of their main rivals for the lucrative northern fur trade but could not exploit their victory. Although small-scale Anglo-Indian trading continued throughout the seventeenth century, the beaver trade never fulfilled its initial promise.[27]

Though never of major economic significance, the fur-trading activities of Claiborne, Fleet, and the Calverts had the unanticipated effect of ensnaring Virginia and Maryland within an entirely Native diplomatic configuration. By this means the long-term environmental history of the Potomac, expressed through well-established patterns of exchange and diplomacy, left its mark on the charter generation of English settlers along the Potomac. It guided colonists even in such fundamental matters as the location of St. Mary's City, for the historical interplay of nature and culture had made towns on the inner coastal plain too strong for the English to encroach upon, thus making it possible for the tayac to direct the Marylanders to a location dictated by the Algonquians' pattern of land use, the colonists' expected place within the region's exchange system, and the tayac's diplomatic interests.

"Papists"

Far from settling matters, the Calverts' victory over their Virginia-based fur-trading rivals and political enemies marked the beginning of over a decade of troubles along the Potomac. Pursuing the fur trade had committed Marylanders to an alliance with the tayac, which consequently pitted the new colony against both the powerful Susquehannocks and their allies amongst Virginia's most consequential men, who in turn had highly influential patrons in London's merchant community. This diplomatic configuration outlived the Marylanders' hopes for a major fur trade, and it had dire results for the colony. Repeatedly attacked by Susquehannocks and twice conquered by Virginians, the Maryland colony barely survived the troublesome times of the 1640s and early 1650s.

The English on the Potomac remained militarily weak and few in number in the 1640s. Maryland attracted only a trickle of migrants in the half-dozen years after the initial voyage in 1634, and the south bank of the Potomac remained the nearly exclusive preserve of Wicocomocos, Onawmanients, Patawomecks, and Tauxenents. Most colonists were men, which suppressed the birthrate (with six men for every woman, Maryland could hardly be expected to grow much through natural increase). New colonists commonly sickened in the unfamiliar environment, falling to dysentery, malaria, and other diseases in their weakened state. This pervasive sickness took its toll in many ways: in death, of course, but also in unstable community leadership, disrupted family life, decreased productivity, and vulnerability to Indian attacks. The numbers dramatically illustrate Maryland's weakness: in 1640 no more than 450 colonists found themselves surrounded by at least 5,000 Algonquians along the Potomac and Patuxent rivers, and pressed between 7,600 hostile Virginians to the south and 6,000 of the Virginians' Susquehannock allies to the north. They had no choice but to maintain their alliance with the Piscataway tayac, but if the historic enmity between the Susquehannocks and the Potomac River nations flared up again the Marylanders risked getting caught in the crossfire—made all the more deadly by the inclusion of leading Virginians within the Susquehannocks' diplomatic orbit.[28]

And that, in fact, is precisely what happened. In 1642, four years after Maryland men had destroyed Claiborne's settlement on Palmer's Island, the Susquehannocks resumed their raids into the heart of the tayac's territory. Supplied with guns from New Sweden, the Susquehannocks attacked the Piscataways and killed colonists near St. Mary's City. The Jesuits had to abandon their mission at Piscataway after Susquehannock warriors killed the men stationed at the mission and plundered their supplies, and Maryland's government scrambled to organize its meager populace for defense. Financial problems, lack of manpower, infighting within the colony, and doubts about the loyalty of Kent Islanders hampered Maryland's attempts at fighting back. When Maryland troops did venture into the field in 1643 the Susquehannocks easily repulsed them. This embarrassing defeat was compounded by a bad tobacco harvest, which made it difficult to raise funds in the annual levy to pay for the campaign. The colony did manage to maintain a garrison on Kent Island and a small presence at the Piscataways' main town, but on the whole Maryland could do little to protect itself, let alone the hard-hit Piscataways.[29]

Fresh off their defeat at the Susquehannocks' hands and nervous over rumors of a Piscataway-Susquehannock peace (which would leave them entirely without allies), Marylanders feared the worst when they learned of a coordinated series of Powhatan attacks along the York and James rivers on 18 April 1644.[30] Powhatan's aged brother Opechancanough had orchestrated this sudden coup, which took the lives of about four hundred Virginians in a single day. Unlike 1622, however, thousands of Virginians survived the attack. Their revenge was swift and direct. County militias quickly mobilized to destroy the cornfields of the enemy nations closest to Jamestown, and increasingly well-planned campaigns over the next two years featured progressively larger and more mobile forces.[31]

In Maryland Opechancanough's attacks fueled fears of a pan-Indian alliance. In a panic, Maryland council member John Lewger begged Fleet to employ his "skill in the Indian language, and long conversation and experiences in the Indian affaires" in order to prevent a "generall league or plott for the cutting off of the English in Maryland." Fleet declined the invitation, but even without his intervention the "generall league" never materialized.[32] This probably came as no surprise to Fleet, who was in a better position than any other colonist to know that a Susquehannock-Piscataway alliance was highly unlikely and that Opechancanough's highly localized coup was not part of a broader Indian "plot."

Indeed, the real danger to colonists along the Potomac came from their own countrymen. The troubles began on the other side of the Atlantic, where events progressively weakened the Marylanders' toehold on the Potomac. An Irish uprising in 1641 reduced Lord Baltimore's income from his lands there and thus prevented him from adequately funding the Maryland venture. The Irish uprising was one link in a chain of events that rapidly escalated into a civil war within England, pitting Royalist forces against supporters of Parliament. Baltimore's patron Charles I enjoyed some initial victories, but a series of Royalist defeats in 1644 rendered him unable to provide much assistance to Baltimore. Since one of the main grievances against Charles I was that he seemed overly tolerant of Catholicism, Parliament's victories in 1644 made the Roman Catholic and Royalist Calvert family highly vulnerable to political attacks.[33]

Thus Baltimore had little recourse when his enemies descended upon Maryland. Claiborne returned to Virginia in 1643, having spent his five-year absence developing contacts among important Puritan merchants and political figures in England. Restored to Virginia's council in 1643, Claiborne served as major general of the colony's militia during the Anglo-Powhatan War of 1644–46. Richard Ingle, a Virginia-based employee of one of Claiborne's Puritan backers in London, opened the door to Claiborne's return to Kent Island by invading Maryland in 1645. Bearing authorization from the now-ascendant Parliament, Ingle and his men plundered colonists' homes, destroyed government records, and shut down Jesuit missions. Claiborne seized the opportunity to recapture Kent Island in 1646, using militiamen who were supposed to be fighting Opechancanough's warriors on the Pamunky River.[34]

By 1646 Maryland had nearly vanished. Disease and low birthrates continued to take their toll, and many colonists fled from Ingle's rule. (Ironically, some of them took up new residences in Virginia, on the south bank of the Potomac.) Including Kent Island, Maryland's population had dropped to less than 200; colonists on the Western Shore were probably fewer in number than the 130 passengers who had disembarked from the *Ark* and the *Dove* in 1634. For the moment, tiny New Sweden on the nearby Delaware River nearly matched Maryland's population. Even Ingle and Claiborne left Maryland.[35]

Fortunately for Lord Baltimore, the new Virginia governor William Berkeley's Anglican orthodoxy was making Virginia a hostile environment for a group of ultra-Protestants who had recently gathered on the south side of the James River. Led by Virginia councilor Richard Bennett, a number of these Puritans helped Calvert to recapture Maryland in 1646, and they ended up staying in Maryland. Then, in 1648, Baltimore replaced his recently deceased brother with a new governor, William Stone. Stone, a powerful Virginian and a solid Protestant, brought the colony back from the brink of extinction by restocking it with still more disgruntled ultra-Protestant émigrés from Virginia. Rising tobacco prices attracted additional immigrants, helping to more than triple the population between 1646 and 1650. Seven hundred colonists now inhabited Maryland, fully half of them Protestants. Baltimore took the further precaution of arranging for the passage of the 1649 Act Concerning Religion, a bill carefully crafted both to market Maryland as a haven for all manner of Christians and to protect Maryland's Catholics from the new Protestant immigrants.[36]

Still the enmity of Claiborne and his Susquehannock allies dogged the Potomac nations. The Susquehannocks struck repeated blows against the Potomac Algonquians, climaxing in a flurry of raids in 1648 in which they attacked nine nations along the Potomac and carried the Patawomeck werowance into captivity.[37] Meanwhile, Claiborne enlisted militant Protestants within Maryland and in England in a campaign to convince Parliament that Baltimore's colony harbored a dangerous nest of Papists. Richard Bennett pitched in by denouncing both Baltimore and Virginia's Governor Berkeley for their royalism. Claiborne and Bennett found their opportunity when George Thomson, one of their closest allies in the London merchant community, assumed leadership of a key parliamentary committee, through which he secured a commission for Bennett and Claiborne to reduce Virginia and Maryland to Parliament's authority. Backed by a parliamentary fleet, the two men first forced the capitulation of Governor Berkeley at Jamestown, then sailed to St. Mary's City. There they replaced Lord Baltimore's government with a committee of ten men drawn mainly from the ranks of recent immigrants from Virginia. Back in Virginia, the two men engineered their own appointments as governor (Bennett) and secretary of state (Claiborne).[38]

In the first major break from the region's sixteenth-century diplomatic configuration, Claiborne and Bennett celebrated their triumph over the Calverts by engineering a July 1652 peace treaty between the Susquehannocks and Maryland (which was regarded as binding upon Maryland's Algonquian allies as well). The timing of the treaty was good for Susquehannocks, for the Five Nations had just obliterated their most formidable northern enemies, the Hurons. The Susquehannocks replaced the Hurons as the Five Nations' favorite enemy.[39] Under these circumstances the Susquehannocks were well advised to make peace on their own southern flank, the better to concentrate on defending themselves against the Five Nations. The Susquehannocks conceded to Maryland all of the northern Chesapeake, with the notable exception of Kent and Palmer's islands, which, the treaty specified, still belonged to Claiborne. Claiborne, it appeared, had won his long battle against Lord Baltimore's colony.[40]

Yet the Susquehannock treaty, while a watershed in the region's history, marked neither Claiborne's ultimate triumph nor the end of Maryland's troubled times. Baltimore's appointee William Stone remained governor, and he retained considerable support among the populace. Then too, parliamentary rule in England declined steadily in popularity after 1652, undermining Claiborne's power base. The completeness of Claiborne's victory over the Calverts also worked against him, for it emboldened Protestants to take an excessively hard line against Catholics. They barred Catholics from voting and sharply restricted religious freedom. The new assembly also moved the provincial records, including precious land records, from St. Mary's City to the Protestant-dominated Patuxent River.[41]

The result was a civil war within Maryland, sparked by the January 1655 arrival of a ship bearing the news that Oliver Cromwell, Lord Protector of England, had restored Maryland to Lord Baltimore. When the Puritan commissioners refused to give up power, Governor Stone dispatched armed men to retrieve the provincial records from the Patuxent and to recruit men for an armed attack against the Puritan stronghold of Providence, on the Severn River. Things came to a head in March 1655, when fifty men were killed or wounded in a Sabbath-day battle. The Providence men won handily, capturing Stone and inflicting most of the casualties.[42]

Although the Providence men prevailed on the battlefield, Baltimore's supporters won the peace. In Virginia Governor Berkeley returned to office and undermined Claiborne's power by courting popular support as assiduously as he did the patronage of great men. Meanwhile, Claiborne was losing interest in the northern Chesapeake. In 1652 he joined Fleet and other Virginians in a new endeavor: the southern deerskin trade with Indians between the James River and the Savannah River. Fleet and Claiborne won grants of land in the Piedmont near the modern-day Virginia–North Carolina line, and the Virginia assembly gave them a fourteen-year license on the Indian trade in that region. Fleet's and Claiborne's interests in the northern Chesapeake switched from the Indian trade to the accumulation of land and equity within Virginia, which did not generally bring them into conflict with Marylanders.[43]

Claiborne and Bennett finally came to terms with Baltimore in 1657, signing what amounted to a peace treaty in which Maryland Protestants agreed to submit to proprietary rule, Claiborne acknowledged Maryland's legitimacy, and Baltimore granted a general amnesty to his opponents.[44] The deepest crisis, however, had passed a decade before, when Maryland had virtually ceased to exist. Since then Baltimore's risky strategy of recruiting Protestants to live in and govern the province had paid off. Increasingly healthy, numerous, wealthy, and secure, colonists in the 1650s began for the first time to significantly alter the Potomac landscape. Drawing from Virginia's example, and ever faithful to the English ecological imagination, they established a new economy based on tobacco, corn, and heavy meat consumption. Although the resulting annual subsistence cycle bore a marked resemblance to that of the Algonquian peoples of the Potomac, nevertheless after 1650 one could view the shoreline on the outer coastal plain and know it for an English-made landscape. The difference between the fur-trading pinnace of the early 1630s and the tobacco shed of the 1650s marked an important shift in colonists' ideas about their proper place within the Potomac environment. Although this shift had yet to fully transform the Potomac in the 1650s, it had already established the patterns by which the newcomers would live, and it set them on a collision course with their Algonquian hosts.

CHAPTER SIX

"You Come Too Near"

As late as 1650 neither grain traders, nor fur traders, nor even the first generation of English planters had done much to change life along the Potomac. Forty
years after the establishment of Jamestown and fifteen years after the founding of
Maryland, Algonquians still outnumbered the English. They had escaped the full
impact of the newly introduced diseases that so often decimated Native communities upon contact with Europeans, and they remained in the same places that
their ancestors had occupied in 1608. The Piscataway tayac still held sway over
the north bank. Although the Powhatan menace had been eliminated, the older
threat from the north persisted: as in the sixteenth century, Iroquoian raiders
still posed the greatest immediate danger to most villagers. Trade still supported
the authority of werowances, and the basic Algonquian subsistence cycle and life
cycle remained intact.

The third quarter of the seventeenth century, however, marked an abrupt re-
versal in Algonquian fortunes, as powerful environmental and political forces
transformed life along the river. Thousands of new colonists flooded the Potomac basin, altering the river's ecology by their very presence. Although their subsistence practices superficially resembled those of their Algonquian neighbors,
underlying differences in the English planters' land ethic virtually guaranteed
conflicts between Natives and newcomers. English livestock, English surveyors,
and English law were the key to systematically dispossessing the Potomac nations, and many colonists were eager to hasten the process by outright chicanery
and brute force.

Troubling hints as to what would happen if English colonists gained a firmer
foothold along the Potomac appeared as early as the 1630s. Maryland backed
up the claims of the new Piscataway tayac Kittamaquund, who ascended to that
position by assassinating his elder brother Wannas; Jesuits exploited a severe
drought and famine to gain converts; Governor Calvert exploited the same trag-

edy to persuade Kittamaquund to cede to the English the right to select future tayacs; colonists allowed their swine and cattle to ravage Indian fields and then complained when Indians killed the offending livestock; and a local planter shot the Wicomico werowance while he was hunting near the mouth of St. Mary's River.[1]

Of course, these episodes seem more ominous in retrospect than they did at the time. The Maryland colony grew weaker in the 1640s, not stronger, and as yet very few Englishmen lived on the Virginia side of the river. When Kittamaquund died in 1641, Maryland's government did not presume to choose his successor. The Jesuits' converts unconverted at will. Nevertheless the Kittamaquund affair, the Jesuits' exploitation of the drought, the shooting of the Wicomico werowance, and strife over free-ranging livestock all previewed the ways in which colonists would use their power if they ever gained the upper hand.

Trials

The fact that it took nearly a half-century for English colonists to begin to achieve dominance over the Algonquian peoples of the Potomac was partly a consequence of how they imagined the river fitting into greater Britain. Before 1640 the Potomac was regarded primarily as a source of grain, furs, and allies, all of which required the existence of functioning Native American communities. All along, however, there were some who thought that the Potomac was destined to become part of a settler colony in which English people largely replaced Indians. Lord Baltimore and some of his prospective colonists had in mind a colony with a more varied and mature economy and society than that of tobacco-dominated Virginia. Initial riches from the fur trade would help the colony to gain a foothold, and eventually, given the "almost incredible" fertility of the colony's soil, they anticipated that the land would yield up exports of silk, naval stores, grain, flax, potash, meat, wine, iron, and dairy in addition to tobacco. Colonists would never want for food because numberless fish, woods teaming with game, and abundant berries would add diversity to an already rich diet of beef, pork, corn, peas, beans, melons, and fruits.[2]

Such lists of "commodities that may be procured" in Maryland drew upon several sources. Thoroughly English environmental sensibilities surfaced in the assertion "that with good husbandry," colonists could transform the area's "great store of marish [marsh]" into "as rich medow, as any in the world," an essential element of an ideal English arable farm where livestock fed on the meadows' grasses would produce power, manure, dairy, and meat. English market conditions suggested other commodities to be obtained from the new colony: iron, for instance, or naval stores that might otherwise have to be purchased from foreigners. Then there was the Mediterranean example. Surely the Potomac would yield up goods produced at roughly the same latitude in Italy—so silk, figs, citrus, and olives went on the list. Finally, nature's bounty would free up hands for the planting of Virginia's main export: "one man may in a season, well plant so much as will yeeld a hundred bushells" of corn, plus beans and peas, "and yet attend a crop of tobacco."[3]

Yet despite their dreams of orange trees and olives, Maryland colonists ended up eating the same foods that had sustained people along the Potomac for centuries: corn, fish, and deer. Lord Baltimore advised colonists to bring two hoes apiece but no plows or tack—that is, tools needed for planting corn and tobacco but not for grain and dairy. He also suggested that they bring trade goods, primarily to acquire cattle and swine. According to Baltimore's calculations a single servant's labor would yield £49 annually in tobacco, corn, beans, and peas in addition to improved equity from building, fencing, clearing, raising cattle, and gardening.[4]

Not surprisingly, tobacco quickly moved toward the center of the Potomac economy. By 1637 it was so common that it served as a form of currency, and in 1639 the General Assembly, worried that planters would focus on tobacco to the detriment of their diets, required that tobacco growers plant two acres of corn per household member. Maryland's tobacco exports reached about 100,000 pounds in that year, and by 1660 the two Chesapeake colonies combined to export roughly five million pounds to English ports alone (a figure that does not include the tobacco carried away by Dutch traders, who often out-competed English merchants). By the end of the 1650s the average worker in Charles County, Maryland, produced over 1,600 pounds of leaf per year. No one in the county even owned a plow, as workers were too busy cultivating tobacco and corn—hoe crops—to waste time growing row crops such as wheat.[5]

Planters integrated tobacco into an overall annual subsistence cycle that bore a marked resemblance to that of their Algonquian neighbors. In the late fall, when Piscataways and Patawomecks headed for their upland hunting camps, colonists, too, ate plenty of waterfowl, deer, and the deer's domesticated equivalents: cattle and hogs. Wild fish and game accounted for at least a quarter of the meat in colonists' diets before 1660, and cattle and swine for the rest. Like Algonquians, they supplemented this meat-heavy winter diet with corn stored from the harvest. Later, as the previous year's harvest ran out and game and livestock waxed thin in the spring and early summer, Indians and colonists alike turned to fish and fowl. Produce—particularly wild fruits and roots for Algonquians and analogous garden crops and orchard fruits for colonists—mingled with fish and game through the heart of the summer. An abundance of grains, legumes, and melons fed Natives and newcomers in the late summer and early fall. The end result was a varied diet with enough diversity to insulate colonists against the catastrophic consequences of the failure of one food source.[6]

With a few modifications, tobacco cultivation meshed well with this Algonquian-like annual subsistence cycle. Planters sowed and mulched tobacco seedbeds in January and February and tended the seedlings carefully throughout the late winter and early spring. Beginning in March workers hoed up thousands of nearly knee-high hills; in these hills they later planted corn (beginning in April) and transplanted tobacco seedlings (beginning in late May). This was an exceedingly busy time of year: on rainy days workers hurried to transplant the tender tobacco seedlings from their seedbeds to the newly hilled fields, while on other days they weeded, repaired hills, culled, and transplanted stalks in the cornfields; in addition, peas, beans, and other garden crops had to be planted in late April and May, and tobacco seedlings that had yet to be transplanted still required careful tending. In the interstices of the late winter and springtime planting season, workers tended to livestock (which frequently became mired in marshes during these months), built and mended fences so that the newly planted crops would be safe from browsing animals, and pruned orchard trees.[7]

Since tobacco seedlings could be transplanted only on rainy days, workers often took all of June to get the fields planted. At the same time the cornfields required much weeding, and the first tobacco to be transplanted to the fields already needed hoeing and hilling. By early July, however, the corn was high enough to shade out the weeds, and the tobacco had all been transplanted. For the next three months the tobacco fields required most of the planters' attention. At first, while the plants were small, they required almost continuous weeding. Workers also had to guard the plants against hornworms, large, ravenous pests that feasted on tobacco leaves. To kill them, laborers plucked the worms from the leaves and crushed them with their feet—a particularly disgusting chore that one expert called "a nauseous occupation."[8] Beginning in July, as the first plants reached the four-foot mark, laborers used their hardened thumbnails to lop off the top of each plant to keep it from flowering and also nipped budding new leaves (called "suckers") at the shady bottom of the plant. These operations prevented the plants from expending their growth on flowers and new leaves and instead forced growth into the strongest leaves in order to produce better-quality tobacco.[9]

The first plants were normally ready to harvest in September, but planters could not go by the calendar alone. They had to pay careful attention to the state of the leaf and choose just the right moment to begin the harvest. This required exquisite judgment, for if cut too soon the leaves would not cure properly, and if left too long in the field they might be ruined by frost. In general, the leaves had to begin turning yellow before the harvest could begin, and they had to be dry enough to snap when bent. When the time came, laborers had to work fast: choosing a dry day, they cut the stalks and left the plants on the ground to dry for a few hours, then hung them on horizontal poles, and hung the poles on fences or scaffolds so that the leaves could wilt in the sun. When the leaves were sufficiently wilted, or if rain threatened, workers moved the poles into a small clapboard to-bacco house for additional curing. There they remained for over a month, until the leaves were not "so dry as to crumble, or so damp as to endanger a future rotting of the leaf." Then the leaves were stripped from the stalks, bundled to-gether, and placed in piles until there was time to pack them into enormous casks, known as "hogsheads." By December all of the tobacco should have been in casks, ready for shipment in the early spring.[10]

While the tobacco leaves were curing, workers busied themselves with the rest of the harvest. They harvested and stored the corn. They harvested fruit, dried some of it, and made cider from the late apples (October was referred to as "cyder time"). This was also an opportune time to plant new fruit trees. Autumn was also the time for slaughtering hogs and cattle—enough, by one estimate, for each adult male on the farm to eat two hundred pounds of meat during the year, "and proportionate amounts for women and children." Preserving the meat took more work: salting, smoking, and storing it in casks. Once these tasks were done, the workload lessened; but still, during the winter months, there were fields to be cleared, fences to be made and mended, and firewood to be chopped.[11]

When the demands of tobacco cultivation conflicted with food production and other necessary tasks, tobacco profits financed subtle yet revealing modifi-cations to the colonists' superficially Algonquian-like subsistence cycle. Tobacco left little time for the handiwork that occupied Algonquians in their spare mo-ments, but it did allow colonists to purchase cookware, weapons, textiles, and other manufactured goods instead of making them. Similarly, the prime fishing season coincided with the busiest time of the agricultural year, so colonists often hired Indians to do their fishing for them. Paying others to fish freed up time for hoeing, hilling, and otherwise preparing the fields so that workers could quickly transplant tobacco seedlings in April or early May. Similarly, hiring Indian hunt-ers in the late fall and early winter allowed planters to concentrate on stripping, stemming, and prizing the previous summers' tobacco and on preparing and planting seedbeds in anticipation of the next season. Consequently, seasonal changes in what colonists *consumed* more closely resembled Algonquian ways than did seasonal changes in *the work colonists performed.*[12]

Colonists also adopted agricultural techniques similar to those of their Algonquian neighbors. Ideally (in English terms) colonists would have completely cleared a field, improved it with marl, dung, and other treatments, plowed, established a crop rotation, and otherwise labored to sustain its productivity over the course of many generations. Planters along the Potomac did none of these things. Instead they grew mostly plants native to America, using methods developed by Native Americans. They girdled trees and planted their corn and tobacco on small hillocks scattered among the rotting stumps, sometimes mixing multiple crops together in a most un-English fashion. Weeds proliferated in the hot sun, and nematodes and fungal infections proliferated whenever tobacco was grown, feeding off the plants' roots; consequently yields steadily declined even when the soil retained some fertility.[13] Given these declining yields, together with the relative abundance of land and the scarcity of labor, it made better sense to leave stumps in the field than to clear it completely; it was more rational to hoe around the stumps than to plow; and it was best to avoid heavy soils that would make hoe agriculture too laborious to be worth the effort. Abandoning each field after a few years made more sense than employing labor-intensive methods such as fencing, manuring, and mowing meadows.

In addition to occupying a place in the planters' annual subsistence cycle analogous to that of deer in the Algonquians' world, livestock also took the place of deer in the landscape, running unfettered and multiplying so rapidly in the woods that planters often could not say how many they owned. "Hoggs runninge wilde in the woods" wore earmarks identifying their owners, but even apparently docile cattle and swine might at any moment fall into the company of feral animals. Jane Deeba's sow, for example, went "wild" in the woods near her neighbor William Churne's house, where she "drew Cherne's hoggs . . . much from home." Yet planters could normally expect these inherently social animals to stick together within a predictable range, for even occasional contacts by farmers with animals that were bred to domesticity served to maintain a bond between them. Handling newborn animals, soothing calves and piglets while marking their ears, and occasionally setting out corn and husks habituated livestock to their humans and gave animals an incentive to stay close to home.[14]

Since English farmers generally grew the same crops as their Algonquian neighbors, using similar techniques, preferred the same types of soils, and grazed their animals in the same places that Indians hunted theirs, it should come as no surprise that the newcomers established themselves in exactly the sort of place in which one might reasonably expect to find a Patawomeck, Mattawoman, or Tauxenent settlement. They sought out freshwater springs and reasonably level, well-drained, and fertile soils, close by the waterways that served as the highways of the day (usually on sheltered, navigable tributaries rather than on the Potomac itself). St. Mary's City, of course, was built atop a Wicomico hamlet, and the first English homesteads on the south bank of the Potomac were adjacent to the main settlements of the Chicacoans. Elsewhere English planters chose land that had been held in reserve by an Algonquian nation but not recently worked. On the Patawomecks' lower Aquia Creek, for, example, a land rush in 1654 resulted in patents to at least 8,318 acres near the creek's confluence with the Potomac, territory that had been too exposed to attacks by northern Iroquoians for the Patawomecks to safely inhabit.[15]

Approaching an English farm in early summer, a traveler from England would have been struck by the similarities between colonists' and Algonquians' fields. Coming at the farm by water, the visitor might first espy a clearing dominated by rotting, waist-high stumps. In one field small hillocks of broad-leafed tobacco plants at four-foot intervals would rise halfway up the stumps, while in an adjoining field workers hoed between knee-high cornstalks. Either in the interstices between the cornstalks or in a separate garden grew a variety of garden stuffs: melons, beans, "sallats," and other foods to enliven the summer diet; nearby were at least a few fruit trees, and often an entire orchard. Fields could be irregular in shape: since workers did not use plows, they could easily work around patches of waterlogged or infertile soil.[16]

Nearby one would find a small house, no larger and no more permanent than an Algonquian yeahawkan. Built to endure only until the declining fertility of the adjoining fields necessitated a move to new fields, houses typically had dirt or plank floors. Builders framed the structure around posts set directly into the ground. Clapboard siding, wooden shingles, and (sometimes) clay plaster imperfectly sealed the house from rain and drafts. The inhabitants cooked on a hearth at the foot of a wattle and daub chimney at one end of the building or in a small, separate kitchen just a few steps away from the main house. Wealthier planters' yards sometimes included other outbuildings: a second small dwelling for members of the household, a barn, a nursery, or a dairy. The remnants of recent meals fermented in pits or heaps of refuse just outside the door of each building; not coincidentally, one might see several farm dogs gathered there.[17]

Confronted with such scenes, newcomers from Europe found planters' husbandry wanting. The Anglican clergyman and scientist John Clayton thought it "strange in how many things . . . they are remise, which one would think English men should not be guilty of." Thomas Glover, a Northern Neck physician, shook his head over the failure of planters to drain and "improve" the region's abundant marshland and lamented that "when the strengthe of their ground is worn out they never manure it." Glover also found the cattle more impressive for their numbers than for their quality. They "might be much larger than they are," he thought, "were the inhabitants as careful in looking after them and providing fodder for them as they in England are."[18]

Had colonists completely abandoned their English environmental sensibilities? Growing Native American crops, using techniques learned from their Indian neighbors, and neglecting the ideals of "improvement" and sustainability—no wonder European observers thought planters "the slovenliest husbandmen imaginable."[19] And surely the similarities between the seasonal rhythms of Algonquians' and colonists' lives rendered the newcomers a little less English, a little more the product of their American environment.

Yet a closer look at a typical Potomac farmstead reveals that such seemingly prosaic colonial practices as earmarking livestock, fencing, producing surplus tobacco, establishing dispersed settlements, and erecting outbuildings actually signaled fundamental differences between English and Algonquian ways of living upon the land. These visual clues also pointed to several important continuities between the English ecological imagination as applied in the mother country and along the Potomac.

Earmarking and otherwise tending to livestock exemplified the English penchant for domesticating and cultivating natural resources. Livestock increasingly supplanted wild game, just as cultivated orchards replaced wild fruits, and garden produce took the place of the Algonquians' wild roots. The great majority of households had swine, and by the 1660s nearly all owned cattle; even small planters routinely accumulated twenty domestic animals. From a low of only 365 cattle in 1624, Virginia's bovine population swelled, by one account, to 20,000 cattle in 1649, in addition to "innumerable" swine. Northern Neck colonists owned their fair share of this hoard: county clerks there recorded dozens of disputes over livestock ownership, hundreds of the earmarks used to distinguish one person's livestock from another's, and numerous inventories of the possessions of people who died without leaving wills. Such inventories almost invariably included livestock, even when the deceased owned little else. John Nightengale, for example, died in 1660 with only thirteen personal possessions to his name, but those possessions included a bull and two steers. As domestic animals proliferated, they also increasingly crowded out wild game in the colonists' diets: after 1660, beef and pork accounted for nearly all of the meat consumed throughout the year.[20]

Livestock could roam freely through the woods because English settlement was scattered. Seventeenth-century planters on the Potomac typically lived between a quarter-mile and one and a half miles from their nearest neighbors, and they actively farmed only a minority of their property at any given time. This spacing left plenty of room for land dedicated to range, timber, and long fallows. Moreover, large-scale land speculators left open still more room for livestock to roam: a mere thirty Virginians owned over a hundred thousand acres on the Northern Neck in the late 1650s, far more than they could plant or lease. Besides, English farmers clung to the main waterways, leaving most of the uplands, marshes, and swamps either unclaimed or uncultivated. Uplands and wetlands served as a commons where livestock could multiply without much effort or capital investment on the planter's part. Marylander Dick Willan, for instance, absolutely relied on common grazing areas: he protested against a rumored land grant adjoining his own property on the grounds that "if any body did seate that land it would ruin him in his stock."[21]

Colonists further domesticated the woods by launching a systematic attack against wolves. The actual extent of wolves' depredations among domestic animals is questionable, but colonists clearly believed that they posed a major threat to livestock; and besides, wolves were associated with nature at its most menacing and primeval. Virginia and Maryland offered bounties of one hundred to two hundred pounds of tobacco per wolf's head, a significant sum amounting to perhaps one-eighth of a tobacco-worker's annual production. Consequently annual reckonings of public expenses almost invariably included entries such as "for a woulfe head paid to an Indian," or "three wolves puppies' heads not kild with shott or taken in a pitt but taken in their denn." At one meeting, the Stafford County Court paid bounties to forty different men for fifty-seven wolves, all of them shot, trapped in a pit, or "from an Indian." The justices of the Westmoreland County Court, "being deeply sensible of the great increase of those pernicious vermine," offered *three* hundred pounds of tobacco per head. This, the commissioners hoped, would effect the "totall extirpation" of these seemingly "invincible" creatures.[22]

Fences signaled a second major continuity between English and colonial environmental sensibilities: the deeply embedded habit of subdividing the landscape into separate spaces for specialized purposes. All manner of fences boxed off portions of Potomac farms: worm rail fences, post-and-rail, board palings, wattle palings, hedges, and stone. Though English fences kept livestock within a carefully tended pasture or fold, Virginia and Maryland law required planters to fence animals *out* of their fields. Nevertheless the logic was similar: fences made it possible to reconcile two potentially conflicting functions by segregating them into different spaces. With fences to prevent livestock from trampling or devouring crops, woods and wetlands could serve as the equivalent of English pastures and folds. Fences also set apart gardens from livestock pens, orchards from tobacco fields, and kitchen yards from cornfields.[23]

This specialization of function within each space transformed biologically diverse, complex ecosystems into greatly simplified biotic communities. Though not so radically simplified as a modern American farm, these carefully delineated spaces represented a real change from Algonquian-made landscapes and a real continuity with English ways. Only the English planter's garden approached the more diversified system of an Algonquian field; the remaining spaces, whether devoted to calves, tobacco plants, or corn, tended to be dedicated to the maximal production of a single item.[24]

Fences also signaled a third major continuity between English and colonial environmental sensibilities: an abiding concern with *boundaries,* within which the owner exercised nearly exclusive use rights. The Native peoples of the Potomac were primarily concerned about maintaining access to and (if necessary) control over the places where critically important resources were to be found: their fields and fisheries, marshes and hunting grounds. Although individual families had their own fields, the Algonquian property system as a whole emphasized rights to specific *uses* of the land, such as the privilege of gathering reeds or hunting deer. Mattawomans, Portobaccos, and Patawomecks had no need of surveyors to bound the land, for it was the distribution of tuckahoe or the path of migratory fish runs, rather than an abstract yet immutable boundary line, that determined where one might gather or fish. The English, in contrast, thought first of boundaries, not cores. They carefully surveyed the outer edges of each piece of property, recorded the markers that established the outer edges of that property, and periodically came together as a community for a procession in which the neighborhood confirmed its outlines.[25] Within those boundaries the owner had very nearly exclusive rights, and he retained those rights regardless of the uses to which that land was put. The first Englishman to take up a land grant might envision it as a tobacco farm, but he and his successors were largely free to put it to other uses. They could even treat it as a commodity in its own right.

Carefully bounded lands, together with other visible departures from Algonquian ways such as cultivating surplus tobacco and tending to livestock, also reflected a fourth major difference between Natives and newcomers: the logic of

merchant capitalism. While Indians and colonists alike had to arrange their subsistence cycle to guarantee ample food supplies during each season, colonists ad-
ditionally wished to accumulate more wealth with each passing year. Thus they
devoted much time and energy to "improving" their farms by clearing fields,
planting orchards, fencing in gardens and calf pastures, building homes, and
erecting tobacco barns. Similarly, cattle, swine, and horses constituted equity as
well as food: breeding livestock amounted to compounding interest, a near-
necessity for building wealth and ensuring family security. Livestock could do as
much to increase a household's wealth as growing tobacco did: it was not unusual for a deceased planter to leave behind livestock amounting to over half the
value of his personal property. Planters also sold beef and pork to feed sailors, to
newcomers who needed to start their own herds, and even to other colonies.[26] In
sum, the burgeoning herds of the Potomac Valley served purposes other than the
simple subsistence needs of colonists. Colonists slaughtered and consumed beef
and pork according to the same seasonal rhythm in which Algonquians hunted
and consumed deer, but they also increasingly identified their long-term prospects with the size of their herds.

Similarly, the ubiquitous tobacco barn clearly announced that colonists invested tobacco-growing with a radically different set of meanings than it carried for Algonquians. Algonquians grew small amounts of tobacco, which they
smoked in order to smooth the way for better relationships with spiritual beings,
with neighboring peoples, or amongst themselves. Colonists, on the other hand,
grew large quantities of tobacco for sale in far-flung markets. Chesapeake exports
to England swelled from roughly a million pounds in 1640 to nearly forty million
pounds per year in the late 1690s.[27]

The profits from this enormous trade paid for still more land, laborers, orchards, and livestock. Planters' estates reflected this tendency to channel profits into investments: the average value of St. Mary's County estates more than
doubled during the 1660s, then increased at a rate of about 1 percent per year
through the end of the seventeenth century.[28] The appearance of their homes also
reflected the priority given to building equity: 70 percent of St. Mary's County
households lacked so much as a chair. Bedsteads, cupboards, chests of drawers,
and even chamber pots were almost unheard of. Most households owned a bare
minimum of cookware and eating utensils. Middling to wealthy planters often
owned furniture, fine plate, and a variety of cookware and eating utensils, but
they still made do with less than people of comparable wealth in England. In
sum, one could rarely find obvious indicators of wealth such as brick mansions,
fine silver, and pampered quarter horses; instead one had to look to subtle clues

such as farm improvements and servants' quarters in order to distinguish between rich, middling, and poor planters.[29]

Commercial relations also fostered dispersed settlements, a readily visible marker of the gulf between colonial and Algonquian social relations. Colonial farmers needed large quantities of reserve lands to support swidden agriculture and to provide ample range for their livestock, and they needed to stay close to navigable waterways in order to market their tobacco to ships that plied the rivers; thus each farm typically stood well beyond hailing distance of its neighbors. Tobacco processing and marketing also took place mostly on the farm and thus did not promote town-building.[30] The contrast between nucleated Algonquian towns and dispersed English plantations reflected their inhabitants' divergent social visions: one, in which survival was a collective enterprise and wealth constituted power primarily because it allowed a person to give things away, and another in which survival was an individual enterprise and wealth constituted power primarily when one accumulated it and kept it within the family.

Some planters quartered servants and slaves in a separate outbuilding, which served as a visual reminder of an exploitative labor system that was entirely consistent with England's deeply hierarchical, ranked society. A farmer, it seemed, could accumulate wealth only by controlling the labor of other men and women: only 18 percent of the non-labor-owning planters who died in Charles County during the 1660s had succeeded in building an estate worth over £50, but those who did own unfree laborers could reasonably expect to amass at least £90 of personal belongings.[31]

Indentured servants, mostly impoverished Englishmen joined by a scattering of poor women and Irish, had given up their labor and their freedom for four to seven years, in exchange for which they received transportation to America, rudimentary clothing, room and board during their servitude, and modest "freedom dues" when their agreement expired. Servants could not marry, work on their own account, or travel without their master's permission. Nor could they choose who they worked for: most sold themselves to a merchant in an English port, who then resold their indenture to a planter along the Potomac. Although the law forbade masters from committing gratuitous acts of cruelty against their indentured servants, some planters bent on wringing as much work out of their servants as possible erred on the side of severity. Planters could have a servant whipped or sold to another master. The servants' primary defenses were appeals to established custom and to the courts. The courts, though dominated by planters who relied on indentured servants, were more evenhanded than one might imagine: although they frequently added months or even years to the terms of servants who broke their agreements and deprived their masters of their labor by running away or getting pregnant, the justices usually ruled in favor of servants who complained of fraud or mistreatment at the hands of their masters.[32]

By the 1660s colonists along the Potomac had found a way to integrate their new home into the landscape of greater Britain by integrating Native American crops and agricultural techniques into a fundamentally English economy and ecological vision. Their success could be seen with the naked eye, in the fences, tobacco sheds, rooting swine, gardens, orchards, and boat landings along the lower Potomac. So, too, could the social arrangements that made this economy possible, for the prevalence of bound labor was evident in the bodies of the people working the fields, in their clothing, and in their housing.

Contrary to modern stereotypes about soil-exhausting tobacco and land-destroying Europeans, the environmental impact of these seventeenth-century settlements was limited. Changes there were, of course; for example, colonists, in contrast to the Algonquians, did not habitually set fire to the woods and thus allowed a lush understory to grow up where formerly the forests had had a more park-like appearance. The decline in woods-burning, the rich forest-edge environments created by colonists' fields, and the colonists' systematic campaign against wolves likely created new opportunities for deer and other creatures to thrive. By the most fundamental measures of environmental health, however, seventeenth-century colonists did not radically change the natural world. Algonquians and English tobacco planters used similar agricultural techniques, with similar consequences. Core samples of river-bottom sediments reveal only modest changes in erosion rates, soil quality, and aquatic life in the mid-seventeenth century. The rate of sedimentation (an indicator of soil erosion and exhaustion) rose incrementally rather than abruptly, as did the volume of ragweed pollen (associated with deforestation and disturbed soils), and nutrient loading (associated with fertilizers, which promote the growth of algae and other suspended organisms at the expense of bottom-dwelling grasses, crabs, and oysters).[33]

In contrast to their modest effects on the ecosystem, expanding colonial settlements had a catastrophic effect on their Algonquian neighbors. The similarities between Natives' and newcomers' subsistence cycles and farming techniques created a deadly competition for the habitats that sustained tobacco planters and Algonquian farmers alike. And whereas the clear differences between the environmental sensibilities of English grain and fur traders and those of Potomac Algonquians had once fostered close diplomatic and trade relations, after 1650 the more subtle differences between Algonquian and English farmers fostered misunderstanding, violence, and oppression. English animal husbandry, conceptions of property, and notions about market relations created serious hardships for Indians along the Potomac, all at a time when the introduction of deadly diseases by the swelling colonial population were rendering the Potomac nations less capable of dealing with the English assault. Indeed, the changes wrought by English colonists in the 1650s and 1660s revolutionized life on the Potomac.

Vicious Cycles

The colonists truly began to gain the upper hand over their Indian neighbors after 1646. Calvert reconquered Maryland that year and adopted the new political strategy that attracted hundreds of Protestants to the colony. Meanwhile, in Virginia, the assembly was paving the way for a land rush into the Northern Neck. The assembly began its October 1646 session by ratifying the treaty ending the recent Anglo-Powhatan War, which forbad colonists from traveling north of the York River unless they had permission to cut timber or recover livestock. Yet the very same assembly also exempted the recipients of land grants north of the York from the usual requirement that they begin to clear fields and build dwellings on the land within three years. By freezing the clock rather than voiding the grants, the burgesses clearly signaled their intention to violate the treaty they had just ratified. And as if that signal was insufficiently clear, they also formally recognized the small settlement of Chicacoan on the lower Potomac, which was far beyond the northern limits of English settlement according to the 1646 treaty.[34]

Although Virginia made no new grants or patents on the Northern Neck between 1644 and 1648, a 1648 statute authorized the resumption of grants and patents north of the York River beginning in September 1649. The result was a major land rush. William Claiborne saw it coming: acting as treasurer for Virginia, he appointed his protégé William Cocke as surveyor to the Northern Neck well ahead of time. Cocke and his successor, Gervase Dodson, went right to work, and by the end of 1650 a wave of new patents was rolling up the river. The new patents clustered around the very tributaries that had long supported Algonquian communities. The Wicocomoco River, Chicacoan River, Yeocomico River, and the Onawmanients' Nomini Bay came first, with many of the new patents clustering around the lands of James Claughton and John Mottrom, well-established Indian traders who had left Maryland after 1639 to settle on the Chicacoan River. By 1653 the English communities at Wicocomoco, Chicacoan, and Nomini Bay had grown large enough to support Anglican parishes. The English grew so thick on the land that Northumberland County, which had previously encompassed the entire Northern Neck, hived off Lancaster County (on the Rappahannock

River) in 1651 and Westmoreland County (on the Potomac above the Yeocomico River) in 1653.[35]

The upriver march of English plantations triggered a recurring cycle of events at each major tributary of the Potomac. Proximity led to conflicts over land use, often sparked by the English practice of using unpatented lands as free range—and thus unleashing cattle, horses, and swine upon unfenced Indian fields. As one outer chief lamented, "Your cattle and hogs injure us you come too near to us to live and drive us from place to place. We can fly no further let us know where to live and how to be secured for the future from the hogs and cattle."[36] Sometimes those conflicts were engineered by malicious colonists who regarded Indians as insufficiently civil and perhaps only partly human—as, in the words of one Marylander, "the brutalls of the forrest."[37] But even when all parties were well-intentioned, the result was to undermine Indian autonomy, for Indians and colonists alike took their differences to local courts and provincial authorities, who insisted that they, and not Native polities, possessed sovereignty over the Potomac. When escalating local tensions threatened to break into violence, the inevitable colonial response was to disarm Indians, which was usually the final prelude to their dispossession. Finally the dwindling Algonquian community migrated to a more congenial location, typically moving in with a nearby Algonquian nation to create a new composite society.

Often the trouble was rooted in conflicting notions about territory, which were reflected in different ways of mapping the world. When Native people drew maps, they depicted not boundaries but core areas; and when they contested terrain they tried to protect places, not "territories" over which their claims to ownership or use rights were evenly spread. Native maps often featured multiple circles arranged to illustrate some relationship between them; sometimes the circles represented places, while at other times they represented primarily social, political, or cosmological relationships. The relationships being mapped were occasionally recorded in a fixed medium such as wood, stone, or hide, or even

---

"Description . . . from an Indian called Jackanapes." The original version of this map was performed by Jackanapes, a Mattawoman who had been taken captive by the Iroquois and lived among them for some time. During a meeting with Maryland's governor and council, Jackanapes arranged pinecones on a table and provided an extended commentary on the conditions within and between each of the Indian nations so represented. Only afterward was this dynamic performance reduced to paper. From *Arch. Md.*, 15: 383. Courtesy of the George Peabody Library, The Johns Hopkins University, Baltimore.

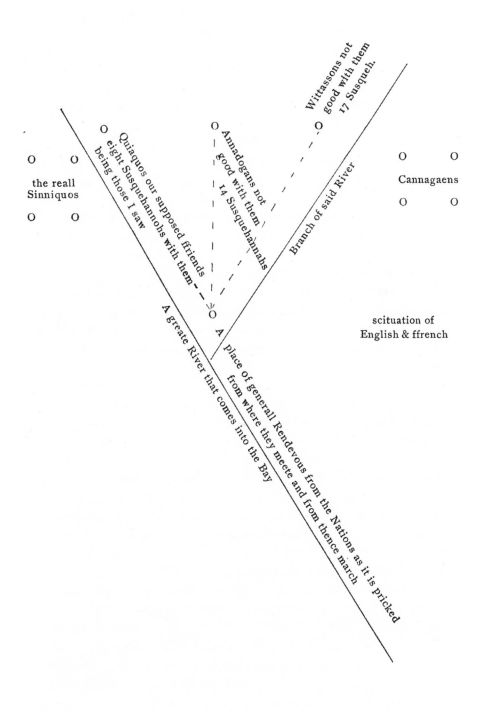

the reall
Sinniquos

Quiaquos our supposed ffriends
eight Susquehannohs with them
being those I saw

Annadogans not
good with them
14 Susquehannahs

Wittassons not
good with them
17 Susqueh.

Branch of said River

Cannagaens

scituation of
English & ffrench

A greate River that comes into the Bay

place of generall Rendevous from the Nations as it is pricked
from where they meete and from thence march

encoded in architecture. Usually, however, maps were *performed* by their makers, who drew in the dust or arranged objects on the ground, as supplements to the real map, which was spoken rather than drawn. In one meeting with Maryland's governor and council, an emissary from the Iroquois used pinecones to represent the different towns of the Five Nations and their neighbors, to explain the relationships between those towns and various outsiders, and to illustrate the best overland route from Potomac country to Iroquoia.[38]

In contrast, English maps and surveys focused on boundaries and sought to meet a universal standard of accuracy in representing spatial relations; they presented the land as a bare mathematical entity. As Peter Nabokov notes, Indians were often perplexed by invisible boundaries that were "not done on foot for obvious purposes of remembering how to reach favored hunting and foraging spots, but through imaginary lines and for highly suspicious reasons." The concept was so foreign that "the frightening political applications" of surveys took a while to sink in, by which time the damage was already done. A planter who had gone to the trouble and expense of having his land surveyed and patented knew in his bones that the newly established boundaries—barriers, really—were absolutely legitimate. Planters were dismayed by the Indians' lack of respect for those barriers, while Algonquians were surprised by the vigilance with which English people maintained boundaries that often had no apparent relationship to the core areas of English or Algonquian land use.[39]

Algonquian independence was also undermined by the regular face-to-face contact that grew out of an increasingly informal intercultural trade. Though this trade was no longer central to the colonists' economy after 1650, it still had a great deal of significance for diplomatic and intercultural relations along the river. Algonquian villagers built canoes for their English neighbors and provided deerskins, beaver pelts, corn, and meat; in return they got the usual mixture of "trucking stuff" including wampumpeake, metal tools, and guns.[40] Colonists also increasingly employed their Indian neighbors as farmhands. Maryland's Governor Stone recognized this as early as 1652, when he issued a temporary proclamation against hiring Indians but excluded "any Indian cowkeeping youth" from the ban. Passing references to Indian employees in court records suggest that this was not an unusual practice. In 1653, for example, "John Little's Indian" was embroiled in two different court cases: in the first case "Little's Indian" ran away in the company of an English servant and took refuge at "the Indian Cabbin," and in the second case Little said that their neighbor, Mrs. Potts, "was dishonest with the said Littles Indian boy in his corne field" and that "he did see said Mrs. Potts back durty." Later, when both colonies began to require licenses to employ Indians, wage-earning Algonquians appeared regularly in the county court proceedings where such licenses were recorded.[41]

As a result of such intimacies a surprising number of colonists learned to "speak to the Indians." In 1665, for instance, a servant concealed in a field during an Indian attack called out to the Mattawoman men who were attacking the farm, asking them "in Indian Kaquince machissino Chippone why hee did so." The man "answered in Indian, because he would." Soon one of the men tracked her down and said, "Pops innahayo a woman with child, and struck at her with his tomajauke, three times." She lived, and she remembered what had been said "in Indian." In another instance, Susan Attcheson and James Nevill carried on a passionate, adulterous, and astoundingly indiscreet affair. They were caught having sex in the woods and in front of her own hearth as others lay sleeping in the same room. At their neighbor George Reed's house, Nevill threw a servant out and "swore that he would swive" Attcheson before the witness "was as far as the cowpen"—and was as good as his word, for the servant, hearing their cries, returned and forcibly uncoupled the pair. As one might imagine, this behavior attracted considerable interest in the neighborhood; thus on another occasion a small crowd gathered after a servant saw Attcheson climb into a hayloft with Nevill, and then heard "a busling in the loft." The crowd included an Indian, who climbed the ladder for a closer look, then "spake in Indian" to tell onlookers that "Nevill and Susan was at sack a sacke."[42]

The increasingly familiar relations that fostered informal trade, the hiring of Indians as wageworkers and servants, and bilingualism among colonists significantly weakened the ability of the Potomac nations to resist the slow-motion British invasion of their territories. In the sixteenth century the funneling of copper and beads through the hands of chiefs had given werowances privileged access to spiritual power and allowed them to elicit the support of their people by the judicious distribution of gifts, both of which helped chiefs to consolidate in their hands the authority necessary to coordinate the resistance against the northern raiders who were laying waste to settlements above the fall line. In contrast, the increasingly widespread distribution of spiritually potent, exotic trade goods now subverted the legitimacy and political power of werowances, weakening their hold over their people and thus undermining their ability to muster an effective resistance against English intruders. Casual trade and wage labor may also account for the forbearance shown by Algonquian villagers toward the colonists who encroached upon Native lands and allowed their livestock to run wild through Indian fields, for Algonquians found it difficult to regard trading partners as enemies even when conflicts arose.[43]

And conflicts there were. When colonists took up residence at Nomini Bay, they came into sustained contact with the Onawmanients. The Onawmanients signed away the smaller of their two towns in 1650, claiming the west side of Matchotic Creek for themselves while allowing English colonists to settle on the east side. The river, however, proved an inadequate barrier against colonists and their livestock. The Onawmanients (now known as Matchotics) complained in 1651 that Isaac Allerton was "intruding a plantacon upon them." Virginia's governor and council directed the Northumberland County Court to eject Allerton if it found that the Matchotics "were not content with his being there," but the commissioners reported that the werowance, Peckatoan, was willing to let Allerton stay, provided he erected no more buildings and that he kept his livestock on the other side of the river from the Matchotics' main town. Despite this upbeat report, tensions continued to mount over free-ranging livestock, the boundaries of the Matchotics' territory, and the Matchotics' hunting rights.[44]

Each conflict provided an opportunity for Virginians to claim sovereignty, as Virginia's councilors and Northumberland County's commissioners had implied when they mediated between Allerton and Peckatoan. So did a 1650 Virginia statute that guaranteed each werowance a reservation containing fifty acres for each bowman within his nation; although this provided much-needed protection against the encroachments of Allerton and his ilk, it also presupposed that Virginia, not Indians, possessed the sovereignty that made a land grant legitimate. And when (in this increasingly tense climate) colonists grew nervous at the sight of gun-toting Indian hunters in the woods, the provincial governments again asserted their sovereignty by banning Indians from owning guns. Maryland's Governor Stone revoked all licenses to employ Indian hunters in 1650, and two months later the Northumberland County Court entertained complaints that the leading planter at Chicacoan, John Mottrom, had given guns to "the Indians." Later in 1651 the Northumberland court reaffirmed its intention to enforce the law against arming Indians, lest the practice lead to "a Massacre."[45]

Matchotic-planter tensions truly came to a head between 1656 and 1660. Dodson surveyed the Matchotics' land for a reservation in the summer of 1656, but the controversy over their conflicting land claims with Isaac Allerton continued unabated. Additional land grants tightened the noose around the small reservation, multiplying the opportunities for strife. Violence finally erupted in 1659, when three Matchotics beat to death John Cammell, who had been a neighbor of theirs since at least 1653. The Matchotics reluctantly handed over two of the alleged killers, but the entire community took to the woods when George Caquescough and Yeotassa were executed for the murders. The county commissioners, hearing that the Matchotics were "endeavoring (with the assistance of other In-dians) to make a warr upon us," spent a considerable sum that summer on men and supplies for "goeing the march." The Matchotics returned to their town early in 1660, but colonists had already begun taking up lands within the reservation. The county commissioners decided that these brand-new claims outweighed the Matchotics' generations of residence, and they directed a party of colonists to "cammand" the Matchotics' "present departure from off the said land, otherwise to burne their cabins and cut up their corne." The Matchotics took the hint and left, regrouping thirty miles up the Potomac on a peninsula formed by the Upper Matchotic River and Chotank Creek. Known to the English as "Appamatucks," they remained there until at least 1669.[46]

The Onawmanients/Matchotics/Appamatucks were hardly alone in their plight. The same cycle of events, replicated on a half-dozen tributaries on either side of the Potomac, also culminated in the dispossession of the Chicacoans, Cuttatawomens, and others in the late 1650s.[47] Take, for example, the case of the Wicomicos, who were increasingly hemmed in by colonists: from St. Clement's Manor at the mouth of the Wicomico to Westfield Manor at its head, new settle-ments marched up the west bank of the river that had long been the Wicomico homeland. In 1651 the Wicomicos asked for a reservation near Choptico Bay at the head of the Wicomico River. The statute creating the thousand-acre re-serve placed the inhabitants under the stewardship of Robert Clark, a promi-nent Maryland planter, surveyor, and council member. The reserve allowed the Wicomicos (now known as the Chopticos) access to good fisheries, freshwater marshes, and extensive swampy woodlands, all of which were critical to their subsistence needs, but it was inadequate as a hunting territory, and it did not protect Choptico fields from marauding swine and cattle. Indeed, the Chopticos were under such pressure from their neighbors that some began keeping live-stock themselves.[48] The implications of keeping livestock were far-reaching: hogs necessitated fences and other adjustments to the landscape, and relying even in part on domesticated animals instead of hunting surely necessitated some recon-sideration of Choptico masculinity.

All of the Chopticos' concessions and adaptations, however, were insuffi-cient to appease their neighbors, who in 1660 launched a legal assault that effec-tively squelched Choptico resistance for the next thirty-five years. Bypassing the county court in favor of the more easily controlled St. Clement's Manor Court, a jury of local inhabitants issued a barrage of presentments against their Indian neighbors. Four men were fined twenty lengths of roanoke (a very substantial sum) for "breakinge into the Lord of the Manners orchard," and two boys were fined *forty* arms' lengths of roanoke for "being taken with hoggs flesh." Another man was fined twenty lengths for taking a shirt from Edward Turner, though the jury did not know exactly who the culprit was. The community as a whole was fined twenty lengths for "takeinge away Christopher Carnells cannowe from his landinge," and their werowance was presented for "killing a wild sow." The jury concluded by recommending "that Indians ought not to keepe hoggs for under pretence of them they may destroy all the hoggs belonginge to the Mannor and therefore they ought to bee warned now to destroy them."[49]

Meanwhile colonists flowed over and around the Chopticos' lands, leapfrogging up the Potomac to the Portobacco River. Soon there were so many planters along the Portobacco that it could no longer be effectively governed as part of St. Mary's County, so in 1658 Maryland established Charles County, with Portobacco itself as the county seat. By 1660 the Portobaccos had to contend with six hundred English invaders in their midst. Many Portobaccos retreated farther up the Potomac, but even there they felt the pressure of English expansion: the Portobaccos' *werowansqua* lamented that her people had "left their towne standing by the water," allowing "the English to seate on theire ancient plantations." Yet the English, "not being . . . contented with what land is allready freely granted," took up land "very nigh unto the said Indians" and allowing their hogs and cattle to destroy the Portobacco fields. Beset by English livestock, by a series of droughts, and possibly by an epidemic that had been killing off many of their English neighbors over the past two years, the werowansqua thought that the Portobaccos "must of necessity come to famine." Not surprisingly, many Portobaccos left their homeland altogether, taking refuge at the falls of the Rappahannock River.[50]

Remarkably, the vicious cycle of English expansion, local conflicts, and Indian dispossession that had begun in the 1650s actually intensified as English population growth accelerated in the 1660s and early 1670s. Due largely to immigration, colonists along the Potomac multiplied from less than 200 in 1646 to nearly 1,400 in 1654, and then to about 7,200 in the mid-1670s.[51] Moreover, rapidly increasing worker productivity at midcentury meant that each tobacco worker and each farm took up more and more space: in the 1650s a typical farmhand cultivated about 2.2 acres during the course of a year, but by 1700 he could handle about 3.7 acres. The amount of livestock also grew rapidly during these years, with similar consequences. Thus with each passing year each individual farm took more Native men's hunting territory out of commission and sent forth a greater number of swine, cattle, and horses to ravage Algonquian women's fields. This swelling population jumped from one major tributary to the next, arriving at the lower reaches of the inner coastal plain ("the freshes") in the late 1660s; in Charles

County alone planters took up an additional 7,700 acres per year between 1660 and 1674. The population also grew denser, gradually filling in the spaces between farms and thus increasing the potential for intimacy and conflict with nearby Algonquian communities. In 1662, for example, about twenty-five families lived within a half-dozen miles of the Cole family's farm on St. Clement's Manor. By 1673 sixty families occupied the same territory, which was just downriver from the Choptico reserve.[52]

Notwithstanding the marked similarities between Algonquian and English diets, agricultural practices, and subsistence cycles, Indians and colonists occupied different landscapes; even when they lived in close proximity, sharing overlapping spaces, they imagined their relationships with that common ground in very different ways. As the English population mushroomed after 1650, both the similarity in their subsistence cycles and the differences between their ecological imaginations caused conflicts between Natives and newcomers. These conflicts were repeatedly resolved in favor of English planters—yet another reminder that the control of nature is closely linked to power relations within and between human societies.

But what was it that gave the newcomers the upper hand after 1650? What was it that allowed them to ride roughshod over their neighbors then, when they had not been able to do so before? For answers to these questions we must look not only to English population growth, English notions of property, boundaries, and sovereignty, and to the disruptive effects of English livestock but also to the biological causes of a drastic decline in the Algonquian population of the Potomac Valley.

CHAPTER SEVEN

Microbes, Magistrates, and Migrations

The waves of colonists washing over the outer coastal plain after 1650 amounted to a biological problem for Algonquian societies; they were, in the words of one historian, a "biotic factor" as well as a political and economic force.[1] And like any other species whose population grew sixfold in the space of a single genera- tion, the colonists forced other organisms within the same ecosystem to adjust to their growing presence. The tobacco planter, a mammal that preferred the same habitat as the Algonquian, prevailed mainly by outnumbering its rivals for the land. By the end of the 1650s it was evident that more and more colonists would soon be arriving and that the newcomers would want to take up still more land on the inner coastal plain. The Native peoples of the Potomac would never again outnumber the English.

In fact, the Native American population was rapidly dwindling. A Virginia census of 1669 found only 320 Indians on the south bank of the Potomac—a catastrophic 80 percent decline from 1608, most of which can be dated to after 1650.[2] Some of this decline was due to migration, for in the 1650s and 1660s many refugees from the south bank moved across the Potomac, combining their num- bers with the Piscataways on the north bank or relocated across the Northern Neck to the falls of the Rappahannock River. Others remained on the south bank but went unrecorded in the census. Yet migrations and undercounting account for only a small part of the overall decline.[3] Thanks to a combination of warfare, dispossession, and epidemic diseases, most of the Native peoples of the Potomac were gone by 1675, and the great majority of the survivors were confined to res- ervations.

Microbes

One obvious explanation for the precipitous decline in the Algonquian population is that exotic epidemic diseases from Europe and Africa had finally reached the Potomac. The list of Eurasian diseases unknown in America before 1492 is impressive: it includes yellow fever, malaria, smallpox, typhus, measles, cholera, chicken pox, whooping cough, scarlet fever, and many strains of influenza.[4] The horrifying effects of these diseases on Native populations with limited or compromised resistance to them is well documented: accounts of decimated villages in which the survivors could not even properly bury the dead abound. But these diseases did not simply leap from newcomers to Natives at the moment of first contact.

In fact, epidemics of the new diseases often did not afflict Native American communities for a generation or more after first contact.[5] Most of these diseases are crowd diseases, and neither Algonquians nor colonists in the Potomac Valley constituted much of a crowd before the 1650s. Some, such as influenza, were prone to "use up their fuel" on a small shipboard population before a vessel could cross the Atlantic, the voyage serving as an effective quarantine.[6] Smallpox, the most feared killer of Native Americans in contact-era situations, had an especially hard time crossing over to the Chesapeake region: it was not yet endemic in the British Isles in the mid-seventeenth century and thus could hardly have been expected to travel from there to America on a regular basis. Moreover, smallpox, too, was so fast-acting that it could burn through a ship's population in less time than it took to make the crossing.[7] Moreover, smallpox is most easily spread by children, who made up only a small proportion of the Potomac's already miniscule colonial population before 1650.[8]

Surely it is no coincidence that the Algonquian population decline began in earnest at midcentury, for it was at that very moment that conditions were ripe for the introduction and spread of influenza, malaria, and other diseases to vulnerable communities along the Potomac. Midcentury changes in shipping patterns increasingly favored the transmission of Eurasian diseases. The typical route from Europe or Africa took westbound travelers first to the Leeward Islands (the outer ring of Caribbean islands), then north and eastward along with the prevailing winds and tides. The introduction of faster sailing vessels in the 1640s and 1650s, combined with increased transatlantic shipping traffic caused by a midcentury sugar boom in England's West Indian colonies, increased the odds that microorganisms would make the crossing to the Caribbean. Once established there a virus or other organism could make the leap to the North

American mainland with relative ease. The sugar boom was followed closely by a rapid growth in the tobacco trade, which attracted far more ships than in the past and thus increased the odds that some diseases would cross the Atlantic to the Potomac.[9]

This sequence of events may account for the timing of malaria's expansion through the Chesapeake region. The most brutal symptoms of malaria, an ascending series of fever spikes over the course of about two weeks, are caused by the body's reaction to the presence of a parasite of the *Plasmodium* genus. *Plasmodium* depends upon a complex cycle of transmission from mosquitoes of the *Anopheles* genus to a vertebrate host (such as a human), and back to another *Anopheles* mosquito. The adult *Plasmodium* resides in the *Anopheles* mosquito, and the vertebrate host serves "as the nursery within which the parasite spends its asexual 'childhood.'" After lodging briefly in the liver, the parasite enters the bloodstream and begins attacking red blood cells, which triggers the series of fevers as the body attempts to kill off the unwelcome guests. Although the body's immune system normally triumphs over the parasites dwelling in the bloodstream, some *Plasmodium* remain lodged in the liver, from whence they erupt again some months later, reentering the host's blood and thus providing *Anopheles* mosquitoes another opportunity to transmit the parasite from one host to another. Clearly this is a complicated disease, and it does not easily spread from one place to another. *Plasmodium vivax,* the milder of the two species that attack humans, became endemic on the coastal plain only after 1650, when "the occasional, seemingly random cases of the early decades" gave way to regular seasonal outbreaks. *Vivax* kills about 5 percent of its newly infected hosts, and infected people tend to suffer from relapses. A more virulent species, *Plasmodium falciparum,* which kills up to 25 percent of its hosts, also took hold in the region at midcentury.[10]

Plasmodium-bearing mosquitoes do not discriminate between Europeans, Africans, and Native Americans. If Europeans had malaria, then so did their Algonquian neighbors. Moreover, English, African, and Algonquian people all continued to suffer the consequences of malaria even after their initial bouts with the parasite. Malaria has been called the "great debilitator," because it saps one's ability to resist other illnesses. By one estimate, for every death caused directly by malaria "another five deaths are actually due to malaria acting in concert with other diseases." Residents of the Potomac commonly suffered from this one-two punch of debilitating malaria followed by deadly visitations of other diseases.[11]

Rapid English population growth along the Potomac and increasing intimacy between Natives and newcomers in the 1650s and 1660s provided an increasingly hospitable environment for the introduction of new disease organisms. The colonial population was by virtue of its size alone increasingly capable of incubating diseases that could lay waste to Native communities: whereas in 1634 a new strain of influenza might burn through the English population of barely one hundred souls before it could reach an Algonquian village, by the 1670s the over seven thousand colonists along the river could sustain an outbreak for months—plenty of time for it to infiltrate a Piscataway village. Moreover, immigration from England's disease-ridden port cities to the Chesapeake region peaked between 1650 and 1680, providing a steady flow of opportunities for killer germs to make the crossing.[12] At the same time the native-born English population was slowly increasing, which meant that the number of children, the most efficient carriers of the deadly smallpox virus, was on the rise. Above all, the rapid spread of the English population in the 1650s meant that Indians and colonists saw much more of each other than in the 1630s and 1640s, when Marylanders had lived well away from most Indian communities and Virginians were few and far between on the south bank. Along the Choptico River and Potomac Creek, Little Hunting Creek and the Portobacco, colonists negotiated and traded with their neighbors, hired them as hunters and laborers, and passed through their villages. Every one of these contacts carried with it the possibility of disaster; if it resulted in the transmission of smallpox or typhoid, the result could be the death or dispersal of half a community's population.

The horror, though, was not limited to the transmission of diseases. Colonists were not passive agents in the Indians' demographic collapse; if they were, Native populations would have eventually rebounded. Like all humans, the peoples of the Potomac had immune systems capable of battling parasites, bacteria, and viruses. After 1650, however, their resistance to disease was severely compromised by a wicked combination of drought, hurricane damage, war, crop damage by colonists' livestock, and the dispossession and displacement of entire communities, all of which combined to undermine Algonquian health.[13]

The real problem was not that colonists introduced new diseases but rather that they exploited their Indian neighbors' momentary weakness by taking over critically important fisheries, fields, and hunting grounds at a moment when their previous owners were diminished in numbers, damaged in their health, sick at heart, and struggling to function as members of a community. The result was a cycle of decline in which social breakdown, war, dispossession, disrupted food supplies, and disease undercut fertility and forced many into early graves.[14]

The precise nature of the diseases afflicting the Potomac nations is unclear. We can safely assume that malaria struck Indians as well as Europeans and that whatever it was that killed and incapacitated many colonists in 1662 and 1663 (and the major influenza outbreak of 1675–77) also struck Algonquian communities. It seems fair to guess that malaria and other diseases acted in concert—that for Indians as for colonists death rates increased each fall when malarial fevers struck and continued their rise through midwinter, as respiratory infections stressed immune systems past their breaking points. Smallpox probably did not strike along the Potomac until after 1667, but other diseases sufficed to eliminate much of the Native population along the Potomac before that date; smallpox, when it did arrive in the last third of the century, only compounded the damage already wrought by oppression, disease, and more oppression.[15]

Magistrates

The mistreatment of the Patawomecks by their English neighbors exemplified the savagery with which the newcomers exploited the slightest weakness. The Patawomecks' troubles began in 1651 and 1652, when Mary Brent and Giles Brent, a former Maryland councilor who had moved across the Potomac during the turbulent 1640s, patented several thousand acres along Aquia Creek. The real land rush into Patawomeck territory came in 1654, when 12,600 acres were newly patented or sold by absentee landowners. By the mid-1650s there was no more talk of Patawomeck power, nor any sign that they were numerous enough to mount any resistance against the encroachments of English planters; from the silent assumptions of English record-keepers, we can infer that much of the Patawomeck nation had succumbed to disease or moved away since the late 1640s. In 1655 the Patawomeck werowance agreed to allow Gerrard Fowke, a substantial planter who patented over 3,000 acres along Potomac Creek, to "build himself an house upon the same land where the Kinge [werowance] now liveth," to bring in servants to plant tobacco, and to "keep what cowes he pleases." The werowance also permitted Giles Brent to build, plant, and graze his livestock along Aquia Creek, but Brent took more than he had been given.[16]

Not content with partial victories, Brent and other leading planters tried in 1661 to get their hands on the remainder of the Patawomecks' lands. This time Deputy Governor Francis Moryson intervened: anxious to avoid a costly Indian war, he appointed an outside committee to mediate the dispute and warned against appointing militia officers who had a material interest in starting a war against the Patawomecks.[17] Moryson was right to worry about Westmoreland County's leadership, for soon afterward the county's most prominent citizens tried to frame the Patawomecks' werowance, Wahanganoche, for murder. They brought Wahanganoche to Jamestown, where the burgesses appointed a special committee to handle the incident. The committee saw right through the Westmoreland men's ploy: Wahanganoche, they discovered, had turned over the real murderer for prosecution by English authorities, but Brent, Fowke, John Lord, and Captain George Mason had deliberately allowed the killer to escape and then detained Wahanganoche in order to remove a major obstacle to the dispossession of the Patawomecks.[18] The great men of Westmoreland were convicted of contempt, issuing illegal warrants, and "aspersing the honourable governour in declareing falsely that their unjust proceedings were done by his authority." All paid enormous fines, posted bond for future good behavior, and were stripped of their offices. Future disputes, it was decided, would be handled by special commissioners appointed by the governor. Since so many of Westmoreland's leading men were now disqualified from office, the burgesses directed that the county be dissolved for the time being, and reincorporated into Northumberland County.[19]

Colonel Fowke and his coconspirators were soon back in office, however, and in 1663 they mounted an armed expedition against the Patawomecks. Though the burgesses ordered that "all the charges ... expended in the late expedition against the King of Potomacke was cast upon [Westmoreland] County," they did not otherwise punish the men who carried out the attack. In fact, the burgesses seemed to turn sharply against the Patawomecks: in September 1663 they required the Patawomecks to give over hostages to the English and to join in Virginia's military expeditions whenever they were asked; if they did not comply, they would be considered an enemy nation. A murder near the Patawomeck homeland in 1664 led to further persecutions. Though blame was not fixed solely on the Patawomecks, they were much suspected of some involvement in the crime. Such suspicions surely contributed to the passage of a 1665 statute asserting that the governor would henceforth appoint all werowances, and of a second law that approved "the sale of the king of Potomacks land." A year later the Governor's Council responded to persistent accusations that the Patawomecks were responsible for recent killings on the Northern Neck by declaring war, ordering "their utter destruction if possible and that their women and children and their goods ... shall be taken to be disposed of." The war eliminated the Patawomecks as an independent polity, and when the burgesses ordered a census of Indian warriors in 1669 no Patawomecks were recorded.[20]

Some Algonquians slipped into slavery. As early as 1650 several Northumberland men "took from the King of Patuxin [in Maryland] two Indian women and ninety three deer skins and three beaver skins." The Chicacoan-based trader John Mottrom, though opposed to the theft and determined to "satisfy the said king" for it, did not contest the definition of the two women as commodities. Clearly there was no sense that Indians could *not* be enslaved. Thus when the dispossession of the Potomac nations began in earnest in the second half of the 1650s, passing references to Indian slaves began appearing in public records, as when a witness in a civil suit referred to "an Indian belonging to" a neighbor. Litigants in other civil suits contested the ownership of enslaved Indians or protested the failure of the defendant to deliver Indian slaves who had been paid for. Even Philip Calvert, the chief legal officer of the Maryland colony and brother to the proprietor, owned Indian slaves: in 1665 he complained that Thomas Wynne and Elizabeth Wynne had been illegally trading with "Frank Indian and dyvers others of the slaves of Philip Calvert," and in 1675 he sued John Quigley for assaulting "a certain man slave named Robin an Indian . . . by trade a sawyer and carpenter."[21]

Provincial authorities permitted and even encouraged Indian slavery. In 1649 Virginia's burgesses ruled that Indian children living in white households could not be sold to another party, while another law discouraged the "stealinge of Indians"; Maryland followed suit, taking an equally bold stand against kidnappings in 1654. Yet Virginia continued to wield enslavement as a weapon against Indians. Some of the captives taken during the Anglo-Powhatan War of 1644–46 were sold into slavery, and the treaty ending that war made servants out of other captives. In 1660 the burgesses authorized Northumberland County to sell some Wicocomocos "into a forraigne country" if they failed to pay for damage done during the conflict over the bounds of their reservation, and in 1666 Governor Berkeley authorized the militia to enslave Indian women and children during the war against the Northern Neck nations.[22]

Migrations

When a Native community was hemmed in by English invaders, buffeted by disease, and threatened with servitude, migration came to seem like a good idea. Many Portobaccos, for example, relocated to the falls of the Rappahannock River. There they lived with the Nandtanghtacunds in a community that was by 1666 known as "Portobacco." Other Potomac River groups took refuge among the Nanzaticos, another Rappahannock River group that was apparently based on a Nandtanghtacund core.[23] These consolidated communities were quite substantial. The 1669 census counted 60 "bowmen" at the Portobacco town and another 50 at Nanzatico, for a combined overall population of perhaps 450, and the Wicocomoco community at the end of the Northern Neck contained nearly 300 people (including its Chicacoan and Cuttatawomen inhabitants). Though small by modern standards, these composite communities seemed large enough to their colonial neighbors, all the more so since Algonquian settlements were much more concentrated and urban than were English communities. The 450 Indians on the upper Rappahannock, for instance, lay just over the narrow Northern Neck from Stafford County (the newest Potomac River county), which contained barely 1,100 colonists in 1674. Similarly, Northumberland County's 1,100 colonists could not help but notice the 300 Wicocomocos among them.[24]

Colonists all along the river noted the presence of Doegs, a shadowy group that was particularly unwilling to accommodate their English neighbors. The Doegs may have originally emerged from the remnants of the Tauxenent nation after its destruction by Nacotchtanks and northern raiders in the 1620s, but by the time the name "Doeg" first began to appear in the written record in the 1650s, it seemed to refer to a series of communities that presented an alternative to life on the reservations that were then being created.[25] Theirs seems not to have been a settled life; indeed, no surviving records mention Doeg women or Doeg fields. Doegs turned up just about everywhere: high up the Maryland side of the Potomac in 1651; far downriver on an island on the Lower Matchotic River in 1653; then back upriver on an island at the "freshes" near the mouth of Occoquan Creek in 1658. In the 1660s there was a "doeggs path" crossing the Northern Neck from a point near Potomac Creek, but there was also a "Doegs Neck" many miles away, on a tributary of Piscataway Creek. References from the early 1670s put the Doegs both in Maryland and in Virginia (on the future site of Mount Vernon, between Dogues Creek and Hunting Creek), while maps drawn in 1670 and 1676 show Doegs on the Rappahannock River at the terminus of the "Doeg's Path" (near the modern-day hamlet of Dogue, which is near still another "Dogue Run").[26]

The elusive Doegs seem to have neither sought out contact with the English, nor gone out of their way to avoid conflicts. In 1658 they fell afoul of Giles Brent, who accused them of killing three of his cattle. When the Westmoreland County Court summoned the "Great man of the Doeggs," three men appeared and denied Brent's charge. That did not settle matters between the Doegs and the Virginians, though: five years later the burgesses demanded that the Patawomecks "joyne and pursue the *Doeggs*," who had "confessed to be actors" in recent killings on the Northern Neck. The hunt continued for years: the 1666 declaration of war against the Patawomecks authorized the "utter destruction" of the Doegs as well. Marylanders, too, found that Doeg men were apt to strike back at the colonists who were overrunning the Potomac. When Indians killed an entire family in St. Mary's County in August 1665, the evidence pointed toward a party of sixteen

Doegs. Hunted by Virginians and about to be hunted by Maryland militiamen, the Doegs hastily signed a treaty with Maryland that ended the investigation into the St. Mary's County killings. They did not, however, confine themselves to a reservation, preferring instead to continue living within the interstices between colonial settlements on both sides of the Potomac and on the Rappahannock.[27]

"Let Us Have No Quarrels"

Notwithstanding the dispossession of a half-dozen nations in less than twenty years, the colonists' rout of their Algonquian neighbors was far from complete at the end of the 1660s. The most notable exceptions were the Piscataways and their remaining tributary nations, including the Nacotchtanks, Pamunkys, and Mattawomans. For them the cycle of intimacy, conflict, depopulation, and dispossession that played out elsewhere along the river was somehow slowed, if not arrested. In part this was because a belt of hilly, infertile lands along the north bank of the Potomac above the Nanjemoy River discouraged English planters from taking up lands there. Although the Potomac counties did not exactly languish (Charles County's population grew by 21 percent in the 1670s), planters looking to take up new lands increasingly looked instead to the Eastern Shore: home to only 365 colonists in 1660, the Eastern Shore swelled to 3,275 colonists in 1670 and 7,300 in 1680. Those few farmers who did venture up the Potomac to the Nanjemoy River or beyond lived a hardscrabble existence even by the standards of seventeenth-century tobacco planters. They owned smaller farms than other planters along the Potomac, had fewer servants to work their fields, and almost never owned slaves.[28] Consequently, while the Wicocomocos, Matchotics, Patawomecks, and Chopticos were drowning in the flood of colonists who had flowed upriver during the 1650s and 1660s, Algonquian migrants from elsewhere along the Potomac found refuge in this core area of the tayac's paramount chiefdom. Protected by their geographical location and with their numbers augmented by the influx of migrants, the Piscataways and their neighbors managed to retain their sovereignty.

It helped that Piscataway and Maryland authorities still believed that they shared certain political and diplomatic interests. In October 1654, Maryland's assembly called for new limitations on interactions between Indians and colonists. Colonists could no longer sell guns to Indians, and no one could "entertaine" Indians "except they come upon the publique Treaty." Although many Indians surely chafed at these limitations, the Piscataways, and particularly the tayac, actually benefited from them. In 1654 they still lived well upriver from the English settlements and thus had little need to be "entertained" by colonists. The tayac did, however, need help in reminding the tribute-paying members of his paramount chiefdom that he was indeed their chief. The 1654 assembly provided such help by ruling that only the tayac and his great men could come into the Maryland settlements to negotiate treaties (and receive gifts) on behalf of the Potomac nations.[29]

The Piscataways and Marylanders alike sought out opportunities to renew their alliance. In February 1659, for example, word arrived at St. Mary's City that Weghucasso, tayac since the 1640s, was dying. Although the governor and council boldly announced their intention to "endeavor the making of a new Emperour in case he dye," in the end they did no such thing; instead Philip Calvert met with nine representatives of the Piscataway, Portobacco, and Nanjemoy nations to renew the peace "formerly made with Weghucasso." Far from choosing the new tayac, Calvert asked about the means of succession. He also followed Algonquian diplomatic protocol by accepting a gift offered by the new tayac Uttapoingassenem "in token of his perfect friendship" and by listening attentively as the Piscataways explained what they needed from their Maryland allies. Calvert promised to "call the Council" to respond to these requests. Similar diplomatic exchanges took place over the next several years as a series of accidents led to a rapid turnover in the tayac's office. Although the succession was always in question (each tayac between 1636 and 1666 died without leaving a brother or nephew to succeed him), Maryland never exercised its claim to choose the tayac. Instead they met repeatedly to renew diplomatic relations; and although Marylanders were not particularly impressed with the protocols of Algonquian diplomacy, they nevertheless participated in "some few Indian Ceremonies."[30]

The willingness of Maryland's leaders to engage with the Piscataways as allies, however, was increasingly at odds with the wishes of Maryland's frontier farmers. Poor soils above the Nanjemoy River and close diplomatic relations may have slowed the cycle of intimacy, conflict, depopulation, and dispossession, but they did not entirely halt the process. English farmers filled in the banks of the Portobacco and Nanjemoy rivers in the 1660s and moved up some of the small creeks feeding those rivers. A few even took up lands in the midst of the densest Indian populations remaining along the Potomac: on Mattawoman Creek, Piscataway Creek, and the Anacostia River. By 1675 there were about forty tracts north of Mattawoman Creek alone. Significantly, the surveyors of these tracts frequently used Indian fields as boundary markers.[31]

We can gain some insight into how Maryland officials and the tayac managed this situation by examining their response to a bloody incident in Charles

County in August 1665.[32] For Thomas Haslings and Bennet Marchegay, it began shortly after they had finished worming and cutting suckers from a tobacco field. Sitting down to smoke, they talked about their neighbors—their *Indian* neighbors. Marchegay said that they had recently "deserted their towne" and gone up to Piscataway Creek; noting that "they did not come about as they used to do," he opined that "as soone as their meetings are broake up that they will give us a clap." Just then they heard screams from the direction of the nearby home of Agatha Langworth. Langworth had been lying "sick on her table" when four Mattawoman men burst through her door. Langworth knew three of them by sight: Maquamps, Chotike, and "the old fisherman alias Inuoyce." Chotike swung his tomahawk at Langworth, but her dog chased the men from the room. After circling her house several times seeking another way in, the men "went through the orchard and the cornefeild," where Langworth's servant Elizabeth Brumley was looking after the Langworth children. Langworth immediately flung open a window "and hollowed and cryed Indians, Indians." From the house, Langworth heard her children crying "good nindians, good nindians" as Brumley tried to gather them together. Brumley called for "Jonny" to be quiet, but it was too late: Maquamps caught him and cut him down with his tomahawk. Brumley fled into the brush, carrying a girl with her. Maquamps followed, tracking Brumley and the girl "with the boyes head under his arme." As he approached their hiding place, he "lay downe the childs head . . . and struck att her [Brumley] with his tomajauke, three times" then left her for dead. Eventually Marchegay, Haslings, and another neighbor drove the Mattawomans away, but by then Jonny and one other child were dead and Brumley was gravely wounded.

Although the series of events leading up to this tragedy were surely a variation on the by-now familiar pattern—an English planter's hogs caught rooting about in a Mattawoman field, a Mattawoman hunter's "trespass" onto an Englishman's farm in pursuit of a white-tailed deer, and perhaps some harsh words between a Langworth and a Mattawoman—the denouement did not follow the established script.[33] Whereas similar incidents involving the Matchotics and Patawomecks provided the excuse for colonists to drive their neighbors from the land, in this instance the actors played out a different story. Chotike and Maquamps were, of course, quickly apprehended, tried, and executed, and on the day Chotike and Maquamps were sentenced to death, the Mattawomans sent one of their "Great Men," Nancotamon, to ask whether they should "remove further of[f] into the woods." But rather than seize this opportunity to "drive the Indians further off," the governor insisted "that it was most for the safety of the Province to continue them neer us" and directed that "theire land be with all convenient speed layd out for them by certaine meets and bounds, within which noe English man shall take up any land."[34]

In other words, the Langworth childrens' deaths led to the creation of a reservation. The new arrangements began to take shape just six months after the trials of Maquamps and Chotike. Delegates from several Algonquian nations arrived in St. Mary's City just as a new session of the General Assembly was beginning in April 1666. In keeping with the forms of Algonquian diplomacy, the visiting delegation made its presentations first. Mattagund, speaking for the Piscataways, began by accepting the principle that "if an Indian kill an English let him be delivered up" but then pointed out that English law did not offer equal protection to Indians: "Mrs. Langsworth's children were killed and the murtherers were delivered," Mattagund noted, but "they found a man Indian dead in the path killed by the English for which they have no satisfaction." Then there was the problem of conflicts over livestock: "let us have no quarrels for killing hogs no more than for the cows eating the Indians corn," he pleaded, for "your hogs and cattle injure us." Mattagund was followed by the Nanjemoy speaker Choatike, who added an appeal to make the Nanjemoys independent of the tayac. Still following Algonquian procedure, the English delegation retired to discuss Choatike's and Mattagund's proposals. The meetings resumed the following day, when the parties quickly reached a new agreement.[35]

The new treaty included concessions on both sides. It confirmed the governor's "sole power of constituting and appointing" the Piscataway tayac; it confirmed the practice of trying Indians in Maryland courts; it required Indians to fence in their own fields; and it prohibited Indians from wearing paint or carrying weapons in the presence of colonists. It also prohibited the Algonquians from allowing "foreign Indians" among them or from undertaking any new treaties (or wars) without the governor's permission. At the same time, it confirmed that "the priviledge of hunting crabbing fishing and fowleing shall be preserved to the Indians inviolably"; that Indian women and children could take refuge among the English whenever the threat posed by northern raiders became particularly dire; that the Nanjemoys would not be subject to the tayac; that each nation would remain in its current location unless "by the consent of their Matchcomics"; and that the governor would have their lands surveyed. It also resolved several disputes with individual Englishmen in favor of the Indians. The governor himself would travel to Piscataway to formally ratify the treaty.[36]

Over two years passed before the bounds of a new reservation could be surveyed, for the landmark 1666 treaty begat still more negotiations. Most communities opted to live on a large new reservation spanning the head of Mattawoman

Creek and the head of Piscataway Creek, "within which bounds the said several Nations of Indians . . . are to retreat and draw theither." The distance between these two markers was ten miles by air, and the reservation encompassed or was adjacent to a tremendous variety of wetlands, uplands, and fisheries.[37] Excepting the Chopticos and the Nacotchtanks, most of the signatories already lived within the bounds of the new reservation. In the end the Chopticos chose to remain at their reservation on the Wicomico River, while the Nacotchtanks abandoned their old homeland for the new reservation.[38]

The Treaty of 1666 gave the nations on the north bank of the Potomac a new lease on life. It was by no stretch of the imagination a victory, for it was the end product of a generation of struggles that perfectly illustrated the close connections between the control of nature and the exercise of power over other humans. Nevertheless, the creation of the new reserve did carve out a space within which Indians might maintain a considerable degree of cultural integrity and political autonomy. A Pamunky woman could still cultivate her own fields, find tuckahoe in the nearby marshes, and raise her children as Pamunkys; a Mattawoman man could still fish, hunt, and trade with people from neighboring nations; and the werowances and matchcomicos could still govern the day-to-day doings within each nation. There was still something to govern as well: the Piscataways, for instance, still fielded eighty warriors in 1676, nearly as many as they had in 1608.[39] Notwithstanding the Maryland governor's claim to appoint the tayac, in practice the office of the paramount chief followed, as nearly as possible, the old rules of succession. And although the Treaty of 1666 apparently ceded control over diplomatic affairs to the governor of Maryland, in reality this made little difference in either the tayac's or the governor's diplomatic policies, because they now both faced the same major problem: the unforeseen consequences of their 1652 alliance with the Susquehannock nation. Soon, that alliance would plunge Virginia, Maryland, and their Algonquian neighbors into a generation of almost unremitting warfare and unrest.

CHAPTER EIGHT

"Away with All These Distractions"

In the early 1670s it must have seemed to English planters along the Potomac that Indians would soon disappear from the scene. Granted, the Treaty of 1666 had set aside a large reservation for the Piscataways, Nacotchtanks, Mattawomans, and Pamunkys, while the Chopticos held on to their patch of land on Maryland's Wicomico River. Smaller groups lingered at Matchotic Creek and the Wicomico River, the towns of Nanzatico and Portobacco remained on the Rappahannock River, and Doegs were scattered throughout the coastal plain. Recent events, however, had given land-hungry planters every reason to believe that they would soon find a way to dispossess the remaining Algonquian communities. Planters could reasonably anticipate that English swine and cattle would continue to ravage Indian fields; that the county and provincial governments would look the other way when English planters and their animals encroached on Indian lands; and that when local conflicts turned violent the provincial governments would fail to protect the Indians. The Doegs had no legal claim, by English reckoning, to any particular lands. Nor did it seem necessary to maintain Indian communities as buffers against northern nations such as the Iroquois or Susquehannocks, for they had rarely visited the Potomac in recent years. Colonists increasingly knew their Algonquian neighbors not as sovereign peoples but as dependents: as hired hunters, fishers, farmhands, servants, and even as slaves. Some planters were so confident in the Indians' imminent demise that they obtained land grants pending "the Indians deserting the said land."[1]

This confidence was misplaced, however, because it failed to account for the momentum of historical forces that English planters had not created and could not fully control. Instead of completing the rout of the Potomac nations in the 1670s, colonists found themselves caught up in events that had their origins in the long-ago adoption of agriculture by the Potomac nations, in the onset of the Little Ice Age in the fourteenth century, and in the rise of chiefdoms in the sixteenth century. Virginians and Marylanders were surprised when hostilities between northern Iroquoians and Potomac Algonquians flared up in the 1670s, once again drawing the colonists into their struggles. These conflicts were profound and prolonged, engulfing Algonquian and English communities alike. The result was a long generation of wars and civil wars that were not fully resolved until the eighteenth century.

The Trouble with Susquehannocks

The Maryland-Susquehannock alliance of 1652 had freed the Susquehannocks to concentrate on battling their Five Nations enemies and had spared Maryland and the Potomac nations from Susquehannock raids. But the Potomac nations had never regarded the Susquehannocks as true friends, nor had they established a trading relationship with their former enemies. Moreover, the treaty did not really make them safe from northern raiders because the Susquehannock alliance amounted to a declaration of enmity against the Five Nations.

At first this problem was not so evident, for Five Nations warriors channeled their energies into raids deep into the western Great Lakes during the 1650s. Iroquois warriors enjoyed so much success there, however, that they began to seek out new adversaries in the 1660s. Canadian Jesuit missionaries reported that the Iroquois "are haughty enough to disdain the conquests to which they are accustomed" and instead "are pushing their way farther down toward the South" into the Susquehannocks' territory and along the Potomac. In December 1660 the Piscataways reported that the Iroquois had recently killed five of their men and threatened to destroy their towns, just "for being freinds to us [Maryland] and the Sasquehannoughs." Governor Calvert, they hoped, would help them to fortify the main Piscataway town.[2]

Would the Iroquois threat extend to the Susquehannocks' colonial allies? In 1664 reports filtered in of Iroquois warriors passing near upriver settlements. The commissioners of newly created Stafford County, Virginia, dispatched seven horsemen to "discover which Indians" had committed a murder "above at Patomeck," and less than two weeks later Marylanders captured a renowned Iroquois warrior on their frontier. His presence gave credence to the Susquehannocks' assertion that the Iroquois were responsible for recent attacks on Maryland settlements. The Piscataways' nearly simultaneous capture of two Oneida warriors seemed to confirm the Susquehannocks' accusations, for under torture the Oneidas said that sixty warriors had already come to "kill the English and the Indeans," and had already "cutt of[f] one house." Another hundred men, he warned, had "gone to the head of the bay to kill English."[3]

As additional accounts circulated of Iroquois penetrating all the way to St. Mary's County, Maryland's councilors declared war against the Five Nations and offered bounties for each enemy warrior captured or for "both his eares if he be slayne." Although the Iroquois mounted no major offensives, Maryland rangers patrolled the colony's frontiers almost continuously from 1664 to 1668. The Susquehannocks and Piscataways seized this opportunity to strengthen their relationships with Maryland, scrambling to demonstrate their friendship by handing over men suspected of committing crimes against colonists to be tried in Maryland courts.[4]

In Virginia, however, influential colonists along the Potomac exploited fears of Iroquois attacks to acquire more of their Algonquian neighbors' lands. In 1664 the Northern Neck counties blended preparations for defense against northern raiders with preparations to eject the Patawomecks and Doegs. Similarly, Stafford County's ban on Indians hunting near "English habitations" may have prevented nervous colonists from mistaking their Algonquian neighbors for Seneca intruders, but it also fit the established pattern of disarming Indians just before dispossessing them—which they did in the 1666 war against the Northern Neck nations. With the Iroquois threat fading and the Patawomecks eliminated from the scene, the Potomac fell quiet, for the colonists at least.[5]

The conflict between the Five Nations and the Susquehannocks, however, was approaching its climax. French missionaries noted the presence of Susquehannock captives in a predominantly Mohawk town near Montréal, and they frequently reported on clashes between the Susquehannocks and Five Nations, such as a 1671 skirmish in which sixty Iroquois warriors on their way to attack the Susquehannocks were ambushed and routed by their enemies. Though it seemed to one missionary that "God preserves the Andastogouez [Susquehannocks] . . . and favors their arms," the Susquehannocks had by this point been reduced to perhaps three hundred warriors.[6]

By 1673 the war had turned decisively against the Susquehannocks. Anxious Maryland officials worried that they might be next and wondered whether it might make more sense to ally themselves with the ascendant Five Nations rather than with the dwindling Susquehannocks. By backing the winners Maryland might not only avoid war with the Iroquois but also lay claim to the Susquehannocks' lands. Instead, though, Governor Calvert removed the Susquehannocks from their land through what was ostensibly a display of kindness: to the surprise of many, he invited the entire Susquehannock nation to move to Maryland.[7]

The governor's idea was controversial among Marylanders, and the Susque-hannocks met with a cool reception when they arrived in February 1675. Some Marylanders worried that the newcomers would corrupt "our Indians"; others, that the Susquehannocks' true purpose was to reconnoiter "the strength of the province and the advantages they may for the future take should they be evily in-clined." A few maintained that since the Susquehannocks "are such absolute en-emies to the Senecas . . . it will so exasperate the Senecas for us to entertain them" that they would target Maryland for destruction. The assembly hoped that the Susquehannocks would settle at a safe distance from other communities, prefer-ably at the Great Falls of the Potomac, but eventually the Susquehannocks were given an abandoned village at the mouth of Piscataway Creek, on the Algonquian reservation that had been created in 1668.[8]

The Susquehannocks' return to the Potomac was a disaster. Even as they were negotiating for possession of the town site at the mouth of Piscataway Creek, rumors spread among the colonists "of the many murthers and outrages comit-ted . . . by the Susquehanna Indians." Just days after reluctantly agreeing to seat them along the Potomac, the Maryland assembly proposed raising fifty thousand pounds of tobacco for peace negotiations with the Five Nations—or, if need be, for war against the Susquehannocks.[9] Nothing came of that initiative, but clearly the men who governed Maryland were inclined to think the worst of their guests. Frontier planters, who had long since demonstrated their preference for Indian removal, could be counted upon to harass the Susquehannocks. So could the Piscataways, Mattawomans, Nacotchtanks, and Pamunkys, who had not invited the Susquehannocks to live among them.

The war, when it came, began as "a dispute over pigs." In July 1675, accord-ing to one account, "certain Doegs . . . on the Maryland side" had been "abused and cheated by Thomas Mathews," who had failed to pay them "for such Indian trucke as he had formerly bought of them." For "satisfaction" of these debts, a party crossed over the Potomac to steal some hogs from Mathew. An English party pursued them by boat; the Doegs and Susquehannocks, encumbered by the stolen hogs, were soon overtaken and "beaten or killed." Upon hearing this tale, "a warr captain with some Indians" swore revenge. By one account, they "came over to Potomake and killed two of Mathewes his servants."[10] Another account, probably written by Mathew himself, mentions only one killing in the Doegs' reprisal: Robert Hen, a herdsman Mathew had hired to tend to his livestock in upper Stafford County. On a Sunday morning, recalled Mathew, "people in their way to church, saw this Hen lying thwart his threshold, and an Indian without the door, but chopt on their heads, arms and other parts, as if done with Indian hatchets." The Indian was dead, but Hen still clung to life. The churchgoers demanded to know "who did that?" Hen managed to gasp, "Doegs, Doegs," and then died.[11]

Colonel George Mason and Captain Giles Brent quickly raised over thirty men and set out after the Indian attackers. Traveling all night, they caught up with their prey across the river in Maryland. Each officer took a group of militiamen into the woods, creeping along through the dawn light. The men under Captain Brent came upon a Doeg cabin and called out in "the Indian tongue" for a "*Matchacomicha Weewhip i.e.* a Councill." When the Doegs' leader came out, Brent seized him by the hair and held a pistol to his head, telling his captive that he had come for the murderer of Robert Hen. The Doeg man broke loose and was immediately gunned down by Brent, setting off a mêlée in which ten more Doegs were killed. The shooting awoke the inhabitants of another cabin nearby, who "rushed out and fled" directly into a hail of bullets fired by Mason and his men. Fourteen died in that initial volley, but one survivor ran to Colonel Mason and "with both hands shook him (friendly) by one arm saying *Susquehanougs Netoughs i.e.* Susquehanaugh friends." Mason instantly grasped the potential consequences of his mistake, "whereupon he ran amongst his men, crying out 'for the Lord's sake shoot no more, these are our friends the Susquehanoughs.'"[12]

Considering that they had just lost more than two dozen men, the Susquehannocks' and Doegs' initial responses were fairly muted. Several months after this incident, Virginia's Governor Berkeley thought that they had killed perhaps two or three people on either side of the Potomac in retaliation, but even that modest death toll exceeded the tolerance of Virginia's anti-Indian majority. Thus in late August Berkeley asked Colonel John Washington and Major Isaac Allerton of Westmoreland County to look into reports that the "the Doegs and Sucahanna Indians . . . have murthered two more English men cutt up severall fields of corne and tobacco and destroyed several stocke of cattle" in upper Stafford County.[13]

By late September a joint assault was underway, with Virginia militia (under Washington and Allerton) and Maryland militia (under Thomas Truman) converging on the Susquehannocks' fortified town on Piscataway Creek.[14] As the siege began, several "great men" of the Susquehannocks came out to parley with Washington, Allerton, and Truman. The English commanders ordered the "great men" seized and bound, and they ordered that they be taken to see the graves of ten Susquehannocks who had recently been killed by the English. Truman reportedly said that the captives "deserved the like" as those who had already been buried, while another witness recalled that Washington "said what should we keep them any longer let us knock them on the head and we shall get the forte to day." Then, "after further discourse," the captives "wer carried forth from the place where they were bound and they knocked them on the head."[15]

The decision to murder five leading men under a flag of truce could not have been more provocative. Both sides settled into a weeks-long siege, during which the defenders managed to pick off fifty of their besiegers and take several horses. The Susquehannocks and Doegs bided their time, and on a moonlit night in early November they stole away from the fort. As they left they "knocked ten men o'th head, who lay carelessly asleep in there way" then burst upon the English encampment "hollowing and firing att them without opposition." The English failed to give chase until the following morning, and even then it seemed to at least one Virginian that they merely went through the motions: "for fear of am-buscades," they "would not overtake these desperate fugitives."[16]

As the Susquehannocks repaired to the southern Virginia Piedmont to re-cover from the long siege, colonists waited for the other shoe to drop. For the first time since 1668, rangers were dispatched to patrol the heads of the rivers, and some of the "most exposed small families withdrew into our houses of better numbers." A few even fortified their homes with "pallisadoes and redoubts." The Susquehannocks' Algonquian enemies also prepared for war. In Maryland the Mattawomans and Piscataways negotiated rewards for each Susquehannock or Doeg they brought in, and they sought permission to "infort" their towns against retaliation, while on the Northern Neck George Mason contracted with "certaine Indians" to kill or capture their mutual enemies.[17]

The Susquehannocks finally struck back in January 1676, when "a party of those abused Susquahanocks in revenge of the Maryland business came sud-dainly down upon the weak plantations at the head of Rapahanock and Poto-maque and killed at one time thirty six persons." From there they worked their way south, attacking English households at the heads of the York and James rivers. News and rumors of additional raids on Virginia's frontiers continued all through the winter of 1676, and Maryland, too, was "much disturbed by the natives." The Susquehannocks, it was said, "draw in others (formerly in subjec-tion to the Verginians) to there aides"; together the Indians "dayly commited" an "abundance of . . . murders" and tortured their captives. Among those killed were the overseer and a servant of a James River planter named Nathaniel Bacon, "whose bloud hee vowed to revenge if possible." Not surprisingly, the Susquehan-nocks were summarily rejected when they sent emissaries to propose a peace.[18]

Conscious of his inability to even find the Susquehannocks (he could say only that they had "fled towards the mountains"), fearful of a general Indian war, and keenly aware of the difficulty of raising men and money for a major military campaign, Governor Berkeley decided upon an essentially defensive strategy. He proposed to build forts at the heads of the rivers, to be garrisoned by five hundred men. Horsemen would range between the forts but would not go on the offensive without the express permission of the governor. To prevent weapons and ammunition from falling into the wrong hands, all Indian traders were stripped of their licenses; new commissions would have to be issued by the county courts.[19]

Many Virginians disliked Governor Berkeley's measured response to the crisis. The proposed forts were derided as useless except to those who would profit from their construction, and the new measures to prevent the colony's Indian traders from selling arms or ammunition were widely regarded as part of an attempt to create a monopoly over the Indian trade. Berkeley, it was said, "for the lucre of the beaver and otter trade . . . privately gave comission to some of his friends to truck with them." Worse still, "those persons furnished the Indians with powder, shott, &c.," so that they were better armed than the English.[20]

Some Virginians resolved to take matters into their own hands. Nathaniel Bacon, the James River planter who had lost two members of his household in the Susquehannock reprisals, accepted an invitation to lead one such group of self-appointed soldiers. Bacon and his followers were mystified by Berkeley's insistence on distinguishing allied Indians from Virginia's enemies. This, it was said, "made the people expostulate and say, how shall wee know our enimyes from our friends are not the Indians all of a colour?" Rather than distinguish between Indian groups, the "common cry" was to do "awaye with these forts, away with all these distractions, wee will have warr with all Indians . . . wee will spare none."[21]

The Baconites hastened to put their anti-Indian sentiments into practice by attacking Virginia's Indian neighbors and allies near Jamestown and along the Virginia–North Carolina line. This was all too much for Governor Berkeley, who declared Bacon and his men rebels. The civil war that followed came, for most Virginians, to overshadow the Indian war that had spawned it. Although Bacon's men continued to harass their Indian neighbors, they also chased Berkeley from office, burned Jamestown, established their own government, and set about punishing Berkeley's supporters.[22] Though most of the fighting between Englishmen took place off to the south, the civil conflict divided residents of the Northern Neck and Maryland as well. Baconites and Berkeley loyalists along the Potomac sporadically harassed each other, mostly by requisitioning each other's horses, boats, food, and homes. The strife even carried over into Maryland, where sixty men gathered to demand new rights and privileges from the colony's proprietors, including relief from the taxes levied to pay for the Susquehannock War.[23]

Along the Potomac, however, the Susquehannock War took precedence over

Bacon's Rebellion. Indians took the lead, as Piscataway and Mattawoman warriors jumped at the opportunity to attack the Susquehannocks. By May 1676 they had already earned the gratitude of the Maryland assembly, which voted to give them 130 barrels of corn, 60 pounds of powder, 200 pounds of shot, and over 100 matchcoats. The Mattawoman werowance earned additional rewards for capturing Indians fleeing from Bacon's pogrom, and Joe Tike, an especially valued Indian scout, was awarded a horse. The Potomac nations maintained their enthusiasm for the war even after the Susquehannocks made peace with the Five Nations and returned to their old home on the Susquehanna River in the summer of 1676, and they protested when Maryland officials decided to invite the Susquehannocks to come in for peace talks.[24]

Despite the Potomac nations' enthusiasm for the Susquehannock War, local planters remained highly suspicious of their Indian neighbors. Maryland's assembly voted "that hostages be required from the friend Indians," and the council decided to keep rangers in the field in order to keep an eye on the Potomac nations. The Matchotics and Nanzaticos fared even worse. The Nanzaticos aroused suspicions because they scattered into the interior after hearing news of Bacon's depredations, so in July 1676 men drawn from the Potomac and Rappahannock river counties sailed to the Nanzaticos' town at the head of the Rappahannock to expel those who had returned from the woods. Somewhere along the way the Matchotics also fled their homes along the Potomac and told the Mattawoman werowance that they "had a mind to come over to his fort." They were turned away for fear of retribution from the English.[25]

By the fall of 1676 the many-sided conflict between Baconites, Berkeleyites, Susquehannocks, Marylanders, Mattawomans, Piscataways, Nanzaticos, Matchotics, and other groups seemed to be winding down. Bacon died in October while pursuing Indians up the Piankatank River, putting an end to the rebellion for all but a few die-hard Baconites. The Susquehannocks had returned to their homeland, submitted to the Five Nations, and formed a new alliance with New York. A new treaty between Virginia and its tributary Indians seemed to restore the peace. The Nanzaticos returned to their homes on the Rappahannock River, and the Matchotics came back to the Potomac. Berkeley fell into disgrace and was sent back to England to answer for his role in Virginia's civil war. He died in July 1677, shortly before he was to go before the king; now both the governor and the rebel were gone.[26]

That is where historical accounts of Bacon's Rebellion normally end, but people living along the Potomac knew better. Potomac planter Francis Moryson predicted that "fears and rumors of rebellion maye continue here this 20 yeares," while Maryland's governor and council still felt it necessary in December 1676, two months after Bacon's death, to identify rebellion-minded planters and "lop off such rotten members as doe endanger the whole." Even those "rotten members" agreed that the conflict was far from over: in January 1677 the authors of the anonymous pro-Bacon "Complaint from Heaven with a Huy and crye and a petition out of Virginia and Maryland" wrote that only the first act had been performed: "now," they warned, "begins the second part of the late tragedy." They predicted a "longe destructive warr" that would pit the peoples of the Potomac against the new Susquehannock–Five Nations alliance, Maryland's proprietors against the common man, Indians against English, and Catholics against Protestants.[27]

"Now Begins the Second Part of the Late Tragedy"

The "Complaint from Heaven" expressed the sentiments of Maryland and Northern Neck planters who believed that even Bacon's analysis of their troubles had not gone far enough. Like Bacon, the authors rejected the distinction between Indian allies and Indian enemies (they even claimed that the Piscataways had been in league with the Susquehannocks during the late war). But the conspiracy against English liberties did not end there. It also included Lord Baltimore, the proprietor of Maryland, who (they said) had arranged for the failure of the siege of the Susquehannock fort in 1675 and had promoted attacks by Five Nations warriors. Worse, the proprietor was secretly in league with the French, the Jesuits, and the pope himself: "the platt form is" that "Pope [and] Jesuit [are] determined to over terne England with feyer, sword, and distractions, with themselves, and by the Maryland Papists, to drive us Protestants to Purgatory . . . with the help of French spirits from Canada." Behind the Indians, French, Maryland's Catholics, and the pope, of course, stood the devil himself.[28]

The "Complaint from Heaven" is remarkable for its wildly paranoid style, manifest errors of fact, and lapses into spluttering incoherence. Yet the charges its authors made resonated deeply with colonists along the Potomac, for it integrated several chronic sources of fear and conflict into a single story that seemed to explain the pervasive sense that corruption within and encircling menace without threatened the very existence of Virginia and Maryland. This newly synthesized conspiracy theory inadvertently reinforced the centuries-old division between northern Iroquoians and the peoples of the Potomac. This division, originally the product of the transition to agriculture, the onset of the Little Ice Age, and the resulting transformations of Iroquois and Algonquian political cultures and diplomacy, had long since taken on a life of its own. By 1677 the fourteenth-century origins of this division were forgotten; it was enough for Potomac Algonquians to know that the Susquehannocks and Iroquois were their enemies, for the English to know that the French were their greatest foes, and for the English and the Algonquians to agree that they had some enemies in common.

Everyone, whether Mattawoman or Virginian, Catholic or Protestant, anticipated more attacks by Susquehannocks and Iroquois warriors in 1677, unless a treaty could be made with the Five Nations and their new Susquehannock dependents. In April a delegation led by Eastern Shore planter Henry Coursey left Albany, with instructions to include Virginia and "all our other low land Indians in amity with us." This instruction, it was recognized, might "prove the harder part of the negotiation," given the enthusiasm with which the Mattawomans and Piscataways had prosecuted the Susquehannock War. Nevertheless Coursey returned with a treaty that seemed to promise that the Five Nations would prevent angry Susquehannocks from seeking vengeance against the people who had turned on them in 1675.[29]

Despite a few rumors of northern Indians harassing "the neighboring Indians" in the spring and early summer of 1678, Coursey's treaty gave Marylanders the confidence they needed to resume the dispossession of their Algonquian neighbors. In early August a family of three colonists was killed at the head of the Patuxent River, not far from the Chopticos' and Piscataways' reserves. One of the family survived long enough to be questioned. When John Burroughs asked her how many men had been in the attack, she held up four fingers; and when he asked her if "the rogue Wassetass," a prominent Piscataway man, had been one of the attackers, she lifted "up hear [her] hand and putt on her head upon the place where she was wounded." Maryland's councilors immediately demanded a "Matchacomico" with the Piscataways, which met on 19 August. The Piscataways, unaware of the true reason for the meeting, began by complaining that they'd been attacked recently by Susquehannock and Iroquois raiders. The councilors, however, refused to talk about this until the Piscataways produced the killers, including Wassetass. The Piscataways insisted that northern Indians must have done the murders, but the councilors were equally insistent that the culprits were Piscataways.[30]

The standoff continued into the fall. Perhaps in retaliation, rangers in Charles County were directed that they should not range above the Piscataway fort but rather "between Pascattoway and the English plantations," thus protecting the colonists but leaving their allies open to attacks. The Piscataways, desperately in need of their Maryland allies, finally cracked. At a dramatic meeting in January

1679 they agreed to hand over Azazames and Manhowton, two of the men accused of the August murders. Wassetass, the Piscataways insisted, had nothing to do with the killings; and besides, they asserted, Wassetass had been "killed in the late reencounter between them and the Susquehannocks and could not be delivered up." Azazames and Manhowton were executed by a firing squad that very evening. Still the negotiations continued, and eventually the Piscataways conceded that Wassetass was alive. They promised to produce him by mid-February but once again failed to deliver.[31]

There matters stood until March 1679, when a Seneca emissary appeared first at the Piscataway fort and then before the governor and council. The emissary, a Potomac native who had been captured and assimilated into an Iroquois community, explained that two Iroquois towns had taken in a great many Susquehannocks and that "through the insinuation and instigation" of the Susquehannocks those two towns had come to share the Susquehannocks' hatred of the Virginians, Piscataways, and Marylanders. The Susquehannocks' "greate man," he said, had recently promised that he "would never have any peace with the English, or the Pascattoway, Choptico, or any other Indians" in Maryland or Virginia; moreover, he bragged that Susquehannocks had "lately killed some English in Maryland but the English had laid it upon the Pascattoway Indians." These revelations clearly shook up the council. It immediately began to lay plans for a renewal of Coursey's 1677 treaty with the Five Nations, promised guns and ammunition to the Piscataways, and declared that Wassetass was innocent of the August 1678 murders (no mention, however, was made of the two Piscataway men who had already been executed).[32]

Despite English and Five Nations attempts at firming up Coursey's 1677 treaty, the Susquehannocks (frequently accompanied by Five Nations warriors) continued to wage intermittent war against the people who had betrayed them with such apparent ease. New York's governor Edmund Andros attempted to use his influence to "stop and prevent . . . futere Indian mischiefs in Virginia and Marilond," and Virginia sent its own delegation to Albany in 1679 to reaffirm the treaty and to negotiate the return of captives. Northern Indians were nevertheless reported to "dayly infest" Virginia's frontier, and a springtime clash between Virginia rangers and a party of northerners left three colonists dead. Additional attacks in August and September 1679 killed six colonists and three hundred cattle. Planters fled the upper reaches of the Northern Neck, rangers went out in many counties, and the Chopticos, Mattawomans, and Piscataways contemplated a separate expedition of their own.[33]

Even as the northern war heated up, the peoples of the Potomac continued

to regard each other with suspicion. In 1680, for example, Virginia's council petitioned the king for relief from the "sudden and sculcking incurssions" of "neighbour or pretended forreigne Indians," who they suspected of fobbing off their
own misdeeds on the Iroquois or of having "induced" the northerners to attack
Virginia's frontiers. Some planters along the Potomac continued to spread rumors that the Piscataways and Susquehannocks were part of a grand Catholic-
French-Indian conspiracy. The Algonquian peoples of the Potomac reciprocated,
worrying about their English neighbors as well as about Senecas and Susquehannocks.[34]

Frightening incidents multiplied during 1680 and 1681, adding to the sense
that matters were coming to a head. Susquehannocks laid siege to the Piscataway
fort for much of the summer of 1680, swearing that they "would have revenge for
their greate men killed [in] the late warr." Then, in February 1681, a large party of
Susquehannocks and Senecas trekked through snowy woods and along icy rivers
to the Potomac River, where they fell upon the Mattawoman nation. The raiders
carried away numerous prisoners, including the werowance, and in a matter of
hours had nearly destroyed the Mattawomans as a people. This devastating raid
shocked residents of the Potomac Valley, for its timing (midwinter, well outside
the ordinary season for warfare) and the large number of warriors in the attack
signaled that something unusual was afoot. A Piscataway emissary to Maryland
reported that the destruction of the Mattawomans "struck such dread and terror
in the Pascattoway" that they dared not venture out to fish or plant corn. This
midwinter raid was followed by still more ominous signs. In late May warnings
spread that two hundred "Sinnico" (a generic term for northern Indians) guided
by the captured Mattawoman werowance were on their way to lay siege to the
Piscataways' main town and "by presents to draw the Pascattoways with them,
but if they cannot to destroy them."[35]

This was a worrisome confluence of events that the Potomac nations interpreted as a sign of their impending destruction at the hands of their northern
enemies—unless, of course, the English could be persuaded to honor their treaty
obligations. English conspiracy theorists, however, had no difficulty in absorbing the Mattawomans' and Piscataways' military defeats into their vision of a
vast Catholic plot. Indeed, the conspiracy theorists may have benefited from the
bewildering array of rumors that circulated in the spring of 1681, for people who
were confused by these rumors likely found the simplistic association between
Catholics, Indians, and the French a comforting alternative to figuring out a terribly complicated situation.[36]

By June 1681 a full-blown panic gripped the Potomac Valley, particularly after news spread of the murder of five Englishmen and a woman at Point Lookout (at the mouth of the river). Jackanapes, an escaped Mattawoman prisoner of the Susquehannocks, said that ten Senecas and ten Susquehannocks had broken off from the siege of the Piscataway fort "to goe downe Pottomock River . . . to hunt for other Indians" and had attacked the English household at Point Lookout instead. Though Jackanapes's explanation seemed most satisfactory to Maryland's governor and councilors, Protestant conspiracy theorists added the murders at Point Lookout to the list of Catholic atrocities.[37]

News from England encouraged the notion that these events were part of an international plot, for popular anti-Catholicism there had surged throughout the 1670s and peaked in 1679–80. James, the heir to the throne, had recently been revealed as a Catholic. A controversial alliance with the French, coupled with Charles II's refusal to disband a thirty-thousand-man army, had aroused fears of "a design . . . to change the lawful government of England into an absolute tyranny, and to convert the established Protestant religion into downright Popery." In 1678 the nation thrilled to the news of the "Popish Plot," in which Jesuit conspirators were supposed to have arranged for the assassination of Charles II, an Irish uprising, and a French invasion. By 1681 about thirty-five people had been executed for their part in the "Popish Plot." Also in 1678, the House of Commons learned that France's Louis XIV had made a secret pact to subsidize Charles II in return for a Catholic-friendly English foreign and domestic policy. This revelation led directly to the Exclusion Crisis, a precarious two-year period in which Parliament repeatedly attempted to pass a bill excluding Catholics (read, "James") from the throne.[38]

Into this combustible mixture of news and rumors stepped Josias Fendall, a Charles County planter who "kept all the late proceedings in England at home at his house." Fendall and others had been trying for months to lay the groundwork for a Protestant uprising against the Catholic "traytor" Lord Baltimore; now, in the days following the killings at Point Lookout, Fendall invoked these documents in order to recruit participants. The Protestant plot was soon exposed, and by mid-July Fendall was under arrest, but as late as 17 July some forty armed supporters led by George Godfrey (an officer in Maryland's Potomac ranger corps) still dared to lay plans to spring Fendall from jail.[39]

Events during the remaining summer months did nothing to dissipate colonists' fears. The northern Indians, bragging that they had already "brought the Pascattoways heads to be as small as a finger," asked Maryland's governor to join them in wiping out the Piscataways. The mixed force of northern Indians continued their siege of the Piscataway fort, cut down their corn, and took captives. Hungry warriors confiscated cattle and hogs from frontier planters and shot at them if they resisted. Virginia and Maryland rangers ceaselessly patrolled the woods, on guard against "strange Indians" and "neighboring Indians" alike. Maryland and Virginia officials fretted about "Rank Baconists" who remained at large.[40]

By August the tayac and Governor Calvert were both eager for peace with the northern nations. While Calvert sought to renew Coursey's 1677 treaty by working with the Five Nations, separate negotiations between the Piscataways and the northerners were mediated by Nacotchtank and Mattawoman captives living in the north. The Iroquois, however, chose a third path. On 16 August, ten Onondagas and Oneidas came to St. Mary's City and declared that they wanted a long-term peace with Maryland, regular trade relations, and an exchange of prisoners. In return they wanted free rein to "see if they can make an end of" the remaining Algonquian communities along the Potomac. Relief, however, came neither through negotiations nor through force of arms. Instead the northerners simply decamped in early September—perhaps because the siege had failed, or because the men wanted to go home, or because of pressure from home to stop upsetting the English. The panic that had gripped the Potomac at midsummer gradually dissipated over the course of the fall and winter.[41]

Most of the factors that had combined to create a general panic in the summer of 1681 remained in play throughout the 1680s. There were periodic stirrings from unreconstructed Baconites and colonists worried about Susquehannock and Five Nations warriors sweeping down out of the north. Like Virginia's burgesses, who lived "in dayly dread and horror of our neighbouring Indians joining with them," Maryland's legislators felt bound to protect their Algonquian allies lest they be driven into the arms of the Iroquois "and in that case become another enraged enemy with the Susquehannahs." Such fears were revived nearly every summer during the 1680s, and often with cause; in 1687 an estimated three hundred Senecas raided the heads of the rivers, taking prisoners and killing "Christians" and Algonquians alike.[42]

In response, Virginia and Maryland maintained rangers on the Potomac frontier while also working to strengthen and polish what was increasingly coming to be known as the "Covenant Chain." The term had appeared in the treaties negotiated during Henry Coursey's 1677 mission to Albany, and it proved a flexible metaphor that structured negotiations and treaties between the Five Nations and a variety of other Indian nations and European colonies. Maryland renewed the

1677 treaty in 1682 and 1685, again including Virginia and its neighboring Indians in the agreement, while Virginia initiated and signed a separate agreement in 1684, which was renewed barely two years later.[43]

A series of bad harvests and epidemics helped to sustain the colonists' general anxiety and pessimism about the future. A major storm in August 1683 badly damaged corn and wheat crops, necessitating bans against exporting food, and in midsummer 1684 a "very promising" tobacco crop was "by 40 days of continuall rain almost totally lost." Wheat crops on the Eastern Shore were damaged as well, further reducing the colonies' food supplies. And four years later, in 1688, Virginia's Governor Effingham declared a day of fasting and humiliation because "it has pleased Almighty God for the two last years to visit the inhabitants of this poore country with frequent violent sicknesses" (possibly smallpox) and a "great drought threatning an extreame dearth of corne."[44]

The more fundamental causes of malaise during the 1680s, however, lay in the choices that earlier generations of colonists had made when deciding how to live upon the land. The colonists' collective decision to build their lives around a single dominant crop, tobacco, restricted their ability to respond flexibly to changing circumstances. The 1680s marked the beginning of a thirty-year period in which tobacco prices, which had been falling throughout the seventeenth century, bottomed out, while demand for the product in the saturated English market stagnated. Unlike in earlier decades, there were no major improvements in productivity, packaging, or shipping to offset low tobacco prices. And since the merchants' route from England to the Potomac passed first through the West Indies, Carolina, and more southerly reaches of Virginia, ships often filled their holds before reaching the Potomac.[45]

Labor also ran short. As the Potomac's colonial population shifted from one dominated by young adult migrants to a more demographically balanced community that included children and superannuated workers, the proportion of productive workers to the overall population fell significantly; each worker's labor thus had to support more people. Moreover, improved prospects in England kept prospective indentured servants at home, and those who did migrate were drawn to Pennsylvania and other new colonies that offered greater opportunities than Virginia or Maryland. (Maryland's rangers were directed to guard not only against northern Indians but also against servants and sailors who tried to run away to Pennsylvania.) Slaves could not make up the difference, as the Atlantic slave trade had yet to deliver many Africans to the Potomac. The African American population of the Chesapeake colonies as a whole increased but slowly during the 1680s, and as a result of the Potomac's location near the end of the slave traders' voyages relatively few slaves were available to planters along the river. The widespread oppression of enslaved Africans would later help white planters to improve their standard of living, but that time had not yet arrived.[46]

The troubles with tobacco inspired some planters to diversify their activities. The steady accrual of knowledge amongst Englishmen about fishing and oyster-ing helped here. (Indeed, St. Mary's River oysterers became too proficient for their own good: oysters taken there in the mid-1640s averaged 3 inches of length, but by the 1690s they averaged only 1.2 inches.) Other colonists began to master the highly technical craft of building fish traps. When Richard Martin of Stafford County recorded a deed in 1687, for example, he gave his occupation as "wear-maker," while Michael Webb was prosecuted in Westmoreland County for "stop-ping up the passage of Machotix River" with weirs and stakes. Similarly, orchards planted earlier in the century were reaching maturity in the 1680s, and new plant-ings continued apace. Planters' livestock continued to multiply, and a few began selling dairy products. Many planters added sheep to their herds: fewer than 10 percent of all Charles County households had owned sheep in the 1660s, but by the 1690s that figure had risen to nearly a third; 10 percent owned equipment for carding and spinning wool. Some planters even turned to growing wheat, though this, like nearly all forms of diversification, proved more popular on the Eastern Shore and on the far northern Chesapeake than it did along the Potomac.[47]

The combination of Indian troubles and economic stagnation put the brakes on the upriver spread of the colonial population. Marylanders had patented forty-two new tracts above Mattawoman Creek between 1661 and 1675, but be-tween 1676 and 1686 they took up only two new parcels, and Charles County's population rose but incrementally during these troubled times. On the Virginia side of the river, the number of tithables crept upward from 1,561 in 1674 to 1,726 in 1682, and the population actually fell by about 7 percent in the westernmost county of Stafford. New arrivals and colonists on the move preferred the relative safety of the Eastern Shore or the relative fertility of the Patuxent River to the more exposed position and less fertile soils of the Potomac.[48]

Although the Algonquian peoples of the Potomac also won a reprieve from the destruction that had seemed imminent in the great panic of 1681, they well understood that the forces arrayed against them remained in play. Wrathful Susquehannocks and their Five Nations allies were far more likely to attack the Piscataways and Chopticos than Virginians or Marylanders; in 1682, for instance, two Indians taken captive in Maryland "were burned as usual, at a slow fire, with heated irons, and were afterward eaten" by their Iroquois captors.[49] Susquehan-nock and Five Nations warriors regarded any of the Native peoples of the Chesapeake region, who they called "Conoys," as fair game.[50] Northern raids against Conoys loomed as a major issue in every treaty negotiation between the Five Nations and the southern colonies. In July 1684 Governor Effingham castigated the northerners for "fighting with our friend and neighbour Indians." A renewed Covenant Chain, he said, must include a promise that the northerners "doe not hinder or molest our frind Indians from hunting att our mountanes it haveing been there country and none of yours, for they never goe into your country to disturbe any of you." Virginia's burgesses noted that "the terror" of northern raiders "hath forced those few remaineing of the neighbour Indians to draw inwards soe that few (if any) of these are to be found at the head, or to the west of the great rivers." The 1684 treaty, coupled with troubles in the west that diverted the attention of Iroquois warriors, gave the Potomac nations something of a respite between 1685 and 1688, but even then the northerners did not completely relent.[51]

Nor did the English neighbors of the Potomac nations completely relent in their encroachments on Indian lands, fisheries, and hunting grounds. The pace of such encroachments was slower than in the 1650s and 1660s, but incident after incident chipped away at the foundations of the Algonquians' subsistence practices. In November of 1683, for example, Virginia's council eliminated one of the two reserves on the Rappahannock River by forcing the Rappahannocks and Nanzaticos to "be united and incorporated." The Rappahannocks' relocation took place under the guise of protecting them from "the incursions of the Seneca Indians," but the Potomac nations could not have missed the fact that the council had assumed that it was free to dispose of Indian lands.[52] The awareness that they could do little to prevent provincial authorities from making such arbitrary decisions must have weighed heavily upon the Chopticos when, just two years later, they found themselves besieged by their neighbors. In September 1686 William Assonam, the Choptico werowance, complained to Maryland's council that "severall of the English living near his people doe extreamely molest and disturb them in throwing down their fences and destroying their corn and provisions." Two years later the new Choptico werowance, Tom Calvert, was still seeking relief. Robert Frazier, he told the council, had thrown down the Chopticos' fences "and let his catle in and soe destroy all their beanes."[53]

Other incidents made it harder for Indians to fish or hunt. Colonists who learned to make weirs took over fishing spots that had once sustained Native communities. And as the English population gradually thickened on the ground and came to make more intensive use of the lands they claimed, conflicts over hunting grounds on the coastal plain also arose—at a time, unfortunately, when Algonquians feared to tread in their traditional hunting grounds above the Great

Falls. In 1687 a Mattawoman man who had gone to "the Indians hunting quarters" in Stafford County was found "lyinge upon his back with his mouth open and the stopper of his powder horne in his mouth." He had been shot from behind. Suspicion soon fell upon Thomas Norman: according to the Mattawoman werowance, Norman had "often been angry with them" because he claimed the hunting quarters as his. Norman, who was ordered to pay compensation to the Mattawomans and "prohibited from carryinge a gune into the woods," was likely deterred from breaking the terms of his settlement because he had posted a £100 bond for his good behavior. His Algonquian neighbors, however, were also likely deterred from hunting in some places for fear of falling afoul of another Englishman like Thomas Norman.[54]

Other intimacies with the English also threatened the survival of Algonquian communities. The fur trade—mostly deerskins now—continued to be of importance to some Algonquian hunters. Some also made substantial sums by bringing in wolves' heads, for which county courts paid generous bounties. Others worked as paid hunters. Rather than strengthening ties between sovereign peoples, however, the fur trade increasingly financed Algonquian alcoholism: as the Choptico werowance complained, "drinke is brought into the towne by the English and soe the Indians buy it for skins and that keeps the Indians poore, and makes them drunke."[55] Paid employment in turn shaded into servitude and slavery. In 1682 Virginia changed its law so that Indian servants could more easily be detained and even enslaved. Through a technicality of this law the distinction between servants, involuntary servants for a period of years, and slaves hinged on their ages, so that local officials were required to inspect prospective slaves and determine how old they were.[56]

On the whole, though, the sense of impending doom that had permeated the region in 1681 had lessened considerably. In 1689 it had been more than a decade since an Algonquian community had been dispossessed. Algonquian political systems and cultures appeared to be intact: each nation had both a werowance and an outer chief, and the werowance's mantle was still passed on according to the old rules of succession. The foodways, bodily decorations, and use of shell beads by Algonquians in the 1680s also suggested a fair degree of continuity. Northern raids had fallen off in recent years, and the French menace (while still on some colonists' minds) had not materialized. Rangers and Indian interpreters were laid off.[57] Protestant-Catholic strife had been reduced to background noise.

CHAPTER NINE

"Frightened Away by Some Threatening Discourses"

The partial reprieve of the 1680s did not last long. The Potomac nations barely survived the 1690s, and shortly after the turn of the century they were forced to leave the Potomac basin altogether. The final destruction of the Potomac nations as independent polities came about through a combination of forces. As usual, hostilities with the northern Iroquoians—conflicts rooted in the environmental history of earlier centuries—compounded the Potomac nations' difficulties. In the 1690s, however, the greatest dangers lay closer to home, as English farmers and provincial governments joined forces to dispossess their Indian neighbors and allies. The process by which this happened was by now all too familiar: bit by bit, English planters captured more and more of the elemental sources of power, taking prime fields and other resources out of the hands of Indians and transferring the energy derived from corn, fish, and other products into the hands of colonists. And like earlier generations of colonists over the centuries, the victors in these contests then deployed these newly acquired sources of energy to expand their power over still more places and people. To make matters worse, the provincial governments of both Virginia and Maryland increasingly threw their weight behind the frontier farmers' cause, abandoning their old alliances of mutual protection with the Piscataways and other nations in order to follow a new script in which there was no role for the Potomac nations.

"Popish" Plots

What triggered this shift on the part of provincial authorities was an earthshaking event in far-off England: the "Glorious Revolution" of 1688. The Glorious Revolution, in which the Catholic James II was ousted and replaced with James's daughter Mary and her husband (the militant Dutch Protestant William of Orange), gave the sort of men who had endorsed the "Hue and Cry" an opportunity to hitch their cause to that of the winning side in England. Once again characterizing the Calvert family as part of a grand Popish plot in league with Indians, Frenchmen, and the local Catholic minority, the anti-Calvert faction in Maryland rose up and took over Maryland's government in the name of William III and Protestantism. The new, neo-Baconian regime they established steadily increased the pressure on Indian communities until finally, in the mid-1690s, the Algonquians cracked. By 1697 most Algonquians had abandoned their reservations, and by 1705 not a single functioning Native American polity remained along the river. The survivors decamped to Pennsylvania or persisted in small, informal communities within the dominant English society.

When news arrived that James II had fled to France and been replaced by William III, rumors began to circulate along the Potomac that leading Catholic colonists had hired "the Indians" to "kill the Protestants." As usual, the key to the new Popish plot was said to be the Five Nations, who were presumed to be under the sway of the French: when unleashed by their Popish puppet-masters, the Iroquois would strike simultaneously in Virginia and Maryland. As the rumors spread in late March and early April 1689, terrified Stafford County residents "fled to their forts" and put their troops and rangers on high alert. The woods on both sides of the river resounded with "the beating of drums and volleys of shott" as Protestants readied for a desperate battle against overwhelming odds. Provincial authorities, concerned that these rumors might serve as a pretext "to stir up and carry on a rebellion in both colony's," quickly exposed the story as a hoax perpetuated by Burr Harrison, John West, George Mason, and other neo-Baconites in Stafford County. Their plan, concluded Virginia's council, was to use the hysteria as a pretext for their own uprising. In April the Stafford County men most deeply involved in the hoax were arrested and examined; one, George Mason, was removed from the Commission of the Peace and from his militia command.[1]

Undeterred, John Coode (a central figure in the anti-Catholic scare of 1681) and seven other leaders of Maryland's anti-proprietary faction met in Charles County in July 1689 and issued an explanation "of the reason and motive for the appearing in arms of His Majesty's Protestant subjects in the province of Maryland." Loyal Protestant subjects of William III, wrote the Protestant "associators," were "in eminent danger by the practices and machinations that are on foot to betray us to the French, Northern and other Indians . . . and others invited to assist in our distruction, well remembering the French Jesuits." Coode and his fellow associators marched downriver toward St. Mary's City, picking up supporters along the way. When they reached the capital, Lord Baltimore's council capitulated without firing a shot. The associators also won the public relations battle, successfully representing themselves to William and Mary as having delivered Maryland out of the hands of the enemy "in defence of their Majestyes soveraigne right and title to this province."[2]

Though both colonies readied themselves for war against northern Indians and Frenchmen, the real source of conflict between Indians and colonists along the Potomac was less a matter of geopolitics than of overcrowding. William Cole, reporting to the Board of Trade in October 1690, wrote that "the Indians are very few, and many people settle among them contrary to law," so that "a disturbance is feared between the English and the Indians." Every new colonist on the Northern Neck made it a little bit harder for Indian men to hunt, while every new farmer who established himself above Mattawoman Creek brought more hogs, horses, and cattle to destroy Indian women's crops.[3] The Potomac nations, wary of the new leadership in Maryland and of the reliably anti-Indian elite in Stafford County, did their best to avoid conflict. The tayac, for example, directed his people to "beware that they did no hurt to the English men or to their stocks," and the leader of a hunting expedition to Stafford County swore that if he thought one of his party was going to do any "mischief," he would "knock him in the head or rather tomahawk him."[4] Algonquian circumspection, however, only delayed the showdown.

As in 1675, the final conflict between the Algonquian and English peoples of the Potomac was sparked by the death of an animal. In early December 1691, Virginia rangers tracked down "six strange Indians" suspected of robbing colonists' cornfields and killing a mare and brought them before the Stafford County Court. The "chiefest of the prisoners" turned out to be "the King of the Doegs," who had "been taken a prisoner about fourteen years since by the Senecar Indians from the Nanjatica Indians." He had remained with the Iroquois until the fall of 1690, when he had come to live with the Mattawomans on their Maryland reserve; then, after getting in a corn crop in 1691, he crossed over to Virginia to explore the possibility of returning to the Nanzaticos. Several Englishmen corroborated his story. But why had his party killed a mare? The Doeg explained that "a young man of the Mohooks [Mohawks] . . . did rashly and without his consent kill the said mare." In the end the Nanzaticos agreed to pay restitution for the damaged livestock, and the "six strange Indians" went home with the Nanzaticos.[5]

This affair happened just before Virginia's rangers were scheduled to disband for the winter, but as a consequence of the incident the rangers remained afield for many more months (as did Maryland's). Virginia's council, though concerned not to "occasion a warr with the Indians" by treating them too harshly, ordered that justices of the peace arrest any Indians who "shall report any news which may alarum the inhabitants" until the news could be checked out. Stafford County protested against Indians resident in Maryland crossing the river to hunt or trade and demanded that they "send over some of their great men to informe the nearest magistrate" of their itinerary before entering Virginia.[6]

The Mattawomans, Chopticos, and Piscataways were scheduled to meet with Maryland's governor and council in May, but the "six strange Indians" episode and other events in the winter and spring of 1691–92 cast a pall over the proceedings. On the very day that the werowances and great men were to meet with the governor and council, they were kept waiting while the council listened to reports of recent Indian attacks. Elizabeth Kersley testified that she had been assaulted in late April by several "strange Indians" who burst "out of the lapp of a fallen tree" near her father's house in Charles County. They scalped her, stripped her naked, "and left her for dead." As they left they stuck a decorated arrow or stick in the path. A similar stick, "painted with severall men and women upon it," was found at a nearby farm where a mare had been shot through the heart. In another recent incident, this time near the Choptico reserve, a mare and several sheep were found shot to death with arrows.[7]

The council's next item of business after hearing these stories was to renew its treaties with the tayac and the Mattawoman and Choptico werowances. Rather than talk peace, however, the councilors interrogated the tayac Ochotomaquath and the two werowances about the recent "injury and violence" done to colonists. Under questioning the Piscataways all denied any knowledge of the late "mischief" but admitted that they did have some Delaware Indians living among them. The Mattawoman werowance Maquantah identified the ornamented stick found near Elizabeth Kersley as the work "of the French Cannada Indians" and said that the marks upon it indicated that the owner had killed three people and taken eight prisoners. The Choptico werowance, Tom Calvert, also denied any involvement and said that the arrows were not made by Chopticos. Scoffing at these "shifting and frivolous excuses," the councilors demanded a confession. Finally the Chopticos acquiesced, saying that they were "sorry . . . and promise never to do the like."[8]

To the undoubted relief of Ochotomaquath, Maquantah, and Tom Calvert, the treaties of 1666 were quickly reconfirmed the very next morning, but no sooner had the gifts been exchanged than the governor and council resumed their interrogation of the chiefs. In the same rancorous spirit, the tayac asked for an order preventing the carrying of liquor to the Piscataways and for another order forbidding the English from interfering with Indians' lawful hunting and fishing, even though these were already guaranteed by the treaty just concluded. Closing on an appropriately sour note, the Piscataways and Chopticos asked for relief from the colonists who were encroaching upon their lands, to which the governor replied by assigning two men who already had rocky relationships with their Indian neighbors to look into and adjudicate these complaints.[9]

Less than a week after the treaty was concluded, ten Indians attacked a slave-woman in Maryland, stabbing her "under the right breast" and lifting "a peice of skin the breadth of a crown piece" from her scalp. In the wake of this attack rumors and signs of other strange Indians kept both Indian and English residents on high alert; among other reports, Jacob Young said that he had spotted some Senecas at the Piscataway fort, and Stafford County rangers followed "the track of a great many Indians" who had taken captive a servant in George Mason's household. Virginia and Maryland created additional troops of rangers to patrol the upper Potomac "in this time of eminent danger."[10]

For once the reports of large bodies of strange Indians lurking on the upper Potomac turned out to be true. An earlier generation of Five Nations warriors had driven many people out of the eastern Great Lakes and Ohio country into the western Great Lakes and Illinois country. By the 1680s, though, a combination of "ecological and economic instability" in these western communities, together with a French alliance and a series of military victories over the Five Nations, had sent many people washing back into the east. Many went to Pennsylvania and the Ohio country, while others ended up as far south as the Savannah River. Several of these groups, including Shawnees, Delawares, and Miamis, turned up in Maryland in July 1692. Although they included numerous women and children and were asking for a place to settle in peace, their sheer numbers, their uncertain identities, and their familiarity with the French were all cause for concern. Most worrisome, some of the refugees really were French: as traders or soldiers at western posts such as Ft. St. Louis, on the Illinois River, they had been so fully integrated into Native communities that they joined in the diaspora of the 1680s and 1690s.[11]

To "Be Reputed as Ennimy's"

Though a great deal of effort went into sorting out the mystery of the western Indians and their French companions, the kidnapping of Mason's servant in June 1692 was followed by two years of little or no violence between Indians and colonists.[12] There may have been clashes between the Potomac nations, the western newcomers, and the northern nations, but by this time colonists paid less attention to and recorded less information about the Potomac nations than ever before. When colonial officials did communicate with their Algonquian neighbors, it was in the same imperious tone that had prevailed in the 1692 treaty "negotiations." As an additional sign of how marginal the Potomac nations had become to colonists, Maryland's council offered in April 1693 to "enter into a league" with the Susquehannocks; though no treaty was made, the very suggestion betrayed either utter ignorance of or complete indifference to the Potomac nations' interests.[13]

The most ominous development for the Potomac nations was the appointment of Francis Nicholson as Maryland's governor in 1694. It was already a difficult time: the corn crop was poor, and the winter of 1694–95 was exceptionally harsh: courts closed because few people dared travel, and "through the excessive sharpness" of the winter "a great mortality among swine, cattle, and horses" killed tens of thousands of animals belonging to colonists and Indians alike. By June 1695 Indians had already "made great complaint for want of corn," but still another rainy, "unseasonable" summer yielded but "half crops" of corn that year.[14]

Nicholson's policies compounded the Algonquians' problems. In July 1695 the tayac sent Nicholson a gift of one hundred raccoon and fox skins, but when the two men met, Nicholson "told him that neither his Majesty nor himself required any present from him"; instead, Nicholson said, the tayac must pay the symbolic tribute that had been negotiated in earlier treaties. In the idiom of Algonquian diplomacy, the message was ringingly clear: Nicholson had rejected the tayac's offer to renew their relationship and dismissed the notion of Indian sovereignty. Nicholson took an equally hard line when the tayac confessed in October 1695 that he could not "well rule his young Indians," who were increasingly prone to "run out to the southward and bring in prisoners to the forte." Nicholson admonished the Piscataways to "be obedient to their Emperor and to the articles of peace," yet at the same time he undermined the tayac's position by offering to listen to the young men's complaints. Once again Nicholson had dismissed the tayac as an independent authority, the better to assert English sovereignty over Indian people. Later that same day Nicholson and the assembly opened the Piscataway reservation to colonists. Within a year a new county that encompassed the reservation—Prince George's—was up and running.[15]

Even the prospect of renewed raids by northern Indians, which had traditionally led provincial authorities to think in terms of alliances with their Algonquian neighbors, now became another occasion for asserting English sovereignty. When northern Indians killed a ranger at the Potomac garrison in the spring of 1696, Nicholson brought in the tayac and werowances and gave them their marching orders. The tayac Ochotomoquath, he directed, would serve as the "comander of all the Indians on the Western Shoar," under a sealed commission similar to that given any other colonial official; in this capacity he would answer directly to Nicholson. Meanwhile the Pamunkys and Chopticos would abandon their villages "to go under the Emperor of Piscattoway and live together." When they balked at leaving their homes and abandoning their crops, Nicholson yielded a little but warned that if they failed to relocate as soon as their corn was in, "they should be reputed as ennimy's."[16] Whatever its military benefits, this plan meshed well with a simultaneous campaign to chip away at Indian landowner-ship. In May 1695 Colonel John Addison was directed to "inquire whose land the Choptico Indians hold, and under what circumstances," a prelude to the loss of their reservation, and in July 1696 Nicholson's council proposed surveying and "adjusting" the boundaries of all Indian lands. They also gave the tayac and we-rowances permission to sell their lands to Englishmen.[17]

Not surprisingly, the Potomac nations began to crack under the pressure. English farmers moved onto reservation lands, then blamed Indian "rogues and doggs" when their livestock went missing. Colonists harassed Indian hunters, fishermen had their traps cut, and at harvest time colonists pulled down fences and rode their horses through Indian fields. A St. Mary's County man demanded that the Chopticos pay him rent for the reservation to which they had been con-fined since 1651, even as another colonist was living on that land without the Chopticos' consent. Some people began to abandon the reservations altogether in the summer of 1696, taking refuge above the Great Falls of the Potomac, and after another brutal winter in which snow lay "3 foot deep for a month together," even more people left their homelands. Smallpox broke out that winter, too, pro-viding still another incentive to flee from the crowded coastal plain.[18]

When one of the Piscataways' most reliable trading partners turned against them during the winter of 1696–97, the estrangement was nearly complete. In February 1697 sixteen "Senecas" came to the home of James Stoddard and offered to sell him their furs and pelts. Stoddard traded with them right under the eyes of several Piscataways who were staying in hunting cabins at his house, either oblivi-ous or indifferent to how the onlookers might feel about his new relationship with their longtime enemies. Stoddard even agreed to trade with the northerners again during the spring. The Piscataways abruptly left their cabins to alert the tayac, and a few weeks later one of them asked another planter if he might hunt for him instead of Stoddard because "in the spring tyme some mischiefe would be done at James Stoddarts." On 2 April, shortly after the northern fur traders had visited Stoddard's house for the second time, Stoddard was in the fields with his slaves when he "heard one of my Negroes cry out." The victim lingered for four days before dying of his wounds from an arrow, a blow to the head, a scalping, and the loss of an ear.[19]

Colonists told the tayac that "the whole countrey" suspected his people of the killing, and in the days after the murder the English "daily threatened" the Piscataways with reprisals. Colonel Addison "taxed them severely with the mur-ther" and said that the Piscataways "went to and again doing this mischiefe in the woods like wolves." When Addison "spoke angry" to the tayac, the Piscataways, concluding that "all the English were likewise angry," hastened to build them-selves a fort. Addison was not impressed: the English, he boasted, could destroy the Piscataways' fort with just thirty men. The tayac, thinking that Addison spoke for the governor, prepared to leave the reservation.[20]

"A Weak Inconsiderable Enemy"

By mid-April 1697 most Piscataways, Mattawomans, Pamunkys, and Chopti-cos had evacuated their reservations and taken up new quarters on the south side of the Potomac. One group of about one hundred people under the Matta-woman werowance established themselves in Stafford County, less than a day's ride above the main English settlements. A second, much larger group led by the tayac settled in some sixty miles above the nearest English farms in Stafford County. There they planted crops, built a new fort, and laid plans (as they told a Maryland delegation) "to live peaceably there and to pass to and fro freely with-out trouble as formerly." Fortunately it was a "very plentiful year" for corn, and in the absence of prickly English neighbors villagers could gather, fish, and hunt unmolested.[21]

Relocating to the interior was nevertheless a risky move that presented several major challenges. The first was to find a new village site with access to fresh wa-ter, good hunting, fishing, and gathering and adjacent to good fields. The second problem was that this new village had to be defensible; after all, the interior had been largely depopulated since the sixteenth century, and it was still very much in the path of northern warriors traveling to attack southern nations such as the Tuscaroras and Catawbas. The third challenge was that the refugee communities, which contained no more than a hundred warriors divided into two different camps, would have to negotiate a safe place within a regional diplomatic configu-ration that was as complex as ever; at a minimum they would have to establish new relationships with the Susquehannocks, the Five Nations, and the governments of Virginia and Maryland.

A fourth problem rendered each of the other challenges more difficult: the refugees had to reckon with the fissures that had opened up within their community. Now, in addition to the obvious differences between Piscataways, Chopticos, Mattawomans, and other distinct groups, the tayac and the werowances had to deal with considerable dissent from within. Chiefly authority had been in decline for the past two generations, so much so that it was no longer possible to present a united front to the world. Consequently it took several years to map out and clear the path that the peoples of the Potomac would take; in the meantime there was more violence, considerable confusion among colonists as to the Algonquians' intentions, and a great deal of uncertainty as to whether any of the Potomac nations would survive as a polity.

Algonquian dissidents even went so far as to sabotage peace negotiations between the Potomac nations and the colonial governments. Even before the evacuation of the reservations, a Pamunky named Esquire Tom met with some northerners encamped in the Potomac interior, led by Monges, "a great man" of the Susquehannocks. Monges still bore a grudge against Virginians, Marylanders, and Piscataways, by whose hands "his nation was ruined" at the time of Bacon's Rebellion. Monges "still had tears in his eyes when he thought of it," but the series of Covenant Chain treaties that had been signed since 1677 prevented him from taking his revenge directly. Now, however, Esquire Tom and other dissidents from the Potomac nations shared his feelings. Esquire Tom, they agreed, would kill some Englishmen in such a way that the tayac would be blamed; then, when the English attacked the tayac's village, Monges and Tom would both have "double revenge" against their enemies.[22]

Esquire Tom and his companions chose as their target the Wiggington farm on Aquia Creek, where they surprised Mrs. Wiggington as she was making butter. She fled, but they "knockt her down" as she tried to climb a fence. While she was unconscious they removed most of her scalp and "ript up" her right breast, wounded three of her children, and looted her house. As planned, Esquire Tom spread word that the tayac was responsible for the attack.[23]

Direct negotiations between the tayac and Maryland officials came to a halt after the attack against the Wiggingtons, and relations were dealt another setback by the killing of a Maryland ranger in September 1697. A horse belonging to the ranger, John Baker, had gone "out of pasture." Baker pursued the horse several hundred yards from the garrison house, from which distance the other rangers heard him shout and discharge his gun. Racing toward the sounds, the rangers found Baker dead, "with the head and his right arm cutt off to his elbow and both carried away." Thirty additional men were quickly dispatched to the area, but the killers were never found.[24]

Clearly Maryland needed to come up with a more comprehensive plan to deal with the departure of the Potomac nations, the presence of northern Indians in the Potomac interior, and the possibility that the French might exploit any conflict between the English and the Indians. A large committee of experts in Indian affairs was formed and presented its proposals to the council just four weeks after Baker's death. Many of the refugees, they thought, sincerely wished to return to their reservations. In the meantime, they recommended, Maryland should call out more rangers and militiamen, procure a "substantial boat" capable of ferrying horses across rivers, keep up the hunt for Esquire Tom, and work closely with the Virginians. Virginia's governor and council, however, sharply rebuffed suggestions that they might cooperate more with Maryland. Virginia's council completely rejected Maryland's proposals and castigated Nicholson for having sent emissaries into Virginia to treat with the Piscataways without first consulting Governor Andros.[25]

William Dent, one of the Marylanders who had borne Nicholson's letter to Jamestown, thought that the tayac must have had "some knowledge of our late negotiation" with Andros and of his "unneighbourly answers," because the Virginians' rejection of the Maryland proposals was followed closely by news that the Piscataways were "preparing a very great present for the Governour of Virginia." It does seem that the Potomac nations were hedging their bets by opening diplomatic relations with provincial authorities in Jamestown. It may even have worked, for the provincial government left the newcomers alone for a time.[26]

Suddenly, however, news from Europe upset the Algonquians' diplomatic calculations: in December 1697 Governor Nicholson announced the "joyfull news of a peace" with France. Freed from concerns that their conflicts with Indians might merge with the conflict with France, colonists adopted a much more belligerent stance toward the Potomac nations. Several weeks after the peace was announced, a Piscataway man who returned to Prince George's County was robbed and "frightened away by some threatening discourses." Maryland's assembly also changed its tune, declaring that the question of whether the Piscataways would return to their reservation "was of no great consequence to them." When Nicholson persisted in consulting the assembly on Indian affairs, he was told that the Piscataways were "a weak inconsiderable enemy." If the governor wished to declare them as enemies, that would be fine with them: they "doe not much regarde whether any message be sent to them [the Piscataways] or not, or whether they doe come in or stay out."[27]

Predictably, Governor Nicholson's "better judgement" was to take a hard line against the Indians. He let it be known that he "could have the Emperor of Piscattoway and his Indians knocked in the head but that he lets them alone to be sick and starve in the mountains." Nicholson also made a separate peace with the Susquehannocks, Delawares, and Shawnees living upon the Susquehanna River and graciously accepted the gifts they offered in the course of the negotiations— a clear indication that he knew what he was about when he so pointedly refused gifts from the Piscataways.[28]

Virginia officials, too, were increasingly hostile to the Potomac nations, in part because Nicholson was reassigned from Maryland to Virginia in December 1698. In March 1699 Nicholson summoned the tayac to Williamsburg, in language that did not bode well for the tayac and his people: the Stafford justices were to find "that Indian, commonly known by the name of the Emperour of Piscattoway, who, about two years agoe, fled from his Majestys province of Maryland," along with "some of his great men, (vulgarly so called)," and "command him" to appear before Nicholson.[29]

The tayac, however, remained one step ahead of Nicholson. The Stafford County Court dispatched Giles Vandercastle and Burr Harrison to deliver Nicholson's summons, but the tayac had moved to an island in the Potomac River at the far western edge of the Piedmont. To get to the island the Virginians had to cross a difficult ford of about four hundred yards. The island, which they estimated to be a mile long and a quarter-mile wide, had a partly completed fort at a high point at its upper end. At least twenty-seven cabins clustered within and near the fort, and the inhabitants seemed to have plenty of corn. Here the two refugee communities—the tayac's village and the smaller "Pomunky" settlement led by the Mattawoman werowance—had reunited. Vandercastle and Harrison estimated the remote, easily defended village's military force at "eighty or ninety bowmen." The tayac, secure on his island, mischievously answered Nicholson's imperious summons by telling Vandercastle and Harrison that he was "very bussy and could not possibly come or goe downe, butt if his Excellency would be pleased to come to him, sume of his great men should be glad to see him."[30]

By then the tayac had less need of Maryland, for he had reached an understanding with the Five Nations and their dependent allies in Pennsylvania, including even the Susquehannocks. Though Piscataway Island was directly in the path of Iroquois warriors heading south on mourning wars, there is no evidence that they bothered the Potomac nations. Quite the opposite: by July 1697, just months after moving into the interior, the tayac had already accepted some Senecas into his village, saying that they "are now all one people." Virginians who visited Piscataway Island in 1699 and 1700 found Senecas living there and were told by the tayac that he had "maid peace with all the Indians." The Piscataways and Susquehannocks even combined forces against the "Wittowees" (Miamis), one of the western nations that had moved east during the 1690s; in 1699, for example, the Susquehannocks captured two Miamis and brought them to Piscataway Island.[31]

Although negotiations continued for several years, in the end the Potomac nations sensibly decided against returning to the reservations.[32] Instead they looked to Pennsylvania, whose proprietor, William Penn, was anxious to regularize relations with his increasingly diverse array of Indian neighbors. The Shawnees who had passed through Maryland in the 1690s ended up in Pennsylvania, as did numerous Delawares returning from the west. The Susquehannocks (now known as the "Conestogas") had just moved again, this time to the site of their old fort on the Susquehanna River (in the vicinity of modern-day Harrisburg). In March 1701 Penn invited each of the Susquehanna River groups to Philadelphia to negotiate a major treaty. The Piscataways, in need of a colonial ally but having failed to reach a satisfactory settlement with either Virginia or Maryland, invited themselves to the Philadelphia meeting.[33]

The Piscataway delegates came back from Pennsylvania having committed their people to a radically new set of diplomatic relations centered on the Susquehanna River (instead of the Potomac) and encompassing Pennsylvania and Iroquoia (rather than Virginia and Maryland). The tayac's brother Ahookassongh, his outer chief Weewhinjough, and two other Piscataways joined representatives of the Conestogas, Shawnees, and Five Nations in agreeing to trade only with Pennsylvanians, to sell certain lands near the Susquehanna River, and to protect Pennsylvania from Indian attacks. Penn reciprocated by pledging to protect his Indian allies from the English, by recognizing Indian land claims, and by including the Piscataways in this relationship, provided they lived "within the bounds of this province." The Piscataways also accepted a subordinate relationship to the Conestogas, who "agreed to answer to the said William Penn . . . for the good behavior and conduct of the said Potowmeck Indians."[34]

With that the Piscataways finally broke out of the centuries-old diplomatic configuration that their ancestors had helped to create. Leaving Virginia and Maryland behind, they went over to the side of their longtime Susquehannock and Five Nations enemies, and to the side of Pennsylvania, Maryland's increasingly bitter colonial rival. The break was decisive and permanent: although the "Conoys," as they were known in Pennsylvania, would retain a distinctive identity there and in further peregrinations through New York and Canada, and although individual people and families stayed behind along the Potomac, the Potomac nations were no more.

CHAPTER TEN

"I Can Not Live in This Beautiful Land"

With the Piscataways out of the way, the interior seemingly lay wide open to resettlement by English colonists, and those who had already explored the interior saw great opportunities there. Maryland ranger Richard Brightwell, for example, found the Piedmont "extraordinarily rich." Louis Michel, who sought to establish an enclave of Swiss Protestants in America, was drawn to "the rather unknown western regions" of the Potomac interior, "of which the Indians here have wonders to tell, on account of their high mountains, warm waters, rich minerals, fruitful lands, large streams and abundance of game." In 1707 Michel enlisted several Indians and Indian traders from Pennsylvania to guide him as far as the lower Shenandoah Valley. Michel was particularly impressed with the area around the Piscataways' island, and set about trying to settle his Swiss colony there. One of his associates, Baron Christoph von Graffenried, visited the island in 1712 and declared it "a remarkably beautiful spot." He "examined the admirable situation of the same region of country and in particular the charming island of the Potomac River above the falls" and "discovered still finer land" beyond the mountains. When the upper Potomac site proved unworkable, Graffenried lamented "that I can not live in this beautiful land."[1]

Given these recommendations, and given the real attractions of the interior—the rich Piedmont bottomlands along the Potomac and its tributaries, and the fertile soils and fine pastures of the Shenandoah and Cumberland valleys—it seems strange that planters did not rush to take up lands there. On the contrary, the expansion of European settlements actually slowed, and only a bare trickle of planters flowed into the interior. So little did the frontier expand that after the creation of Prince George's County, Maryland, in 1696 no new county was created on either side of the Potomac until 1721. In 1706 Prince George's County still had only about 460 households, all of which were below the fall line and most of which were on the Patuxent River rather than on the Potomac; the district of New Scotland, which encompassed roughly the same terrain as the modern-day District of Columbia, had only 20 resident landowners. On the Virginia side, no one took a land grant above the falls until 1709, and the pace at which land grants were issued did not really quicken until 1717. Even then the grants were thinly strung along the Potomac bottomlands and islands and up Goose Creek, well below the Blue Ridge. Though the dribble of migrants above the falls increased to a trickle in the mid-1720s, it did not swell into a regular flow until the 1730s and did not really take off until the mid-1740s.[2]

Why didn't land-hungry colonists rush into the interior? What delayed the resettlement of this vast and fertile region for a full generation after the departure of the Potomac nations for Pennsylvania? Why did it finally happen when it did (in the 1730s) and where it did (far upriver from the Great Falls, mostly in the Shenandoah, Cumberland, and Monocacy valleys)?

The answers to these mysteries can be found at three different knots in the web of connections between the environment, the colonists' ecological imaginations, and the human relations that went along with their chosen ways of living upon the land. First, this was a problem of cultural ecology. Each society must create a workable system for living with and within its natural surroundings, and the tobacco culture adopted by the planters of the lower Potomac was, during the early eighteenth century, ill suited for expansion into the Piedmont and interior valleys. Second, "changes in the land" predating colonization continued to shape life in the interior. Even though the last of the Potomac nations had just joined forces with the Susquehannocks, Five Nations, and other northern groups, the Potomac interior was still caught in the centuries-old gap between northern and southern Indian nations. The fault line between north and south, which had for many generations lain between the Susquehanna River and the Potomac, had now opened up to include almost the entire span between the Susquehanna and the Carolinas. People who ventured into the interior still found themselves caught in the resulting crossfire. Third, although English notions about boundaries and exclusive property rights—a way of registering their power over nature—had proved to be a remarkably effective tool for dispossessing Indians in the second half of the seventeenth century, in the early eighteenth century these same ideas worked to *discourage* the resettlement of the interior by European colonists: due to sketchy geographical knowledge, Indian land claims, and overlapping colonial and proprietary boundaries, no one could be certain who had the right to dispose of lands in the interior. The various parties with a stake in the colonization of the interior took over four decades to work out these problems, finally resolving their differences only in the mid-1740s.

The Limits of Tobacco Culture

At the beginning of the eighteenth century, colonists along the Potomac still exported very little besides tobacco. They had built their lives "upon smoke," so much so that their settlement patterns, labor systems, and farming practices all conformed to the demands of producing tobacco for export. The tobacco trade had always had its ups and downs, but it was decidedly flat in the first two decades of the eighteenth century, after which it recovered in fits and starts. Low prices combined with disruptions to shipping during the Anglo-French wars of 1689–97, 1702–14, and 1744–48 to chip away at planters' profits. It didn't help that Potomac planters lived too far north to grow sweet-scented tobacco, which would have brought higher prices and was cheaper to ship than the Orinoco variety that they were able produce.[3]

This stagnant economy was the source of several major changes in social and political life along the river in the first half of the eighteenth century. It seems to have affected the growth of slavery along the Potomac, and it led to the decline of white immigration, the departure of many poor whites, and the rise of a dominant gentry class. At the same time, the economy was never quite bad enough to force planters to abandon tobacco as their staple crop; nor did the significant social changes of the early eighteenth century inspire any significant modifications to the colonists' ecological imaginations, to their way of living within nature along the Potomac, or to the environment itself. Nor did it involve substantial migration above the Great Falls; that would have to await better tobacco prices.

Planters adopted several strategies for dealing with flat prices. Mostly they tried to produce more tobacco despite their low profit margins, hoping to improve their incomes through sheer volume. Since there were no major improvements in worker productivity during this period, the only way to do this was to put more laborers in the field. Since the supply of indentured servants had long since dried up, those laborers came largely from Africa. This put Potomac planters at something of a disadvantage, because acquiring slaves remained more difficult than it was elsewhere in the Chesapeake region (in part because Scottish merchants, who rarely dealt in slaves, dominated the Potomac market). Thus, while elite planters who had connections and relations along other rivers may have had some access to new slaves, middling sorts who might have been able to afford slaves if they lived elsewhere tended to be shut out of this labor market on the Potomac. Many resorted to purchasing convict servants from England.[4]

Nevertheless, slavery did grow in importance along the Potomac, a development that further discouraged white indentured servants from coming to the Chesapeake colonies for fear that the slaves' low status would rub off on them. In Prince George's County the number of slaves per household roughly doubled between 1704 and 1755, while the number of white servants per household fell precipitously. By 1710 slaves made up 26 percent of the population of Maryland's lower Western Shore, and in 1755 that figure had risen to 38 percent.[5]

Another strategy was to fish more, raise more sheep, spin thread or weave cloth, take on additional work as an artisan or professional, or otherwise diversify into new economic fields. In bad times planters tried growing small surpluses of corn or grain for export, or they purchased new tools for home manufactures such as spinning wool. While they generally set their tools aside as soon as the depression eased off, families used them again during the next bad patch (and then acquired more tools and skills, thus gradually accumulating the means for greater self-sufficiency over the course of several depressions).[6] A few even invested in iron mines, furnaces, and forges, such as the Accokeek Furnace in Stafford County (active 1729–53), the Neabsco Creek works in Prince William County (established in 1738), and the Pine Forge (1725) and Vestal Iron Works (1742) on the Shenandoah River.[7]

For the most part, however, Potomac residents did not take diversification too far. Most planters already produced enough food for themselves and so could not save much by producing more corn or wheat. Outside markets for grain were not well developed; and to the extent that they were developed, Potomac planters were not well positioned to compete against farmers on the Eastern Shore or in Pennsylvania and New York. Manufacturing required more capital than small farmers could muster. Even making cloth depended upon exchanges between households, for few could afford all of the things needed to produce cloth. Besides, growing tobacco left little time for other activities. Any new tasks had to take place in the interstices of the rigid annual round of work required to cultivate tobacco.[8]

Still another strategy was to migrate to a frontier area with more plentiful and less expensive land. It was difficult and costly to move heavy hogsheads of tobacco overland, so the falls posed quite an obstacle to would-be Piedmont planters (at least while profit margins were so close to the bone; later, when prices improved, more tobacco was grown in the interior). It made better sense to purchase relatively expensive lands below the falls (or better yet, to inherit them).

The recipients of seventeenth-century land grants subdivided their holdings for lease or as bequests to their children, and occasionally for sale. Old land grants were finally surveyed and patented, and marginally cultivatable lands that had been overlooked or disdained by seventeenth-century settlers were finally taken up. Consequently, between 1700 and 1720 new farms mostly filled in the gaps within existing settlements rather than pushing the frontier farther upriver. As with other strategies for coping with the flat economy of the early eighteenth century, this remedy worked better for the rich than for the poor, for starting a new farm was an expensive proposition.[9]

Those who already owned slaves and land weathered these decades better than poor whites did, so much so that many poor immigrants and ex-servants departed for Pennsylvania and other colonies. New heads of household normally acquired their first land and slaves, the two things tobacco planters needed most, by inheritance rather than by starting from scratch. The statistics speak volumes: 85 percent of the sons of tenant farmers who owned no slaves also failed to acquire land or slaves. In contrast, 98 percent of the sons of land- and slaveowners also ended up with both land and slaves. An astonishing proportion of those without family ties, slaves, or land moved away altogether (75 percent of such men living in Prince George's County in 1733 left over the next decade), but householders who owned land or slaves were generally able to stay put.[10]

The near-cessation of white immigration coupled with the departure of poor whites from the coastal plain left property-owning creoles in command of an increasingly African American population (who, unlike poor whites, could not claim their rights as Englishmen). It also allowed wealthy planters to consolidate their positions. Certain intermarried families with substantial land- and slaveholdings came to dominate life in their communities. Most couples lived within two miles of each other before they married, and increasingly they married kin. In Prince George's County between 1700 and 1730, 10 percent of all married couples were blood relations, and another 8 percent had other kin ties (such as marrying in-laws). After 1730 the practice became even more common: 22 percent of all marriages united blood relatives, with 10 percent marrying a first or second cousin. As a result property stayed within a circle of kin and neighbors, preventing the children of local elites from being downwardly mobile and simultaneously strengthening their sense of group identity. Women typically brought to the marriage slaves and other portable wealth, while men inherited their family's land.[11]

The wealthiest of these intermarried clans came to think of themselves as a separate gentry class and employed at least some of their wealth to set themselves off from yeomen and tenant farmers. Unlike yeomen, who owned property but still had to work with their own hands, members of the gentry lived by collecting rents and supervising the labor of servants and slaves. Although much gentry wealth was reinvested, well-off eighteenth-century planters also lived much more comfortably than their seventeenth-century forebearers. Some built impressive brick or framed two-story homes. The classic great house, such as the Lee family's Stratford Hall in Westmoreland County, was built around a large central passage extending from the front door to the back entry; on either side, the hallway was flanked by four large, high-ceilinged rooms with plank floors on the ground level and smaller chambers upstairs. The interior design was roughly symmetrical, and the exterior perfectly so. Modeled quite directly on contemporary English country homes, such buildings were not just comfortable places to live: they also served as reminders of their owners' gentry status. So, too, did the expansive gardens that graced some of these homes. Painstakingly laid out in geometrical designs, and often situated to accentuate the grandeur of the main house, these gardens not only announced their owners' control of nature (dramatized by the contrast with the surrounding woods) but also indicated that the inhabitants were blessed with more leisure and good taste than most onlookers (speaking through the idiom of decorative but otherwise unnecessary crocuses, irises, daffodils, violets, marigolds, and hyacinths, and attractive but equally nonfunctional walkways and benches).[12]

Manners as well as material possessions served as markers of gentry rank. The ideal of open-handed hospitality for which the Chesapeake gentry became famous emerged after 1700. An entire ethic of gentry "condescension" (the word has changed meaning; at the time it simply meant a natural and generous way with ordinary folks) and deference by their inferiors was encoded in their dress, in their bodies (gentry women could, and did, avoid the sun), in everyday civilities and small gestures, in seating arrangements at church and in other public places, and even at play: gentlemen, for example, owned quarter horses, while common folks swelled the crowds and bet on the races.[13]

The native-born gentry gained a near-monopoly on local political office, serving as vestry members, justices of the peace, sheriffs, militia officers, members of the assembly or council, and provincial officeholders. Such offices had always gone to the well-off, but after 1700, appointments were increasingly based on family connections as well. With the exception of a few wealthy merchants, immigrants and self-made men had little chance of preferment. Instead a handful of extended families strengthened their hold on political office, sending generations of their young men to the bench or to the assembly. In Prince George's County, just four families filled 70 percent of the legislative seats in the half-century after 1725. As one might predict, such men were very much attuned to the needs of their own class, kin, and neighbors. Justices of the county courts, who functioned as peace officers, judges, and county commissioners, responded to petitions from their fellow gentry for roads and other internal improvements, while members of the council granted large tracts of western lands to members of the gentry. The assemblies of both colonies also attended to the gentry's needs (by, among other things, reorganizing the legal system to better accommodate slaveowners).[14]

The final piece in the consolidation of gentry power was an alliance with the yeomanry. Many yeomen were the relatives of gentry, and they all shared a common identity as free white men in an increasingly black, enslaved world; besides, as landowners, as tobacco planters, and as at least aspiring slaveowners, the yeoman's interests overlapped considerably with those of his gentry neighbors. Moreover, members of the gentry frequently acted as patrons who might help yeomen to realize their aspirations, or at least to hold on to what they had.[15]

In short, the eighteenth-century gentry were the ultimate beneficiaries of the tobacco-and-slaves landscape created in the seventeenth century. Had the tobacco economy failed altogether, colonists would have been forced to enter into a very different relationship with the natural environment of the Potomac Valley, one that might well have supported a more just and equitable society. The tobacco economy, however, remained sufficiently viable that the flat economy of the early eighteenth century neither overturned the social order nor much changed the relationship between culture and nature established by previous generations.

Nor did planters much alter the environment itself. By clearing additional fields, planters along the Potomac contributed to a slight uptick in the rates of siltation downstream from their farms, and increases in levels of ragweed and pine in those silt deposits reflect both the gradual increase in cleared fields (where ragweed thrived) and in old fields (where pines thrived). The increase in siltation rates and ragweed levels was very modest, though: ragweed levels were at most double those of precolonial times, accounting for no more than about 3 percent of all sediments (compared to over 10 percent in the nineteenth century). This increase was very much in proportion to the rate of population growth—as one might expect, given the continuity of agricultural practices over the centuries. Some researchers have found hints of aquatic oxygen depletion in areas affected by this increased siltation, but even there the evidence is ambiguous: the organisms that serve as markers of oxygen depletion also thrive during unusually wet years, of which there were many in the early eighteenth century. Wolves suffered the most from the English presence (they were nearly eradicated from the coastal plain), but deer, fish, and oysters were still plentiful (the seines and oyster tongs that would later be used to deplete them were only just beginning to show up in a few scattered households). In short, the forests, underbrush, and top-soil of the coastal plain remained largely intact, water quality was substantially unchanged, and wildlife depletion was mostly the result of hunting rather than habitat loss.[16]

Tobacco had served Potomac planters very well in the seventeenth century, and it would do so again. Building their world around the production and marketing of tobacco fit nicely with their fundamentally English way of imagining the proper relationship between people and nature. It was consistent with the English tendency toward distinctive local specializations, and it gave planters a secure place within the transatlantic British economic system. It had given many people the opportunity to enjoy greater wealth than they would have had in England and to pass that wealth on to their children. It had also been the instrument of colonial expansion and of the dispossession of the Native peoples of the Potomac.

By the early eighteenth century, however, the boom was long over. Once the instrument of opportunity for whites at the expense of Indians, tobacco now became the instrument of wealth and power for a few whites who inherited slaves and good land, and it provided yeoman farmers who owned reasonably good soils with a competency, though not much more. Tobacco was also the instrument of frustrated opportunities for ex-servants and other poor whites, and the instrument of permanent servitude for a rapidly growing African American population. Although the region's tobacco culture worked well enough to survive the slow economy of the early eighteenth century, it did not, for the moment, work so well as to inspire planters to grow much tobacco above the head of navigation at the Great Falls.

"Not Safe for Any Christians"

The few Europeans who did live or work above the falls before 1720 were Indian traders. When Louis Michel explored the interior in 1707, he had with him several French-speaking guides who had already traded as far west as the Illinois River. One of them, the Frenchman Martin Chartiere, had lived among the Shawnees on the Illinois River and had joined a Shawnee party in the eastward migrations of the 1680s and 1690s. In all likelihood he had already traveled through the Potomac interior with the Shawnees in 1692, and when they finally settled into a new village on the Susquehanna River, he was well situated to enter the Indian trade. After the Michel expedition Chartiere established a post on the north bank of the Potomac at the mouth of the Monocacy. Soon Israel Friend (at the mouth of the Antietam), Edmond and John Cartlidge (based at Conestoga), Charles Polke (at the great north bend of the Potomac at modern-day Hancock, Maryland), Charles Anderson (based on the Monocacy), and others were trading in the area.[17]

Indian traders gravitated to the Potomac interior because the Indian presence there had not ended with the departure of the Potomac nations. Five Nations, Shawnees, Delawares, Conoys, Nanticokes, and Conestogas came from the north to hunt, fish, trade, negotiate, or wage war against their enemies, while Catawbas, Cherokees, Tutelos, Tuscaroras, and others headed north for the same reasons. Indian traders established themselves along the main trails hoping to exchange their rum, powder, and other goods for deerskins and other considerations. Unlike the Indian traders, however, other colonists hesitated to put themselves in the way of so many Indians, from so many places, traveling for so many reasons.

European farmers avoided the interior lest they find themselves caught in the crossfire between northern and southern Indians. It was a testament to the profound and enduring significance of the environmental, cultural, and political forces that had transformed the Potomac interior between 800 and 1600 that the diplomatic configuration forged before the arrival of European colonists persisted into the eighteenth century. Although neither Indians nor colonists could have been aware of the centuries-long interplay of nature and culture that had led to the depopulation of the Potomac interior and the creation of a crossfire zone there, they were perfectly aware that it was a dangerous place to establish farms and villages.

Indeed, after 1701 Five Nations and Susquehannock warriors poured even more of their energy into raids against their southern enemies. The shift followed the "Great Peace of 1701," a pair of treaties at Montréal and Albany that extricated the Five Nations from a series of conflicts in the west that had reduced them to less than two thousand warriors, cost them most of the territory they had gained in the mid-seventeenth century, and caused them some humiliating defeats at the hands of western nations allied with the French (who had also inflicted severe damage on Iroquois villages). Thus the twin treaties of 1701 amounted to a declaration of neutrality in the imperial contests between the French and the English, and by extension a peace with the Indian allies of the French.[18]

Establishing peace with the western nations did not, however, eliminate the cultural imperatives that inspired Iroquois men to go to war. Five Nations warriors therefore redirected their efforts toward the south. Increasingly joined by

Susquehannocks, Shawnees, Conoys, and other refugees who had settled in Pennsylvania, they attacked Tutelos and Nottoways in the southern Virginia Piedmont, and Tuscaroras, Catawbas, and Cherokees in the Carolinas.[19] The available sources, which surely recorded only a small minority of this activity, are riddled with accounts of armed Iroquois and other northerners in the southern woods. In 1703, for instance, Shawnees attacked the Nottoways of southern Virginia, taking the Nottoways' chief and several other captives back with them to Pennsylvania. Four years later a New Yorker reported that "most of the Five Nations were out against the Flatheads" (a generic name for their southern enemies). Other English observers stumbled upon an encampment of several hundred northern Indians at the foot of the Blue Ridge "on their return from making warr with the southern Indians from whome they had taken divers prisoners" and recorded the passionate declaration of a Seneca man that "when I think of the brave warriours that hav[e] been slain by the Flatheads I can govern my self no longer . . . the heatred I bear to the Flatheads can never be forgiven."[20]

The "Flatheads" gave as good as they got. In 1704 forty warriors appeared on the Potomac and besieged the Piscataways, saying "that they (of Carolina) had been for many years attacked and injured by some Indians from the northward, whom they had always hitherto taken to be those of Canada, but now found who they were, viz: the Senecars and those of Potomock and Conestogoe, and that they were resolved to be revenged, and [to] that end three nations had joyned and would shortly come up and either destroy or be destroyed by them."[21] On one occasion a "considerable body of Southern Indians" caught and killed several members of a party of Conestogas and Iroquois "near the head of Potowmack River," while in another instance "the Southern Indians being at last provoked beyond measure, came out this Spring to meet the mighty warriors of [the] Five Nations, and pursued them with slaughter almost as far as Patowmeck River."[22]

War parties spent weeks and even months on the road to reach their enemies, sometimes walking more than a thousand miles before they returned home. Traveling mostly between the spring fishing season and the winter hunting season, they broke into small groups of ten to fifty. Stopping as necessary to rest, fish, and hunt, these small groups generally followed the north-south grain of the interior river valleys and mountains. Starting in the vicinity of Conestoga, some trails cut overland to the Monocacy River, crossed the Potomac at the Piscataways' island, and then branched into several trails running down through the Piedmont. Others looped westward before traveling southward down the Cumberland Valley along Antietam or Conococheague Creek and then (after crossing the Potomac River) through the Valley of Virginia along the Opequon, the South Branch, or the Shenandoah. From the upper Shenandoah Valley near modern-day Staunton, Virginia, travelers could choose among several routes leading to the Cherokees' mountain fastnesses, the Catawbas' Piedmont towns, or the villages of North Carolina and the Virginia Southside.[23]

These north-south Indian trails traversed the lands best suited for European colonization. War parties preferred level terrain on the valley floors, just as farmers avoided steep, erosion-prone gradients. They sought reliable springs, abundant game, and good fishing, all of which were equally attractive to white planters. In short, colonists who ventured to settle in the backcountry were bound to encounter armed Indians. The consensus was that it was not worth the risk. In 1711 representatives of the Conestogas, Five Nations, and Shawnees warned William Penn against settling "some people upon the branches of the Potomack," saying that "as they are at present in warr with the Toscororoes and other Indians, they think that place not safe for any Christians." It was folly to "scituate betwixt them and those at warr with them." Martin Chartiere seconded that advice, telling the prospective settlers that "we ought not to expose ourselves to such danger without expecial necessity." The leader of the would-be settlers later recalled that he "believed him and postponed the matter to a convenient time."[24]

The Tuscarora War of 1711 made the backcountry seem more dangerous than ever. The Tuscaroras, an Iroquoian people in the Carolinas, had long suffered from colonial encroachments. When surveyors began marking off land for a large new settlement of Swiss and Palatines in Tuscarora territory, many Tuscaroras rose up, killing 120 colonists and capturing others. South Carolina's government organized retaliatory raids in 1712 and 1713 in which hundreds of Catawbas, Yamasees, and other Carolina Indians (aided by a smaller number of colonists) destroyed Tuscarora towns, killed or enslaved over 2,000 people, and sent the survivors fleeing into the woods. Some stayed in North Carolina, but many more drifted north toward Iroquoia. Five Nations warriors had often raided the Tuscaroras before 1711, but their similar languages and their shared enemies now turned these former enemies into allies; the Five Nations, after all, needed to augment their shrinking population, while the Tuscaroras needed a home. By the 1720s the Tuscaroras were recognized as the Iroquois League's sixth nation.[25]

The southern Shawnees also fell afoul of the other Carolina nations. In the 1680s and 1690s the same eastward diaspora from the western Great Lakes that had sent Shawnees to Maryland and Pennsylvania also landed a large Shawnee group on the Savannah River. After 1700 their relations with South Carolina deteriorated, and by 1707 they were at war with the colony. Although they patched things up with the colonists, they had a falling-out with the Catawbas in 1711.

Consequently groups of Savannah Shawnees migrated to Pennsylvania, where they moved in with their fellow Shawnees along the Susquehanna.[26]

Some Shawnees and Tuscaroras established short-lived villages in the Potomac interior on their way north. Local traditions in the nineteenth century maintained that various creeks named after the Tuscaroras—in the Shenandoah Valley near modern-day Martinsburg, West Virginia, on the Potomac near the mouth of the Monocacy River, and midway up the Monocacy at Frederick, Maryland—commemorated places where Tuscaroras had paused for a season or two on the way to Iroquoia. Shawnees also settled in the Potomac interior. Opessa, a Shawnee leader at the Susquehanna River town of Pequehan who had welcomed the influx of Savannah River Shawnees in 1707, headed a group that left Pequehan for the upper Potomac in 1711. By 1722 they were settled in on the upper Potomac near Tonoloway Creek, well to the west of the usual paths between Iroquoia and the southern nations.[27]

The presence of Tuscarora and Shawnee refugees in the Potomac interior, on the Susquehanna, and in Iroquoia only intensified the crossfire over the Piedmont and valleys, for they persuaded their new Five Nations hosts to join them in still more attacks against the Flatheads. When some of Virginia's tributary Indians killed several Tuscaroras in 1713, Governor Alexander Spotswood reported that "this brought the rest down on our frontiers." "The rest" included participants from Canada and the western nations: in 1716, for example, the Five Nations tried to recruit New England Algonquians "to goe out to war against the Flat-head Indians."[28]

The Tuscarora War forced colonial authorities to reconsider their frontier defenses and their Indian diplomacy. This was especially true of Virginia, where some people could still remember when Governor Berkeley's insufficiently fierce Indian policy had led to Bacon's Rebellion. "A Governour of Virginia," Spotswood told a colleague in New York, "has to steer between Scylla and Charybdis, either an Indian or a civil war, for the famous insurrection in this colony called Bacon's Rebellion, was occasioned purely by the Governour and Council refusing to let the people go out against the Indians, who at that time annoyed the frontiers."[29]

Mindful of popular anti-Indian sentiment and faced with reports of "stragling parties of Northern Indians" committing murders and harassing Indian traders and neighbor Indians as they passed through Virginia, Spotswood revived an old idea: settling non-English Protestants beyond the frontier in order to buffer the colony against Indian attacks and to challenge the French for control of the interior of the North American continent. The idea had been around for some time—for at least as long as Protestant Scots had been placed in Catholic Ireland.

The Ulster precedent may have been the inspiration for the suggestion in 1677 that six or seven hundred "good resolute Scotts Highlanders" be sent to the frontiers, "beeinge men supposed onely fitt to encounter with the Indians, and keep the French robbers at a distance," or for Nicholas Hayward's 1689 proposal to settle French Huguenots on the Potomac frontier. Virginia's burgesses had similar considerations in mind when they passed legislation in 1701 offering generous land grants and tax breaks to frontier communities, in return for which they were to build a fort and provide one armed, free, "warlike Christian man" for every five hundred residents.[30]

Within weeks of the Tuscaroras' destruction of the Swiss colony in North Carolina, negotiations began to relocate the survivors to Virginia, where (Spotswood hoped) they would "be of great advantage to this country and prove a strong barier against the incursions of the Indians if they were properly disposed above our inhabitants."[31] Devastated by the Tuscarora War, and remembering his associate Louis Michel's glowing account of the lands on the upper Potomac, Graffenried accepted Spotswood's invitation to go up the river to select a new location for his colony. Although that did not work out, about forty of the New Bern refugees established Germanna on the Northern Neck, several miles above the falls of the Rappahannock River. There they built palisades and a blockhouse, which Spotswood was certain would "awe" the Indians traversing the frontier "and be a good barrier for all that part of the country."[32]

Spotswood also tried using allied Indians as buffers. In November 1713 he proposed a new approach to frontier defense, telling the burgesses, "I am perswaded that the setling [of Indian allies] along our frontiers without all our inhabitants . . . would be a better and cheaper safe guard to the country than the old method of rangers." In 1714 Virginia established Ft. Christanna on the Meherrin River, astride a main north-south trail through the Piedmont south of the James River. Here three hundred Saponis, Tutelos, and Occaneechees, Siouan-speaking residents of the southern Piedmont, moved into a new village defended by a substantial fort with five cannons. They were supposed to serve as frontier "border guards," to host a regular Indian trading fair, and to endure attempts at converting their children.[33]

Ft. Christanna, however, turned out to be more of a magnet for northern raiders than a buffer against them. In April 1717 a hundred southern Indians, mostly Catawbas, gathered at the fort to renew their relationship with Virginia. The visitors surrendered their arms to the Virginians and set up camp "under the wals of the fort." At dawn the next morning, fifty northern warriors attacked, killing five southern Indians, wounding two others, and taking prisoner six Catawbas, including "the cheiftman" Wittmannetaughkee. One of the prisoners later escaped and returned to confirm that "the party were sinnekes a term which they give all ye 5 nations." The attackers also included northern Tuscaroras and Savannah Shawnees.[34]

The 1717 attack on Ft. Christanna was an important turning point. It set off a sustained burst of north-south warfare, which in turn set off a burst of diplomatic activity that would eventually open the backcountry to colonial farmers. Northern warriors remained in the south throughout the summer of 1717, harassing the Saponis and others who remained at Ft. Christanna, and in 1718 Spotswood reported that they were still "very numerous in our frontiers." The raids continued in 1719, 1720, 1721, and 1722, and Iroquois and Conestoga diplomats, who normally blamed the young men for violence while presenting themselves as peacemakers, now defended the warriors' actions.[35] Southern Indians also turned more aggressive. In the spring of 1717, five Pennsylvania Indians ran into trouble "beyond the furthermost branch of Potomack" when one of their party was "shot with two arrows in his side, and his head cutt off, and carried away" by a band of thirty men from the south. Two years later the Conestogas were still complaining to Pennsylvania officials that "Southern Indians come out to warr against the Five Nations, and the Indian settlements on Susquehanna," making it unsafe to hunt on the upper Potomac. In 1720 the southerners killed twelve northern warriors, including two Shawnees—more than twice as many people as had been killed in the northern attack at Ft. Christanna, and certainly more men than the villages of the north could spare.[36]

The attack on Ft. Christanna also inspired the first serious diplomatic initiatives between Virginia and the Five Nations since the 1680s. A veteran Indian trader was dispatched "to persuade the Senequa Indians . . . to come into Williamsburgh in order to treat." Spotswood enlisted the aid of his fellow governors, and he even traveled to Pennsylvania and New York in the fall of 1717. There he emphasized what he saw as the single most important provision of any new treaty: that northern Indians must stay to the west of the Blue Ridge and not "concern themselves with the English [of Virginia] or their neighbouring Indians." Pennsylvania's Governor William Keith joined in the effort, working tirelessly over the next several years to talk the Susquehanna River communities out of joining raiding parties headed for the south.[37]

Five Nations and Virginia representatives finally came to together at Albany in August 1722. There the Iroquois agreed to stay west of "the high ridge of mountains which extend all along the frontiers of Virginia" and to leave Virginia's tributary Indians alone, though they confessed that they had hoped for the "total extirpation" of the groups at Ft. Christanna. The Five Nations also seized the opportunity to claim dominion over the Tuscaroras, Conestogas, Shawnees, and Conoys by asserting that they spoke for all of these groups when they promised to stay west of the Blue Ridge (a claim that they further advanced at Albany by ceding lands around the Conestogas' town on the Susquehanna River to Pennsylvania's Governor Keith).[38]

And yet even the Albany Treaty of 1722 did not stimulate a land rush into the Potomac interior, for it exposed still another problem: the vexed issue of boundaries. The Five Nations claimed the interior to the south of their homeland by right of conquest, but how far south did that claim extend? Did the Conestogas, Shawnees, and Conoys have similar claims? Other boundaries were equally vague. Where did Maryland begin and Pennsylvania leave off? Virginia and Maryland? Within Virginia the Northern Neck had been granted in 1649 to a group of proprietors who were free to dispose of their land without reference to the provincial government, but where were the boundaries of the Northern Neck? Each of these disputes had been simmering away for decades, but with the imminent prospect of substantial settlement above the fall line it suddenly became important to settle them soon. Thus the Treaty of 1722 set off a scramble between nations, provincial governments, and private interests to set up boundaries that would establish their claims to the Potomac interior. And until those claims could be sorted out, colonists above the fall line could not be certain that the person from whom they had obtained their land truly had the right to dispose of it. Until they were certain, most potential settlers declined to invest their labor and capital on the upper Potomac.

CHAPTER ELEVEN

The Trouble with Boundaries

In 1722 two of the three main barriers to backcountry settlement had been lowered, though not fully removed. Tobacco incomes improved somewhat, especially in 1719 and 1720, and the crossfire between northern and southern Indians lessened in the wake of the 1722 Albany treaty. Consequently a few more colonists ventured into the Piedmont, and land speculators began to take a greater interest in the Potomac interior. Already in 1722 Maryland authorities were concerned about the safety of Marylanders living in the Piedmont, and by 1724 Philemon Lloyd could write (albeit with considerable exaggeration) that "we have many settlements lately made" at the mouth of the Monocacy River. On the Virginia side as well "many late settlements" spread to the base of the Blue Ridge during the 1720s, including an "Irish settlement" on the south bank of the Potomac opposite the mouth of the Monocacy.[1]

Wealthy, well-connected Tidewater residents were particularly quick to survey and patent lands above the fall line. Surveyors, rangers, and militia officers who lived near the Great Falls and were familiar with the terrain above the cataracts were also well represented among the first grantees. Stafford County's Colonel Thomas Lee, for example, who was authorized to grant lands on the Northern Neck, bestowed upon himself prime tracts along the Potomac River and Goose Creek. Similarly Daniel Dulany the Elder, Maryland's attorney general, partnered up with Major John Bradford of upper Prince George's County to survey and patent a series of 100–300-acre tracts of the very richest bottomlands in the Piedmont. By May 1724 the two men owned 4,500 acres in the area, and when Bradford died in the mid-1720s his son (also named John) continued the relationship, even arranging for tenants on these properties. Dr. Charles Carroll, another wealthy Marylander, accumulated warrants for 30,000 acres of backcountry land during the 1720s, and Charles Carroll of Annapolis patented the 10,000-acre Carrollton tract at the mouth of the Monocacy in 1723. These men had an eye for the best lands: like most of the patents taken out in the 1720s, theirs clustered along the islands and bottomlands of the Potomac, the Monocacy River, and Goose Creek.[2]

Exactly how many colonists dared to move into the Piedmont during the 1720s is hard to say, because squatters and tenants left few traces in the records, but their number seems to have been small. This collective hesitancy to take up farms in the interior might be partly attributable to the expense of hauling heavy hogsheads of tobacco around the falls (though with improving tobacco prices this was less of a problem) and partly to continued fears of Indians. But above all, farmers needed to have secure and unencumbered title to their lands; otherwise they might pour out their sweat and their life savings on a farm only to discover, in the end, that in the eyes of the law they had never owned it in the first place. To enjoy secure title to their lands they needed to know which government or proprietor really owned that piece of land.

The problem was that there was no shortage of people who claimed sovereignty over the Potomac interior, including the Six Nations, Conestogas, Conoys, and Shawnees, the proprietors of Pennsylvania, Maryland, and the Northern Neck, and the crown colony of Virginia. Most of these parties asserted their rights to large swaths of territory, often staking out extreme positions in anticipation of the extensive negotiations that would clearly have to take place. Consequently their claims overlapped outrageously: Maryland's proprietor granted lands to the north of Philadelphia, for instance, while the Six Nations insisted that nearly the entire backcountry was theirs by right of conquest. Not surprisingly, given the complexity of the situation and the numerous claimants involved in this high-stakes contest, it took more than two decades of war, diplomacy, litigation, lobbying, and politics to determine the victors.

Any solution to the boundary disputes would have to involve the Six Nations, Conoys, Shawnees, Delawares, and Conestogas, for these nations were still very much forces to be reckoned with. Much of the public record of Virginia, Maryland, and Pennsylvania in the second quarter of the eighteenth century was concerned with Indian affairs, for even at this late date the three colonies were compelled to assimilate themselves into the latest version of the diplomatic configuration that had been created during the fourteenth, fifteenth, and sixteenth centuries. It was a splendid illustration of the ways in which "changes in the land" prior to the arrival of the English continued to shape life along the Potomac long after the advent of colonization.

"We Are Like to Be Disturbed by Idle People"

The depths of the confusion over who really owned the land above the falls, and over what that might mean, was illustrated by several episodes leading up to the Albany Treaty of 1722, beginning with the Piscataways' departure from the upper Potomac at the turn of the century. When the Piscataways moved to their island in the middle of the Potomac in the winter of 1699, they negotiated with Virginia in hopes that a Virginia connection would serve them better than had their Maryland alliance. But when the hard-line governor Francis Nicholson was transferred from Maryland to Virginia that same winter, they asserted that their island lay within Maryland, not Virginia. Then, when this latest round of negotiations with Maryland failed, the Piscataways changed their tune one more time, negotiating with William Penn in 1701 for "free leave . . . to settle upon any part of Patowomeck River within the bounds of this province"—meaning Pennsylvania. Although the Piscataways stayed put on their island, Pennsylvania secretary James Logan wrote that they had come "to settle within this government."[3]

In effect, the Piscataways had managed to move from Virginia to Maryland to Pennsylvania without actually going anywhere. The Piscataways stayed at the island until the end of 1704, a terrible year in which they were threatened with destruction by Virginians, Marylanders, and Catawbas, and visited with "a great mortality . . . supposed of the small pox" that killed fifty-seven people and left the survivors so prostrated that they did not even harvest their corn. Only then did they abandon their village, leaving the Potomac altogether to establish a new village upon the Susquehanna River near Conestoga.[4]

If the Piscataways' stationary migration demonstrates the confusion over the boundaries between Virginia, Pennsylvania, and Maryland, Baron Christoph von Graffenried's aborted attempt at establishing a Swiss colony above the Great Falls in 1712 shows with equal clarity the confusion over who had the right to grant lands on the Northern Neck. Graffenried ultimately decided against settling on the Northern Neck, he told Governor Spotswood, because while Spotswood had led him to believe that he would be settling on crown lands, he found "claims made to it both by the Proprietors of Maryland and the Northern Neck." Baltimore claimed the southernmost branch of the Potomac as his boundary, which (depending upon what watercourse one identified as the southern branch) might well make the Swiss colony part of Maryland. In contrast, Spotswood and Northern Neck proprietor Thomas, Lord Fairfax, asserted that Virginia extended to the northernmost branch of the Potomac. Spotswood and Fairfax, however, parted ways on the question of how far west the Northern Neck extended. Spotswood said that it ended at the fall line, making the entire interior crown land. Fairfax, however, claimed everything below the "first springs" of the Potomac and Rappahannock rivers, which would add over four million additional acres of interior lands to his domain. These complexities were too much for Graffenried. Fearful of Indian attacks, deeply in debt, and put off by "the uncertainty of the property of the soil, whether belonging to the Queen or the proprietors," Graffenried threw up his hands and departed for Europe.[5]

A third incident, the 1722 murder of the prominent Seneca warrior Sawantaeny, introduced still another set of claimants to the Potomac interior. Sawantaeny spent his winter hunting near the confluence of the Potomac and Monocacy rivers. He had a cabin there, kept by his Shawnee wife Weynepreeueyta, a cousin to "Savannah, Chief of that nation." Brothers John and Edmond Cartlidge, Indian traders who lived at Conestoga, knew where to find him. The Cartlidges, accompanied by Aiyaquachan (a Conoy), Acquittanachke, Metheegueyta (Shawnees), William Wilkins, and Jonathan Swindel (servants), rode up to Sawantaeny's cabin toward dusk on a February evening. As they settled in to trade for Sawantaeny's pelts and furs, John Cartlidge treated Sawantaeny to enough rum to make him tipsy, but soon he began to insist that the Seneca man pay for his drinks. Together they got drunk.[6]

When they awoke the next morning Sawantaeny said that he must have more rum, "for that he had not received all he had bought." John Cartlidge disagreed, and in the ensuing scuffle Sawantaeny cracked his neck against a fallen tree. From this point the witnesses' accounts varied quite a bit (not surprisingly, as most of them were drunk) but they agreed that someone had a gun, with which one of the Cartlidge brothers clubbed Sawantaeny in the head so hard that the gunstock broke. John then kicked Sawantaeny in the face until he "bled at the mouth and nose and was unable to speak, but rattled in the throat." His skull was cracked, as were several ribs; on later inspection, his brains could be seen through a wound in his skull. After the Cartlidges left, Sawantaeny came into his cabin, lay down on a bearskin, and "said his friends had killed him." He died the next day, leaving Weynepreeueyta all alone. She left to find help, and during her absence a Cayuga man and a Conestoga woman traveling in the company of "the Hermaphrodite of the same place" came upon the scene and buried Sawantaeny.[7]

News of Sawantaeny's murder reached Maryland before it reached Pennsylvania, spreading rapidly through the network of Indians, traders, surveyors, and frontier settlers to reach provincial authorities at Annapolis on 21 February, about ten days after the killing. Maryland's governor Charles Calvert wanted nothing to do with the matter. Well aware that Sawantaeny had been "one of the chief men of the Sinicar Nation" and fearful that Maryland's frontier inhabitants would suffer the consequences of the Cartlidges' actions, he and his councilors immediately resolved to "let the Indians know, that the murderers are under the Pennsylvania Government and that we are no ways concerned in it." They dashed off a quick note to Pennsylvania's Governor Keith urging him to handle the situation and washed their hands of the affair.[8]

Keith faced a serious dilemma. On the one hand, he had to take Sawantaeny's death very seriously, because the Iroquois alliance was so important to Pennsylvania. On the other hand, the Cartlidges were important cultural intermediaries who kept Indians and Pennsylvania authorities informed of each others' doings, served as translators at treaty negotiations, and carried on a regular trade that kept diplomatic channels open and maintained the sense of reciprocity that made peaceable relations possible. The Five Nations also had an incentive to smooth over the problem: it had been their idea to sign Pennsylvania to a Covenant Chain treaty the previous fall, as they were attempting to play Pennsylvania against New York in order to gain concessions from both colonies.

Keith instantly dispatched two emissaries to Conestoga. They began by presenting a wampum belt, speaking words of condolence, and dispatching a Cayuga man to Iroquoia with gifts "to cover our dead friend" and "to wipe away tears." But they also did the work of English magistrates, interrogating the witnesses under oath and recording their answers in depositions. The Cartlidges were taken to Philadelphia, where they were alternately jailed and released as authorities struggled to reconcile English legal procedure with Pennsylvania's diplomatic interests. The diplomatic interests ultimately triumphed. Though dissatisfied with the meager gifts initially offered in condolence for Sawantaeny's death and insistent that the Pennsylvanians come to Iroquoia to perform the proper ceremonies in person, the Iroquois nevertheless argued that the Cartlidges should be set free. "One life," they said, "is enough to be lost." And so Pennsylvania acquiesced, settling the matter the Iroquois way. The Cartlidges returned to their former lives, and with Sawantaeny's death requited, Governor Keith was free to attend the Albany treaty negotiations that fall.[9]

The story of Sawantaeny's death on the banks of the Monocacy raises several questions that are relevant to the mystery of why colonial farmers were so reluctant to move above the fall line even after the 1722 treaty at Albany. For example, why was a Seneca man from what is now western New York camping at the Monocacy? Where did Weynepreeueyta go looking for help? Why was a Cayuga man there to find his body? Why were the Cayuga man, the Conestoga woman, and the hermaphrodite wandering around together so far from home?

The short answer to these questions is that Indians still had a variety of claims on the Potomac interior. Weynepreeueyta may have gone to the Susquehanna River for help, or she may have sought out relatives at the new Shawnee village farther up the Potomac River; she had a choice because the cabin on the Monocacy lay within a web of rivers, trails, kinship connections, and trade relationships connecting the two Shawnee communities. Sawantaeny was hunting there, and his body was discovered by the Cayuga, the Conestoga, and the hermaphrodite because the Potomac interior, though very thinly inhabited, was much used. Though the crossfire effect made it a dangerous place during the wartime months of summer and fall, in the winter and spring the Potomac interior became part of a vast commons in which northern Indians ranged more freely to hunt, fish, gather, and process meat and hides. The circulation of Shawnees, Conoys, Conestogas, and Iroquois through this great commons both reflected and reasserted their claims to the land.[10]

Moreover, provincial authorities in several colonies fostered and recognized some of those Native American claims—for their own reasons, of course, which are evident in the negotiations to bring the Cartlidge brothers to justice. Again, there are some obvious questions: why were Pennsylvania traders so much at home on the Monocacy? Why were the Cartlidges tried in Pennsylvania instead of in Maryland? And why did Pennsylvania authorities defer so much to Seneca ways of doing justice? Again there is a short answer: colonial officials recognized Indian land claims in order to strengthen their own land claims. By implicitly recognizing the Five Nations' claims to the backcountry, the 1722 treaty set the stage for later transactions in which the Iroquois could sell land to Virginia, Maryland, or Pennsylvania. When provincial authorities trumpeted the reputation of the Iroquois as lords of the forest, they fostered the impression that such sales were valid. Similarly the presence of Pennsylvania traders along the Potomac, doing business with Pennsylvania's Conoy, Shawnee, Conestoga, and Iroquois allies, strengthened the impression that this was already functionally part of Pennsylvania, and that land there could legitimately be conveyed to Pennsylvania by any of these groups.

Such complicated dynamics between rival colonies and Indian nations were very much in play in the summer of 1722, when the long-running Pennsylvania-Maryland boundary dispute flared up again. On 15 June Governor Keith warned the Conestogas, Conoys, and Shawnees that "you and we are like to be disturbed by idle people from Mary Land, and also by others who have presumed to survey lands on the banks of Sasquehanna." Perhaps, suggested Keith, it would be best to give "a large tract of land" on the west side of the Susquehanna to the proprietor, "for when the land is marked with his name upon the trees, it will keep off the Mary Landers . . . from coming to settle near you to disturb you." The Indians saw right through Keith's ploy and responded by demanding that Pennsylvania first recognize the primacy of their claims to the lands on the west side of the Susquehanna over the claims of the Five Nations: even though they "know that the Five Nations have not any right to these lands," the speaker said, and only the Cayugas even "pretend to" that right, it seemed prudent to address the land issue at the forthcoming conference at Albany.[11]

In his representations of this exchange to provincial authorities, Keith deftly turned the original discussion at Conestoga inside out. He wrote to the council that "the Indians" were "very much pleased" with his suggestion that they cede lands to the proprietor in order to block the Marylanders' progress up the river. Then Keith informed Maryland's Governor Calvert that he had "at the earnest request of the Indians, order[ed] a survey to be forthwith made upon the banks of Sasquehanna, right against our Indian towns." Keith warned that Marylanders ought not to "encroach upon what these Heathens call their own property," for "mischief" would surely result. He enclosed a copy of the warrant for surveying the "Mannor of Springetsbury."[12] Thus Keith transformed a transparently self-interested Pennsylvania proposal that was coolly received by the Indians into a spirited campaign by Indians to give land to Pennsylvanians.

Keith's game amounted to a land-laundering scheme: he recognized the Susquehanna nations as having title to lands claimed by both Maryland and Pennsylvania, then obtained those lands from the Indians. If the Indians' original claim was good, then so was Pennsylvania's. Maryland could not play this game, or at least not against Pennsylvania—not after having cast out the Potomac nations, and not after having neglected, since the 1680s, to maintain regular diplomatic relations with the various Native American claimants to the backcountry. Instead Maryland continued to press its case in the English courts and on the ground, arguing over the language of Maryland's and Pennsylvania's original charters while also making their possession of the disputed lands an accomplished fact by settling, surveying, and patenting them.

By the late 1720s the maneuvering had begun in earnest. In 1727 the Five Nations approached Pennsylvania authorities with a proposal to sell them the lower Susquehanna River, notwithstanding the presence of Conestoga, Shawnee, and Conoy towns there. Pennsylvania officials did not immediately take up the offer, but they watched with interest and considered the question of which group's land claims they ought to endorse as relations among the Iroquois, Shawnees, and other Susquehanna nations deteriorated.[13]

While the Conestogas, Maryland, Six Nations, Pennsylvania, and Shawnees jockeyed for control of the lands between the Potomac and the Susquehanna, Virginia's governor William Gooch was taking the initiative against Lord Fairfax, proprietor of the Northern Neck. In 1728 Gooch, who had only recently arrived in Virginia, warned the Board of Trade that uncertainties about Virginia's boundaries "discouraged the people from taking up his Majesty's lands, and making settlements" on the frontier. A year later, as Fairfax's agent Robert Carter dispatched surveyors to lay out the bounds of proprietary land grants in the Shenandoah Valley, Gooch informed imperial authorities that "the eagerness of the inhabitants to take up lands amongst the great western mountains, has renewed a contest" between Fairfax and the crown government, "which for a long time had layn dormant, touching the right of granting the lands."[14]

Gooch decided to preempt Fairfax's claim to the Shenandoah Valley by awarding generous land grants and filling them with farmers as quickly as possible. In June 1728 Gooch and his council granted 26,000 acres on the west side of the Blue Ridge. Two years later, on 17 June 1730, they granted 50,000 acres of prime valley land to John Van Meter, Isaac Van Meter, and Jacob Stover. Later in 1730 Gooch granted another 100,000 acres to Alexander Ross and Morgan Bryan of Pennsylvania. By the beginning of 1732 Gooch had granted at least 370,000 acres beyond the Blue Ridge, mostly within territory claimed by Fairfax.[15]

Gooch and his councilors knew only the rough outlines of the valley lands they were so freely dispensing. Unburdened by excessive geographical knowledge, in 1730 Gooch granted 50,000 acres on the north side of the Potomac between Antietam and Conococheague creeks, territory that even the most expansive interpretation of Virginia's boundaries would not encompass. Gooch evidently suspected as much: in 1732 he granted John Robinson 20,000 acres on the Monocacy River "*if* the said lands appear to be within the bounds of this colony." Robinson's grant lay in an area where Lord Baltimore had already granted tens of thousands of acres. The Penn family claimed the area, too, as did the Conestogas.[16]

Nevertheless Gooch knew exactly what he was doing. In the first flurry of large land grants in the valley in 1730, Gooch argued that the king should seize control of as much of the Northern Neck as possible. The original grant to the proprietors posed no problem, according to Gooch, because the fall line marked the upper end of the Northern Neck and thus excluded the Piedmont and Shenandoah Valley.[17] Gooch also justified the massive backcountry land grants by reviving the idea of buffer settlements, "since by that means we may . . . prevent the French surrounding us."[18] There were also the Indians to worry about, for the crossfire between southern and northern Indians seemed to be intensifying again in the late 1720s. The northerners seem to have been drawn into a conflict between the Saponis and Nottoways in southern Virginia, which (Gooch complained) exposed "our frontier inhabitants . . . to the barbarous insults of these Indians." Already it had begun: "in November last about a dozen families of our outward inhabitants were, with guns and arrows forced by them from their habitations." Perhaps even more ominously, Shawnees living on the upper Potomac were taking in runaway slaves.[19]

Robert Carter also knew what Gooch was doing. He challenged each new grant as soon as it was awarded and did a little preemptive granting of his own: he bestowed upon himself and a partner 58,000 prime acres on the northwest branch of the Shenandoah and another 50,000 acres upon Robert Brooke. Carter, who had started with an inheritance of 1,000 acres, eventually accumulated 300,000 acres, much of it by granting Fairfax lands to himself. More Fairfax lands went to his family and friends, much of it in the disputed territory.[20]

In the decade after the 1722 treaty at Albany the backcountry was very much on the minds of a wide range of people, from Native spokesmen to colonial governors and from would-be settlers to members of the king's Board of Trade. Nearly a dozen different Indian nations, colonies, and proprietors struggled to establish the boundaries within the Potomac interior that would most favor their own interests. Among the English each faction maneuvered to control and benefit from the movement of colonists into the backcountry. In spite all of this interest, however, surprisingly few people moved into the Potomac interior in the 1720s. Those who did were mostly Shawnees, runaway slaves, and Indian traders beyond the Blue Ridge, and squatters or tenants in the Piedmont.

"To Have the Country Settled"

In late September 1731 the magistrates of newly established Lancaster County, Pennsylvania, met to supervise the raising of a new courthouse. As the walls of the new building went up, the Conestoga spokesman Tagotolessa arrived with some unwelcome news: although a long series of Pennsylvania officials beginning with William Penn "had promised them they should not be disturbed by any settlers on the west side of the Sasquehanah," a group of Marylanders had nonetheless settled there, and "one Crissop, particularly, is very abusive to them when they pass that way." Thomas Cresap, a larger-than-life Yorkshireman who had married a local woman who herself "carried a rifle, two pistols, a tomahawk, a scalping knife, and, in her boot, a small dagger," was no diplomat. By January 1732 Cresap and his fellow Marylanders had made themselves so obnoxious that Tagotolessa was moved to warn Maryland's Governor Calvert against granting any more lands on territory claimed by the Conestogas, including the upper Potomac: "I hear you intend to come and run land out above Andahetem [Antietam Creek], and I heartily desire you not to do it," wrote Tagotolessa. "I would have you not to press too much upon us for we have give no body land yet but Israel Friend at the mouth of Andahetem . . . You must not think to force us out of our own."[21]

Tagotolessa's warning was to no effect. There were already eight small clusters of settlement at Monocacy by 1732, as owners of the grants issued in the 1720s and early 1730s had gradually parceled them out to tenants or purchasers or begun to work the land themselves. Throughout the 1730s Maryland grantees encouraged settlement by selling off or leasing their lands to new arrivals. Charles Carroll, for instance, appointed an overseer at his 10,000-acre Carrollton Manor in 1734 and signed a number of farmers to long-term leases; meanwhile at "Dulany's Lot," Daniel Dulany parceled out 3,800 acres to new owners or lessees.[22] Maryland officials also continued to grant and patent land above the fall line, promoting both the filling in of existing settlements and their extension into the northern reaches of the Monocacy, on the Potomac above the Monocacy, and in the Cumberland Valley.[23]

Seventeen thirty-two also saw the first substantial migrations of Europeans to the Shenandoah Valley. Although a few colonists may have trickled into the Shenandoah as early as 1726, the seeds of a substantial new community in the lower valley were sown by a group of migrants led by Jost Hite. Hite had recently purchased the rights to 40,000 acres in the valley and had obtained a grant of 100,000 acres from Virginia's council. Hastening to make these paper claims a reality, Hite left for the Shenandoah in late 1731 at the head of sixteen families. When spring came around these families were already at work clearing fields and dwellings at Opequon Creek.[24]

Ironically, many of these new backcountry residents were Pennsylvanians, New Yorkers, or New Jerseyites rather than the Marylanders who so annoyed Tagotolessa. Jost Hite was a German native who had lived in New York and Pennsylvania since 1710. More than half of the original sixteen families accompanying Hite to Opequon Creek in 1732 were his descendants. Similarly, in Maryland the large Van Meter clan came down from New York and New Jersey to live along Carroll Creek and the middle reaches of the Monocacy River. Even Tagotolessa's longtime associate Edmond Cartlidge, the Conestoga-based Indian trader, translator, and killer of Sawantaeny, relocated to the upper Potomac and accepted an appointment as justice of the peace for Prince George's County, Maryland.[25]

Lord Baltimore had a big head start in peopling the interior, but Thomas Penn, who had just taken over the proprietorship of Pennsylvania after a succession dispute following his father William's death, did his best to meet the challenge. Confident that the Iroquois or some other nation would soon cede additional territory, he began selling land beyond the Susquehanna River. Though the strategy was a risky one, it caught the Susquehanna nations at a moment of weakness. The Shawnees, Conestogas, and Conoys were likely suffering from influenza and smallpox epidemics (these diseases raged throughout the colonies in 1730–33 and hit Pennsylvania especially hard), while internal dissension and pressure from settlers was already forcing some groups to move farther up the Susquehanna or over the mountains to the Ohio country. So many migrants flooded into areas that had been closed to settlement before 1732 that the Penn family's revenues skyrocketed: in the thirty-one years between 1701 and 1732 they took in a total of only £12,610, but in the next thirty years they collected £214,709.[26]

Meanwhile, Lord Fairfax and Virginia governor William Gooch redoubled their efforts to lay claim to the Northern Neck above the falls. In 1732 alone Gooch and his council doled out 125,000 acres of crown lands in the Shenandoah Valley, and though their pace inevitably slowed they continued to give out large chunks of land. The council also encouraged the rapid settlement of the interior by making Shenandoah Valley grants conditional on the establishment of one resident family for each 1,000 acres of the grant. By 1735 about 800 people lived in the Opequon settlements alone, and a nascent local government began to take shape.[27] Gooch also worked hard at creating the right impression among the authorities in London who would adjudicate the Northern Neck boundary controversy. In July 1732 he commissioned a survey and map designed to represent the contested terrain as properly belonging to the crown. He also pushed the buffer settlement argument harder than ever, implying that a decision for Fairfax would play into the hands of French Papists and Indian savages.[28]

Fairfax countered with his own spate of large grants in 1732, and, urged on by his brother and agent William, he, too, began to press his case with officials in London.[29] The Board of Trade took up the matter in 1733 and directed Gooch and Fairfax to appoint commissioners to "survey and settle the marks and boundaries" within two years. In the meantime, they ordered, there were to be no more grants in the disputed areas. But rather than alert Gooch to the board's directives, Fairfax pocketed their orders while he wound up his affairs in England and arranged to move to Virginia, where he could personally oversee the surveying of the Northern Neck's boundaries. Thus Gooch did not learn of the board's order until October 1735, nearly six months after Thomas Fairfax's arrival in Virginia.

Gooch dragged his feet as well, alternately ignoring, resisting, and protesting against the moratorium on new land grants as much as he dared.[30]

Although the rivalry between the provincial government and the proprietor undoubtedly frightened off a few prospective settlers, the competition between them also meant that a person wishing to acquire a farm in the Shenandoah Valley could choose from among a variety of locations and terms of sale. Grantees offered land at attractive terms and often allowed purchasers to select irregularly shaped lots that encompassed only the choicest soils and access to roads and waterways. One could also purchase directly from Fairfax or claim "Treasury Rights," which allowed one to buy up to four hundred acres at a very competitive price. The competition between the various sellers kept prices for unimproved tracts at or below £3 per hundred acres throughout the 1730s.[31]

Settlers could also, at last, be fairly sure of the title to their land. In 1736, in anticipation that the surveys and maps ordered by the Board of Trade would settle the boundary dispute, both Fairfax and the provincial government assured Shenandoah Valley residents that they would recognize each other's patents. Lord Fairfax himself traveled to the valley to tell settlers at Opequon that he would not turn anyone out of their home, for he merely "wanted to have the country settled." Virginia's burgesses concurred, declaring in an August 1736 act "For confirming and better securing the Titles to Lands, in the Northern Neck" that land grants issued by Fairfax's agents were valid.[32]

1736

The planting of nascent communities in the interior in the early 1730s had inspired those who claimed sovereignty over the Piedmont and valleys to redouble their efforts to control the distribution of lands there. By 1736 those efforts had begun to bear some fruit. In Virginia the struggle between crown and proprietor yielded a set of comprehensive surveys and maps that greatly clarified the situation, even though the Board of Trade did not render its decision for another decade. Meanwhile the Iroquois entered into a special relationship with Thomas Penn that strengthened each party's claims to sovereignty over backcountry lands and people, thus setting in motion a chain of events that would culminate in the 1744 Treaty of Lancaster—an event that, perhaps more than any other single event in the eighteenth century, opened the way for migrants to flood into the southern backcountry.

Everyone involved in surveying the Northern Neck recognized that it was a high-stakes affair. Fairfax, for one, was unwilling to trust the surveyors with so much responsibility. The commissioners, he insisted, could report on but not decide the issue. Gooch made a show of protesting but secretly agreed with Fairfax (he predicted that whatever their findings "it will be too crabbed a matter for the Commissions to adjust").[33] The crown and proprietor each appointed three commissioners, each of whom could be relied upon to promote his patron's interests. The rival commissioners in turn appointed their own men to do the actual surveying and mapping.[34]

The commissioners and surveying teams met at the falls of the Rappahannock in late September 1736. There they identified the main issues: were the "main springs" of each river at the fall line or above it? If the latter, which branch of the Rappahannock was the river's main trunk? Then they broke into two groups, one to survey the Potomac and one to survey the Rappahannock.[35] For the next two months they struggled through and over rapids, shoals, cliffs, and dense underbrush, dragging their chains and other instruments every step of the way. Their horses tended to wander off or fall down. The hired men quarreled over provisions and complained about the slow pace at which the party moved. Many quit. As the freezing rains of mid-October set in, they decided to forgo the horses and travel by canoe or on foot. When the surveying teams returned, they were "so very much fatigued," according to Gooch, that they needed extra time to recuperate before they could prepare their reports for the commissioners.[36]

Fairfax's commissioners and the crown's men issued rival reports in August 1737, which merely reiterated the most extreme claims of their patrons. The king's commissioners said that the Rappahannock and Potomac each ended at the falls, an understanding based on long usage; the Indians, they wrote, had begun the practice, which colonists had continued (and indeed, Gooch and other provincial authorities had been careful to call the upper Potomac the "Cohongarootan" at every opportunity). Even if they had to concede that point, the king's commissioners wrote, Fairfax's claims were still exaggerated, for the northernmost branch of the Rappahannock was broader, deeper, and longer than the southern branch. Not surprisingly, Fairfax's commissioners claimed the opposite of whatever the crown's representatives wrote. If the king's men had their way, they reckoned, the Northern Neck proprietary would contain 1.48 million acres; if Fairfax's men prevailed, it would encompass 5.28 million acres.[37]

As soon as his commissioners' report and map were finished, Fairfax bolted for London. There he went to work on the political front, distributing an especially attractive version of the map drawn from his survey and otherwise drumming up support for his position. In May 1739 representatives of Fairfax and Virginia presented their full arguments before the Board of Trade, which rendered its opinion in July. Though their report did not explicitly endorse either of the combatants' positions, it did advocate a literal interpretation of the patent, which would tend to favor Fairfax's stance: since the king's patent specified that the Northern Neck extended to the "first springs" of the Rappahannock and Potomac, and in English usage rivers did not terminate at the head of navigation, the only real issue was which branch of the Rappahannock was the main trunk. The board's report, however, was merely advisory. The Privy Council itself would have to make the final decision, and since Fairfax was still out of favor with the ruling party he did not press for an immediate decision. Nor, for some reason, did the colony's agent. The case was shelved until a more propitious time.[38]

Even though the surveys of 1736–37 did not yield an immediate ruling on the boundary question, they did promote a second burst of migration in the Shenandoah Valley. Mary McDowell Greenlee's family was typical of this new group of settlers. They began by moving from Scotland to Ulster, and from there to Carlisle, Pennsylvania. Mary Elizabeth McDowell married her second cousin James Greenlee in 1736, just as their family was considering the glowing reports about the upper Shenandoah Valley sent by another Irish relative, John Lewis, who had settled at Beverley Manor (a large tract in the far upper valley surrounding modern-day Staunton, Virginia). Elizabeth's brother John McDowell went ahead to scout out farm sites at Beverley Manor, but along the way he encountered an Opequon resident named Benjamin Borden. Borden said that "he had about 10[0],000 acres of land . . . if he could ever find it," and he offered 1,000 acres to whoever could guide him there. John, who just happened to be carrying his surveying equipment, took Borden up on the offer. The McDowell/Greenlee clan migrated to the Borden Tract (adjacent to Beverley Manor), where John became Borden's right-hand man. There they were joined by other Scots-Irish migrants with names like McClung and McCown, many of whom were kin or former neighbors (in Ulster or in Pennsylvania) of the McDowells. Soon their neighborhood was known as the "Irish Tract."[39]

The McDowell family's migration to the upper valley was very much connected to the Northern Neck boundary dispute and the surveys of 1736–37. The surveys had clarified the potential future boundaries of the Northern Neck, and Gooch and the council once again began to issue large land grants, this time to the south of Fairfax's most expansive claims. In 1736 they bestowed upon William Beverley and his partners Beverley Manor, which turned out to contain nearly 120,000 acres, and in 1739 they confirmed Borden's 92,000-acre grant. Soon a dozen neighborhoods of Scots-Irish like the McDowells' were scattered along river and creekbeds in the upper Shenandoah Valley.[40]

The surveyors' notes and maps from 1736–37 also revealed the continuing Indian presence in the interior.[41] Some Indians still went to the Potomac interior to trade, hunt, and fish, but a growing proportion were on their way to war. The crossfire over the interior valleys had never let up entirely; in 1733 and 1734, for example, the Conoys were blamed for the killing of several Virginians. Shortly after this incident war parties from the south penetrated all the way to the Susquehanna River, where they captured two Indian children on one occasion and killed eight men on another. With all of this activity backcountry residents could not help but be aware that they lived there "against the inclinations of those natives." The Presbyterian minister John Craig wrote that war parties of twenty to fifty men "must be supply'd at any house they call at with victuals" or they would simply help themselves. David Shriver also wrote that warriors regularly stopped at his family's farm, displaying their trophies and requesting food and lodging, "to which there could be no resistance; of course none was attempted."[42]

By May 1736 reports of rising tensions between northern Indians and the "frontier inhabitants" moved Virginia's council to invite the southern and the northern nations to a treaty conference. For the next two years messages and letters flew between the Cherokees, Catawbas, Virginians, Shawnees, Pennsylvanians, and New Yorkers, but the Catawbas and Iroquois could not be brought to the table. The Six Nations sent word to Virginia in the spring of 1737 that they would like to have a treaty with the Catawbas, but the Catawbas, who had just lost eleven people to Iroquois raids, were "so exasperated that they will hearken to no terms of accomodation, at least till they have their revenge." Catawbas attacked the Shawnees in their Ohio country villages the following summer, after the Shawnees had been assured that "peace was making so that they was in no fear." The meeting place became an issue as well, with the Six Nations declining to come to Virginia for a treaty but leaving open the possibility of a meeting at Albany.[43]

By then Gooch and other Virginians were not so sure that they wanted to be peacemakers. In early April 1738 word arrived in Williamsburg that northern Indians had killed a colonist near Beverley Manor, under which circumstances the councilors were happy to accept a proposal that the peace treaty at Albany be postponed. There was more wrangling over where the negotiations would take place and who would pay the expenses. Then, in late summer, a party of northern Indians that had been battling Catawbas all the way from South Carolina to the Potomac was accused of killing eleven Virginians "on the back of the mountains."[44]

Virginians responded by beefing up their frontier defenses. The council voted to make John Lewis of Beverley Manor an irregular captain and to supply his men with powder, ammunition, and thirty-eight guns. The burgesses gave the governor greater powers over the militia, exempted frontier settlers from certain taxes, liberalized naturalization procedures (to draw foreign Protestants to the frontier), and provisionally created two new counties: Frederick in the lower valley and Augusta in the upper valley. The catch was that Frederick and Augusta would not become counties right away. The governor could, in an emergency, quickly activate the frontier counties even if the burgesses were not in session, upon which the new counties could quickly form their own militia companies. But many Virginians were uncomfortable with the idea of allowing the foreigners who predominated in the valley to govern their own counties, so unless military circumstances necessitated their activation the valley residents would remain within Orange County, whose county seat was east of the Blue Ridge.[45]

Though anxious to avoid a war, imperial officials in London had some sympathy for the Virginians' increasingly combative attitude. The Board of Trade insisted that officials in each colony must better control "their" Indians. The critical task was to "perswade the Indians that all the English through that whole continent of America have but one common prince and father." Gooch agreed and warned that well-armed backcountry residents would no longer "suffer the heathens to insult them with impunity." Gooch also lost sympathy for the Iroquois as he came to understand that their interpretation of the boundary established by the 1722 treaty differed from his own: as the Iroquois understood it, they were to stay to the west of the Blue Ridge, making the Shenandoah Valley their main route to points south; but as Gooch understood the treaty, they were supposed to stay to the west of the Shenandoah Valley.[46]

At the end of the 1730s, then, the most volatile boundary issue of all was the question of what was Indian country and what was English territory. Pennsylvania, as it happened, had already begun to address that issue. In September and October of 1736, at the exact moment that surveyors for Fairfax and the crown were beginning their work, Six Nations representatives came to Philadelphia to revise their treaty with Pennsylvania. In essence they agreed to a special relationship that Thomas Penn had first proposed in 1732: Pennsylvania declared that the lower Susquehanna River and the backcountry belonged to the Six Nations by right of conquest, and the Iroquois agreed to sell the lower Susquehanna Valley to Pennsylvania. This was clearly a fiction. The Delawares, Shawnees, Conestogas, and Conoys who actually inhabited these places, of course, rejected the logic that allowed the Iroquois to sell their lands out from under them.[47]

Both the Six Nations and the Penns put their 1736 agreement to work right away. The Penns used it to justify the notorious "Walking Purchase" of 1737, a shameful episode in which colonial authorities defrauded the eastern Delawares of much of their best land; the Iroquois defended the Pennsylvanians on the grounds that the Delawares had no right to the land anyway, as it belonged to the Iroquois by right of conquest.[48] Similarly, the Iroquois used Pennsylvania's endorsement of their land claims to press for reparations from Maryland and Virginia. Using Pennsylvania's Conrad Weiser as their scribe, the Iroquois representatives to the 1736 treaty told the governors of Maryland and Virginia that "we expect some consideration for our land now in their occupation."[49]

The Six Nations' proposal to sell backcountry lands to Virginia and Maryland, like the final settlement of the Northern Neck–Virginia and Pennsylvania-Maryland boundary disputes, was put on the back burner in the late 1730s. So, too, were colonial efforts to end the crossfire between northern and southern Indians: though the fighting continued, warriors traversing Virginia and Maryland seem to have avoided additional conflicts with colonists. At the time it must have seemed as if the various claimants to backcountry lands were stalemated. Who knew how (or when) the Privy Council would determine the Northern Neck's boundaries? How much of the Monocacy and Cumberland valleys lay within Pennsylvania? How far would the Six Nations press their claims to the southern backcountry? Yet all of the ingredients for resolving these issues were already in place, thanks to the events of the 1730s. The migration of large numbers of Marylanders to the Monocacy Valley proved especially decisive, as did the Six Nations–Pennsylvania treaty of 1736, the Northern Neck survey of 1736–37, and the failure of the Catawba-Iroquois peace initiative. All of these developments came together in the 1740s, first in a diplomatic crisis that threatened to explode into a bitter and destructive war engulfing all of eastern North America and then in a treaty and a Privy Council decision that defused the diplomatic crisis and finally resolved the most pressing boundary disputes.

CHAPTER TWELVE

The Backcountry Transformed

Farmers considering a move to the Potomac interior in the early 1740s were well advised to proceed with caution. Part of the problem lay in their cultural predilection for boundaries, which was near the heart of the English relationship with the natural world. The need for precisely defined boundaries had spawned an elaborate system of surveys, plats, patents, and deeds. All of this generated considerable paperwork, which had to be coordinated and recorded by a central bureaucracy such as a provincial government or the land office of one of the great proprietors: Fairfax, Baltimore, or Penn. But which bureaucracy would rule? And what about Native American claims to the same lands? In the early 1740s the uncertainty bred by this situation rapidly escalated into a serious diplomatic crisis. The crisis, however, was neatly resolved by the 1744 Treaty of Lancaster, a watershed event that spared backcountry residents from a war they were not prepared to fight and solved most of the outstanding boundary disputes over the Potomac interior. Shortly afterward, the Privy Council rendered its long-delayed decision in the Northern Neck boundary dispute. The effect of these developments was to suddenly throw open the backcountry to colonial farmers, who could now know with some precision which proprietor or colony had won the right to sell or grant lands there.

Finding colonists to repopulate the backcountry proved not to be a problem, because the Treaty of Lancaster and the resolution of the Fairfax-Virginia boundary dispute coincided with the peak of eighteenth-century German and Scots-Irish emigration through Philadelphia. Thousands of emigrant farmers and artisans rushed into the booming interior settlements after 1744. There, in a marked contrast to the tobacco-and-slaves economy and landscape of the coastal plain, German and Scots-Irish farmers created a distinctive landscape tailored to the demands of a grain-and-dairy economy.

These migrations from central Europe and the British borderlands perpetuated the centuries-old division between the coastal plain and the interior. Once again, the decisions made by Native Americans in the centuries prior to the arrival of Europeans turned out to be binding on their successors, for the geography of war and diplomacy that they had created during the ecological crisis of the fourteenth, fifteenth, and sixteenth centuries persisted even into the mid-eighteenth century, a full two generations after the departure of most Conoys for Pennsylvania. Although they surely would have preferred some other result, the Algonquian and Iroquoian peoples who had forged that regional diplomatic configuration over the centuries had effectively regulated the timing, extent, and character of European colonization in the backcountry.

Reopening the Backcountry

On 30 June 1742, Jacob Pattasahood, a Nanticoke from the Eastern Shore, came before Maryland's council to warn of yet another "Popish Plot." Pattasahood said that he had visited the Conoys' town on the Susquehanna River, where he learned of a scheme among the French and Indians to "cut off the English inhabitants in Pensilvania Maryland and other adjacent parts." The Senecas, he noted, were about to go to Philadelphia to collect the last payment for the Susquehanna River lands they had sold in 1736. Once they had done so they and "other Indians" would begin preparations for an autumn attack: "in roasting ear and apple time" they would "fall upon the back inhabitants and at the same time the French who was to come by sea."[1]

The Six Nations were indeed at Philadelphia in July 1742 to renew the treaty of 1736 and to collect payment for selling the lower Susquehanna out from under the Conoys—a payment that included guns and ammunition. At Philadelphia, the Onondaga orator Canasatego complained about the people of Maryland and Virginia, "from whom we have never received any consideration" for backcountry lands. "We now renew our request," Canasatego said, emphasizing that "that country belongs to us in right of conquest, we having bought it with our blood and taken it from our enemies in fair war." If no payment was forthcoming "we are able to do ourselves justice, and we will do it, by going to take payment ourselves." Pennsylvania's council immediately dispatched a special courier to warn governors Ogle and Gooch of Canasatego's "threats . . . against the inhabitants of Maryland."[2]

Maryland's Governor Benjamin Ogle dashed off a warning about the "conspiracy" to Virginia's Governor Gooch, and Gooch in turn smoothly integrated Pattasahood's and Canasatego's warnings into a single story about imminent attacks against Virginia's western frontiers. Gooch "sent powder and ball to our people" in the Shenandoah Valley and ordered frontier militias to "keep constant patroles in large body's." By the fall of 1742 most Shenandoah Valley residents had heard about the impending Indian attacks. They were under orders "to be on their guard, to seize and examine all Indians they shall find."[3]

Clearly this was not a good time for Iroquois warriors to pass through the Shenandoah settlements. But pass through they must, for (as one Six Nations orator explained) they were "ingaged in a warre with the Catabaws which will last to the end of the world, for they molest us and speak contemptuously of us, which our warriours will not bear." In October twenty-nine Iroquois on their way to fight Catawbas stopped near a ferry across the Susquehanna River. There their leader, a seasoned Onondaga warrior named Jonnhatty, met with Lancaster County magistrate John Hoge, who granted them a pass to travel through Pennsylvania. Hoge, who had apparently heard of the Shenandoah residents' preparations, warned Jonnhatty that "the back inhabitants of Virginia might perhaps use them ill if they traveled that way."[4]

Jonnhatty's party pressed on anyway, following the main road through the most crowded portions of the Shenandoah Valley. The atmosphere became evermore threatening as the Iroquois approached the upper valley. Indians who broke off from the main party to scout out the road were harassed by armed colonists. At John McDowell's house some of the Iroquois accepted an invitation to come inside. Those who remained outside soon grew alarmed and organized an escape, but they were quickly overtaken by forty militiamen under McDowell's command. Each side later claimed to have approached the other under a white flag, and each side later claimed that their opponents had fired upon them without warning. At any rate a bitter struggle resulted, at such close quarters that some of the men fought with their axes. Eight to eleven colonists died in the forty-five-minute battle (including McDowell) while the Iroquois lost between four and ten men. The Iroquois turned around and went home.[5]

Though the rumors of war that brought about the skirmish at the Borden Tract were false, the skirmish itself threatened to bring on a real war. Virginia's council only inflamed matters with its initial response, which was to activate the new counties of Frederick and Augusta so that they could form their own militia units. As both sides spread their versions of what had happened, a few key people immediately realized what was at stake. Governor George Thomas of Pennsylvania feared that the Iroquois would "make war upon our fellow subjects in Virginia," and Lieutenant Governor George Clarke of New York warned against steps that might "involve all the colonies in a war." In case of a war with Virginia, the

Six Nations would have to abandon their neutrality between France and England. "If we lose them and the French gain them," wrote Clarke, "what will become of all the provinces is but too obvious to every one."[6]

To forestall this chain of events, Thomas quickly dispatched the experienced diplomat Conrad Weiser to the multiethnic Susquehanna River town of Shamokin, where he recruited his Oneida counterpart Shickellamy to help defuse the situation. Shuttling back and forth between Shamokin and Onondaga, they met with Canasatego and Jonnhatty and participated in ceremonies intended to heal the breach between Virginia and Iroquoia. On their second visit to Onondaga, Weiser and Shickellamy participated in a full council of the Iroquois League, at which they completed the rituals necessary to bury the incident. They also scheduled a major treaty to be held at Lancaster, Pennsylvania.[7]

The Lancaster treaty convened on 25 June 1744 in the very same courthouse where, in 1731, the Conestoga sachem Tagotolessa had first raised the issue of Marylanders establishing farms in the backcountry. Predictably, the Iroquois asserted that they had acquired the backcountry by conquest, while the English expressed their astonishment at such claims: "if the Six Nations have made any conquest over the Indians . . . on the west-side of the Great Mountains of Virginia, yet they never possessed any lands there," the Virginia delegates pointed out. "That part was altogether deserted, and free for any people to enter upon."[8]

Though neither Virginia nor Maryland was willing to concede that the Six Nations had a valid claim to the backcountry, the treaty they negotiated nevertheless included payments of £300 for Maryland's western lands and £200 for Virginia's, in return for which the English gained almost uncontested rights to the Potomac interior. The treaty also bound the Six Nations to an English alliance just as another war between England and France was beginning, thus eliminating a serious strategic threat from the north and west. Meanwhile, the Six Nations retained their right to pass through Virginia and Maryland and had reason to believe that their hunters and warriors would henceforth be better treated by backcountry residents. The Six Nations also received confirmation of their privileged relationship with the English.[9]

After the 1744 Treaty of Lancaster the problem of overlapping and contested boundaries, which had been given such urgency by the Albany treaty of 1722, was nearly settled. The provincial governments of Virginia and Maryland never again felt the need to purchase lands within the Potomac interior from an Indian nation. As far as the English were concerned, the question of the Six Nations' southern boundary had been definitively settled, and there were no other Indian nations' claims that needed to be addressed. That left just two important boundary disputes to be settled: the Fairfax-Virginia dispute over the boundaries of the Northern Neck and the Pennsylvania-Maryland controversy. Coincidentally, the dispute over the boundaries of the Northern Neck proprietary was finally resolved by a Privy Council decision in 1745. Assured by Fairfax that he would confirm all Virginia patents and waive all past-due quitrents within the Northern Neck, the Privy Council decided the case wholly in his favor. The new boundary would connect the headwaters of the southernmost branch of the Rappahannock (today's Rapidan River) with the headwaters of the northernmost branch of the Potomac.[10]

The Treaty of Lancaster and the Privy Council's decision in the Northern Neck controversy ended centuries of conflict over who might live in the Potomac interior. The backcountry had been highly—and often violently—contested since at least the fourteenth century, when the onset of the Little Ice Age had forced a reshuffling of peoples throughout the region. The results of the last of these contests may not have been just, but they did enable migrants to purchase back-country land without having to worry much about whether their title was good or whether they would be caught in a crossfire between northern and southern warriors. Indians who were angry that the Six Nations had sold their land out from under them nevertheless had to accept, for the time being, that their claims to the broad arc of territory from the lower Susquehanna River to the upper Shenandoah Valley had effectively been extinguished. As a result many Conoys, Conestogas, Shawnees, and Delawares retreated farther north up the Susquehanna or headed west into the Ohio Valley. Except for a finger of land along the disputed Maryland-Pennsylvania line, the way was finally open to a backcountry land rush—if, that is, enough migrants could be found to inhabit those lands.

"Out of the Hibernian Hive"

John Craig was but one of nearly five hundred Irish migrants to arrive on the Delaware River in 1734. Born in 1709 in County Antrim, at the northeast extremity of Ulster, Craig had returned to his family's native Scotland to earn his M.A. from the University of Edinburgh in 1732. Like many recent university graduates, he struggled to find his way after graduation. Though he yearned to enter the ministry, his experiences in Edinburgh led him to question "my own abilities for such an important office." Moreover, he was tempted by the prospect of inheriting a substantial Ulster farm from his parents and by a competing offer of a croft worth £60 per year from a Scottish uncle. Either opportunity might be combined with a career as a physician, which trade he briefly studied. Ultimately, however, he decided to go to America. After disembarking at New Castle, the favored Delaware River port for ships from Ireland, Craig looked up "an old acquaintance," the Reverend Benjamin Campbell. Campbell, the Presbyterian minister at New Castle, took Craig under his wing. He oriented Craig to his new surroundings with "a very just account of the country," advised Craig on the current politics of the Presbyterian ministry, "which turned out greatly to my advantage," and strongly advised Craig "to seek a living in a healthy place of the country" (the importance of which Campbell demonstrated by dying of malaria soon after Craig's arrival).[11]

Armed with Campbell's advice and with letters of recommendation from ministers in Ulster, Craig attended a synod of thirty-three Presbyterian clergy at Philadelphia in September 1734. Here he found himself among like-minded men who spoke in familiar accents: though the synod was riven by controversies between traditionalists and evangelicals, Craig was well received by the largely Scots-Irish clergy who remained "steady to the Presbyterian principles and against all innovations." One of them, John Thompson of Chestnut Level, Pennsylvania, took Craig into his home and acted as his "mentor and surrogate father in America." In Chestnut Level Craig taught school and studied for the ministry. After several years he accepted a call from "a new settlement in Virginia of our own country people."[12]

Arriving in Augusta County in 1740, Craig found himself (by his reckoning) some two hundred miles from the nearest Presbyterian clergymen. That distance, however, did not insulate his community from the controversies that routinely tore at the fabric of Presbyterian congregations. Like his colleagues in Ulster, Craig struggled to maintain "Presbyterian order and Rules of Government" without offending the established Church of England. At the same time Craig had to contend with "New Side" sentiments among his own congregants, some of whom invited evangelical preachers "to come and preach and convert the people of my charge and free them from sin and Satan and from me a carnal wretch."[13]

Meanwhile Craig put down roots. He "purchased a plantation, and began to improve upon it," and in 1744 he married Isabella Russell, "a young gentle woman of a good family and character born and brought up in the same neighbourhood where I was born." Together the newlyweds set about producing nine children and somehow juggled their pastoral duties, housekeeping, farming, and child-rearing, initially with "neither servant nor slave to help us, only employing hirelings when we could find them." When their first child died in infancy and many of their horses and cattle perished during the first years of their marriage, rumors spread that the children and livestock were "killed by witch craft." Eventually, though, Craig found his footing. He grew hemp and other crops, and his herds grew (with the help, eventually, of five slaves). He established a school and helped to establish thirteen new churches. He died in 1774, leaving as his most personal legacy a large brood of Presbyterians: seven generations later, over 80 percent of his descendants adhered to the same faith.[14]

Craig's story was far from unique. As he tended to his congregation, mingled with his fellow residents of the upper Shenandoah Valley, and preached through-out the backcountry, he must have compared stories with the people he encountered and found that they overlapped in significant ways. Whether Scots-Irish or German, the new migrants tended to follow paths blazed by earlier generations of migrants, as Craig did when he gravitated to Benjamin Campbell in New Castle, to John Thompson of Chestnut Level, and to the Ulster Presbyterian congregation at Beverley Manor. German-speakers gravitated toward other Germans, Irish to Irish, Catholics to Catholics, and Lutherans to Lutherans, creating a patchwork of surprisingly persistent ethnic enclaves in the Potomac interior.

Unlike Craig, however, most German, Scottish, and Irish immigrants migrated because of economic pressures and political instability. In continental Europe the main source of migrants was the southwestern German-speaking principalities along the upper Rhine. Many residents of the small political entities of this region were subjected to a vexing combination of ancient feudal obligations and burgeoning new bureaucracies. As a result families had "little room for innovation, individual action, or flexibility in response to crisis." A single war, political change, or poor harvest could push people over the edge. Thus harsh winters in 1708–10 led to famine and a burst of migration, as did wars in 1733–38 and 1741–48 and bad harvests in 1740–41, 1745, and 1749. All told, the southwest German states lost at least 900,000 people to emigration in the eighteenth century, of whom about 85,000 went to British America. Many of them were people "who owned some property, but not enough to support their families or to make it through occasional hard times."[15]

Similar forces also led hundreds of thousands of Scottish and Irish migrants to move to England, continental Europe, and America. Famine and disease drove perhaps 40,000 Scots to Ulster in the 1690s, where many took up new leases that had fallen vacant during the Williamite wars of the early 1690s.[16] There they found low prices for land but also weak markets for their produce—until, that is, a 1697 Act of Parliament opened England and Scotland to duty-free linen from Ireland. Exports soared: Ulster sent 700,000 yards of linen to England in 1704, 1.5 million in 1710, and 6.4 million in 1740. Yet not everyone benefited equally. Land and leases became more expensive, and many tenants were on shaky ground.

Thousands were forced to leave when a change in the English/Irish exchange rate produced a sharp drop in exports in 1717, smack in the middle of four consecutive weak harvests. Similarly, bad harvests in 1727–29, 1735–36, 1740–41, and 1745–46 prompted bursts of out-migration. Irish immigration to the Delaware River ports spiked with each subsistence crisis, jumping from less than 500 in 1734 to over 1,300 in 1736, from barely 400 in 1738 to over 2,000 in 1741, and from less than 300 in 1744 to over 800 in 1745 and in 1746.[17]

The cumulative effect of these migrations was to pave the way for a boom in migration that brought tens of thousands of migrants from Germany, Ireland, and Scotland between 1745 and 1755. By then letters and visits home by earlier generations of migrants created an awareness on the part of potential migrants that the interior behind Philadelphia might be a good place to go; the merchants who provided them with passage from Amsterdam, or Derry, or Edinburgh had a well-developed "trade in strangers" by which a multitude of immigrants could be efficiently carried to Philadelphia; and the migrants who crossed over before 1745 had established a number of ethnic enclaves in the backcountry that were capable of absorbing large numbers of countrymen, coreligionists, family members, and old-world neighbors.[18]

Whereas an average of 744 Irish immigrants per year passed through Delaware Valley ports between 1734 and 1744, an average of 1,321 made the journey between 1749 and 1754. The accelerating pace of German migration was even more dramatic: 1,236 per year entered through Philadelphia in the two decades prior to 1749, but over 9,000 came in 1749 alone. They were followed by between 4,500 and 7,600 Germans in each of the next six years, for an average of nearly 8,000 annually between 1749 and 1754. The nearly 40,000 Germans who arrived in these peak years accounted for almost half of all German immigration through Philadelphia in the entire colonial period.[19] The population of the Potomac interior soared. Though reliable figures for the entire region are not available, the evidence from several of its constituent parts is clear enough: about 10,000 settlers lived west of Virginia's Blue Ridge in 1745, 17,000 in 1750, and nearly 21,000 in 1755; western Maryland above the falls of the Potomac grew from several thousand residents in the 1730s to 10,000 in 1748 and 14,000 in 1755; and roughly 5,000 European colonists lived in Pennsylvania's portion of the Cumberland Valley by midcentury.[20]

Once in the Potomac interior the new migrants filled out existing ethnic communities rather than pressing the frontier discernibly to the west. Migrants who had arrived in America through Philadelphia or New Castle typically headed west across the Susquehanna River and then looped west and south to settle amongst their own kind. Thus newcomers from the upper Rhine might go directly to the

German-dominated middle and upper Monocacy River and its tributaries or to enclaves along the lower and middle Antietam and Conococheague creeks in the Cumberland Valley. Still others went on to the central Shenandoah Valley. Scots-Irish settlers generally avoided these German-dominated areas, looping around to the north and west to create settlements on the upper Conococheague and Antietam, on the western fringe of the Cumberland Valley, and in the northern and southern extremities of the Shenandoah Valley. English settlers, with enslaved Africans in tow, followed the Potomac River upstream and settled near the river or on Goose Creek and along the lower reaches of the Monocacy and Shenandoah rivers.[21]

Although this residential segregation was far from total, it was readily apparent to contemporary observers. The Beverley grant in the upper Shenandoah Valley came to be known as the "Irish Tract," while an Irish emigrants' guidebook commented on the clustering of Irish Presbyterians in the upper Cumberland Valley, "owing to the swarms that, for many years past, have winged their way westward out of the Hibernian Hive." Francis Campble, upon arriving in one such community, wrote that "the entire people of this settlement is of Irish origin and Presbyterian in faith." A party of German Moravians traveling through the Cumberland Valley in 1753 noticed the same thing, but were less pleased about it: they went out of their way "so as not to be too near the Irish Presbyterians" and were relieved when they passed into the German-dominated lower Cumberland Valley, where they could take their lunch at "a German inn," purchase hay from a kindly "old Swiss," and buy "some kraut from a German."[22]

The communities that resulted from this influx exhibited a peculiar combination of solidarity and fragmentation. On the one hand, ethnic, linguistic, religious, and other differences broke the backcountry into hundreds of different groups. Even speaking a common language was not always sufficient to inculcate a sense of community between neighbors, for the "British" and "Germans" each included a diverse array of peoples speaking different dialects, coming from different regions, and professing different faiths. The "British" included English, Scots, and Irish, and the Irish included Scots-Irish and southern Irish. German-speakers identified themselves as Swiss, Palatines, Saxons, or Westphalians. The English included Anglicans, Catholics, and Quakers, while the Irish included all of these and Presbyterians as well. John Craig struggled against the evangelical Presbyterian "New Lights," and mainstream German Protestants (mostly Lutherans and German Reformed) spent much of the 1740s and 1750s battling radical sects such as the Dunkers and Moravians. Though the Lutherans and Reformed carried the day, this struggle nonetheless contributed to the cultural fragmentation of the Potomac interior, for the perceived threat posed by the sectarians led established churches to distrust any significant interaction across denominational boundaries.[23]

On the other hand, we have already seen how many new migrants lived from the very outset among their own countrymen, coreligionists, and family members. Attending church and school together, exchanging labor and goods, and intermarrying quickly added threads to the web of connections that had brought such people together to begin with. Each wave of new migrants strengthened local linguistic and religious solidarities, albeit at the expense of meaningful relationships with neighbors who were cultural outsiders. So, too, did a series of information networks that helped to guide new migrants safely to backcountry communities, maintain relationships with those left behind, and obtain publications and educated clergy from centers of religious activity in Scotland, Ireland, and the German states. A few well-placed cultural brokers made it easier for such communities to go about their business without having to assimilate much to English ways. In Frederick County, Maryland, for example, David Shriver acted as the local "umpire . . . to preserve peace and harmony" among Germans, who preferred to avoid the English-language courts that meted out an unfamiliar form of justice, while Jost Hite served as a liaison between Germans and Scots-Irish in the lower Shenandoah Valley.[24]

People like Craig, Shriver, and Hite were part of the charter generation of backcountry colonists. Like other migrants to the Potomac interior in the 1730s and early 1740s, they created communities and local institutions that structured the daily lives of those who arrived during the peak migration years of 1749–54. They established connections with English authorities, merchants, and powerful patrons and land speculators such as the Fairfaxes and the Dulany family and otherwise learned the ropes well enough to smooth the way for later arrivals. Above all, they learned some important lessons about how one might live on the land above the fall line: what crops they might grow, what livestock they might keep, how they might organize the spaces on and between their farms, how they might exchange and market their produce, and how they might integrate their emerging social order with the landscape they were creating.

The New Backcountry Landscape

Newcomers to the Potomac interior encountered a varied landscape that had been marked, but not yet transformed, by humans. Members of a family arriving as part of the great midcentury rush of migrants into the backcountry would have caught their first sight of the Potomac interior from a high point near the ferry crossing over the Susquehanna, where they could see off to the southwest the first of the long, south-by-southwest-trending ridges that rib the backcountry. From this point onward they would rarely be out of sight of the mountains, for the main valleys are never more than thirty miles in width. The ridges bordering the Monocacy, Cumberland, and Shenandoah valleys rise between 700 and 2,500 feet above the valley floor, and on their steep slopes the travelers could see rocky outcroppings amidst a forest dominated by pines. The creeks and rivers at the heart of these valleys often flowed over limestone and shale formations, forming shallows and rapids that made navigation impossible, so the newcomers rode or walked. The main roads hugged the valley floors and skirted the most promising farmlands, which allowed migrants to study the topography, soils, and vegetation for themselves, while also examining their predecessors' farms to see what choices others had made.

Travelers on these roads paid especially close attention to the vegetation, from which they inferred much about the quality of the soil. Hardwoods were believed to cover the best soils, and pines the worst; ground covered with grass, brush, or scrub was also considered suspect. Newcomers saw precious little open space, however; apart from cleared fields nearly all was forest except for a few meadows and marshes along the waterways. Oak made up about 70 percent of the hardwood forest, hickory nearly 15 percent, and pine, walnut, and other species the remaining 15 percent.[25] These woods teemed with fish and wildlife. Andrew Burnaby, visiting at midcentury, remarked that the Shenandoah River had "plenty of trout and other fish," while hunters were able to keep up a steady trade in deerskins and elkskins. There were fiercer animals as well: the men surveying the Fairfax line in 1747 killed several bears, and though wolves were nearly extinct on the coastal plain, hunters in the interior killed thousands of wolves throughout the middle and late eighteenth century.[26]

Scattered through these woods were patches of cleared fields clustered about small cabins. Narrow paths branched off the main roads, hinting at additional farms beyond view of the road. The Moravian missionaries who passed through in 1753 encountered a farm or tavern at intervals of one to five miles in the lower Cumberland Valley, while in the middle and upper Shenandoah Valley settlements were thinly dispersed along the waterways, with large gaps in between the loose neighborhoods that had been established by 1750. Even in the more thickly settled lower Shenandoah Valley, there was typically a quarter- to a half-mile gap between farms.[27]

What, then, to do with this landscape? The diary of James McCullough, a

County Londonderry native who settled in Antrim Township, Cumberland County, Pennsylvania, provides an excellent starting point for understanding the relationship between backcountry farmers and their land. McCullough's story was in many ways typical. He and his wife Martha sailed from Belfast in the winter of 1745–46, then sojourned in Delaware for several years. There they had two children, John and Jane (or Jean). In the winter of 1749–50 the McCulloughs moved to a two-hundred-acre farm on the west branch of Conococheague Creek, where they soon had another son. McCullough's brother and other relations lived nearby. Naturally they joined the local Presbyterian church.[28]

McCullough was less typical, however, in that he kept a journal in which he recorded transactions, plantings, and harvests and remarked upon local happenings. From the names of the people who appear in his journal, we can readily see that his neighborhood was dominated by Scots-Irish newcomers, and in his phonetic spellings we can hear the story of his family's migrations from Scotland to Ireland to Pennsylvania: "ray" for rye, "yeards" for yards, "stript" for striped, and "inins" for onions. Above all, we can trace the agricultural cycle he adopted, glimpse something of the ecological imagination that lay behind his annual rounds, and discern something of the social relations that were encoded within that ecological imagination.

The cycle began in late winter, with lambing and sheering sheep, calving, and preparing the ground for his flax and oats. By the end of March, McCullough was ready to sow the flax and oats, after which he turned to plowing, harrowing, and planting his cornfield. (Unlike Tidewater planters McCullough plowed all of his fields—even for corn, which remained a hoe crop among even the most experimental planters below the fall line.)[29] That work was usually done between May and early June, though under exceptional circumstances he might still be planting corn in early July. During the remainder of May and June the McCulloughs busied themselves with a variety of tasks. Though no one job was overwhelming, the work added up: among other things, they planted potatoes, got the garden started, and cut hay. McCullough hoed regularly, and also "moulded" the cornfield, spreading earth about the stalks to suppress weeds. The neighborhood's bulls were also ready to get down to business in May and June, so (reading between the lines recording the bare facts of such transactions) we can well imagine McCullough emerging from his barn to receive suitors for his bull's services—or, on other occasions, swinging down from his horse in another man's farmyard and negotiating to have his cow Chirley "bulled." If all went according to plan, the pregnant Chirley would give birth the following spring, and give good milk until her next pregnancy.

The pace quickened considerably in mid-June, and by early July McCullough was in a permanent crisis mode: within a two-week span he harvested the rye and wheat; reaped the flax and oats; gathered the sheaves of grain and stood them up to dry and ripen in shocks; threshed the grain; rhetted the flax stalks (fermenting them in water so that the fibers could be separated prior to spinning and weaving linens); hauled grain to the mill; mowed and dried the hay; and sowed buckwheat, a second flax crop, and turnips. McCullough needed help to get through this mountain of work, especially in the early 1750s, when his sons were still too young to contribute. He may have hired workers; there is some hint of this in his relations with Dinas McFall, who boarded with the McCulloughs. Certainly he exchanged labor with other farmers: his accounts for the summer of 1754 show that he worked at least sixteen days reaping rye and wheat on the farms of Adam Armstrong, Cormick Dorman, Ephraim Smith, and Samuel Torintine.[30]

By late July the crisis had passed, and McCullough began to prepare for the winter by planting fodder and sowing a crop of winter wheat. The potatoes were ready for harvest and storage. The garden crops began to come in, which would have been primarily Martha's responsibility (perhaps with the sporadic and marginally helpful assistance of her small children). By mid-September all of the wheat was in the ground, and in October McCullough harvested the fodder and a corn crop. Though McCullough's operation emphasized dairy and wool rather than meat production, this was also the time to slaughter any surplus animals.

McCullough used the fall and winter to clear new fields and made other improvements to the farm. In one winter, for instance, McCullough "did begin . . . the great swamp to clear" and "did finis the swamp at the barens," converting both to meadow, while another winter he cleared a new field. This was much harder work than on the coastal plain, where farmers planted tobacco and corn in small mounds situated between the rotting stumps of the trees they had felled. McCullough, in contrast, needed a clean field for his plow and harrow; thus he had to uproot all of the stumps by hand using a mattock (a double-headed tool with a pick-and-blade on a sturdy handle). McCullough could not devote his entire off-season to clearing new fields, however, for there were also fences and outbuildings to build and repair, including the barn, a sheephouse, and a calfhouse.

Above all, the McCulloughs turned to textile manufacturing in the autumn and winter. The family owned a willying machine for cleaning wool and flax, at least one spinning wheel, and a loom on which they wove linens, tow cloth (made from flax fibers too short for high-grade linen), woolens, linsey (a wool-linen blend), bagging, check cloths, handkerchiefs, hickory (a heavy twilled cotton), and other textiles. They also coordinated the work of other textile producers:

while the bobbins shuttled back and forth on a winter's night at the McCulloughs' home, in other households people were at work producing textiles to be distributed by McCullough. The McCulloughs may have advanced materials to some of these producers or hired them directly (again, their boarder Dinas McFall may have earned his keep this way), but the details of these relationships are not spelled out in the journal.

So what would such a farm look like? A visitor to the McCulloughs' farm in June, riding up the path along the west branch of the Conococheague, might well have passed onto their farm without knowing it, for as late as 1767 they had cleared only thirty-two of their two hundred acres.[31] If it was late afternoon, the light angling in from the west would have given the leaves and grass an almost luminous cast, and the season's moderate heat and humidity would have brought out the scents of fresh-mown hay somewhere up ahead. Another two minutes at an easy trot might have carried the lightly perspiring horse and rider to the edge of one of the farm's two meadows, where small, scattered bundles of hay lay drying. Back into the woods, then, until "the far field" appeared through a line of trees; here the rye, heavy with seeds, looked nearly ready for harvest. Then on through a gap in the oak and hickory into another meadow, not yet mown; on a modest slope over to the right, in "the field over the meadow," the flax awaited its harvest.

Finally, from a brief rise at the end of the second meadow, the rider could see the McCulloughs' farmyard. A log cabin with smoke spiraling out of the chimney stood on a slight rise, with bare, packed-down earth and a broad outcropping of shale for a front yard; near the front door a large wooden Ulster churn promised fresh butter if the rider was invited to stay for supper. Close by the cabin was a carefully fenced kitchen garden, and behind it the potato furrows; beyond these loomed the darkening woods. Thirty yards from the house a barn stood with the door open; inside it the rider might have glimpsed tools at the ready for reaping and threshing the grain crops, a corn rick, as well as the last scraps of the potato stalks, straw, and hay that had fed the livestock over the winter. On one side of the barn, between the barn and the potato field, stand a calfhouse and a sheephouse, with the animals penned or staked and tethered nearby. On the other side of the barn, several horses are quietly grazing in a pasture. Above the barn, in "the upper field," the winter wheat stands awaiting the harvest; below and beyond the barn, oats and freshly moulded corn grow calf-high in carefully delineated fields, marked off and protected by sturdy fences from marauding deer and livestock.

The McCulloughs' farm reflected an ecological vision that overlapped considerably with that of Tidewater farmers, but there were important differences as well. McCullough, for instance, rotated crops and manured fields in order to maintain their productivity, while Tidewater planters continuously cleared new fields and abandoned old ones after just a few years.[32] The barn, the pasture, the oats, and the hay in the first meadow suggested that the McCulloughs' horses and cattle were far more coddled than their Tidewater cousins. The sheer diversity of goods the McCulloughs produced contrasted sharply with the tobacco-centered farms of the outer coastal plain, signaling a less profitable but more fluid, adaptable, and secure economic strategy. The potatoes, oats, rye, and wheat pointed to a more varied diet that included plenty of bread, oatcake, porridge, dairy, and whiskey. The narrow, rutted roads that carried visitors to the McCullough farm made it evident that the family would not be able to ship large quantities of their products to faraway markets, and the lack of black faces or of separate quarters to house gangs of servants and slaves betokened a different set of social relations.

The farm more closely resembled the sort of operation the McCulloughs had grown up with in Ulster. They tended the same animals, grew the same array of crops, and produced the same textiles as the relatives and neighbors they left behind. They used the same tools and techniques and followed similar seasonal rhythms. McCullough and his neighbors built houses and outbuildings comparable to what they had known in Ulster and Scotland (albeit using different materials), with similar spatial divisions serving similar social and economic functions. They wore the same fabrics and clothing and ate the same foods, and they rendered the backcountry landscape even more familiar by giving its features names from their past, such as "Antrim," "Cumberland," "Derry," and "Donegal." In short, Ulster-born visitors to the McCullough farm would have seen little to offend their sensibilities.

The Conococheague farmers' penchant for economic diversification, their poor prospects for an extensive long-distance trade, and some hints as to their social relations all found expression in McCullough's bookkeeping methods. McCullough's journal functioned in part as a record of debts incurred and accounts receivable. Evidently he noted transactions in the journal when he was away from the farmyard, then entered them in a single-entry account book at home. These journal entries point to the dense web of economic relations between backcountry residents, which made neighbors—rich and poor, tenants and landowners, single men and families—highly interdependent. They reveal the McCulloughs' emphasis on economic security and farm-building, and they reflect the close-fitting relationship between the region's "exchange economy" and its dispersed settlements. They do not, however, give any indication that McCullough was doing much business with people beyond his corner of the Cumberland Valley or that his goal was to maximize his cash income.[33]

Although McCullough and his neighbors reckoned both accounts due and accounts receivable in pounds, shillings, and pence, they used almost everything *but* cash as a medium of exchange. For example, McCullough provided Adam Armstrong with shirting, linsey, and bagging and worked five days reaping Armstrong's rye and wheat, which they agreed was worth £2.0.7; after the harvest Armstrong sent McCullough several bushels of wheat to extinguish that debt. Other exchanges were more complex and long-running. In October 1750 McCullough received 22s 6d worth of textiles from Thomas Montgomery. In November McCullough sent Montgomery a New Testament and a strip of linen, which shaved 3s 7d from his balance, and in January he earned 3s 9d credit for a gallon and a half of molasses. In midsummer 1751 McCullough was still chipping away at the debt, using as mediums of exchange a combination of labor (15d), molasses, and linen (for another 15d), but no cash. The account remained open until at least the summer of 1752, and perhaps longer (the journal's record of accounts is incomplete).

Since no cash changed hands, these were not exactly full-blown market transactions, but neither were they "barter." In a market transaction the parties exchange cash, goods, and services with the goal of maximizing profit on that transaction; and in a barter transaction the parties agree in advance on what goods and services will be exchanged without attempting to calculate their value in cash. McCullough's dealings were different. Unlike a market or barter transaction, each debt was incurred without any prior agreement about the form repayment would take. Unlike a barter agreement, each debt had to be recorded in pounds, shillings, and pence, so that credits could eventually be recorded in the same idiom. And unlike a market transaction, the goal in McCullough's accounting was not to create an imbalance between accounts due and accounts receivable that could only be rectified by his collecting cash from his trading partners; on the contrary, the goal was to achieve equilibrium by making the accounts balance without using cash. Since accounts were kept open indefinitely, the credits and debits rarely matched up exactly (as they would in either a market or barter transaction), so that one party or the other normally had a small outstanding debt. On the rare occasions when McCullough did acquire cash, it was usually a small amount, and he normally lent it out or used it to even out an account that he could not balance by providing goods or services.

McCullough's way of living within the backcountry environment was fairly typical of backcountry farmers, for the landscape and society of the Shenandoah Valley, Piedmont, and Cumberland Valley were variations on a single regional theme. McCullough's two hundred acres would have made him a small-to-middling farmer in most of the backcountry, and the mixture of meadows, small fields, and unimproved lands on his property closely resembled that of a typical farm in the Shenandoah or Monocacy valleys. Shenandoah and Piedmont farmers tended virtually the same array of crops and livestock as McCullough, arranged themselves in a similar pattern of dispersed settlements along the main creeks, and grew flax, raised sheep, and owned tools to prepare flax and wool fibers for the spinning wheel and loom. Like McCullough, they built their homes and outbuildings mostly out of logs. And as in the McCulloughs' neighborhood, the Shenandoah and Piedmont farmers' dispersed settlements and diverse economy were of a piece with the exchange economy that they had constructed. Routing exchanges through a web of account books rather than through a central marketplace meshed nicely with the needs of people in a dispersed landscape and diversified economy who were bent on achieving a competency and building productive capacity on their farms.[34]

And yet there were differences as well; subtle ones, but sufficient to raise questions about the relative significance of culture and environment in the creation of the backcountry landscape. An attentive traveler through the lower Shenandoah Valley might have noticed a scattering of tobacco fields and of slaves (8 percent of the population in 1754), neither of which were part of the landscape in McCullough's neighborhood. The Piedmont and lower valley population included numerous English planters who carried slaves up from the coastal plain and who knew how to grow and market tobacco. By midcentury tobacco prices had risen, making it more feasible to grow tobacco above the Great Falls; besides, tobacco could be used to pay taxes and other obligations in Virginia and Maryland. English planters who had moved up from the Tidewater were also less fond of flax, spinning wheels, and looms than their Irish and German neighbors. And there were other differences: although the farmers of the lower Shenandoah grew roughly the same array of grains as people on the upper Conococheague, corn and wheat were more prominent than in McCullough's neighborhood, and buckwheat and potatoes were practically unknown. There were also larger herds of cattle, which were used for their hides and meat as well as for dairy; in fact, some men were employed as drovers to herd surplus cattle to coastal markets. Livestock often ran free in the woods.[35]

Throughout the backcountry, the first generation of landowners had often surveyed and patented their lands without much reference to the preferences of provincial authorities. Many of these tracts were oddly shaped "water-hogging parcels" that cherry-picked the most fertile bottomlands and limestone soils. In 1734, for example, Robert Brooke surveyed a twenty-four-sided tract for Isaac Perkins that took in a long strip of meadows and bottomlands along a branch of Opequon Creek, with an additional spur up another creek.[36]

Such surveys ran contrary to the interests of the proprietors, large-scale land speculators, and provincial authorities, and as migrants flooded into the backcountry at midcentury, these men took steps to put their own imprint upon the landscape. After the 1745 Privy Council ruling in his favor, Lord Fairfax moved to the lower Shenandoah Valley to oversee his affairs. Although he stood by his promise to recognize title to lands initially acquired from the provincial government, he took exception to "unequal and irregular surveys" that engrossed "the waters and springs together with the best lands" and therefore left "great tracts useless and untenantable."[37] Virginia law required that the breadth of a tract must be at least one-third of its depth, and Fairfax enforced that requirement. Beginning in 1748 his surveyors (including sixteen-year-old George Washington) went to work reconfiguring existing properties and laying out new tracts to create "a neat, rectangular, gridlike pattern of tracts . . . joined in such a way that each had more or less equal access to water." The result was a less vernacular landscape but also one that opened up opportunities to the new migrants who were pouring into the backcountry.[38]

Though measures such as Fairfax's resurveys modified the vernacular landscape that had emerged in the 1730s and early 1740s, they generally perpetuated the dispersed settlement pattern created by the first generation of European colonists. Towns did not emerge until the interests of the provincial government, local residents, and a prominent landowner converged. That confluence of interests first occurred in the mid-1740s, when the combination of backcountry settlers' demands for the creation of new western counties and provincial authorities' desire to have functioning county militias west of the mountains as buffers against Indians and Frenchmen led to the establishment of Frederick County, Maryland (in 1748), Frederick County, Virginia (1743), and Augusta County, Virginia (1745).

The heart of county government was the county court, which needed a place to meet. Daniel Dulany provided that place for Frederick County, a new county encompassing all of Maryland above the falls of the Potomac. In 1744 Dulany had begged off attending the Treaty of Lancaster because he was anxious to explore western Maryland. He was so impressed by this "most delightful country" that he went on a western buying spree that included "Tasker's Chance," a 7,000-acre tract situated between the Monocacy River and Catoctin Mountain about a dozen

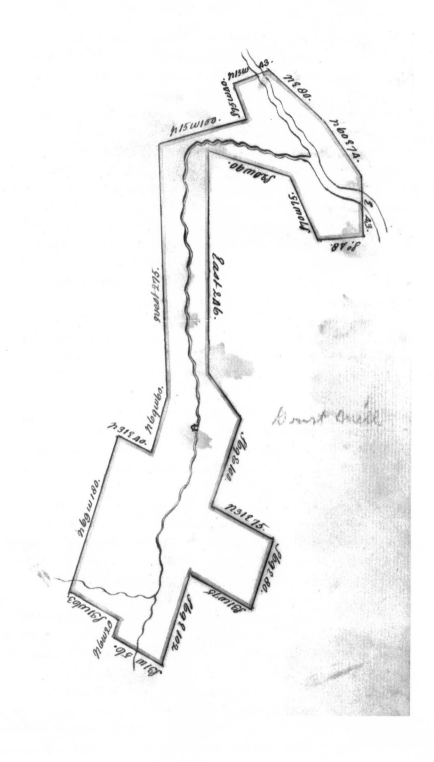

miles north of the Potomac River. Dulany quickly sold off nearly 5,000 acres of Tasker's Chance at prices well below what he had paid but retained ownership of land along Carroll's Creek, where he surveyed 340 lots for a new town named "Frederick." There was a healthy demand for the town lots, largely because Dulany had lured so many farmers to the surrounding area with his cut-rate prices. The 60-foot by 400-foot lots sold at an initial rate of £4–£5 in 1745, and prices rose steadily as Dulany added amenities to make Frederick Town even more attractive. He donated lots for churches, gained permission from Lord Baltimore to hold weekly markets and a biannual fair, and had the town designated the county seat when Frederick County was formed in 1748. By midcentury Frederick Town, with 1,000 residents, was larger than any other town in the Potomac interior (or, for that matter, anywhere in Maryland).[39]

Dulany's venture was unique in that the town attracted a county seat. Elsewhere in the backcountry the county seat attracted the town. Such was the case in Virginia's Frederick and Augusta counties, whose county seats, Frederick and Staunton, were the only other backcountry towns at midcentury. When the threat of war with northern Indians and the French inspired Virginia governor William Gooch to appoint Frederick County's first commission of the peace in 1743, they initially had nowhere to meet. At their second meeting, County Clerk James Wood declared that he had already surveyed a town on a heavily wooded tract he owned west of Opequon Creek, a half-mile from the Philadelphia Wagon Road some thirty miles south of the Potomac. Within a matter of months the court had diverted the main road to run through the new town and had erected a courthouse, a stone office for the county clerk, a log prison, stocks, a pillory, whipping post, and ducking stool. At first Frederick Town, Virginia, was more an administrative center than a town. After a year only eight of the twenty-six lots had been sold, and even those went to people whose primary residences and economic activities were elsewhere. The main street was littered with stumps, and many lots remained uncleared. Though court days brought the town to life, for most of the year the town was quiet. Fairfax helped to secure a 1752 Act of Assembly that established "the town of Winchester" and authorized annual fairs in June and October, but still the renamed town did not become a central marketplace or alter the region's diffuse exchange economy.[40]

Shenandoah Valley survey by Robert Brooke, 1734. Many early surveys in the Shenandoah Valley were irregularly shaped "water-hogging parcels" that encompassed only the best farmlands. Robert Brooke Survey Book, 1732–1734, p. 11, Thorton Tayloe Perry Collection, Virginia Historical Society, Richmond.

In 1753, nearly a decade after Wood's initial survey, only a few hundred people had gravitated to Winchester. Yet the infrastructure was largely in place, should more people decide to come. And come they might: Frederick County had been created under the threat of war, and if war ever threatened again Winchester would provide a refuge for those whose farms were exposed to French or Indian raids, and serve as a gathering place for the county militia and provincial troops. And as it happened, another war with the French and their Indian allies was indeed brewing. For much of the 1750s and 1760s, these renewed conflicts would engulf the backcountry in a bloody—and transformative—war.

CHAPTER THIRTEEN

"The Finest Country I Ever Was In"

The 1744 Treaty of Lancaster had given backcountry farmers more secure title to their lands, and it provided for the more peaceful transit of northern warriors through the backcountry. It did not, however, bring peace to the backcountry. On the contrary, the treaty created new problems and glossed over others, allowing them to fester beneath the surface. It left many Shawnees and Delawares embittered and angry with the Iroquois and the English. It failed to quench the thirst of land speculators and farmers for Indian territory, and it opened up a new intercolonial boundary dispute, this time between Pennsylvania and Virginia. The treaty's provisions also included a nasty little time bomb that, in retrospect, could not have been better calculated to set off a major war against the French and their Indian allies.

Though many backcountry residents suffered when the Seven Years War and Pontiac's War spilled over from the nearby Ohio Valley in the 1750s and early 1760s, others profited greatly. The Seven Years War drew backcountry residents much more fully into a far-flung market economy, so much so that they collectively reconfigured both the backcountry and fall-line landscapes to reflect this commercial orientation: numerous towns emerged in the interior, while on the inner coastal plain Alexandria and Georgetown burgeoned into the eighteenth-century equivalents of the large Algonquian villages of the early seventeenth century. In short, the war permanently altered the farmers' economy and their relationship to the land, created distinctive new settlement patterns at the fall line and in the interior, and set into motion processes of environmental degradation that shape life there to this day.

On the Frontiers of Empire

As the Treaty of Lancaster was being negotiated in the summer of 1744, Governor George Thomas of Pennsylvania noted with some concern that only one representative of the Ohio Valley Shawnees was in attendance. He immediately "set afoot an enquiry into the reason of it," from which he learned "that the Six Nations and the Shawonese are far from being on good terms, and that the latter have been endeavoring to draw the Delawares from Shamokin [on the Susquehanna] to Ohio." The Shawnees and Delawares, he was warned, would oppose the English in the Anglo-French war that began just before the Lancaster gathering.[1]

Although the rumors of Shawnee and Delaware hostility were true, the anticipated attacks on the backcountry settlements did not materialize during the Anglo-French war of 1744–48. French authorities did try to encourage their Indian allies to attack the English, but the war coincided with a series of French economy measures that sharply reduced subsidies for gifts to Native allies. Since exchange and diplomacy were so closely linked, this failure to provide trade goods and presents opened the door to the competition. The governments of Pennsylvania, Virginia, and New York took advantage of the moment, adopting a conciliatory approach to the Susquehanna and Ohio Valley nations. British diplomacy was also made easier because there was (thanks to the war) little pressure from farmers to move in on Indian lands.[2]

The Ohio nations set about establishing a thriving trade and diplomacy with Pennsylvania during the war. By 1747 the Ohio Shawnees and Delawares, together with Iroquois migrants from the northeast ("Mingos"), had established "a loosely confederated network" of towns with a council fire at Logstown, a Shawnee village on the Monongahela River. A year later nearly twenty Pennsylvania traders were doing business at Logstown, while others had penetrated to Pickawillany, a Miami River town in today's western Ohio, and to Cuyahoga, a Mingo town on the site of modern-day Cleveland. By 1748 furs and skins accounted for over a third of Pennsylvania's exports. With this trade came closer diplomatic relations between Pennsylvania and the Ohio Valley Shawnees, Delawares, Iroquois, Wendats, and Miamis.[3]

The Pennsylvania traders' success attracted a host of competitors for control of the Ohio Valley. There were French and British imperial officials, for example, as well as optimists within the Six Nations who still aspired to speak for the Shawnees and Delawares. The most immediate and direct European competition for control of the Ohio Valley came from Virginia, which attempted to use a clause that its representative had buried in the Treaty of Lancaster: in it, the Iroquois ceded "all the lands within the said colony [Virginia] as it is now or hereafter may be peopled and bounded" by its charter. Unbeknownst to the Six Nations (let alone to the Native inhabitants of the Ohio country), Virginia's crown charter encompassed the Ohio Valley.[4]

Virginia's council began granting large blocks of western land shortly after the Lancaster treaty. In the fall of 1745 they granted a hundred thousand acres lying mostly in the Ohio Valley to eighteen men, including Councilor John Blair, and in April 1747 they granted another group sixty thousand acres near modern-day Pittsburgh.[5] Soon afterward Thomas Lee and twelve associates in the "Ohio Company"—most of whom lived along the Potomac, were intermarried, and were acutely aware of the river's potential as a throughway to the Ohio Valley—were granted two hundred thousand acres directly on the Allegheny River, which was expanded to half a million acres in 1749. In return, the Ohio Company was required to settle a hundred families and build a fort for their protection.[6]

The Ohio Company's aggressive pursuit of western lands set off alarms from Williamsburg to Québec and from Pickawillany to Versailles. The machinations of the Ohio Company and other English speculators and traders forced France to attend more closely to its interests in the Ohio country. Employing a combination of force, diplomacy, and trade, the French struggled mightily (and with modest success) to lure the Ohio nations away from the English interest. Though the maneuvers and schemes of the various French and British players failed to bind the Ohio Indians to either the French or to the English, the escalating competition did succeed in convincing imperial officials on both sides that the future of their American colonies depended upon their ability to control the Ohio Valley.[7]

All of this attention from outsiders made the Native inhabitants of the Ohio country nervous. Clustered on the upper Susquehanna and near the Forks of the Ohio, where they nursed memories of the infamous Walking Purchase and other acts of bad faith, the Delawares and Shawnees were well aware that another landgrab (such as that planned by the Ohio Company) would cut into their territory first. Where, they wondered, did "the Indian's land lay"?[8] Thus Delawares and Shawnees were not surprised when, at the 1752 Treaty of Logstown, the Iroquois agreed to allow the Ohio Company to build a fortified trading house at the Forks of the Ohio. That was good enough for the Virginians (did not the Iroquois rule over the Ohio nations?), but to the Shawnees and Delawares it looked like yet another example of an ongoing conspiracy between the Six Nations and the British.[9]

The Treaty of Logstown answered any lingering questions about the Virginians' intentions. But were they serious about those plans? That question was answered in 1753, when George Washington crossed the mountains to demand that the French leave the Ohio to the English (they did not). It was answered even more emphatically in the winter of 1753–54, when Ohio Company employees began building their fort and establishing settlers at the Forks of the Ohio. In April 1754, six hundred French troops expelled the Virginians from their half-completed fort and adjoining settlement and built a much larger fort on the same site, called Ft. Duquesne. When news of this setback arrived in Williamsburg, funds, men, and materials were quickly raised to dislodge the French by force. With twenty-two-year-old George Washington at their head, the Virginians raced over the mountains in near-record time—only to be captured along with Washington's entire company and sent home in ignominious defeat.[10]

These events provided the excuses that war hawks in England and France had been waiting for. Both nations dispatched thousands of troops to America in 1755, including two regiments under Major General (and Commander in Chief) Edward Braddock. After convening a council of English governors at Alexandria, Virginia, in April, Braddock spent several weeks gathering supplies, provincial troops, and Indian allies at Ft. Cumberland, which had quickly sprung up on the site of the Ohio Company's storehouse at Will's Creek. On 10 June Braddock led 2,200 British regulars and provincials with eight Mingo allies up Will's Creek en route to Ft. Duquesne. Along the way he paused to completely alienate a delegation of Delaware chiefs by telling them that after expelling the French "the English shoud inhabit and inherit the land." Warned that if the Delawares did "not have liberty to live on the land they would not fight for it," Braddock replied that "he did not need their help and had no doubt of driving the French and their Indians away."[11]

Braddock was mistaken, of course. Without Indian scouts he was unable to see the ambush coming: on 9 July, just a few miles short of Ft. Duquesne, nearly three hundred French soldiers and militia blocked the path while over six hundred Indians began firing from the woods. Eight hundred British were killed or captured within a few hours, and Braddock himself died during the subsequent retreat. The survivors fled, abandoning tons of weapons and supplies, and even a chest containing Braddock's papers laying out the British strategy for all of North America. Leaving behind hundreds of stragglers, Braddocks' troops raced eastward, with the provincials making for their homes and the regulars making a beeline for Philadelphia.[12]

The war that followed brought death and destruction to the Potomac interior on a scale unknown since the sixteenth century. Shawnee and Delaware raiders buzzed around Ft. Cumberland, completely isolating that far western outpost.

The violence spread throughout the backcountry, and for the next two years the provincial forces and militias of Pennsylvania, Maryland, and Virginia were simply overwhelmed. They could not prevent the destruction of at least five English forts, nor the killing of a thousand colonists and the capture of several thousand more (about 4 percent of the prewar backcountry population). Tens of thousands fled, leaving those who remained more exposed than ever. Augusta County lost half of its population, and Frederick County, Virginia, a third. So few people were left in Hampshire County, a new county to the west of Winchester, that the county court did not meet for two years. From one end of the backcountry to the other, settlers fell back fifty miles or more under the onslaught, leaving crops unharvested and livestock to fend for themselves.[13]

James McCullough's neighborhood was as hard hit as any, and his journal provides an unusual ground-level perspective on these events.[14] Twice in the weeks following Braddock's defeat, the McCullough family "was put to flight by a fals alarm from the Ingens." On 1 November the Great Cove, a Scots-Irish community just west of the McCulloughs' farm, was sacked and burned. This time the McCulloughs fled for six weeks to Marsh Creek, a Scots-Irish enclave thirty-five miles away on the east side of the mountains (near modern-day Gettysburg). Then, that winter, the war truly came to the Cumberland Valley:

> John Creag [and] Richert and John Cocks [close neighbors of the McCulloughs] was taken by the Indins Feberwary 11. . . .
>
> We did move all to Anttetem [Antietam Creek] Apriel the 19—1756 [though they soon returned]. . . .
>
> I did hide welingers and some shafts in a hollow tree upon the top of the hill above the garden and a wolen reed[15] in a hollow tree above the barn amongst the wheat [and squirreled away other irreplaceable tools throughout the farm]. . . .
>
> John [Watson?] killed May the 26 in year [17]56.

And then, a family tragedy: "John and James McCullough was taken captive by the Indins." Both of his sons, aged five and seven, lost at one fell stroke. Would they live? Would they be assimilated into their captors' community? If so, would they want to come back? Would they remember their family, their language, their faith? Subsequent events offered little hope:

> Agust the 27 a verey great slaughter at Putmuck [Potomac] by the Indins wherin was 39 persons killed and taken captives 16 killed at a burring [burial] and 7 killed loading a wagon in the field . . . and Indins did carey away one prisoner from the South mountain. . . .

Robert Clogston his son [and] Bettey Ramsey hir son and cropper [tenant farmer]
was killed Agust 28 [and] hir daughter taken away....

November the 9 John Woods his wife and mother in law and John Archers wife was
killed and 4 children carried off and 8 or 9 men killed near [John] Mc Dowels Fort.

And so it went for another two years. McCullough reported the killing and captivity of neighbors at regular intervals: on 29 March 1757, on 2 April, on 17 April
("Jeremiah Jeck near Putomock was taken captive his two sons killed and one
man and a woman drounded in Putomock making ther Escape"), and 23 April.
In May "Mager [Major] Cambel and Tussey was killed or carried away captives
with 14 other persons near Putomock." McCullough recorded another 13 deaths
and a pair of captivities between 12 May and 15 May before fleeing again to Marsh
Creek. Even there the bad news poured in: McCullough recorded at least 185 more
deaths and captures between mid-May and early October.

Thanks to a combination of Delaware diplomacy and British military successes, the raids against backcountry communities finally began to taper off in
the spring of 1758. A series of Susquehanna Delaware–Pennsylvania talks at Eas-
ton and Lancaster in 1756 and 1757 kept lines of communication open, and toward the end of 1757 the French, whose supply lines across the Atlantic were badly
disrupted, found that they could no longer provide the Ohio nations with arms,
ammunition, and gifts. Moreover, some potential raiding parties from the Ohio
country stayed close to home in order to defend against Virginia-allied Cherokee
warriors. Other Ohio warriors were diverted to fight on the northern front, and
still others were stopped in their tracks by a smallpox epidemic that spread from
Canada to Ft. Duquesne.[16]

Meanwhile, 2,500 provincials and British regulars under Brigadier General
John Forbes marched toward Ft. Duquesne. Blessed with the support of a new
British ministry under William Pitt, Forbes got off to a much better start than
Braddock had. Pitt sent 2,000 regulars to Pennsylvania and agreed to reimburse
the colonies for their war expenses, including the costs of fielding another 5,000
provincials under Forbes. Forbes adopted a cautious approach, taking months
to build roads and bridges, establish base and forward camps, and secure supply
lines. He sent his first advance parties west through the Cumberland Valley from
Carlisle, Pennsylvania, in June 1757, but in August 1758 the base camp had advanced only as far as Rays Town, barely fifty miles west of the McCulloughs' farm
(though there was also an advance camp at Loyalhanna, within striking distance
of Ft. Duquesne). There Forbes's advance stalled. Confident that Forbes would

have to go into winter quarters in the wake of this defeat, the French commander at Ft. Duquesne dispatched many of his French troops to their own winter quarters and released his Indian allies to their villages or to their winter hunts.[17]

Forbes's slow progress toward Ft. Duquesne left ample time for diplomacy, which was an essential component of his plan to capture the fort. By the fall of 1758 many Shawnees and Delawares had been persuaded to stand aside from the Anglo-French struggle. When a British force left Loyalhanna on 20 November for a quick thrust against Ft. Duquesne, French commander François-Marie Le Marchand de Lingery begged for reinforcements from a nearby Delaware town but was turned away and rebuked: "we have often ventured our lives for him [de Lingery]; and had hardly a loaf of bread when we came to see him; and now he thinks we should jump to serve him." When the British reached Ft. Duquesne on 25 November, it had already been evacuated and burned to the ground. The French had retreated to the north and west, and their Shawnee and Delaware allies had retreated into neutrality.[18]

After over a decade of imperial competition, Britain finally had a foothold in the Ohio Valley—though not a firm one, for the Seven Years War ground on for another five years, and British diplomatic blundering after Forbes died in March 1759 brought additional conflicts with Ohio Indians. Delawares and Shawnees, who had expected the British to leave the Ohio Valley after expelling the French, looked on with dismay as the British rebuilt Ft. Duquesne (now "Ft. Pitt"). Land speculators jockeyed for control of the Ohio country and colonial farmers illegally squatted there. Soon these provocations merged with other grievances to yield the pan-Indian Pontiac's War of 1763–65, which spread from the Susquehanna to the Mississippi and lapped at the edges of the Potomac interior. Pontiac's War devastated the Conococheague settlement in 1763, and another attack the following year killed a schoolmaster and ten students; James McCullough's nephew was "bludgeoned and scalped" but survived.[19]

The most lasting and important consequences of the Seven Years War and Pontiac's War in Potomac country, however, stemmed not from the violence itself but rather from the massive and sustained effort to supply the thousands of troops that defended the region and used it as a launching pad for expeditions into the Ohio country. The premium prices offered by army quartermasters and the cash spent by soldiers posted to the backcountry drew residents more fully into a market economy stretching across the Atlantic. This in turn led backcountry residents into a modified relationship with their natural environment, which could be seen in subtle, but significant, changes to the landscape. The changes eventually encompassed much of the Potomac basin, from the upper Conoco-cheague to Beverley Manor and from the freshes of the river to its mountainous upper reaches.

War, Wheat, and the Atlantic Economy

John Carlyle was well known in his own time, but he appears infrequently (and then only in passing) in modern historical writing. Perhaps he wasn't glamorous enough: unlike his peers and business partners along the Potomac—men such as George Washington and Henry Lee—he led no troops and played no role in the politics of the revolutionary era; nor was he primarily a tobacco planter, whose doings have been much studied by historians. In the 1750s, however, this Scottish tobacco merchant was a prominent figure. Carlyle established himself in the mid-1740s near Great Hunting Creek, on the south bank of the Potomac just below the fall line, from whence he traded not only with Tidewater tobacco planters but also with merchants in Winchester and elsewhere in the Potomac interior.

Carlyle was the natural choice to serve as Virginia's commissary of provisions in 1753–54, charged with supplying provincial troops as they marched to and from the Ohio Valley. Carlyle was delighted to have the opportunity to make windfall profits while also advancing the interests of the Ohio Company (of which he was a member). Soon he was bringing in supplies by the shipload and collecting fat commissions.[20] His job became much more difficult, however, when he tried to move these supplies above the falls. Washington, preparing to lead his Virginia provincials to the Forks of the Ohio, complained that it was almost impossible to procure wagons. Even though Carlyle signed contracts with established back-country merchants, transportation and supplies still proved hard to come by. Bacon, beef, flour, and an occasional canoe, wagon, or horse purchased along the way barely sufficed and could not be counted upon at any given moment.[21]

Carlyle endured harsh criticism for the supply shortages, and he was replaced in December 1754 by two Northern Neck merchants based on the Rappahannock River. Governor Robert Dinwiddie also pitched in, devoting much of his own time that winter to supplying the garrison at Ft. Cumberland and preparing for Braddock's assault on Ft. Duquesne. Dinwiddie and his counterparts in Maryland and Pennsylvania scrambled to line up mountains of salt, wagons, draft animals, and other supplies (one order included 600,000 pounds of flour).[22] Still supplies were barely adequate, in part because backcountry residents were at first unwilling to supply wagons or provisions or to work clearing the road from Will's Creek to Ft. Duquesne. General Forbes had the same problem feeding and transporting his men, and he complained that what horses and cattle he was able to find were weak and scrawny.[23]

Backcountry residents, however, were neither unpatriotic nor averse to profits, and as the war wore on they reoriented their lives to supply food, transportation, and labor to support the troops in the field. Once again James McCullough's diary provides a case in point. In the summer of 1755, McCullough twice abandoned his farm due to rumored Indian attacks, though he optimistically planted the usual array of grains and kept up a reduced trade in textiles. In 1756, when scores of his neighbors (including his sons) were being captured or killed, he let his textile business slide and planted little except what was necessary for survival. In 1757, however, he returned to his fields—drawn, perhaps, by the lure of the premium rates paid by quartermasters desperate to supply their troops. In late July, four local men were killed while driving wagons to Ft. Frederick, but McCullough, undeterred, decided to ship his produce there anyway. He also worked for his neighbors, borrowed money, and stepped up his textile sales that fall and winter, apparently to raise money for a return to his former annual round of agricultural and textile production. By the next spring he was back on schedule.[24]

McCullough was but one of thousands who responded to the lure of wartime profits. Military commanders complained about high prices, but they paid nonetheless. In Winchester, construction began in May 1756 on Ft. Loudon, which had massive 240-foot-long, earth-filled log walls linking bastions on each of its four corners. Situated on a rise at the north end of the town, Ft. Loudon drew hundreds of newcomers to the town. There were laborers drawn by the promise of six shillings per day, plus rum, as well as contractors, masons, smiths, and carpenters. Local residents supplied building materials, horses, feed and pasture, clothing, and food and drink (*lots* of drink) for the one to two hundred men stationed at the fort (and, at times, to several hundred Cherokee allies). By one reckoning the soldiers at Ft. Loudon needed over 5,000 pounds of flour and beef each month, not to mention other victuals; and, of course, the men had their own pay with which they could supplement their diets.[25]

Since the army paid for everything with treasury notes, the result of all this activity was an unprecedented influx of currency. Backcountry farmers suddenly had a substantial cash income, while laborers and artisans working on the fort earned two to three times their usual daily rates. Merchants with connections in Philadelphia, Baltimore, Alexandria, and points beyond took notice, snapping up Winchester town lots on which they built taverns and stores. And Ft. Loudon was but one of many new markets for backcountry goods and services. The largest concentration of troops was in Pennsylvania, where Forbes's army vacuumed up food, livestock, and laborers from throughout the Mid-Atlantic and upper South. Forbes's agents sought pork from Maryland and North Carolina, cattle and arms from Maryland, wagons from Virginia, Maryland, and Pennsylvania, and boats to move supplies up the navigable portion of the Potomac between the mouth of the Conococheague and Will's Creek.[26]

The military continued to pay backcountry residents for goods and services even after the fall of Ft. Duquesne in November 1758, for the war with the French was not over and peace with the Indians remained elusive. The several hundred people at Ft. Pitt had to be provided for, and all of the main forts in the Potomac interior remained garrisoned. Andrew Burnaby, traveling through the Shenandoah in the late 1750s, was under the impression that people there made "a sufficient livelihood by raising stock for the troops." There was more than a grain of truth to this: a single buying spree in the fall of 1759, for example, pumped enough cash into the Shenandoah to put more than £4 into the hands of every taxable male in Frederick and Augusta counties. Even the end of the Seven Years War in 1763 did not halt the flow of cash, for Pontiac's War kept the military afield for another two years.[27]

This wartime infusion of cash into the interior permanently altered the region's landscape, economy, and society. To begin with, as part of its methodical westward advance the British Army built a new infrastructure in the backcountry, one that was capable of moving large quantities of supplies between the fall line and the interior valleys. It built new and improved roads, making it far easier to travel directly across the Piedmont and mountains than it had been before the war, thus supplementing the backcountry's traditional orientation toward Philadelphia with new connections to the heads of navigation on the Potomac, Rappahannock, and Patapsco rivers. Braddock's Road was but one of several new and improved links between the backcountry and the Great Falls of the Potomac; other routes made it easier to travel to the falls from Frederick Town, Maryland, or Winchester, Virginia. Even the old road to Philadelphia, once it was integrated into Forbes's Road across southern Pennsylvania, gave northern Cumberland Valley residents improved access to eastern markets.

The wartime economy had accustomed backcountry residents to doing at least some of their business in cash, to risking at least some degree of specialization in anticipation of cash payments, and to producing an excess of certain staple goods for sale to faraway consumers. Many retained that market orientation even after the war; only now, instead of selling to the military, they looked toward coastal and Atlantic markets. They did so with the help of merchants from Philadelphia, Baltimore, Alexandria, Fredericksburg, Falmouth (on the Rappahannock), and

Richmond, many of whom had reoriented their operations toward the back-country during the war.

Backcountry residents shipped hemp, tobacco, horses, whiskey, skins, tallow, cattle on the hoof, and dairy products over the mountains, but above all they exported wheat and flour. The price paid for wheat at Philadelphia doubled between 1720 and 1770, with most of the increase coming after 1758 (partly because sugar planters in the West Indies had to import food from the mainland, partly because of European population growth, and partly because of a series of disastrous harvests in southern Europe in the 1760s).[28] Backcountry farmers responded to this opportunity. Virtually no wheat had been exported from the Northern Neck in 1749, but nearly 4,500 bushels were shipped in 1758, and 7,000 in 1768. Exports mushroomed in the 1770s, so much so that in 1775 a single Northern Neck firm shipped over 800,000 pounds of flour and 44,000 bushels of wheat. Flour exports from Philadelphia, which drew from a vast hinterland extending to the Potomac interior, multiplied six times between 1740 and 1770. In western Maryland a German farmer in 1800 was three times more likely to grow wheat than the farmer of 1749, and German families tripled the volume and value of their wheat crops between 1749 and 1800.[29]

This is not to say that backcountry residents abandoned the regional exchange economy that had served them so well before the war, especially since shipping and marketing goods over the mountains proved to be a complicated business that could be worked out only through years of experimentation. Most hedged their bets, keeping one hand in the local exchange economy while cautiously extending the other hand into the world of long-distance markets. Thus rising exports were not the result of a wholesale commitment to long-distance trade but rather of modest increases in the production for market by thousands of individual backcountry farmers, coupled with backcountry population growth that increased the number of producers contributing to the stream of exports.[30]

Backcountry producers reinvested much of the cash that came in during the war and in the postwar expansion. Many purchased more land in order to build a nest egg for their heirs or speculated in the land market in hopes of subdividing and selling at a profit. This was a good time to invest in land, for a new flood of migrants from coastal regions and from Europe roughly doubled the backcountry population between 1763 and 1775. The result was a brisk land market: Charles Carroll, for instance, more than doubled his receipts from leases on Carrollton Manor.[31]

Reinvested profits also went into farm-building: erecting bigger barns, buying more wagons, horses, and cattle, and otherwise digging in for the long haul.[32] The cumulative results could be impressive, as on a Monocacy River farm advertised in 1777:

> A valuable tract of land, lying in Frederick County, on the mouth of Linganore [Creek] about two miles and a half from Frederick Town, containing 382 acres; on which are a new dwelling house, 28 feet by 20, well under-pinned with stone, with a stone chimney: also a Negro quarter, meat-house, poultry-house, and spring-house, a large barn shingled, with a plank threshing-floor through the middle; about 60 acres of cleared land, 10 of which are well laid down in wheat; about 9 acres of meadow cleared, 5 of which is in Timothy [hay], the other fit for sowing, and much more may be made. On the said land is a convenient seat for a saw-mill, which may be built with a little expence, as a great part of the timber is already got, and part of the dam made. This land is well watered by a fine stream running through the middle, and is remarkably well-timbered.[33]

This was clearly an exceptional property, but even tenant farms were becoming less bare-bone. Christopher Plunk, for example, leased 99 acres in the lower Cumberland Valley in 1767 with a 20-foot by 30-foot log house, a second 18-foot by 30-foot house, a log barn of 60 feet by 28 feet, 2 outhouses, 8 acres of meadow, and 200 orchard trees. All but 40 acres had been cleared.[34]

Backcountry residents also purchased salt, cloth, rum, sugar, powder, shot, knives, buttons, paper, and pins from Philadelphia-based peddlers and coastal merchants, and they invested in tools that could be used to expand a by-employment (smithing, say) into a more significant source of income. A few even invested in larger enterprises such as stores, taverns, and mills. In the upper Shenandoah Valley alone, the number of gristmills increased from thirty-three in 1760 to over ninety in 1775; two mills for the extraction of linseed oil from flax seeds also went up, as did four sawmills and a pair of fulling mills for finishing cloth. The business of marketing and transporting grain encouraged such specialization, for it required the services of merchants, teamsters, boatmen, innkeepers, and stablekeepers. New iron forges sprouted as well, particularly in backcountry neighborhoods where growing populations created a thriving market for nails, farm implements, kettles, and other iron products.[35]

The most conspicuous use of wartime cash windfalls and commercial profits, however, was the founding and growth of towns. Most of the new towns were located at a well-established crossroads or ford along one of the major roads that already had a mill, tavern, or store; in a place, that is, that had already emerged as a gathering place for those specializing in market-oriented crafts or services. Town founders from one end of the Potomac interior to the other discovered that rapid population growth was creating a "minimum threshold of local population density needed to support a distinct concentration of services," that local farmers were sufficiently market-oriented to support an urban class of merchants, artisans, and other specialists, and that people had cash to pay for town lots.[36]

Towns and villages cropped up at regular intervals along the main roads. Hagerstown, Maryland (1762), and Chambersburg, Pennsylvania (1764), sprouted at crossroads in the Cumberland Valley, and each grew into a substantial market town and county seat in the 1770s. A string of smaller towns also beaded the main roads: Leesburg (1758), Woodstock (1762), Stephensburg (1758), Strasburg (1761), Romney (1762), Martinsburg (1778), Sharpsburg (1763), Sheperdstown (1762), Funkstown (1767), and Middletown (1767), among others. Lots in such places initially went for £2–10 but soon rose to at least £20 for a vacant lot and £200 for one with a house or store. The "older" town of Frederick, Maryland, also boomed. The town's savvy founder Daniel Dulany had been holding lots in anticipation of just such a moment; in May 1764 alone he sold 144 lots. At the other end of the Potomac interior, Staunton, like Winchester a county seat before it was a viable town, grew large enough to merit a charter in 1762.[37]

Additional towns emerged below the fall line. Backcountry producers shipped their goods to many of these entrepôts, from Philadelphia to Richmond, but the most important new town on the Potomac was Alexandria. Alexandria was established in 1749 on the site of a tobacco inspection station to which merchants such as John Carlyle had already gravitated, drawn there in part because it had the best natural harbor on the inner coastal plain. In 1752 the Fairfax County Court moved into the town, and a substantial courthouse and jail were built, as were an Anglican church and a school. Alexandria attracted mariners, merchants, storekeepers, ordinary keepers, artisans, lawyers, and manufacturers. Visitors were duly impressed. Andrew Burnaby called it "a small trading place in one of the finest situations imaginable," while the *Maryland Gazette* considered it the gateway to the west, perhaps even to the Ohio country.[38]

Alexandria really began to thrive, however, only when large quantities of backcountry wheat and other produce began to flow eastward after the Seven Years War. With its fine port and privileged access to the Shenandoah Valley, Alexandria was ideally situated to serve as a shipping, service, and distribution center connecting the interior to the rest of the Atlantic world. New lots were surveyed, and old ones were subdivided (or expanded by filling in wetlands). A second public landing was built, new warehouses appeared, and a new public market building was erected. A new distillery took up the better part of three lots. Merchant Harry Piper marveled at the town's growth: "our lotts increase in value,"

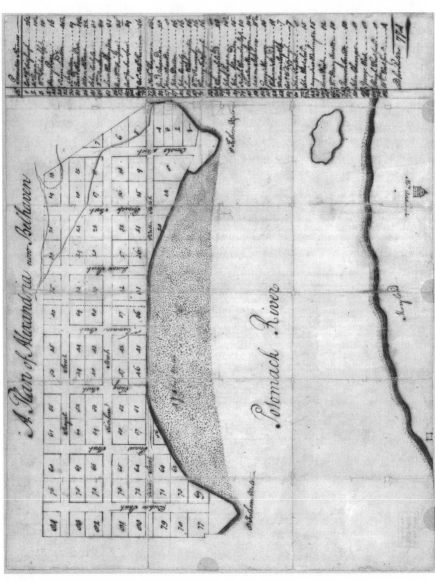

George Washington, "A Plan of Alexandria, Now Belhaven," 1749. Like other towns in the interior and on the inner coastal plain, Alexandria grew steadily through the early 1750s and then much more rapidly during and after the Seven Years War. Courtesy of the Library of Congress, Geography and Map Division, Washington, D.C.

he wrote. "We have I dare say 20 stores and shops now in this town and more are expected . . . and the people are going out of town before day to meet the wagons" bearing wheat and flour from the interior.[39]

The same forces that caused Alexandria to grow also conjured into being new fall-line towns at Bladensburg (1742), Colchester (1753), Dumphries (1749), and Georgetown (1751). On the eve of the American Revolution each of these small towns had 150–450 residents and a handful or two of merchants and factors. Georgetown, though not the largest of these shipping centers, emerged as "a smart town" commanding the lower end of the portage around the Great Falls of the Potomac. On the other side of the Northern Neck, the Rappahannock River towns of Fredericksburg and Falmouth also dealt in wheat, tobacco, and other produce from the Potomac basin, as did the boomtown of Baltimore near the head of the Chesapeake Bay.[40]

Rural residents of the coastal plain also responded to changing Atlantic markets. Planters on the inner coastal plain could see how well backcountry farmers were doing by growing wheat, and many devoted a growing proportion of their acreage (and labor) to the new grain. Most planters did not abandon tobacco altogether, however; rather than making wheat the new tobacco, they made it part of an overall move toward a greater, but still modest, diversification. Corn exports also rose sharply, and those who could afford to experiment with new agricultural techniques kept more livestock and attended more closely to their animals' needs. They began manuring fields, made greater use of the plow, and tested various crop rotations. The largest landowners supplemented their incomes by subdividing western lands and collecting rent from tenant farmers. A few diversified into industries such as iron or commercial fisheries. This could be a big business: an English visitor to Alexandria in 1777 goggled at the sight of "a seine drawn for herrings" that "caught upwards of 40,000 with about 300 shadfish."[41]

* * *

Late eighteenth-century travelers in Potomac country encountered a landscape that had been subtly transformed since the early 1740s. In the vast Potomac interior, there were many more farms than there had been a generation before, with fewer gaps between them and more open spaces where the land had been cleared. At some places large swaths of forest had been cleared around a sawmill or an iron forge. Though log construction was still the norm, an increasing number of homes were built of stone. Farms also had more substantial buildings and a greater number of outbuildings, and some of the modifications and additions clearly served commercial purposes as well as the demands of a local exchange economy. Local roads that had once crossed over streams at shallow fords now passed over milldams, from which travelers could hear the rasping of saws or the rumble of grindstones. The network of trunk roads and side paths that had connected the backcountry in the 1740s had shifted about to converge upon towns and villages, and the trunk roads running northeast to southwest along the grain of the backcountry's mountains and valleys were now intersected by major east-west routes that connected backcountry towns to fall-line ports such as Alexandria.

The inner coastal plain, too, looked different. Here and there were new calf- and sheephouses, milldams and plowed fields, and deforested areas surrounding ironworks and towns—though unlike the interior, these signs of change had to be picked out of a landscape that was still shaped to a considerable degree by the older tobacco-and-slaves economy. The most striking change, of course, was the rise of Alexandria, Georgetown, and other small urban centers on the inner coastal plain. These were highly visible reminders of how much had changed, for new roads tended to converge upon the towns, and they occupied prominent riverfront locations in an age when many people still experienced the coastal plain as a waterscape rather than as a landscape.

These alterations to the landscape of the inner coastal plain dramatized the relative lack of change on the outer coastal plain, which was least influenced by the rise of the grain trade, agricultural innovation, and economic diversification. More than one commentator thought that the outer coastal plain had fallen behind the rest of the region: Isaac Weld, for example, described it as "flat and sandy," with "a most dreary aspect . . . Nothing is to be seen here for miles together but extensive plains, that have been worn out by the culture of tobacco, overgrown with yellow sedge." Weld repeatedly lost his way in this "perfect wilderness," where "no traces of a road or pathway were visible on the loose white sand, and the cedar and pine trees grew so closely together on all sides, that it was scarcely possible to see farther forward in any direction than one hundred yards." What houses he did run across were still impermanent wood structures, and the inhabitants still relied upon a monotonous diet of pork, poultry, and corn. Numerous slaves worked the fields—more, really, than the local economy could justify.[42]

The changes to the landscapes of the inner coastal plain and the interior were more than superficial. They signaled another in a centuries-long series of shifts in the relationship between the residents of the Potomac basin and their natural environment. The alterations to the landscape between the 1740s and 1770s also recorded the social changes that took place during those decades; for as always, how people chose to live within nature had something to do with how they chose to live with one another. The deepening roots of slavery on the coastal plain (and its extension into the interior), the emerging urban social and economic relations in places such as Alexandria, Georgetown, Frederick, and Winchester, the creation of ethnic enclaves in the backcountry, and the different social and cultural formations fashioned by residents of the backcountry, inner coastal plain, and outer coastal plain—all found expression in the new landscapes of the 1770s and beyond.

Isaac Weld, who so detested the outer coastal plain, was but one of many European observers who traveled through North America, recording their impressions in journals, letters home, and published travelogues. None of these visitors had more to say about the Potomac basin than Nicholas Cresswell, the son of a Derbyshire farmer who spent three years in the region. Though not inerrant, his observations were generally very astute; taken together, they nicely capture the state of the Potomac basin on the eve of the American Revolution.

Cresswell first came ashore at Nanjemoy, Maryland, in May 1774. He was not impressed. Though pleased with the hospitality of the residents of this "small village of about five houses," he shied away from the "sandy and barren" land and found the wheat and soft fruit grown there "very indifferent." Though tobacco was an interesting novelty, he had little interest in growing it himself. He also tired quickly of eating "bacon or chickens every meal . . . If I continue in this way I shall be grown over with bristles or feathers." He seemed disturbed by the presence of numerous slaves and concluded that the outer coastal plain was "in general . . . barren and thinly inhabited." Although he had plenty of time to reconsider his harsh first impressions (he was stranded for weeks in Nanjemoy by "a fever with some cussed physical name"), Cresswell saw nothing on the outer coastal plain that could induce him to settle there.[43]

Cresswell found the inner coastal plain more to his liking. Sailing from Nanjemoy aboard a small schooner bound for Alexandria, Cresswell found that he especially liked what he saw above the freshes. He praised the "great number of pleasant houses along the river" and noted that the soils were "much better here than it is lower down the river." The waterways teemed with "incredible numbers" of geese and ducks. Alexandria, too, made a good impression with its brick buildings and thriving trade. The backcountry wheat marketed there was "as good . . . as I ever saw"—so good, in fact, that he felt compelled to explore the places where that wheat was grown. Thus (after another long delay while he lay ill with a "bloody flux") Cresswell set out for the west in late November. The road across the Piedmont took him through a countryside that he found adequate but not particularly impressive: the land was "monopolized and consequently thinly inhabited. Gravelly soil in general." Surely this was not the source of all that high-quality grain and all of those fat hogs that he had seen in Alexandria?[44]

Cresswell was stunned, however, at what he found in the Shenandoah Valley. Declaring it "some of the finest land I ever saw either for the plough or pasture," he marveled at the "excellent pasturages," the level terrain, and the "good wheat and barley" produced by valley residents. The extensive limestone and decidu-ous woods, "which are certain indications that the lands are rich," suggested that the valley's agricultural potential had not yet been fully realized. He also praised Winchester, both for its size and for its appearance. Further explorations of the backcountry only added to his enthusiasm. "Here there is every encouragement," he gushed. The land was cheap and "will produce any sort of grain . . . meadows may be made with little trouble, and the range for stock is unlimited." Taxes were low, and farmers' wheat and livestock brought excellent prices. Cresswell also liked western Maryland, but his heart was captured by the two lower Shenandoah Valley counties: "I am exceedingly pleased" with them, he confided to his journal, "and am determined to settle in one of them."[45]

In the end, however, Cresswell decided against settling in Virginia. He still considered it "the finest country I ever was in," but he had underestimated the seriousness of the dispute between the American colonies and the British govern-ment and could not bring himself to join the society of the rebels who predomi-nated in the places he had visited. His reticence about political matters did not es-cape notice, and despite enjoying the protection of a former Derbyshire neighbor who had moved to Alexandria (and built the town's massive distillery), Cresswell was suspected as a Tory spy. He escaped from Alexandria in August 1776, making his way (after many adventures) to New York City, headquarters for the British Army in North America. From thence he sailed to England. His journal survived all of his travels and was handed down from generation to generation.

Taking the long view, we can see in Cresswell's journal some of the main fea-tures of the region's environmental history: the persistent contrast between the environments, settlement patterns, and societies of the inner coastal plain, the outer coastal plain, and the interior, for example, including their most recent manifestations in the marked differences between the grain-and-dairy agricul-ture of backcountry Germans and Scots-Irish, the tobacco-and-slaves regime on the outer coastal plain, and the reurbanization and partial economic diversifica-tion of the inner coastal plain.

For all his insights into the relationships between nature and society in the

Potomac basin, however, perhaps the most striking thing about Cresswell's journal is what he did *not* see: Indians. The descendants of the Native people who had done so much to shape the region's landscape simply did not register with Cresswell. The Algonquians who had remained behind when the Conoys left for Pennsylvania in 1705 kept to themselves, tucked away in small communities that did not call attention to themselves. The diplomatic configuration that the Algonquian peoples of the Potomac had created between the thirteenth and seventeenth centuries was no longer in effect: northern warriors neither threatened the Potomac frontier nor passed through the Shenandoah Valley on their way south.

There was one exception to Cresswell's silence about Indians: his encounter, in December 1774, with four Shawnee men in Winchester. This exception, however, seems a poignant coda to the long history of Native Americans in Potomac country. A brief conflict between Virginians and the Ohio nations was just coming to a close, and the "four Indian chiefs" were on their way to Williamsburg "as hostages." Cresswell described them as

> tall, manly, well-shaped men, of a copper colour with black hair, quick piercing eyes, and good features. They have rings of silver in their nose and bobs to them which hang over their upper lip. Their ears are cut from the tips two thirds of the way round and the piece extended with brass wire till it touches their shoulders, in this part they hang a thin silver place, wrought in flourishes about three inches diameter, with plates of silver round their arms and in the hair, which is all cut off except a long lock on the top of the head. They are in white men's dress, except breeches which they refuse to wear, instead of which they have a girdle round them with a piece of cloth drawn through their legs and turned over the girdle, and appears like a short apron before and behind. All the hair is pulled from their eyebrows and eyelashes and their faces painted in different parts with vermilion. They walk remarkably straight and cut a grotesque appearance in this mixed dress.[46]

One of the most poignant things about Cresswell's description is his sense of wonder at finding Indians in Winchester, a town that had until very recently been directly on the ancient Warrior's Path and had hosted hundreds of Indians just a few years earlier, during the Seven Years War. Now, after generations of struggle, the valley had been made into a wholly colonial space. Indians had been driven away or gone underground, and except for place names such as "Conococheague," "Choptico," and "Shenandoah," there were no obvious indications that Indians had ever lived in Potomac country.

But had the Native American presence along the river truly been erased? Had the Potomac become something entirely new? And would it even retain the marks of its colonial past, once it had passed through the American Revolution? Out of the Revolution emerged a "First Citizen"—George Washington—and a national capital—Washington, D.C.—both of which were seated on the Potomac River. Would it now become "the Nation's River," reshaped to reflect the new republic itself?

Ahone's Legacy

Much has changed along the Potomac since Nicholas Cresswell made his escape from Alexandria in 1776. The changes range from the patently obvious (a population that has mushroomed into the millions and the rise of an automobile-centered economy, society, and culture) to the nearly invisible (such as radical changes in the prevalence of certain single-celled floating organisms beneath the water's surface), and they are evident from one end of Potomac country to the other.

Although the most visible changes date to the twentieth century, the transformation of the environment was already underway when Cresswell recorded his impressions of the region: thanks to the rise of grain and dairy farming, new farming techniques, the conversion of large swaths of forest to fields, population growth, and the growth of industry, by the 1770s humans were already causing far more extensive environmental changes along the Potomac and its tributaries than ever before, similar in kind (if not yet in scale) to the massive environmental changes of the nineteenth and twentieth centuries.

The colonial tobacco planter's long fallows, hoe agriculture, and small, unruly looking, and stump-filled fields had left much of the land covered with trees, herbs, and shrubs. In contrast, small, independent farmers in the Age of Jefferson were in the process of switching to plow agriculture, which more profoundly disturbed the soil, encouraged the stripping of all vegetation from the fields (including stumps), destroyed the root systems of perennial species (thus altering soil chemistry by starving out the microorganisms that live upon those roots), and encouraged crop rotations and short fallows instead of the older system of allowing old fields to return to forest in twenty-year-long fallows. By the 1820s commercial fertilizers made it possible to more continuously work each field, to put into production marginal soils, and to alter rotations to include fewer replenishing crops such as clover, grass, or turnips. Mechanized gristmills, reapers, and

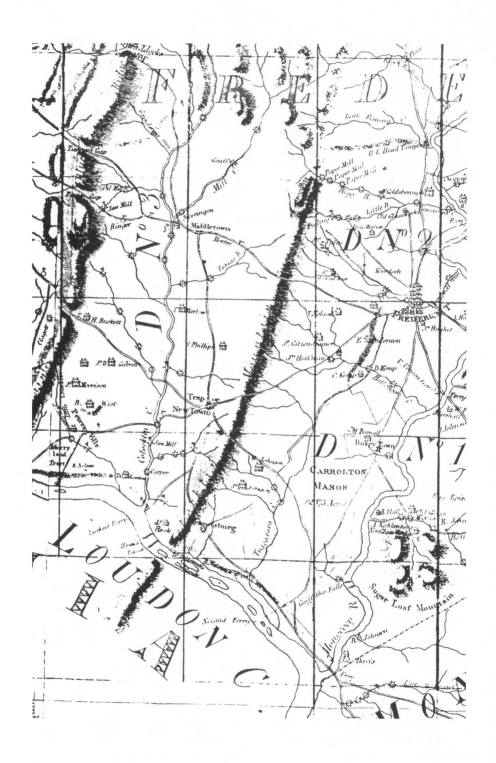

other machines introduced in the century after the Revolution made it possible for each individual farmer to keep more land under cultivation (even before the advent of tractors), while continued population growth put many more farmers in the field. As a result the proportion of land that had been cleared soared from well under 20 percent in the 1730s to nearly 50 percent a century later. Much of the new clearance was on steeper slopes (particularly in the Piedmont) that were prone to erosion. Forest habitat for all manner of creatures was much reduced, as was overall biodiversity. Sedimentation rates increased as much as fourfold, enough to leave once-bustling harbors silted up and landlocked.

Increased runoff from plowing and deforestation also transformed life below the surface of Ahone's waters. Waterborne nutrients and the tiny creatures that fed upon them thrived on the fertilizers and other organic matter contained in the runoff from farmers' neatly cleared fields, causing the water's oxygen content and clarity to plummet. Bottom-dwelling plants and animals either suffocated or were starved for light. At the same time, increasingly commercialized and mechanized harvests were stripping the lower Potomac and the adjoining Chesapeake Bay of oysters. Since oysters cleanse the water by drawing it over their gills and filtering it of sediments and other suspended materials, their depletion further contributed to the transformation of the estuary "from a system of mostly bottom dwellers to one dominated by floating and swimming organisms." As late as 1870 there were still sufficient oysters to filter the entire Chesapeake Bay estuary clean in just one week, but now there are so few oysters that "it would take them almost a year to do the job."[1]

Industry also contributed to the degradation of the environment. Iron furnaces and forges multiplied after the Revolution, and large swaths of forest were cleared in order to feed them. Investors bought up thousands of acres of timberland to support each charcoal-hungry furnace: at Neabsco Creek up to fifty slaves at a time worked cutting and burning wood on the five thousand acres that supported the furnace, and the Keep Triste Furnace, near the juncture of the Shenandoah and Potomac rivers, was fed by ten thousand acres of woodlands.

This 1808 map notes the locations of towns, substantial farms, and other enterprises; this section, encompassing Frederick Town, Maryland (right side, just above center), shows the locations of grist- and merchant mills (marked with a symbol resembling the sun), sawmills (a circle topped by a left-facing flag), and taverns (a circle topped by a right-facing flag). Detail from Charles Varle, *A Map of Frederick and Washington Counties* (Philadelphia: Francis Shallus, 1808; repr. 1983). Courtesy of the George Peabody Library, The Johns Hopkins University, Baltimore.

Crews building railroads and canals felled more trees, and the transportation systems they built carried still more timber to lumber- and papermills. Tanneries cut trees for their bark, used in curing hides, while glassmakers needed wood for both charcoal and potash.

By the late nineteenth century, there were only a few stands of mature trees left anywhere in Potomac country. Consequently erosion, runoff, and siltation increased dramatically, and sedimentation rates reached their all-time peak. Habitats were destroyed, reducing biodiversity, and several disastrous floods were linked to deforestation. Moreover, after the mid-nineteenth century coal mining in the upper Potomac basin "created hundreds of miles of highly acidic and biologically dead streams," while coal-burning factories (and, more recently, power plants) spewed pollution into the air and left toxic ash dumps on the ground. Only recently have the upper reaches of the river begun to recover, and even then only partially: the Jennings Randolph Dam, completed in 1982, acts as a giant acid trap by discharging water from the least acidic levels of the lake in order to avoid further poisoning the river downstream, while lime dumps deacidify the river so that game fish can survive (so long as the lime-dumping continues).[2]

Yet the environmental consequences of two centuries of intensive farming and industry seem almost subtle compared to the transformation of the former homeland of the Tauxenent, Nacotchtank, and Patawomeck Indians into a sprawling urban complex. The inner coastal plain was already the most populous and urban part of the Potomac basin when John Smith voyaged up the river in 1608, and it would likely have supported a typical fall-line city even if the capital of the United States had remained in Philadelphia. George Washington's plans for a federal city below the Great Falls, however, set the stage for the emergence of modern Washington, D.C., a metropolis unlike any of the other fall-line cities strung along the eastern seaboard from Montréal to Augusta, Georgia.

Washington dreamed that the Potomac would become the hub of the eastern seaboard, and he devoted much of his life to making it so. Even as a young man Washington was convinced that the Potomac was the key to binding the yet-to-be-colonized west to his home "country" of Virginia. Washington and his partners in the Ohio Company expected to profit from western settlement by marketing the produce of western farmers and selling them goods imported through Potomac River ports and by taking the unearned increment from rising land values all along the route from Alexandria to the Forks of the Ohio. Although the Seven Years War and a subsequent royal ban on English colonization beyond the Appalachian Mountains thwarted the Ohio Company's plans, Washington and other eastern planters persisted in dreaming of western real estate fortunes.[3]

By the 1760s Washington had come to believe that the Potomac-Ohio connection was important not only to his own pocketbook but also to resolving the
geopolitical issues facing British America. The colonies' population, he predicted,
would soon shift away from the eastern seaboard as farmers flooded into the rich
lands beyond the Appalachians, and there (he feared) they might fall under the
influence of Spain, which had recently acquired Louisiana and thus controlled
access to the entire Mississippi River drainage. The solution, thought Washington, was to channel the western trade through eastern ports. This seemed perfectly reasonable to Virginians, whose crown charter encompassed much of the
west and who were already the recipients of millions of acres of western land
grants. They already tended to think of their colony as the gateway to the west,
and local patriots on the Northern Neck regarded the Potomac as the best possible natural highway through the mountains. Once its shallows were dredged
and its rapids bypassed by canals, Washington predicted, the Potomac would
serve as a "channel of conveyance of the extensive and valuable trade of a rising
empire." In 1762 Washington joined in the first of several efforts to improve navigation on the upper Potomac, and in 1772 he obtained a charter from Virginia to
dredge the upper river and build a series of five canals around the Great Falls and
other rapids (thus opening the river to navigation until it reached a portage to a
tributary of the Ohio River). To his intense disappointment, however, little work
was done on the project before the war intervened.[4]

The Revolution only heightened Washington's sense of the Potomac's strategic importance. Even in wartime the local orientation of the average American
had occasionally led politicians to advance provincial interests at the expense
of the nation's health. In peacetime, Washington feared, the lack of a strong national identity and effective central government would completely undermine
the common good, leading at the very least to economic stagnation and diplomatic impotence, and potentially to disunion, poverty, and the loss of the west to
Britain or Spain. If the United States was to avoid this fate, Washington believed,
it needed a strong national government (hence the Constitutional Convention of
1787) and some way of binding the west to the east—the key to which, of course,
was the Potomac River.[5]

As the nation's first president, Washington threw his influence into the effort
to make the Potomac the nation's hub. He remained president of the Potomac
Company, recruiting new investors and otherwise looking after its interests, and
he worked hard to bring the national capital to the Potomac—and to see that the
urban and architectural design of the new city reflected and promoted his vision
of a strong, centralized national government. In 1790 Congress voted to relocate

the capital from Philadelphia to a hundred-square-mile diamond-shaped tract encompassing Georgetown and the lower reaches of Rock Creek and the Anacostia River. Washington persuaded local landowners to donate land for roads, parks, and government buildings, and he hired the French artist and Revolutionary War veteran Pierre Charles L'Enfant to design the Federal City. In L'Enfant's vision the city was to be dominated by the "grand edifices" of the Capitol building and the "President's Palace." The vast Mall and broad diagonal streets were situated to maximize the visual impact of the Capitol building and President's Palace. Additional public squares were designed to lend a "majestic aspect" to projected buildings such as a "grand church," a national bank, the federal judiciary, a national university, and numerous monuments.[6]

L'Enfant's plan was of a piece with Washington's vision of a strong federal government, which was to be held in check by the separation of powers between three branches of government and by the considerable powers retained by the sovereign states; it was, on paper, "a city that looked like the Constitution." The Capitol and President's Palace were placed far apart (separated, just like their powers) but were connected by Pennsylvania Avenue, with the "judiciary house" interposed between them. The Capitol, home to the popular branch of the government, occupied the high ground, looming over the Mall and looking down on the president's house. The large public squares were dedicated to individual states (a fairly obvious reference to their residual sovereignty). At the same time, however, the states' squares featured monuments to national heroes and were adjacent to federal institutions—thus nicely capturing the ambiguity of the relationship between state and federal power.[7]

L'Enfant's urban design also accommodated Washington's vision of the Potomac as the gateway to the west. Anticipating that the District of Columbia would also become an economic capital once the western trade began flowing along the Potomac, Washington convinced L'Enfant to fully integrate commercial space into the city's design. A canal designed to both facilitate and symbolize the circulation of goods traversed the city, following the northern edge of the Mall from the Potomac until just below the Capitol building, where it turned sharply southward to cross the Mall en route to the Anacostia River. The city market was given a prominent place on Pennsylvania Avenue, near the canal on the site now occupied by the National Archives, and shops were supposed to occupy the spaces between widely separated "grand edifices" and other federal buildings. Georgetown and other nearby ports would handle most of the oceangoing and transmontane trades, and they were sure to boom once the Pawtomack Company opened the way to the west.[8]

Washington's grand idea was never fully realized. His dream of making the Potomac the commercial gateway to the west went practically nowhere: New Orleans captured the western trade after all, and what traffic did connect the east and the west passed over other, easier routes than the shallow upper Potomac and the mountainous portages between the Potomac and the Ohio. Nor was the urban design developed by L'Enfant and Washington fully implemented, for a falling-out between L'Enfant and Washington, tight federal budgets, principled opposition to such a grandiose design for the seat of a republican government, and the failure of the Potomac as a commercial artery into the west all conspired to make the Federal City less impressive than they had hoped. The city filled in but slowly: an English visitor in the 1820s wrote that "I had been told, indeed, that I should see a straggling city; but I had no idea that I should find the houses so very much scattered as they really are . . . The plan of the city is on a vast scale, and it will be many a long year before even one half of it will be completed." Twenty years later Charles Dickens described a city of "spacious avenues, that begin in nothing, and lead nowhere; streets, mile-long, that only want houses, roads, and inhabitants; public buildings that need but a public to be complete." As late as 1899, even after a tremendous burst of building during and after the Civil War, a visitor could still with some justice call the city "distinctly unfinished . . . not yet the city it is manifestly destined to become."[9]

The federal government's massive expansion during World War II and the Cold War, however, turned the sleepy capital into the sprawling headquarters of the most powerful government in the world. Washington, D.C.'s expansion coincided with the rise of the automobile, and together they produced a massive rise in the number of people in the region, in the space they consumed, and in the waste they produced. By 2000 the basin's population had risen to 5.35 million people, three-quarters of whom lived in the Washington, D.C., area. These people consume up to 500 million gallons of water each day, much of which is returned to the river as silt-laden runoff or as treated sewage (and sometimes as untreated sewage; until the 1930s much of the city's sewage ran directly into the river, and even now big storms back up the sewers until they overflow). Most of the Washington, D.C., area is planned to accommodate and even promote automobile traffic, which has led to serious suburban sprawl, deforestation, traffic jams, and water pollution from the runoff from so much oil-splattered pavement. Even where water quality might still support a healthy mixture of aquatic life, roads and other impediments block American shad and other fish from returning to their spawning grounds, with disastrous consequences for these populations. As in other automobile-dominated cities, smog is a problem: in a typical year the

Washington, D.C., metropolitan area ranks among the thirteen worst U.S. cities for air pollution. The triumph of the automobile is so complete that the topography with which earlier, horse-and-pedestrian societies had to reckon with is barely relevant; as *Washington Post* writer Joel Achenbach puts it, "the metropolis so miniaturizes the old river that the city can no longer be described as 'on the Potomac.'" It is now more accurate to say that "Washington is on the southern section of the Boston-to-Richmond urban corridor."[10]

Between the ravages of industry, urban sprawl, and automobiles, the degradation of the environment in the Potomac basin sometimes seems irreversible. In my gloomier moments I wonder what is left of the world that Ahone created for the Native peoples of the Potomac. Are these still Ahone's waters? Or has some other, less generous god taken over? And this environmental destruction seems to have gone hand in hand with cultural genocide: where are the people who Ahone originally placed upon this land and who Okeus taught how to live here? It sometimes seems as if most of the region's ten thousand years of human history have been effaced from Potomac country, for there are few obvious signs of a Native American presence; not even in the region's countless museums and other public history sites is there much mention of a Native American past. Where are the traces of Ahone, or Okeus, or their people?[11]

But such moments of despair are neither helpful nor entirely true to what is plainly visible on the land—if one knows where to look. When I first began to explore the Potomac basin in the 1980s, I immediately recognized that the landscape had been shaped in some places by English tobacco planters' ways of living upon the land, and in other places by the German and Scots-Irish farmers who flooded the backcountry in the eighteenth century. The Native American past, however, seemed far less evident. But as the years went by, and my historical studies and my everyday life both came to revolve around the Potomac, it gradually dawned on me that the trajectory of Native American history before John Smith's visitation in 1608 had not been entirely cut off nor subsumed into the trajectory of Euro-American history. If one knows what to look for, this longer sweep of history is recorded in a still-visible archaeology of land use in which layer upon layer of changing relationships between nature and people are recorded.

In today's landscape the first thing to grab the eye is the highly visible and widely scattered detritus of global consumer culture: fast food restaurants, waterside vacation homes, and the vast suburban sprawl radiating from Washington, D.C. Yet with a minimum of excavation we can discern differences in the human geography and in the landscapes of different parts of the Potomac basin—most notably the outer coastal plain, the inner coastal plain, and the interior above the fall line. The most obvious differences between these three subregions date to the colonial period, when separate streams of emigration from across the Atlantic created a noticeable division between English and Africans below the fall line, and German-speakers and British borderlanders above it. A second division split the coastal plain into two parts: by the middle of the eighteenth century, greater numbers of people clustered into more concentrated settlements on the inner coastal plain than on the outer coastal plain.

These colonial-era distinctions were in turn derived from a similar division that emerged between 700 and 1600 out of a closely linked set of environmental changes, demographic trends, and a great transition from foraging to farming. The forager-farmer transition put humans in an altered relationship with nature, and in that new relationship the very real environmental differences between the inner coastal plain, outer coastal plain, and interior fostered a new configuration of social, political, and diplomatic relations. Colonists had to reckon with those new relations, and in the process of reckoning with them they perpetuated the old three-part division.

Thus Indians in effect governed the timing, extent, and character of colonization. By the end of the American Revolution Native Americans exercised no direct political power along the Potomac, yet their ancestors' presence could still be discerned throughout Potomac country. The ancient Indian influence could be felt even beyond the Potomac, because the region served as a cultural hearth for southern Appalachia, Tennessee, Kentucky, and the southern reaches of Ohio, Indiana, and Illinois. Roughly a million Virginians and Marylanders migrated west between 1790 and 1850, and they managed to recreate in their new homes much of the world they had left behind. The influence of these migrants from Potomac country in the west and the Appalachian South was clearly visible to the naked eye: in their architecture and farmyard layouts, for example, and in the irregularly shaped properties they surveyed (which greatly favored the first arrivals in each neighborhood, just as it had in Potomac country).[12]

So today, when I pause during a hike above the Potomac, or Shenandoah, or Monocacy and open my mind and my senses to the view before me, I feel a greater sense of continuity with the ancient past, and thus a greater sense of hope for the future. At such moments the fragility of Ahone's waters and the enduring legacy of his gifts seem equally clear: we humans may yet manage to reject Ahone's gifts and wipe all traces of the original peoples of the Potomac from the land, but for now these are still Ahone's waters.

One such moment came in April 2006, when I revisited Virginia's Westmoreland State Park, a hilly 1,300-acre tract on the outer coastal plain some twenty-four miles above the mouth of the river and fifty-two miles below the D.C. Beltway. On my first visit to the park, in the brutally hot summer of 1988, I had joined a friend for a long run in the drenching midday heat, then sprawled in the shallows at the park's beachfront. There we felt crowded by the hundreds of beachgoers and boaters and depressed by the garbage that had accumulated along the shoreline. We worried about catching something (a bacterial infection, perhaps) from the warm, sluggish, and slightly malodorous water. A red-and-white striped power-plant stack just upriver at Morgantown, Maryland, weighed on my mind, all the more so because it was one of the smoggiest summers on record.

In 2006, however, the circumstances were different: this time it was a perfect Wednesday in April, my companion was a delightful twelve-year-old daughter, and we had the park to ourselves. My state of mind had also changed. As it happened, I had just encountered a passage from T. S. Eliot's "Little Gidding" that aptly described what had happened in the eighteen years between visits to the park:

> We shall not cease from exploration
> And the end of all our exploring
> Will be to arrive where we started
> And know the place for the first time.[13]

The power-plant stack was still there in 2006, and the solid "thump" of artillery practice at nearby Dahlgren Naval Weapons Laboratory that morning provided an insistent reminder of the enormous destructive power we moderns have at our command. And if anything, I knew in more intimate detail than in 1988 what was wrong with the Potomac basin: unexplained fish kills, for example, and toxic algae blooms, and PCB contamination, and other horrors.[14]

Nevertheless, on this visit to the park I was more open to signs of nature's resilience and to the beauty of what is, despite all of the abuse to which it has been subjected, a relatively wild river. Several minutes into our walk my daughter and I began to see eagles everywhere: perched high in a tall oak tree, plunging into the river to snare a wriggling fish, and circling low over a tangled clearing in search of more food, twice passing within twenty yards of us. Offshore, flotillas of birds marked the migration routes and breeding grounds of anadromous fish. In a nearby marsh we passed near a great blue heron perched high on a tall stump; turtles basked on downed trees and slipped into the water at our approach.

There were also other reasons why, toward the end of all my exploring, I felt more optimistic than in 1988. By now, I was aware that a century of reforestation had restored habitats, suppressed runoff, and otherwise contributed to a healthier river, that American shad had been successfully reintroduced to the Potomac, that acid abatement efforts had made it possible for fish to return to once-dead stretches of the upper river, and that the water was far cleaner than it had been in previous decades. By 2006 I had also learned of earlier victories that had saved the river from even worse environmental degradation: the thwarting of a Corps of Army Engineers plan to create a chain of fourteen dams above the Little Falls (which would have turned the Potomac into the eastern equivalent of that sad case from the American West, the Columbia River) and the successful effort, led by Supreme Court Justice William O. Douglas, to prevent the construction of a planned highway hugging the north bank of the Potomac for nearly two hundred miles above Washington, D.C.

I was also more aware of the continuing Native presence than I had been in 1988. The original peoples of the Potomac have been staging a recovery for the better part of a century now. Directly across the river from Westmoreland State Park, in Charles County, Maryland, and in small communities scattered along both sides of the river, live the descendants of the Algonquian people who greeted John Smith some four centuries ago. Some people stayed behind rather than migrate to Pennsylvania, while others returned to the Potomac rather than continue to follow the path that led the Conoys of Pennsylvania to New York and points beyond. One modern descendant remembered a group of twenty-seven Piscataways who returned around 1800 and "tried to organize the remnants here—the Chopticos, Mattawomans, Accokeeks, and Zekiahs." Though this attempt at reconstituting an Algonquian polity failed, Ahone's children nevertheless lived on throughout the coastal plain. Their presence often went unnoticed by outsiders, partly because they had to lay low at a time when their neighbors harbored viciously racist attitudes toward Native Americans. But always there was someone, in some community, to pass along the stories and to make some attempt at conducting the proper ceremonies. Hidden in plain sight from neighbors and government officials who took it as an article of faith that Indians had vanished from the eastern woodlands, the Piscataways, Patawomecks, and others have never ceased to be, as the Piscataway Nation's Chief Billy Tayac put it, "so intermingled with the earth . . . that when you pick up one fistful of dirt, you pick up life."[15]

Human beings have been "intermingled with the earth" in Potomac country for at least ten thousand years. Never, in those long centuries, has nature been untouched by Ahone's children, but neither has it been completely domesticated. The landscape that has emerged from this synthesis of culture and nature bears the marks not only of the last century of overdevelopment but also of the colonial period and of the thousands of years predating the English conquest. W. G. Hoskins's classic commentary on the English countryside applies equally to the Potomac. "Everything in the landscape," he wrote, "is older than we think."[16]

Hoskins was referring to the tangible, physical remnants of old roads and ancient fields, but Iopassus—our teller of the Patawomeck creation story—might have explained the continuing presence of the Potomac's original inhabitants in other terms. After dying, he said, his people's leading men went down a broad path toward the rising sun, where Ahone, the Great Hare, lived. There they found "their forefathers living in great pleasure in a goodly feild, where they doe nothing but daunce and sing, and feed on delicious fruicts with that great Hare." They remained in this happy state "until they be starke old men" again. Eventually each old man died once more and, reincarnated as an infant, came "into the world againe." By Hoskins's reckoning *or* in Iopassus's account the result is the same. The ancients of the Potomac have a presence there, still.[17]

Abbreviations

AHR	*The American Historical Review*
Arch. Md.	William Hand Browne et al., eds., *Archives of Maryland,* 72 vols. (Baltimore: Maryland Historical Society, 1883–1972)
CRP	Samuel Hazard, ed., *Colonial Records of Pennsylvania,* 16 vols. (Harrisburg and Philadelphia: T. Fenn, 1838–1853). Vols. 1–10 have title: *Minutes of the Provincial Council of Pennsylvania, from the organization to the termination of proprietary government;* vols. 11–16 have title: *Minutes of the Supreme Executive Council of Pennsylvania*
CVSP	William Palmer, ed., *Calendar of Virginia State Papers and Other Manuscripts* (Richmond, 1875; repr. New York: Kraus, 1968)
CWCJS	Philip Barbour, ed., *The Complete Works of Captain John Smith,* 3 vols. (Chapel Hill: University of North Carolina Press, 1986)
DRCHSNY	E. B. O'Callaghan and B. Fernow, eds., *Documents Relative to the Colonial History of the State of New York,* 15 vols. (Albany: Weed, Parsons, 1856–1887)
EJCV	H. R. McIlwaine, ed., *Executive Journals of the Council of Colonial Virginia* (Richmond: Virginia State Library, 1925)
Hening, *Statutes*	Wm. Hening, ed., *The Statutes at Large; Being a Collection of all the Laws of Virginia from the First Session of the Legislature in the Year 1619* (New York: R. & W. & G. Bartow, 1819–1823)
JAH	*Journal of American History*
JR	Reuben Gold Thwaites, ed., *The Jesuit Relations and Allied Documents: Travels and Explorations of the Jesuit Missionaries in New France, 1610–1791,* 73 vols. (Cleveland: Burroughs Brothers, 1896–1901)
LV	Library of Virginia
MdHM	*Maryland Historical Magazine*
MHS	Maryland Historical Society

PA   *Pennsylvania Archives,* 9 series, 138 vols. (Harrisburg and Phila-
            delphia, 1852–1949)
RVC   Susan Myra Kingsbury, ed., *The Records of the Virginia Company
            of London, 1607–1626,* 4 vols. (Washington, D.C.: U.S. Govern-
            ment Printing Office, 1906–35)
VCRP   Virginia Colonial Records Project, Virginia Historical Society
            (microfilm)
VHS   Virginia Historical Society
VMHB   *The Virginia Magazine of History and Biography.*
WMQ   *The William and Mary Quarterly,* 3rd series

A Note on Language and Usage

1. Michael Yellow Bird, "What We Want to Be Called: Indigenous Peoples' Perspectives on Racial and Ethnic Identity Labels," *American Indian Quarterly* 23 (1999),
1–21.

2. Robert Bringhurst, *A Story as Sharp as a Knife: The Classical Haida Mythtellers
and Their World* (Lincoln: University of Nebraska Press, 1999), 17.

3. Daniel Richter, *The Ordeal of the Longhouse: The Peoples of the Iroquois League
in the Era of European Colonization* (Chapel Hill: University of North Carolina Press,
1992), 282. (Italics in the original.)

Introduction. Ahone's Gift

1. William Strachey, *The Historie of Travell into Virginia Britania* (1612), ed. Louis
B. Wright and Virginia Freund, Works Issued by the Hakluyt Society, 2nd series, no.
105 (London: Hakluyt Society, 1953), 101–2. For a slightly different version, see Samuel
Purchas, *Purchas his pilgrimage, or Relations of the world and the religions observed in
al ages and places discovered, from the Creation unto this present,* 3rd ed. (London: William Stansby for Henry Fetherstone, 1617), 954.

2. William Cronon, *Changes in the Land: Indians, Colonists, and the Ecology of New
England* (New York: Hill and Wang, 1983), 48–50, 165, 169; Alfred Crosby, *Ecological
Imperialism: The Biological Expansion of Europe, 900–1900* (New York: Cambridge
University Press, 1986); and Carolyn Merchant, *Ecological Revolutions: Nature, Gen-
der, and Science in New England* (Chapel Hill: University of North Carolina Press,
1989).

3. Several recent assessments of the state of environmental history confirm this
impression, for they cite very little recent work on early America, particularly in the
eastern woodlands. See John Brooke, "Ecology," in Daniel Vickers, ed., *A Companion
to Colonial America* (Malden, Mass.: Blackwell, 2003), 44–75; Mart Stewart, "Southern Environmental History," in John Boles, ed., *A Companion to the American South*
(Malden, Mass.: Blackwell, 2001), 409–23; and Andrew Isenberg, "Historicizing Natural Environments: The Deep Roots of Environmental History," in Lloyd Kramer and
Sarah Maza, eds., *A Companion to Western Historical Thought* (Malden, Mass.: Black-

well, 2002), 372–89. A trickle of new works have appeared in recent years, including Virginia DeJohn Anderson, *Creatures of Empire: How Domestic Animals Transformed Early America* (New York: Oxford University Press, 2004); Judith Carney, *Black Rice: The African Origins of Rice Cultivation in the Americas* (Cambridge: Harvard University Press, 2001); Brian Donahue, *The Great Meadow: Farmers and the Land in Colonial Concord* (New Haven: Yale University Press, 2003); Matthew Mulcahy, *Hurricanes and Society in the British Greater Caribbean, 1624–1783* (Baltimore: Johns Hopkins University Press, 2005); and Mart Stewart, *"What Nature Suffers to Groe": Life, Labor, and Landscape on the Georgia Coast, 1680–1920* (Athens: University of Georgia Press, 1996). Several studies in a related area, the history of science and technology, have also appeared recently: see, e.g., Joyce Chaplin, *Subject Matter: Technology, the Body, and Science on the Anglo-American Frontier, 1500–1676* (Cambridge: Harvard University Press, 2001); James Delbourgo, *A Most Amazing Scene of Wonders: Electricity and Enlightenment in Early America* (Cambridge: Harvard University Press); Sara Gronim, *Everyday Nature: Knowledge of the Natural World in Colonial New York* (New Brunswick: Rutgers University Press, 2007); Amy Meyers, ed., *Empire's Nature: Mark Catesby's New World Vision* (Chapel Hill: University of North Carolina Press, 1999); Susan Scott Parrish, *American Curiosity: Cultures of Natural History in the British Atlantic World* (Chapel Hill: University of North Carolina Press, 2006); and Thomas Slaughter, *The Natures of John and William Bartram* (New York: Knopf, 1996). The list of recent works related to (though not synonymous with) early American environmental history also expands if one includes agricultural history and historical geography. Happily, two notable examples are set in Potomac country: Lois Green Carr, Russell Menard, and Lorena Walsh, *Robert Cole's World: Agriculture and Society in Early Maryland* (Chapel Hill: University of North Carolina Press, 1991), and Warren Hofstra, *The Planting of New Virginia: Settlement and Landscape in the Shenandoah Valley* (Baltimore: Johns Hopkins University Press, 2004).

4. Christian Feest, "Virginia Algonquians," in Bruce Trigger, ed., *Handbook of North American Indians,* vol. 15, *Northeast* (Washington, D.C.: Smithsonian Institution, 1978), 254; Helen Rountree, *Pocahontas's People: The Powhatan Indians of Virginia through Four Centuries* (Norman: University of Oklahoma Press, 1990), 3, 10, 25; James Axtell, "The Rise and Fall of the Powhatan Empire," in *Natives and Newcomers: The Cultural Origins of North America* (New York: Oxford University Press, 2001), 233–58; Richard Dent, *Chesapeake Prehistory: Old Traditions, New Directions* (New York: Plenum, 1995), 280–81. For a more detailed critique of this assumption, see chapter 7 in this volume.

5. Alfred Crosby and William McNeill, who did much to draw to scholars' attention the importance of disease in history, were quite attentive to such details in their most pioneering works; see Crosby, *Ecological Imperialism,* and McNeill, *Plagues and Peoples* (New York: Doubleday, 1977). Some recent works also pay close attention to the timing and locations of specific epidemics; see, e.g., Daniel Richter, *The Ordeal of the Longhouse: The Peoples of the Iroquois League in the Era of European Colonization* (Chapel Hill: University of North Carolina Press, 1992); Richard White, *The Middle Ground: Indians, Empires, and Republics in the Great Lakes Region, 1650–1815*

(New York: Cambridge University Press, 1991); Thomas Hatley, *The Dividing Paths: Cherokees and South Carolinians through the Revolutionary Era* (New York: Oxford University Press, 1995); and Elizabeth Fenn, *Pox Americana: The Great Smallpox Epidemic of 1775–82* (New York: Hill and Wang, 2001). See also David Jones, "Virgin Soils Revisited," *WMQ* 60 (2003), 703–42, and Dean Snow and Kim Lamphear, "European Contact and Indian Depopulation in the Northeast: The Timing of the First Epidemics," *Ethnohistory* 35 (1988), 15–33.

6. Mart Stewart, "Environmental History: Profile of a Developing Field," *The History Teacher* 31 (1998), 361 (quotation; emphasis added). Nevertheless panoramic environmental histories continue to dominate the field's coverage of early America: Cronon's and Crosby's foundational works have been followed by Albert Cowdrey, *This Land, This South: An Environmental History* (Lexington: University of Kentucky Press, 1983); Donald Davis, *Where There Are Mountains: An Environmental History of the Southern Appalachians* (Athens: University of Georgia Press, 2000); Jack Temple Kirby, *Mockingbird Song: Ecological Landscapes of the South* (Chapel Hill: University of North Carolina Press, 2006); Timothy Silver, *A New Face on the Countryside: Indians, Colonists, and Slaves in South Atlantic Forests, 1500–1800* (New York: Cambridge University Press, 1990); and Gordon Whitney, *From Coastal Wilderness to Fruited Plain: A History of Environmental Change in Temperate North America, 1500 to the Present* (New York: Cambridge University Press, 1994).

7. The approach taken here is often labeled "bioregionalism," a term applying originally to the movement for sustainable, ecologically sensitive ways of living within specific landscapes, consistent with what nature *in that place* can sustain. These activist roots have sprouted diverse branches of inquiry in which bioregionalism is an analytical tool for understanding the place of human societies within specific local environments. See Gary Snyder's *Earth House Hold* (New York: New Directions Press, 1969) and *A Place in Space: Ethics, Aesthetics, and Watersheds* (Washington, D.C.: Counterpoint Press, 1995); Dan Flores, "Place: An Argument for Bioregional History," *Environmental History Review* 18 (1994), 1–18; and Michael McGinnis, ed., *Bioregionalism* (New York: Routledge, 1999). Excellent examples of this approach include Richard White, *The Organic Machine: The Remaking of the Columbia River* (New York: Hill and Wang, 1995), and Donald Worster, *Dust Bowl: The Southern Plains in the 1930s* (New York: Oxford University Press, 1979).

8. On knowing nature through labor, see Richard White, "'Are you an environmentalist or do you work for a living?': Work and Nature," in William Cronon, ed., *Uncommon Ground: Rethinking the Human Place in Nature* (New York: W. W. Norton, 1996). For an exemplary merging of broad processes in environmental history and a history of events, see Elliot West, *The Contested Plains: Indians, Goldseekers, and the Rush to Colorado* (Lawrence: University Press of Kansas, 1998).

9. Julian Steward, *Theory of Cultural Change: The Methodology of Multilinear Evolution* (Urbana: University of Illinois Press, 1955), 37 (quotation), which tends to emphasize how people adapt to the rest of nature, is nicely complemented by the great geographer Carl Sauer's emphasis on how people adapt and alter nature to suit themselves (see, e.g., "The Morphology of Landscape," in J. Leighly, ed., *Land and Life: A*

Selection from the Writings of Carl Ortwin Sauer (Berkeley: University of California Press, 1963), 315–50. For recent statements on the field of cultural ecology and related areas, see Carole Crumley, ed., *Historical Ecology: Cultural Knowledge and Changing Landscapes* (Santa Fe: School for American Research, 1994), and Paul Robbins, "Cultural Ecology," in James Duncan, Nuala Johnson, and Richard Schein, eds., *A Companion to Cultural Geography* (Malden, Mass.: Blackwell Publishing, 2004), 180–93.

10. My use of the term "landscape" and means of interpreting the landscapes of the Potomac country owe much to the work of the English scholar W. G. Hoskins and American geographers such as David Meinig. See Hoskins, *The Making of the English Landscape* (London: Hodder and Stoughton, 1955), and David Meinig, ed., *The Interpretation of Ordinary Landscapes: Geographical Essays* (New York: Oxford University Press, 1979).

11. C. S. Lewis, *The Abolition of Man* (New York: Macmillan, 1947), 35 (quotation). On the connections between environmental history and the study of social and political structures, see Stewart, "Environmental History," 354 (quotation); Alan Taylor, "Unnatural Inequalities: Social and Environmental Histories," *Environmental History* 1 (1996), 6–19; Arthur McEvoy, *The Fisherman's Problem: Ecology and Law in the California Fisheries, 1850–1890* (New York: Cambridge University Press, 1986), and Mike Davis, *Ecology of Fear: Los Angeles and the Imagination of Disaster* (New York: Vintage Books, 1998). For a broad application of this insight to the conquest of the Americas right up to the present day, see Donald Grinde and Bruce Johanson, *Ecocide of Native America: Environmental Destruction of Indian Lands and Peoples* (Santa Fe: Clear Light, 1995).

12. Lewis, *Abolition of Man*, 36–37 (quotation).

13. This focus means that less space is devoted to African American experiences than is customary in writings about the colonial Chesapeake. Beginning the narrative in the eighth century has a similar effect, since the widespread enslavement of Africans occurred only in the last of the eleven centuries covered here. Any work focusing on the eighteenth century, however, would have to place slavery at the center of the region's society, economy, and culture. Good entry points into the extensive literature on this subject include Allan Kulikoff, *Tobacco and Slaves: The Development of Southern Cultures in the Chesapeake, 1680–1800* (Chapel Hill: University of North Carolina Press, 1986); Edmund Morgan, *American Slavery, American Freedom: The Ordeal of Colonial Virginia* (New York: W. W. Norton, 1975); and Philip Morgan, *Slave Counterpoint: Black Culture in the Eighteenth-Century Chesapeake and Lowcountry* (Chapel Hill: University of North Carolina Press, 1998).

14. William Cronon, "The Trouble with Wilderness; Or, Getting Back to the Wrong Nature," in Cronon, *Uncommon Ground*, 89 (italics in the original), and White, *Organic Machine*, 111. See also Wendell Berry, *What Are People For?* (San Francisco: North Point Press, 1990).

15. See, e.g., Gary Snyder, "Is Nature Real," in *The Gary Snyder Reader: Prose, Poetry, and Translations* (Washington, D.C.: Counterpoint, 1999), 387–89, and Dave Foreman, *Confessions of an Eco-Warrior* (New York: Harmony Books, 1991), 69.

16. J. Donal Hughes, *American Indian Ecology* (El Paso: Texas Western Press, 1987),

1 (quotation); Vine Deloria, Jr., *We Talk, You Listen: New Tribes, New Turf* (New York: Macmillan, 1970), 186 (quotation; italics in original). This idea was also implicit in the practice of many curators of archaeological collections, who at one time commonly cataloged Indian remains and artifacts as part of "natural history"; see David Hurst Thomas, *Skull Wars: Kennewick Man, Archaeology, and the Battle for Native American Identity* (New York: Basic Books, 2000), ch. 6. I have no intention of arguing that Native American people did not, and do not, live in close relationship with nature; rather, I argue that many Europeans and colonists did as well, and, furthermore, that there was no single way in which Native (or European) people have lived within nature.

17. Peter Nabokov, *Where the Lightning Strikes: The Lives of American Indian Sacred Places* (New York: Viking Penguin, 2006); Paul Nadasdy, "Transcending the Debate over the Ecologically Noble Indian: Indigenous Peoples and Environmentalism," *Ethnohistory* 52 (2005), 291–331; and Robert Sullivan, *A Whale Hunt: Two Years on the Olympic Peninsula with the Makah and Their Canoe* (New York: Scribner, 2000). Charles Mann's populist *1491: New Revelations of the Americas before Columbus* (New York: Knopf, 2005) makes accessible a large body of anthropological and scientific evidence on this score. For more general treatments, see Michael Harkin and David Rich Lewis, eds., *Native Americans and the Environment: Perspectives on the Ecological Indian* (Lincoln: University of Nebraska Press, 2007), and Douglas Ubelaker, William Sturtevant, and Dennis Stanford, eds., *Handbook of North American Indians*, vol. 3, *Environment, Origins, and Population* (Washington, D.C.: Smithsonian Institution, 2006).

18. For a critique of this tendency, see Neal Salisbury, "The Indians' Old World: Native Americans and the Coming of Europeans," *WMQ* 53 (1996), 435–58. The problem lies not with any one book but with the overall pattern. See, e.g., the following books, all of which I happen to admire: Robert Weir, *Colonial South Carolina: A History* (Millwood, N.Y.: KTO Press, 1983); Richard Melvoin, *New England Outpost: War and Society in Colonial Deerfield* (New York: W. W. Norton, 1989); Wilma Dunaway, *The First American Frontier: Transition to Capitalism in Southern Appalachia, 1700–1860* (Chapel Hill: University of North Carolina Press, 1996); Silver, *A New Face on the Countryside;* James Axtell, *The Invasion Within: The Contest of Cultures in Colonial North America* (New York: Oxford University Press, 1985); and Rountree, *Pocahontas's People*. There are exceptions to this rule, such as Bruce Trigger, *Natives and Newcomers: Canada's "Heroic Age" Reconsidered* (Kingston: McGill–Queens University Press, 1985), and West, *Contested Plains*. Within the Chesapeake Bay region, Stephen Potter's *Commoners, Tribute, and Chiefs: The Development of Algonquian Culture in the Potomac Valley* (Charlottesville: University Press of Virginia, 1993) and Helen Rountree and E. Randolph Turner III, *Before and After Jamestown: Virginia's Powhatans and Their Predecessors* (Gainesville: University Press of Florida, 2002), are each the fruits of decades of research, and they do bridge "prehistory" and history. Their concerns, however, differ from my own; they are held together by a focus on ethnogenesis and material culture rather than on environment and place, and they do not much concern themselves with how Native Americans shaped colonial societies.

Chapter 1. Ahone's Waters

1. Richard Dent, *Chesapeake Prehistory: Old Traditions, New Directions* (New York: Plenum, 1995), 194–200; Stuart Fiedel, John Bedell, and Charles LeeDecker, *Cohongorooto: The Potomac above the Falls; Archaeological Identification and Evaluation Study of C&O Canal National Historical Park*, vol. 1 (Washington, D.C.: Lewis Berger Group, 2005), 8–23.

2. This and the following paragraphs are synthesized from John Bratton et al., "Birth of the Modern Chesapeake Bay Estuary between 7.4 and 8.2 ka and Implications for Global Sea-Level Rise," in *Geo-Marine Letters* 22 (March 2003), 188–97; George Fisher and Jerry Schubel, "The Chesapeake Ecosystem: Its Geologic Heritage," in Philip Curtin, Grace Brush, and George Fisher, eds., *Discovering the Chesapeake: The History of an Ecosystem* (Baltimore: Johns Hopkins University Press, 2001), 1–14; John Kutzbach and Thompson Webb III, "Climate and Climate History in the Chesapeake Bay Region," in ibid., 15–39; Grace Brush, "Forests before and after the Colonial Encounter," in ibid., 40–59; Donald Pritchard and Jerry Schubel, "Human Influences on the Physical Characteristics of the Chesapeake Bay," in ibid., 60–83; David Steadman, "A Long-term History of Terrestrial Birds and Mammals in the Chesapeake-Susquehanna Watershed," in ibid., 83–108; Henry Miller, "Living along the 'Great Shellfish Bay': The Relationship between Prehistoric Peoples and the Chesapeake," in ibid., 109–126; Fiedel, Bedell, and LeeDecker, *Cohongorooto*; and Dent, *Chesapeake Prehistory*, ch. 3 and 184–200.

3. Ruth Harris DeFries, "Sedimentation Patterns in the Potomac Estuary since European Settlement: A Palynological Approach" (Ph.D. diss., Johns Hopkins University, 1981), 5.

4. White-water kayakers' guide "Paddling the Potomac," at www.gorp.com.

5. DeFries, "Sedimentation Patterns," 5.

6. Laurie Steponaitis, "Prehistoric Settlement Patterns in the Lower Patuxent Drainage, Maryland" (Ph.D. diss., Binghamton University, 1987), 1–31, 264–68; Jay Custer, "Coastal Adaptations in the Middle Atlantic Region," *Archaeology of Eastern North America* 16 (1988), 121–36; Michael Stewart, "Observations on the Middle Woodland Period of Virginia: A Middle Atlantic Perspective," in Theodore Reinhart and Mary Ellen Hodges, eds., *Middle and Late Woodland Research in Virginia: A Synthesis* (Richmond: Dietz Press, 1992), 12–15; Stephen Potter, *Commoners, Tribute, and Chiefs: The Development of Algonquian Culture in the Potomac Valley* (Charlottesville: University Press of Virginia, 1993), 62–77, 100–114, 138–41; Michael Johnson, "Middle and Late Woodland Settlement Systems in the Interior Fall Zone of the Potomac Valley: Not a Live Oyster in Sight," *North American Archaeologist* 12 (1991), 29–60; Dennis Curry and Maureen Kavanaugh, "The Middle to Late Woodland Transition in Maryland," *North American Archaeologist* 12 (1991), 16–22; Dennis Blanton, "Middle Woodland Settlement Systems," in Reinhart and Hodges, *Middle and Late Woodland Research*, 69–71; J. Michael Stewart, "Prehistoric Settlement and Subsistence Patterns and the Testing of Predictive Site Location Models in the Great Valley of Maryland" (Ph.D. diss., Catholic University of America, 1980), 120, 318, 375; Paul Green, "Forager-

Farmer Transitions in Coastal Prehistory" (Ph.D. diss., University of North Carolina, 1987), ch. 1; William Gardner, *Lost Arrowheads and Broken Pottery: Traces of Indians in the Shenandoah Valley* (Front Royal, Va.: Thunderbird Museum, 1986), 73–75.

7. Marshall Sahlins, *Stone Age Economics* (Chicago: Aldine-Atherton, 1972), 1 (quotation); Elman Service, *Primitive Social Organization*, 2nd ed. (New York: Random House, 1971).

8. Blanton, "Middle Woodland Settlement Systems"; Dent, *Chesapeake Prehistory*, 240–42; William Gardner, "Early and Middle Woodland in the Middle Atlantic: An Overview," in Roger Moeller, ed., *Practicing Environmental Archaeology: Methods and Interpretations* (Washington, Conn.: American Indian Archaeological Institute, 1982), 53–86; Johnson, "Middle and Late Woodland Settlement Systems"; Stewart, "Observations," 12–15; Keith Egloff, "Development and Impact of Ceramics in Virginia," in Theodore Reinhart and Mary Hodges, eds., *Late Archaic and Early Woodland Research in Virginia: A Synthesis* (Richmond: Dietz Press, 1991), 243–52.

9. For oystering on the outer coastal plain, see Potter, *Commoners, Tribute, and Chiefs*, 46–47, 50, 68–75, 100; Gregory Waselkov, "Shellfish Gathering and Shell Midden Archaeology" (Ph.D. diss., University of North Carolina, 1982). For fishing camps and anadromous fish runs on the inner coastal plain, see Alice Lippson et al., *Environmental Atlas of the Potomac Estuary* (Baltimore: Johns Hopkins University Press, 1981), ch. 8; Johnson, "Middle and Late Woodland Settlement Systems," 54–58; Gardner, "Early and Middle Woodland," 60, 78, fig. 2; and E. Randolph Turner and Helen Rountree, "The Powhatan Paramount Chiefdom in Virginia," in Elsa Redmond, ed., *Chiefdoms and Chieftaincy in the Americas* (Gainesville: University Press of Florida, 1998), 276. For the interior, see Fiedel, Bedell, and LeeDecker, *Cohongorooto*, 33–35; Jeffrey Hantman and Michael Klein, "Middle and Late Woodland Archaeology in Piedmont Virginia," in Reinhart and Hodges, *Middle and Late Woodland Research*, 143–45; Stewart, "Prehistoric Settlement," 373, 380–83; Maureen Kavanaugh, *Archeological Resources of the Monocacy River Region* (Crownsville, Md.: Maryland Historical Trust, 1982), 63–69; Gardner, *Lost Arrowheads*, 73–77.

10. Potter, *Commoners, Tribute, and Chiefs*, ch. 2 (quotations on 71, 77).

11. Archaeologists struggle to categorize the ceramics of western Maryland, noting affinities with ceramics from the Shenandoah, Susquehanna, and Ohio valleys. J. Sanderson Stevens, "Examination of Shepard and Potomac Creek Wares at Montgomery Complex Site (44LD521)," *Journal of Middle Atlantic Archaeology* 14 (1998), 96; Frederic Gleach, "A Rose by Any Other Name: Questions on Mockley Chronology," *Journal of Middle Atlantic Archaeology* 4 (1988), 94; Jay Custer, *Delaware Prehistoric Archaeology: An Ecological Approach* (Newark: University of Delaware Press, 1984), 181; Curry and Kavanaugh, "Middle to Late Woodland Transition," 11–12, 16–21; Stewart, "Prehistoric Settlement," 376–80; Stewart, "Rhyolite Quarry and Quarry-Related Sites in Maryland and Pennsylvania," *Archaeology of Eastern North America* 15 (1987), 54.

12. Stewart, "Rhyolite Quarry"; Curry and Kavanaugh, "Middle to Late Woodland Transition," 13–21; Kavanaugh, *Archeological Resources*, 68; Stewart, "Prehistoric Settlement," 58–59, 78–80, and ch. 5; Douglas McLearen, "Virginia's Middle Woodland

Period: A Regional Perspective," in Reinhart and Hodges, *Middle and Late Woodland Research,* 42.

13. Blanton, "Middle Woodland Settlement Systems," 82–87; McLearen, "Virginia's Middle Woodland Period," 43–44; Stewart, "Observations," 13–15.

14. The key word here is "relatively"; as Martin Gallivan notes, "ethnographies of supposedly egalitarian hunter-gatherer and peasant communities demonstrate that true equality may be a social impossibility." Gallivan, *James River Chiefdoms: The Rise of Social Inequality in the Chesapeake* (Lincoln: University of Nebraska Press, 2003), 45.

15. Potter, *Commoners, Tribute, and Chiefs,* 91–94; Steponaitis, "Prehistoric Settlement Patterns," 269–75; Kavanaugh, *Archeological Resources,* 66–69; Curry and Kavanaugh, "Middle to Late Woodland Transition," 11, 15, 24; Gardner, *Lost Arrowheads,* 73–78; Stewart, "Prehistoric Settlement," 120, 375, 382–84.

Chapter 2. Foragers into Farmers

1. Jane Buikstra, "Diet and Disease in Late Prehistory," in John Verano and Douglas Ubelaker, eds., *Disease and Demography in the Americas* (Washington, D.C.: Smithsonian Institution Press, 1992), 87–102; Linda Cordell and Bruce Smith, "Indigenous Farmers," in Bruce Trigger and Wilcomb Washburn, eds., *The Cambridge History of the Native Peoples of the Americas,* vol. 1, *North America,* pt. 1 (New York: Cambridge University Press, 1996), 234–50; John F. Doebley, Major M. Goodman, and Charles W. Stuber, "Exceptional Genetic Divergence of Northern Flint Corn," *American Journal of Botany* 73 (January 1986), 64–69; Jon Muller, "Lower Ohio Valley Emergent Horticulture and Mississippian," in William Keegan, ed., *Emergent Horticultural Economies of the Eastern Woodlands* (Carbondale: Center for Archaeological Investigations, Southern Illinois University at Carbondale, 1987), 243–74; Bruce Smith, "Origins of Agriculture in Eastern North America," *Science* 246 (1989), 1566–71; R. Michael Stewart, *Prehistoric Farmers of the Susquehanna Valley: Clemson Island Culture and the St. Anthony Site* (Bethlehem, Conn.: Archaeological Services, 1992), 26–27, 188, 196–97. On the earliest uses of maize and squash in use in the northeast, see Martin Gallivan and Justine McKnight, "Paleoethnobotany of Native Societies in the Chesapeake: A Regional Synthesis and Revised Chronology," Annual Meeting of the Society for American Archaeology, Austin, Texas, April 2007, and J. P. Hart, "A New History of Maize-Bean-Squash Agriculture in the Northeast," in S. W. Neusius and G. T. Gross, eds., *Seeking America's Past: An Introduction to North American Archaeology* (New York: Oxford University Press, 2006), 600–608.

2. Paul Green, "Forager-Farmer Transitions in Coastal Prehistory" (Ph.D. diss., University of North Carolina, 1987), 1–9, 26–31; Dennis Curry and Maureen Kavanaugh, "The Middle to Late Woodland Transition in Maryland," *North American Archaeologist* 12 (1991), 21–26; Laurie Steponaitis, "Prehistoric Settlement Patterns in the Lower Patuxent Drainage, Maryland" (Ph.D. diss., Binghamton University, 1987), 2, 269–76, 287–88; Joan Walker and Glenda Miller, "Life on the Levee: The Late Woodland Period in the Northern Great Valley of Virginia," in Theodore Reinhart and Mary

Ellen Hodges, eds., *Middle and Late Woodland Research in Virginia: A Synthesis* (Richmond: Dietz Press, 1992), 166; William Gardner, *Lost Arrowheads and Broken Pottery: Traces of Indians in the Shenandoah Valley* (Front Royal, Va.: Thunderbird Museum, 1986), 77–79; Stephen Potter, *Commoners, Tribute, and Chiefs: The Development of Algonquian Culture in the Potomac Valley* (Charlottesville: University Press of Virginia, 1993), 91–100, 143–45. A few corn kernels, squash, beans, and other seeds have been radiocarbon dated to between 900 and 1300: a single maize kernel at a Shenandoah Valley site, corn and beans at another Shenandoah excavation, and another four kernels at Martin's Meadow in the Hagerstown Valley. Other possible finds include bean seeds, squash, and corn kernels at sites scattered along the Monocacy and lower Potomac rivers, but most of these likely date to post-1300 occupations. Walker and Miller, "Life on the Levee," 168–70; Potter, *Commoners, Tribute, and Chiefs*, 138–45, 170–73 (esp. 144–45); J. Sanderson Stevens, "Examination of Shepard and Potomac Creek Wares at Montgomery Complex Site (44LD521)," *Journal of Middle Atlantic Archaeology* 14 (1998), 98–102 (on refinements to dating); Michael Klein, "An Absolute Seriation Approach to Ceramic Chronology in the Roanoke, Potomac and James River Valleys, Virginia and Maryland" (Ph.D. diss., University of Virginia, 1994), 70.

3. Potter, *Commoners, Tribute, and Chiefs*, 170 (quotation).

4. Joan Chase, "A Comparison of Signs of Nutritional Stress in Prehistoric Populations of the Potomac Piedmont and Coastal Plain" (Ph.D. diss., American University, 1988), ch. 6.

5. Stevens, "Examination," and Klein, "Absolute Seriation Approach," 15–28, 326–49, trace these evolutions in ceramic technology.

6. Walker and Miller, "Life on the Levee," 165–67; R. Michael Stewart, "Prehistoric Settlement and Subsistence Patterns and the Testing of Predictive Site Location Models in the Great Valley of Maryland" (Ph.D. diss., Catholic University of America, 1980), 396–97; Steponaitis, "Prehistoric Settlement Patterns," 288; Curry and Kavanaugh, "Middle to Late Woodland Transition"; Gardner, *Lost Arrowheads*, 75–79; Barbara Little, "An Overview of Economic Archeology in the Middle Atlantic. Part I: Subsistence," *Maryland Archeology* 32 (1996), 22–34; Potter, *Commoners, Tribute, and Chiefs*, 77–81, 100–101, 141–43; Maureen Kavanaugh, *Archeological Resources of the Monocacy River Region* (Crownsville: Maryland Historical Trust, 1982), 62–82.

7. Marshall Sahlins, *Stone Age Economics* (Chicago: Aldine-Atherton, 1972), ch. 1; John Blitz, "Adoption of the Bow in Prehistoric North America," in *North American Archaeologist* 9 (1988), 123–47. On climate, see Grace Brush, "Forests before and after the Colonial Encounter," in Philip Curtin, Grace Brush, and George Fisher, eds., *Discovering the Chesapeake: The History of an Ecosystem* (Baltimore: Johns Hopkins University Press, 2001), 51–54.

8. On dietary diversity, see Elizabeth Moore, "Prehistoric Economies during the Late Woodland Period of the Potomac Valley: An Examination of Animal Resource Utilization" (Ph.D. diss., American University, 1994); Christine Jirikowic, "The Hughes Village Site: A Late Woodland Community in the Potomac Piedmont" (Ph.D. diss., American University, 1995); Green, "Forager-Farmer Transitions," 101–4; Jay Custer, "Settlement-Subsistence Systems in Augusta County, Virginia," *Quarterly Bulletin of*

the Archeological Society of Virginia 35 (1980), 1–27; Debra Gold, *The Bioarchaeology of Virginia Burial Mounds* (Tuscaloosa: University of Alabama Press, 2004), 86–98, 123–26; Michael Hoffman and R. W. Foss, "Blue Ridge Prehistory—A General Perspective," *Quarterly Bulletin of the Archeological Society of Virginia* 34 (1980), 185–210. On ceramic technologies, see Walker and Miller, "Life on the Levee," 168–171; Klein, "Absolute Seriation Approach," 15–28; Stevens, "Examination." On teeth and skeletal remains, see Chase, "Comparison of Signs of Nutritional Stress," ch. 6.

9. Potter, *Commoners, Tribute, and Chiefs,* 79, 100, 141; Curry and Kavanaugh, "Middle to Late Woodland Transition," 13–24.

10. Wayne Clark, "Origins of the Piscataway and Related Indian Cultures," *MdHM* 75 (1980), 8, 13–16; Curry and Kavanaugh, "Middle to Late Woodland Transition," 3–38; Green, "Forager-Farmer Transitions," 106, 143; Klein, "Absolute Seriation Approach," 26, 85–86; Potter, *Commoners, Tribute, and Chiefs,* 77–81, 103–48; Richard Slattery and Douglas Woodward, *The Montgomery Focus* (Myersville: Archeological Society of Maryland, 1992), 157. The mounds dating to this period can be found not only in the upper Shenandoah Valley but also in adjoining areas of the Piedmont to the south of the Potomac. Gold, *Bioarchaeology of Virginia Burial Mounds,* ch. 2.

11. William Cronon, *Changes in the Land: Indians, Colonists, and the Ecology of New England* (New York: Hill and Wang, 1983), 41.

12. Concerns about global warming have inspired an explosion of research on climate history, which has complicated earlier portrayals of the Little Ice Age as a relatively uniform coldsnap. Current research on climate change points to switching mechanisms connected to oceanic currents (and to the associated atmospheric circulation patterns). The best-known of these affecting the Potomac basin are the North Atlantic Oscillation and the Jet Stream, relative to which the Chesapeake occupies a transitional position. The Little Ice Age, then, was characterized not by numbing cold, year after year, but rather by a greater tendency toward switching mechanisms that, when activated, caused lower average temperatures and shorter growing seasons. Thus even in the midst of the Little Ice Age some years were hot and dry; others were warm and wet; and still others were cold and wet.

Historians have just begun to take advantage of the new climate research. Though scholars often cite David W. Stahle et al., "The Lost Colony and Jamestown Droughts," *Science* 280, no. 5363 (24 April 1998), 564–67, there is much more still to absorb. Good entry points into this literature include H. H. Lamb, *Climate, History, and the Modern World* (New York: Routledge, 1995); Brian Fagan's adroit popularization, *The Little Ice Age: How Climate Made History, 1300–1850* (New York: Basic Books, 2000); and Thomas Cronin, *Principles of Paleoclimatology* (New York: Columbia University Press, 1999). For studies specific to the Chesapeake region, see Cronin et al., "Medieval Warm Period, Little Ice Age and 20th Century Temperature Variability from Chesapeake Bay," in *Global and Planetary Change* 36 (2003), 17–29; Debra Willard, Thomas Cronin, and Stacey Verardo, "Late-Holocene Climate and Ecosystem History from Chesapeake Bay Sediment Cores, USA," *The Holocene* 13, no. 2 (2003), 201–14; Grace S. Brush, "Natural and Anthropogenic Changes in Chesapeake Bay during the Last 1000 Years," *Human and Ecological Risk Assessment* 7 (October 2001), 1283–96; John

Kutzbach and Thompson Webb III, "Climate and Climate History in the Chesapeake Bay Region," in Curtin, Brush, and Fisher, *Discovering the Chesapeake*, 15–39; "Effects of Climate Variability and Human Activities on Chesapeake Bay and the Implications for Ecosystem Restoration," U.S.G.S. Fact Sheet FS-00-116 (Reston, Va.: U.S. Geological Survey, 2000); and Dennis Blanton, "The Climate Factor in Late Prehistoric and Post-Contact Human Affairs," in Dennis Blanton and Julia King, eds., *Indian and European Contact in Context: The Mid-Atlantic Region* (Gainesville: University Press of Florida, 2004), 6–21.

13. Steponaitis, "Prehistoric Settlement Patterns," ch. 10; Potter, *Commoners, Tribute, and Chiefs*, 100–14; Curry and Kavanaugh, "Middle to Late Woodland Transition," 24.

14. E. Randolph Turner estimates that maize accounted for 75 percent of the calories in the Algonquian diet in 1608. A more likely figure would be well under 50 percent, but the precise figure is less important than the fact that communities now depended upon domesticated plants. Turner, "An Archaeological and Ethnohistorical Study on the Evolution of Rank Societies in the Virginia Coastal Plain" (Ph.D. diss., Pennsylvania State University, 1976), 160, 188–92, 254–57; Potter, *Commoners, Tribute, and Chiefs*, 31–40; Helen Rountree, *The Powhatan Indians of Virginia: Their Traditional Culture* (Norman: University of Oklahoma Press, 1989), 45–46; personal communication from Helen Rountree, October 2001. New bioarchaeological technology has yielded mixed results: while the most current testing methods do seem to confirm that Turner's figures are too high for 1608, let alone for the fourteenth and fifteenth centuries, they are better at detecting the durable shells and pits from wild nuts and fruits than the soft remains of roots, tubers, legumes, and grains; thus they tend to understate the significance of corn, beans, and squash. See Justine McKnight, "Potomac Creek Archaeology: Analysis of Flotation-Recovered and Hand-Collected Plant Remains from the Potomac Creek Site (44ST2)," in Dennis Blanton et al., *The Potomac Creek Site (44ST2) Revisited* (Richmond: Virginia Department of Historic Resources, 1999), appendix B; and Lisa Kealhofer, "The Potomac Creek Site (44ST2): Phytolith Analysis," in ibid., appendix D.

15. Dee Cabaniss Pederson et al., "Medieval Warming, Little Ice Age, and European Impact on the Environment during the Last Millennium in the Lower Hudson Valley, New York, USA," *Quarternary Research* 63 (2005), 238–49; Green, "Forager-Farmer Transitions," 53, 104–6, 139–43; Stewart, *Prehistoric Farmers*, 194, 200–202; Barry Kent, *Susquehanna's Indians* (Harrisburg: Pennsylvania Historical and Museum Commission, 1984), 14–21; Dean Snow, *The Iroquois* (Malden, Mass.: Blackwell Publishers, 1994), 26–46. Why would people along the Potomac be slower to make a full commitment to agriculture? The most likely explanation is that the Chesapeake Bay estuary naturally supported denser populations than could the smaller fish runs and relatively less extensive and less varied wetlands used by the northern Iroquoians, and that Potomac residents thus had less need of intensified plant husbandry. Personal communication from Stephen R. Potter, National Park Service, 8 June 2007.

16. Irving Rouse, *Migrations in History: Inferring Population Movement from Cultural Remains* (New Haven: Yale University Press, 1986).

17. This debate can be traced in Potter, *Commoners, Tribute, and Chiefs,* 119–38, and Blanton et al., *Potomac Creek Site,* 8–12, 98–99, 102–5. See also Jirikowic, "Hughes Village Site," 300–302.

18. Turner, "The Virginia Coastal Plain during the Late Woodland Period," in Reinhart and Hodges, *Middle and Late Woodland Research,* 106–8; Walker and Miller, "Life on the Levee"; Curry and Kavanaugh, "Middle to Late Woodland Transition," 18–24; Blanton et al., *Potomac Creek Site;* Green, "Forager-Farmer Transitions," 139–43; Kavanaugh, *Archeological Resources,* 79–81; Michael Klein and Douglas Sanford, "Analytical Scale and Archaeological Perspectives on the Contact Era in the Northern Neck of Virginia," in Blanton and King, *Indian and European Contact,* 57–58.

19. Blanton et al., *Potomac Creek Site,* ch. 5 (quotation on 92). The decline in the area enclosed by the palisades is calculated from figures on pp. 93, 97.

20. Blanton et al., *Potomac Creek Site,* ch. 5 and appendices B–D; Potter, *Commoners, Tribute, and Chiefs,* 119–25. Maize was ubiquitous at Potomac Creek but did not appear in large quantities, which reflects both the varied nature of the villagers' diet (in which domesticated plants accounted for only a minority of all calories—albeit a substantial and strategically important minority) and the fact that starchy grains and processed foods are difficult to detect using even the most advanced bioarchaeological technology.

21. Richard Dent, *Chesapeake Prehistory: Old Traditions, New Directions* (New York: Plenum, 1995), 250–51; Walker and Miller, "Life on the Levee," 167, 172–82; Gardner, *Lost Arrowheads,* 88–90; Stevens, "Examination," 123; Kavanaugh, *Archeological Resources,* 77–82; Potter, *Commoners, Tribute, and Chiefs,* 130–31, 147–48, 153–55; Klein, "Absolute Seriation Approach," 114–15; and Stewart, *Prehistoric Farmers,* 201–5; Jirikowic, "Hughes Village Site," 303, 313–14.

22. Potter, *Commoners, Tribute, and Chiefs,* 83, 158–61; Donna Boyd and C. Clifford Boyd, "Late Woodland Mortuary Variability," in Reinhart and Hodges, *Middle and Late Woodland Research,* 256–64; Gardner, *Lost Arrowheads,* 90–92; Helen Rountree and Thomas Davidson, *Eastern Shore Indians of Virginia and Maryland* (Charlottesville: University Press of Virginia, 1997), 23; Walker and Miller, "Life on the Levee," 175, 181. On trade, gifting, power, and diplomacy in the eastern woodlands, see James Axtell, *The Invasion Within: The Contest of Cultures in Colonial North America* (New York: Oxford University Press, 1985), 88–89, and Richard White, *The Middle Ground: Indians, Empires, and Republics in the Great Lakes Region, 1650–1815* (New York: Cambridge University Press, 1991), 103, 180–82. For broader perspectives, see Peter Burke, *History and Social Theory* (Ithaca: Cornell University Press, 1992), 70–73, and Sahlins, *Stone Age Economics,* chs. 4–6.

23. For evocative descriptions of the region's aquatic life, see William Warner, *Beautiful Swimmers: Watermen, Crabs and the Chesapeake Bay* (Baltimore: Johns Hopkins University Press, 1976); Alice Lippson and Robert Lippson, *Life in the Chesapeake Bay,* 2nd ed. (Baltimore: Johns Hopkins University Press, 1997); and Jack Wennersten, *Leaning Sycamores: Natural Worlds of the Upper Potomac* (Baltimore: Johns Hopkins University Press, 1996).

24. John Smith, *A Map of Virginia,* in *CWCJS* 1: 18, 159, 162–64 (quotations).

25. Smith, *Map*, 156–57 (quotations); Robert Beverley, *The History and Present State of Virginia*, ed. Louis B. Wright (Chapel Hill: University of North Carolina Press, 1947), 211 (quotations); Stanley Pargellis, "The Indians of Virginia," *WMQ* 16 (1959), 241; Thomas Glover, *An Account of Virginia, its situation, temperature, productions, inhabitants, and their manner of planting and ordering tobacco*, Extracted from the Royal Society of London, Philosophical Transactions, vol. 2, no. 126, 20 June 1676 (repr. Oxford: B. H. Blackwell, 1904), 633. William Strachey, *The Historie of Travell into Virginia Britania* (1612), ed. Louis B. Wright and Virginia Freund, Works Issued by the Hakluyt Society, 2nd series, no. 105 (London: Hakluyt Society, 1953),183, 186, 190, 202–3.

26. Henry Spelman, "Relation of Virginia," in Edward Arber and A. G. Bradley, eds., *Travels and Works of Captain John Smith, 1580–1631* (Edinburgh: John Grant, 1910), cvi–cvii; Smith, *Map*, 164 (quotation); Strachey, *Historie*, 34, 82, 114; Beverley, *History*, 154–56.

27. Quotations from Samuel Purchas, *Purchas his pilgrimage, or Relations of the world and the religions observed in al ages and places discovered, from the Creation unto this present*, 3rd ed. (London: William Stansby for Henry Fetherstone, 1617), 954, and Spelman, "Relation," cxi–cxii. See also Smith, *Map*, 163–65; Strachey, *Historie*, 125.

28. Joseph Ewan and Nesta Ewan, eds., *John Banister and His Natural History of Virginia* (Urbana: University of Illinois Press, 1970), 42; Andrew White, "A Briefe Relation of the Voyage Unto Maryland" (1634), in Clayton Hall, ed., *Narratives of Early Maryland, 1633–1634* (New York: Charles Scribner's Sons, 1910), 43–44; "A Relation of Maryland," in ibid., 86; Spelman, "Relation," cvi; Smith, *Map*, 161–62 (quotations), 245; Strachey, *Historie*, 78, 115, 188, 207; Potter, *Commoners, Tribute, and Chiefs*, 24–26.

29. John Smith, *The Proceedings of the English Colonie in Virginia*, in *CWCJS* 1: 39–40, 79; Smith, *Map*, 150–51, 157–58, 163, 217, 245, 250, 256–57; Smith, *The Generall Historie of Virginia, the Somer Iles, and New England*, in *CWCJS* 2: 194; Beverley, *History*, 153–54; [Gabriel Archer], "Description of the People," in Philip Barbour, ed., *The Jamestown Voyages under the First Charter, 1606–1609* (Cambridge: Hakluyt Society, 1969), 136: 103; "Francis Perkins to a Friend in England," in ibid., 160; Strachey, *Historie*, 128; White, "Briefe Relation," 40–45.

30. For witnesses to hunting birds, see [Archer], "Description of the People," 103; Beverley, *History*, 154–55; Smith, *Proceedings*, 245; Alexander Whitaker, "Part of a Tractate written at Henrico in Virginia," in Samuel Purchas, *Hakluytus Posthumus; or, Purchas His Pilgrimes . . .* (London: Henry Fetherstone, 1625; repr. Glasgow: J. MacLehose and Sons, 1905–1907), 19: 110–11; John Lawson, *A New Voyage to Carolina* (1709), ed. Hugh Lefler (Chapel Hill: University of North Carolina Press, 1967), 50. On clothing: Beverley, *History*, 161–64. On the plentitude of fowl, see Smith, *Map*, 157; Francis Perkins to a Friend in England, 28 March 1608, in Barbour, *Jamestown Voyages*, 136: 160; "Relation of Maryland," 80; White, "Briefe Relation," 45; Ralph Hamor, "Notes of Virginian Affaires," in Purchas, *Hakluytus Posthumus*, 19: 97; *A Perfect Description of Virginia, being a full and true relation of the present state of the plantation . . . being sent from Virginia, at the request of a gentleman of worthy note, who desired to know the true state of Virginia* (London: Richard Wodenoth, 1649), 18. On the preferred habitats of

waterfowl, see Alice Lippson et al., *Environmental Atlas of the Potomac Estuary* (Baltimore: Johns Hopkins University Press, 1981), ch. 9.

31. Detailed testimony about the use of specific wild plants is hard to come by, so one must make inferences based on the availability of plants and slivers of evidence from written records. E.g., arrow arum and arrowheads (tuckahoe) are available year-round, are invariably found in large quantities in freshwater marshes near Potomac village sites, and according to Smith were eaten in June, July, and August. But Tuckahoe roots are actually at their best (and starchiest) in the late winter and early spring, when villagers otherwise lacked a high-calorie carbohydrate complement to their protein-rich winter diet. See Rountree, *Powhatan Indians*, 52–53.

32. Lippson et al., *Environmental Atlas*, ch. 8 and folio map 8; Smith, *Map*, 148, 228 (quotation); Smith, *Proceedings*, 47; Beverley, *History*, 146–51 (quotation on 146); White, "Briefe Relation," 41; Glover, *Account of Virginia*, 602–3; "Relation of Maryland," 80; John Hammond, "Leah and Rachel, Or, The Two Fruitfull Sisters Virginia and Mary-Land" (1656), in Hall, *Narratives*, 29.

33. Shad and rockfish (striped bass) shun the tributaries, spawning instead in shallow freshwater flats; they would have been particularly susceptible to entrapment in tidal pound-style weirs. In contrast, alewives and herrings spawn far up the tributaries, finding their way into improbably small creeks. They can be caught with dipnets, and the shallow waters and swift currents along their migration routes likely lent themselves to V-shaped fish traps. White and yellow perch lay their eggs in the shallows of freshwater tributaries of the Potomac, which called for all three types of fish traps or weirs, depending upon the current and width of the tributary at the places through which they passed. Smith, *Map*, 162–64; Strachey, *Historie*, 74–75, 127; Beverley, *History*, 148–51; [Archer], "Description of the People," 103; Hammond, "Leah and Rachel," 291; Lippson et al., *Environmental Atlas*, 164–79.

34. Rountree, *Powhatan Indians*, 35–38; Strachey, *Historie*, 78–79; Beverley, *History*, 178–84; Smith, *Map*, 158; Gabriel Archer, "Relatyon of the Discovery of Our River," in Barbour, *Jamestown Voyages*, 136: 91.

35. White, "Briefe Relation," 43; Strachey, *Historie*, 100, 102; Smith, *Map*, 169–71; Smith, *Generall Historie*, 144; "Carving Gives Early View of Virginia Hunt Country," *Washington Post*, 8 May 2002, B3.

36. Lippson et al., *Environmental Atlas*, 126–34, 165–80; Gabriel Archer, "Description of the River and Country," in Barbour, *Jamestown Voyages*, 136: 99, 103 (quotation); Archer, "Relatyon," 82–84, 89–91; John Smith, *A True Relation of Such Occurences and Accidents of Noate as Hath Hapned in Virginia*, in *CWCJS* 1: 29; Smith, *Map*, 152–53, 162; George Percy, "Observations Gathered out of a Discourse of the Plantation of the Southern Colonie in Virginia by the English in 1606," in Barbour, *Jamestown Voyages*, 136: 141; "Relation of Maryland," 79–80.

37. John P. Hart, David Asch, C. Margaret Scarry, and Gary Crawford, "The Age of the Common Bean (Phaseolus vulgaris L.) in the Northern Eastern Woodlands of North America," *Antiquity* 76, no. 292 (2002), 377–83; Blanton et al., *Potomac Creek Site*, appendices B, D.

38. Smith, *Map*, 157–58, 162; Beverley, *History*, 141–45; "Relation of Maryland," 73

(corn in the fields on 27 March, or early April by the modern calendar); Percy, "Observations," 137; Archer, "Relatyon," 84, 89; Spelman, "Relation," cxi–cxii; Strachey, *Historie,* 75.

39. Smith, *Map,* 157.

40. Archer, "Relatyon," 83, 92; Strachey, *Historie,* 128; Smith, *Map,* 151, 162; Smith, *Generall Historie,* 289; Smith, *True Relation,* 29; White, "Briefe Relation," 44; Glover, *Account of Virginia,* 632; Potter, *Commoners, Tribute, and Chiefs,* 92–100, 102.

41. Smith, *Map,* 153–54, 162 (quotation); Strachey, *Historie,* 120, 122; Beverley, *History,* 181; Helen Rountree, "Powhatan Indian Women: The People Captain John Smith Barely Saw," *Ethnohistory* 45 (1998), 3, 13–15; Lippson et al., *Environmental Atlas,* 88–90, folio map 4.

42. Spelman, "Relation," cvi; Beverley, *History,* 146–51 (quotation on 149); Smith, *Map,* 146–48, 162–64; "Letter from the Council," in *Jamestown Voyages,* 136: 79; Lippson et al., *Environmental Atlas,* ch. 8.

43. Smith, *Map,* 156–58; Henry Fleet, "A Brief Journal of a Voyage Made in the Bark Virginia, to Virginia and Other Parts of the Continent of America," in Edward Neill, ed., *The Founders of Maryland as Portrayed in Manuscripts, Provincial Records and Early Documents* (Albany: J. Munsell, 1876), 32; Strachey, *Historie,* 79–80; Smith, *True Relation,* 35; John Smith, *Advertisements for the Unexperienced Planters of New England, or Anywhere,* in *CWCJS* 3: 289; "Relation of Maryland," 80; Clifford Lewis and Albert Loomie, *The Spanish Jesuit Mission in Virginia, 1570–1572* (Chapel Hill: University of North Carolina Press, 1953), 90.

44. "Relation of Maryland," 82 (quotation); Strachey, *Historie,* 80–81, 115; Smith, *Map,* 153, 156–58; Beverley, *History,* 143 (quotation), 178; White, "Brief Relation," 44; Percy, "Observations," 142; Potter, *Commoners, Tribute, and Chiefs,* 39–40.

45. Blanton et al., *Potomac Creek Site,* 92–98; Robert Stephenson, Alice Ferguson, and Henry Ferguson, *The Accokeek Creek Site: A Middle Atlantic Seaboard Culture Sequence* (Ann Arbor: University of Michigan, 1963); Dent, *Chesapeake Prehistory,* 249–51, 281–83; Potter, *Commoners, Tribute, and Chiefs,* 45–46; Beverley, *History,* 177 (quotation).

46. On the connections between copper, beads, and political authority, see chapter 3 in this volume. On the increasing incidence of these goods in the archaeological record, see Boyd and Boyd, "Late Woodland Mortuary Variability," 256–57, and Klein and Sanford, "Analytical Scale and Archaeological Perspectives," 59–60. On burial practices, see Christine Jirikowic, "The Political Implications of a Cultural Practice: A New Perspective on Ossuary Burial in the Potomac Valley," *North American Anthropologist* 11 (1990), 368–70, and Potter, *Commoners, Tribute, and Chiefs,* 165, 211–18, 146–47. On the connection between long-distance trade and social ranking, see Potter, "Early English Effects on Virginia Algonquian Exchange and Tribute in the Tidewater Potomac," in Peter Wood, Gregory Waselkov, and M. Thomas Hatley, eds., *Powhatan's Mantle: Indians in the Colonial Southeast* (Lincoln: University of Nebraska Press, 1989), 152–67; E. Randolph Turner, "Native American Protohistoric Interactions in the Powhatan Core Area," in Helen Rountree, ed., *Powhatan Foreign Relations, 1500–1722* (Charlottesville: University Press of Virginia, 1993), 90–92.

47. Potter, *Commoners, Tribute, and Chiefs,* 170–73.

48. Spelman, "Relation," cv (quotation); "Relation of Maryland," 88; Alexander Whitaker, "Letter to Raleigh Croshaw," in Alexander Brown, ed., *The Genesis of the United States* (New York: Houghton, Mifflin, and Company, 1890), 498–99; Whitaker, "Part of a Tractate," in Purchas, *Hakluytus Posthumus,* 19: 111; George Percy, "A Trewe Relacyon," *Tyler's Quarterly* 3 (1921–22), 277; Percy, "Observations," 145; Strachey, *Historie,* 96, 98; Smith, *Map,* 170–72; Beverley, *History,* 202, 210; Glover, *Account of Virginia,* 603; Pargellis, "The Indians of Virginia," 232; "Relation of Maryland," 90.

Chapter 3. *"Kings" of the Potomac*

1. Stephen Potter discusses competing population estimates in *Commoners, Tribute, and Chiefs: The Development of Algonquian Culture in the Potomac Valley* (Charlottesville: University Press of Virginia, 1993), 20–24.

2. Arthur Parker, *The Constitution of the Five Nations; or, the Iroquois Book of the Great Law* (Albany: University of the State of New York, 1916), 16–17 (quote). William Fenton, *The Great Law and the Longhouse* (Norman: University of Oklahoma Press, 1998), 67–73, 128–31, notes that the creation was a process spanning several generations rather than an event that can be assigned to a specific date. He makes an excellent case for dating the beginning of the formation of the league to the mid-fifteenth century and its fruition to the mid-sixteenth century—a range of dates that fits nicely with the evidence of increased raiding along the Potomac during those same years.

3. Daniel Richter, "War and Culture: The Iroquois Experience," *WMQ* 40 (1983), 528–59.

4. Daniel Richter, *The Ordeal of the Longhouse: The Peoples of the Iroquois League in the Era of European Colonization* (Chapel Hill: University of North Carolina Press, 1992), ch. 2; Dean Snow, *The Iroquois* (Cambridge, Mass.: Blackwell Publishers, 1994), ch. 4; William Engelbrecht, "New York Iroquois Political Development," in William Fitzhugh, ed., *Cultures in Contact: The European Impact on Native Cultural Institutions in Eastern North America, A.D. 1000–1800* (Washington, D.C.: Smithsonian Institution Press, 1985), 163–83; Bruce Trigger, *Children of Aataentsic: A History of the Huron People to 1660* (Montreal: McGill–Queen's University Press, 1976), chs. 2, 3.

5. On the Susquehannocks' ordeals, see Richter, "War and Culture"; Barry Kent, *Susquehanna's Indians* (Harrisburg: Pennsylvania Historical and Museum Commission, 1984), 15–18. On their sojourn in the Potomac basin, see Janet Brashler, "A Middle 16th Century Susquehannock Village in Hampshire County, West Virginia," *The West Virginia Archeologist* 39 (1987), 1–30; Robert Wall, "Late Woodland Ceramics and Native Populations of the Upper Potomac Valley," *Journal of Middle Atlantic Archaeology* 17 (2001), 15–37; Robert Wall and Heather Lapham, "Material Culture of the Contact Period in the Upper Potomac Valley," *Archaeology of Eastern North America* 31 (2003), 151–77; and Robert Wall, "The Chesapeake Hinterlands: Contact-Period Archaeology in the Upper Potomac Valley," in Dennis Blanton and Julia King, eds., *Indian and European Contact in Context: The Mid-Atlantic Region* (Gainesville: Uni-

versity Press of Florida, 2004), 74–97. Wall's work suggests that the Susquehannocks came from the lower Susquehanna in the late sixteenth century and remained on the upper Potomac into the early seventeenth century. Not coincidentally, radiocarbon dates at sites in western Maryland and the lower Shenandoah Valley reveal a distinct gap in the sixteenth century: villages occupied in earlier centuries yield a sharply declining number of dates after 1500. Hettie Boyce and Lori Frye, *Radiocarbon Dating of Archeological Samples from Maryland* (Baltimore: Maryland Geological Survey, 1986), 8, 10–11, 19–29, 44; Donna Boyd and C. Clifford Boyd, "Late Woodland Mortuary Variability," in Theodore Reinhart and Mary Ellen Hodges, eds., *Middle and Late Woodland Research in Virginia: A Synthesis* (Richmond: Dietz Press, 1992), 252–53; Richard Dent, *Chesapeake Prehistory: Old Traditions, New Directions* (New York: Plenum, 1995), 256–57, 262; Joan Walker and Glenda Miller, "Life on the Levee: The Late Woodland Period in the Northern Great Valley of Virginia," in *Middle and Late Woodland Research*, 175–82; Maureen Kavanaugh, *Archeological Resources of the Monocacy River Region* (Crownsville: Maryland Historical Trust, 1982), 52, 75–82; R. Michael Stewart, "Early Archeological Research in the Great Valley of Maryland," *Maryland Archeology* 33 (1997), 1–45. The documentary evidence tells the same story: John Smith, who undertook two very thorough reconnaissances of the Chesapeake Bay region in 1608, found no evidence of settlements in the Potomac interior or northwestern shore of the Chesapeake. John Smith, *A Map of Virginia*, in *CWCJS* 1: 151; Smith, *Proceedings of the English Colonie in Virginia*, in *CWCJS* 1: 226.

6. Richter, *Ordeal of the Longhouse*, ch. 3.

7. Henry Spelman, "Relation of Virginia," in Edward Arber and A. G. Bradley, eds., *Travels and Works of Captain John Smith, 1580–1631* (Edinburgh: John Grant, 1910), civ, cxiii–cxiv (quotations). On Chesapeake Algonquian warfare, see also Alexander Whitaker, "Part of a Tractate written at Henrico in Virginia," in Samuel Purchas, *Hakluytus Posthumus; or, Purchas His Pilgrimes . . .* (London: Henry Fetherstone, 1625; repr. Glasgow: J. MacLehose and Sons, 1905–1907), 19: 111; Andrew White, "A Briefe Relation of the Voyage Unto Maryland" (1634), in Clayton Hall, ed., *Narratives of Early Maryland, 1633–1634* (New York: Charles Scribner's Sons, 1910), 43; George Percy, "Observations Gathered out of a Discourse of the Plantation of the Southern Colonie in Virginia by the English in 1606," in Philip Barbour, ed., *The Jamestown Voyages under the First Charter, 1606–1609* (Cambridge: Hakluyt Society, 1969), 136: 133–34, 138; William Strachey, *The Historie of Travell into Virginia Britania* (1612), ed. Louis B. Wright and Virginia Freund, Works Issued by the Hakluyt Society, 2nd series, no. 105 (London: Hakluyt Society, 1953), 44, 60, 74, 85–86, 109, 192, 203; Smith, *Map*, 154, 161, 163, 166–67, 174–75; Smith, *Proceedings*, 227; Gabriel Archer, "Relatyon of the Discovery of Our River," in Barbour, *Jamestown Voyages*, 136: 96, 98; [Gabriel Archer], "Description of the People," in ibid., 136: 103; "A Relation of Maryland," in Hall, *Narratives*, 89; William White, "Fragments Published Before 1614," in Barbour, *Jamestown Voyages*, 136: 150.

8. One Algonquian song, e.g., reminded listeners of foes who had not only lost a skirmish but compounded their humiliation by crying out when tortured, "whe, whe, yah, ha, ha, ne, he, wittowa, wittowa." Strachey, *Historie*, 85–86 (quotation); White,

"Fragments," 150 (quotation); George Percy, "A Trewe Relacyon," *Tyler's Quarterly* 3 (1921–22), 263; Smith, *Proceedings*, 212; Smith, *Map*, 166, 175; *RVC* 3: 228.

9. The theoretical literature on chiefdoms is impressive and ever-growing, and frequently applicable to the Potomac Valley. David Anderson, *The Savannah River Chiefdoms: Political Change in the Late Prehistoric Southeast* (Tuscaloosa: University of Alabama Press, 1994); Elsa Redmond, ed., *Chiefdoms and Chieftaincy in the Americas* (Gainesville: University Press of Florida, 1998); Timothy Earle, ed., *Chiefdoms: Power, Economy, and Ideology* (New York: Cambridge University Press, 1991); and especially Earle, *How Chiefs Come to Power: The Political Economy in Prehistory* (Stanford: Stanford University Press, 1997) provide excellent entry points into this literature.

10. Smith, *Map*, 147–48; *Arch. Md.*15: 251; Gabrielle Tayac, "'To Speak with One Voice': Supra-Tribal American Indian Collective Identity Incorporation among the Piscataway, 1500–1998" (Ph.D. diss., Harvard University, 1999), 63; Helen Rountree, *The Powhatan Indians of Virginia: Their Traditional Culture* (Norman: University of Oklahoma Press., 1989), 117.

11. E. Randolph Turner III, "An Archaeological and Ethnohistorical Study on the Evolution of Rank Societies in the Virginia Coastal Plain" (Ph.D. diss., Pennsylvania State University, 1976), 27–38; Helen Rountree, "A Guide to the Late Woodland Indians' Use of Ecological Zones in the Chesapeake Region," *Chesopiean* 34 (1996), 1–37. See also Smith, *Map*, 153–54, 164. On the diversity and distribution of plants in the freshwater zone, see Alice Lippson, et al., *Environmental Atlas of the Potomac Estuary* (Baltimore: Johns Hopkins University Press, 1981); Alice Lippson and Robert Lippson, *Life in the Chesapeake Bay*, 2nd ed. (Baltimore: Johns Hopkins University Press, 1997), 185–90; and Helen Rountree and Thomas Davidson, *Eastern Shore Indians of Virginia and Maryland* (Charlottesville: University Press of Virginia, 1997), appendix C.

12. Smith, *Map*, 140–41, 147–48; Potter, *Commoners, Tribute, and Chiefs*, 8–24. This list should be taken as an approximation only. Since the main source for this list is Smith's record of his travels, and since Smith only briefly visited the north bank of the Potomac, it is likely that he was somewhat confused about the situation there— especially on the north bank of the inner coastal plain, where he may have lumped two other nations—the Mattawomans and the Pamunkys—in with the Nanjemoys. Smith and other English observers did not necessarily conceive of group identities in the same way as the Algonquian residents of the Potomac, and translation was a problem. Moreover, place names were often conflated with groups' names (this may partially explain the confusing situation on the north bank between Piscataway Creek and Portobacco Creek, an area where new names for Algonquian groups were still emerging in the 1680s). Variant phonetic spellings add to the confusion. The Wicomicos, e.g. (or at least the group on the river of that name), also known as the Chopticos (later in the century, when they lived on Choptico Bay) had an outlying hamlet named Yaocomaco; although this was likely a variant spelling of "Wicomico," and other evidence clearly indicates that the Yaocomacos were subject to the Wicomico/ Choptico werowance, historians have occasionally identified the Yaocomacos as a separate polity. John Smith's 1612 *Map of Virginia* shows a werowance's village named "Cecemecomoco" on the Wicomico River but only a hamlet without a hereditary

chief on St. Mary's River. On the danger of imposing European conceptions of group identity onto the indigenous peoples of eastern North America, see Heidi Bohaker, "*Nindoodemag*: The Significance of Algonquian Kinship Networks in the Eastern Great Lakes Region, 1600–1701," *WMQ* 63 (2006), 23–52.

13. Not all chiefs were men, but the means of succession—from the oldest brother to the youngest, then to the oldest sister, then to her sons—meant that few chiefs were women. Thus the use of "he" here and elsewhere in this volume. As for dating the origins of the tayac's paramount chiefdom, it is worth noting that the range of dates given here is consistent with both the range of dates commonly given for the formation of the Iroquois League and with the archaeological evidence of increasingly hierarchical societies on the inner coastal plain. It is difficult to be any more precise than this. James Merrell calculated an average of nine years in office for each tayac, based on the average tenure between 1634 and 1700, which yielded a founding date of 1534. But Merrell assumed that exotic European-introduced epidemics struck the Piscataways in the sixteenth century, an assumption for which there is as yet no evidence. Merrell was also deliberately conservative in his assessment so as not to exaggerate the paramount chiefdom's antiquity, so 1534 should be taken as the *latest* likely date for the beginning of the tayac's paramount chiefdom. It is also possible that the number thirteen had particular significance for Piscataway people, in which case all such calculations are moot. Then, too, it is entirely possible that other paramount chiefdoms preceded this one. This is simply the earliest for which we have any evidence. *Arch. Md.* 3: 403 (quotation); Merrell, "Cultural Continuity among the Piscataway Indians of Colonial Maryland," *WMQ* 36 (1979), 551.

14. *Arch. Md.* 3: 402–3; "Annual Letters of the Jesuits," in Hall, *Narratives*, 124–25; "Relation of Maryland," 72, 844; *Arch. Md.*, 3: 402–3; Rountree and Davidson, *Eastern Shore Indians*, 26–29; Smith, *Map*, 141–42, 147–48, 173; Smith, *Proceedings*, 227; John Smith, *The Generall Historie of Virginia, the Somer Iles, and New England*, in *CWCJS* 2: 105; Strachey, *Historie*, 44, 49, 56; Wayne Clark and Helen Rountree, "The Powhatans and the Maryland Mainland," in Helen Rountree, ed., *Powhatan Foreign Relations, 1500–1722* (Charlottesville: University Press of Virginia, 1993), 116, 133–34; Merrell, "Cultural Continuity," 552.

15. Strachey, *Historie*, 43–45, 57, 63–69, 104–5, 108; Smith, *Map*, 147, 173, 178. On Powhatan's multiple names, see Margaret Holmes Williamson, *Powhatan Lords of Life and Death: Command and Consent in Seventeenth-Century Virginia* (Lincoln: University of Nebraska Press, 2003), 56–57, and Frederic Gleach, *Powhatan's World and Colonial Virginia: A Conflict of Cultures* (Lincoln: University of Nebraska Press, 1997), 32–33.

16. Kent, *Susquehanna's Indians*, 17–19, 311–19; "Relation of Maryland," 74, 89; Smith, *Proceedings*, 230–32; Smith, *Generall Historie*, 105–6, 119, 165, 170–72, 176; Smith, *Map*, 149–50, 166; "Instructions to Sir Thomas Gates," in Barbour, *Jamestown Voyages*, 137: 237; Spelman, "Relation," cv–cvi.

17. *Arch. Md.* 3: 402–3. The Tauxenents, who were oriented to the Piscataway tayac instead, were the only south-bank nation that did not pay tribute to Powhatan.

18. Elsa Redmond, "The Dynamics of Chieftaincy and the Development of Chief-

doms," in *Chiefdoms and Chieftaincy,* 1–13; Timothy Earle, "Chiefdoms in Archaeological and Ethnohistorical Perspective," *Annual Reviews of Anthropology* 16 (1987), 279–308.

19. Tribute: Spelman, "Relation," cxii–cxiii; John Smith, *A True Relation of Such Occurences and Accidents of Noate as Hath Hapned in Virginia,* in *CWCJS* 1: 69; Smith, *Map,* 158–59, 169, 174; Strachey, *Historie,* 87; Tayac, "'To Speak with One Voice,'" 63. Initiated wars: Strachey, *Historie,* 44, 54, 104. Ordered executions: Spelman, "Relation," cxi; Strachey, *Historie,* 77. See also "Relation of Maryland," 26.

20. Strachey, *Historie,* 88–103 (quotations); Smith, *Map,* 169 (quotation); White, "Briefe Relation," 44–45; "Relation of Maryland" (quotation); "Occurants in Virginia" (1619), in *Hakluytus Posthumus,* 19: 118; Spelman, "Relation," cv.

21. White, "Fragments," 149–50; Smith, *Map,* 169–70; Smith, *Proceedings,* 170; Strachey, *Historie,* 77, 88, 94–95, 100–103; Purchas, *Hakluytus Posthumus,* 19: 954; Spelman, "Relation," vx; Stephen Potter, "Early English Effects on Virginia Algonquian Exchange and Tribute in the Tidewater Potomac," in Peter Wood, Gregory Waselkov, and M. Thomas Hatley, eds., *Powhatan's Mantle: Indians in the Colonial Southeast* (Lincoln: University of Nebraska Press, 1989), 162–64. Piscataway oral tradition describes the dead as intercessors for the living. See Tayac, "'To Speak with One Voice,'" 54, 75.

22. Smith, *Map,* 160 (quotation); Samuel Purchas, *Purchas His Pilgrimage,* 2nd ed. (London: William Stansby for Henry Fetherstone, 1614), 765, quoted in Rountree, *Powhatan Indians,* 135.

23. Smith, *True Relation,* 65; Smith, *Generall Historie,* 156, 243–44, 268; Spelman, "Relation," cii–civ; Ralph Hamor, *A True Discourse of the Present State of Virginia, and the Successe of the Affaires There till the 18 of June, 1614* (London: W. Welby, 1615), repr. in *Virginia: Four Personal Narratives* (New York: Arno Press, 1972), 4–6; Strachey, *Historie,* 46, 101; "Letter of Sir Samuel Argoll," in Purchas, *Hakluytus Posthumus,* 19: 91–93; Williamson, *Powhatan Lords,* 95–123, 132–33; Gleach, *Powhatan's World,* 28–36.

24. *Arch. Md.* 3: 402–3 (quotation); Beverley, *History,* 61; Hamor, *True Discourse,* 13; Earle, "Chiefdoms in Archaeological and Ethnohistorical Perspective," 299; Redmond, "Introduction," *Chiefdoms and Chieftaincy,* 10–12.

25. Smith, *Map,* 169–70, 173; Spelman, "Relation," civ–cv; Strachey, *Historie,* 88–89.

26. White, "Briefe Relation," 45, 88 (quotation); Smith, *Map,* 170–71 (quotation); Smith, *True Relation,* 59; Smith, *Generall Historie,* 124–25; Tayac, "'To Speak with One Voice,'" 75; Spelman, "Relation," cv; Strachey, *Historie,* 97–98, 123; White, "Fragments," 150; Stanley Pargellis, ed., "The Indians of Virginia," *WMQ* 16 (1959), 232–33, 235–36; "Annual Letters of the Jesuits," 124–26.

27. *RVC* 3: 438; Samuel Purchas, *Purchas his pilgrimage, or Relations of the world and the religions observed in al ages and places discovered, from the Creation unto this present,* 3rd ed. (London: William Stansby for Henry Fetherstone, 1617), 955; Spelman, "Relation," cv–cvi; White, "Briefe Relation," 85; Pargellis, "The Indians of Virginia," 234–35; White, "Fragments," 147–49; Strachey, *Historie,* 58, 85–86, 98–100, 104 (quotation); Smith, *Map,* 171–72; White, "Briefe Relation," 43, 45; Hamor, *True Discourse,* 6;

Purchas, *Hakluytus Posthumus,* 19: 93; Beverley, *History,* 84, 108–9 (quotation), 115; and Gleach, *Powhatan's World,* 38–43.

28. Gleach, *Powhatan's World,* 56–59; Christopher Miller and George Hamell, "A New Perspective on Indian-White Contact: Cultural Symbols and Colonial Trade," *JAH* 7 (1986), 311–28; George Lankford, "Red and White: Some Reflections on a Southeastern Metaphor," *Southern Folklore* 50 (1992), 53–80; Williamson, *Powhatan Lords,* 247–54.

29. William Tooker, "On the Meaning of the Name Anacostia," *American Anthropologist* 7 (1894), 389–93; Philip Barbour, "The Earliest Reconnaissance of Chesapeake Bay Area: Captain John Smith's Map and Indian Vocabulary," *VMHB* 79 (1971), 296; Strachey, *Historie,* 46, 56–57, 107, 132; Smith, *True Relation,* 59, 69, 81; Smith, *Map,* 160, 166, 173–74; Smith, *Proceedings,* 242, 247; Hamor, *True Discourse,* 4–6; "Letter of Sir Samuel Argoll," 91–93; Boyd and Boyd, "Late Woodland Mortuary Variability," 256–57.

30. Strachey, *Historie,* 56–57, 61, 63, 87, 107; White, *Briefe Relation,* 43; "Annual Letters of the Jesuits," 125, 127; Spelman, "Relation," cv, cxii–cxiii; Smith, *True Relation,* 69, 81, 93; Smith, *Generall Historie,* 201; Smith, *Map,* 173–74; Smith, *True Relation,* 69, 81; Percy, "Observations," 12–15; Tayac, "'To Speak with One Voice,'" 63; Potter, *Commoners, Tribute, and Chiefs,* 170–73.

31. Strachey, *Historie,* 68–69, 104, 107, 114; Spelman, "Relation," cvi–cxiii.

32. Smith, *Proceedings,* 228, 231–32 (quotation). On trade, gifting, power, and diplomacy, see James Axtell, *The Invasion Within: The Contest of Cultures in Colonial North America* (New York: Oxford University Press, 1985), 88–89; Peter Burke, *History and Social Theory* (Ithaca: Cornell University Press, 1992), 70–73; and Richard White, *The Middle Ground: Indians, Empires, and Republics in the Great Lakes Region, 1650–1815* (New York: Cambridge University Press, 1991), 103, 180–82.

33. Although the emphasis here is on diplomatic relations, the same sort of slippage characterized social and political relations *within* each nation. On the inherent impossibility of monopolizing power, see Anderson, *Savannah River Chiefdoms,* and Earle, *How Chiefs Come to Power,* 4–14.

34. Smith, *Map,* 140–41, displays the locations of most hamlets and villages, which I have compared to the resource maps in Lippson et al., *Environmental Atlas,* supplemented by county tidal marsh inventories for Virginia. See also Strachey, *Historie,* 77; Smith, *True Relation,* 39–40, 43, 81; Smith, *Map,* 145, 148, 161; Smith, *Generall Historie,* 289; Rountree, "Guide to the Late Woodland Indians' Use of Ecological Zones," 1–38.

35. Lippson et al., *Environmental Atlas,* 23–26, 32–47, folio maps 2, 6, 7, 8; David W. Stahle et al., "The Lost Colony and Jamestown Droughts," *Science* 280, no. 5363 (24 April 1998), 564–67.

36. White, "Briefe Relation," 40; "Relation of Maryland," 79; William Byrd, "History of the Dividing Line," in Louis B. Wright, ed., *The Prose Works of William Byrd of Westover* (Cambridge: Harvard University Press, 1966), 257; Stafford County (Va.) Court, Extracts from Order Books, 1664–1692, VHS mss 4st135a1, 15 November 1664; Smith, *True Relation,* 49; Percy, "Observations," 134.

37. Lippson et al., *Environmental Atlas,* ch. 8, folio maps 2, 4, 7, 8.

38. According to John Smith it is *two* hamlets, but he may have erred in seeing the creek as a barrier rather than as a common road uniting a community. Spelman, "Relation," cvi; White, "Briefe Relation," 40; "Relation of Maryland," 79; Gabriel Archer, "Description of the River and Country," in Barbour, *Jamestown Voyages*, 136: 103; Strachey, *Historie*, 78; Smith, *Map*, 140–41, 162; Joseph Ewan and Nesta Ewan, eds., *John Banister and His Natural History of Virginia* (Urbana: University of Illinois Press, 1970), 372; Lippson et al., *Environmental Atlas*, folio map 4.

39. Potter, *Commoners, Tribute, and Chiefs*, 27.

40. Spelman, "Relation," cvi; Smith, *Map*, 157; Strachey, *Historie*, 114; Turner, "Archaeological and Ethnohistorical Study," 192–95; Potter, *Commoners, Tribute, and Chiefs*, 32, 175.

41. Helen Rountree, "Powhatan Indian Women: The People Captain John Smith Barely Saw," *Ethnohistory* 45 (1998), 3, 13–15; Lippson et al., *Environmental Atlas*, 88–90, folio map 4.

42. Smith, *Map*, 140–41; Smith, *Generall Historie*, 167–68; Smith, *Map*, 227; Percy, "Observations," 137.

43. Turner, "Archaeological and Ethnohistorical Study," 257; Lippson et al., *Environmental Atlas*, folio map 4.

44. Dennis Blanton et. al., *The Potomac Creek Site (44ST2) Revisited* (Richmond: Virginia Department of Historic Resources, 1999), 1–3.

45. Strachey, *Historie*, 65, 86.

46. Tayac, "'To Speak with One Voice,'" 59; Spelman, "Relation," cvi; Beverley, *History*, 176; Smith, *Proceedings*, 216; Smith, *True Relation*, 65; Rountree, *Powhatan Indians*, 86, 92–94.

47. Strachey, *Historie*, 62 (quotation), 88–90, 94–95 (quotations); Spelman, "Relation," cv; Whitaker, "Part of a Tractate," 110–11; Smith, *Map*, 173–74; Beverley, *History*, 102.

48. Smith, *Map*, 169–70, 173; Spelman, "Relation," civ–cv; Strachey, *Historie*, 88–89.

49. Strachey, *Historie*, 77, 88, 94 (quotation, 100–103); Spelman, "Relation," vx; Smith, *Map*, 149, 169, 172; Potter, "Early English Effects," 162–64.

50. Strachey, *Historie*, 58, 104; White, "Briefe Relation," 43, 45; "Relation of Maryland," 73, 84, 87; Hamor, *True Discourse*, 6; "Letter of Sir Samuel Argoll," 19: 93; Beverley, *History*, 84, 108–9 (quotation), 115; Spelman, "Relation," 56.

51. The hubbub of the Virginia Council's deliberations, where "they all talke at once," confused a group of Potomac Algonquians. Unable to recognize the event as a council meeting, the visitors asked their hosts "what it meant." John Clayton, "Another Account of Virginia," *VMHB* 76 (1968), 435 (quotation); White, "Briefe Relation," 44; "Relation of Maryland," 87; Gleach, *Powhatan's World*, 39–43.

52. White, "Briefe Relation," 45; "Relation of Maryland," 87; Spelman, "Relation," cv, cxiii (quotation); Strachey, *Historie*, 59–61 (quotation), 80 (quotation), 88 , 90, 95, 104–5 (quotation); Whitaker, "Part of a Tractate," 111; *Purchas his pilgrimage*, 3rd ed., 955; Smith, *Map*, 59, 160, 169–71, 174; Smith, *True Relation*, 53; George Percy, "Observations Gathered out of a Discourse of the Plantation of the Southern Colonie in

Virginia by the English in 1606," in Philip Barbour, ed., *The Jamestown Voyages under the First Charter, 1606–1609* (Cambridge: Hakluyt Society, 1969), 136: 135–37; Pargellis, "The Indians of Virginia," 232–33; "Occurants in Virginia," 118; Karen Kupperman, *Indians and English: Facing Off in Early America* (Ithaca: Cornell University Press, 2000), 92–96.

53. This and the following paragraphs are synthesized from White, "Briefe Relation," 42–43; Strachey, *Historie*, 71–73, 88; Percy, "Observations," 136, 142; Smith, *Map*, 160–61; "Relation of Maryland," 85, 87; Spelman, "Relation."

54. Spelman, "Relation," cxiii; Smith, *Map*, 160–61, 174; Percy, "Observations," 135; [Archer], "Description of the People," 102; Strachey, *Historie*, 71, 90–91.

55. Strachey, *Historie*, 86; Potter, *Commoners, Tribute, and Chiefs*, 24–29.

56. C. S. Lewis, *The Abolition of Man* (New York: Macmillan, 1947), 36–37.

Chapter 4. The Nature of Colonization

1. Scholars focusing on the Jamestown colony have argued that late sixteenth-century Spanish explorations in the region, including a failed attempt at establishing a mission, later shaped relations between the Jamestown colonists and their neighbors. Although Spaniards may have ventured as far north as the Potomac, no evidence survives of their having had much impact on later English-Algonquian encounters this far north. See Helen Rountree, *Pocahontas's People: The Powhatan Indians of Virginia through Four Centuries* (Norman: University of Oklahoma Press, 1990), 15–20.

2. William Cronon, *Changes in the Land: Indians, Colonists, and the Ecology of New England* (New York: Hill and Wang, 1983), 12 (quotation). Carolyn Merchant describes a similar choice (albeit with some qualifications) in *Ecological Revolutions: Nature, Gender, and Science in New England* (Chapel Hill: University of North Carolina Press, 1989), pt. 1.

3. H. C. Darby, *A New Historical Geography of England before 1600* (Cambridge: Cambridge University Press, 1973), 254–55; James Horn, *Adapting to a New World: English Society in the Seventeenth-Century Chesapeake* (Chapel Hill: University of North Carolina Press, 1994), 78–120; Joan Thirsk, *The Agrarian History of England and Wales*, vol. 4, *1500–1640* (London: Cambridge University Press, 1967), ch. 1.

4. Thirsk, *Agrarian History*, introduction; M. W. Barley, *Houses and History* (London: Faber and Faber, 1986), 147–65; J. H. Baker, *An Introduction to English Legal History*, 3rd ed. (London: Butterworth's, 1990), 255–360; Christopher Hill, "Puritans and the 'Dark Corners of the Land,'" in *Change and Continuity in Seventeenth-Century England* (Cambridge: Harvard University Press, 1975), 3–47.

5. Mark Overton, *Agricultural Revolution in England: The Transformation of the Agrarian Economy, 1500–1850* (Cambridge: Cambridge University Press, 1996), ch. 2.

6. Thirsk, *Agrarian History*, 5–8, 18–25, 182–83; Darby, *New Historical Geography*, 259–61.

7. Keith Thomas, *Man and the Natural World: A History of the Modern Sensibility* (New York: Pantheon Books, 1983), 15, 254–58; T. C. Smout, *Nature Contested: Envi-*

ronmental History in Scotland and Northern England Since 1600 (Edinburgh: Edinburgh University Press, 2000), ch. 1.

8. Joan Thirsk, *Agricultural Regions and Agrarian History in England, 1500–1750* (Atlantic Highlands, N.J.: Humanities Press, 1987); Thirsk, ed., *The English Rural Landscape* (New York: Oxford University Press, 2000), pt. 1.

9. Overton, *Agricultural Revolution*, 36–38; Thirsk, *Agrarian History*, ch. 7; Thomas, *Man and the Natural World*, 95, 235; Darby, *New Historical Geography*, 294. For examples of a clergyman-farmer's concern with his livestock and crops, see Alan Macfarlane, ed., *The Diary of Ralph Josselin* (London: Oxford University Press, 1976), 546, 548, 563.

10. W. G. Hoskins, *The Making of the English Landscape* (London: Hodder and Stoughton, 1955), 13–15, ch. 1; Horn, *Adapting to a New World*, 128–30; Thomas, *Man and the Natural World*, 25–26; Donal Woodward, "'An Essay on Manures': Changing Attitudes to Fertilization in England, 1500–1800," in John Chartres and David Hey, eds., *English Rural Society, 1500–1800: Essays in Honour of Joan Thirsk* (New York: Cambridge University Press, 1990), 251–58; I. G. Simmons, *An Environmental History of Great Britain from 10,000 Years Ago to the Present* (Edinburgh: Edinburgh University Press, 2001), 71–87. For examples of areas that have been farmed for many centuries using such sustainable techniques, see the essays in Thirsk, *English Rural Landscape*, pt. 2.

11. Simmons, *Environmental History*, 71; John Richards, *The Unending Frontier: An Environmental History of the Early Modern World* (Berkeley: University of California Press, 2003), ch. 6.

12. *Oxford English Dictionary*; Thomas, *Man and the Natural World*, 17–50, 150–59, 278–79.

13. Barley, *Houses and History*, 247–50; Thomas, *Man and the Natural World*, 92–120; Thirsk, *Agrarian History*, 740–41, 749, 752, 766; Karen Kupperman, "The Beehive as a Model for Colonial Design," in *America in European Consciousness, 1493–1750* (Chapel Hill: University of North Carolina Press, 1995), 272–92.

14. John Awdelay, *The Fraternitie of Vacabondes*, 2nd ed. (London: John Awdelay, 1603), n.p. (quotation); Thomas, *Man and the Natural World*, 41–50.

15. John Derricke, *The Image of Ireland* (London: J. Kingston for Ihon Daie, 1581), n.p. (quotation); Nicholas Canny, *The Elizabethan Conquest of Ireland: A Pattern Established* (New York: Barnes & Noble, 1976), 13–14, 125, and ch. 6; Canny, *Making Ireland British, 1580–1650* (New York: Oxford University Press, 2001), 103, 109, 127–28; Vincent Carey, "John Derricke's *Image of Ireland*, Sir Henry Sidney, and the Massacre at Mullaghmast, 1578," *Irish Historical Studies* 31 (1999), 305–27; Fynes Moryson, *An Itinerary: Containing his ten yeeres travell through the twelfe dominions of Germany, Bohmerland, France, England, Scotland and Ireland* (London: John Beale, 1617), bk. 3, 164 (quotation).

16. Carey, "John Derricke's *Image of Ireland*"; Derricke, *Image of Ireland*, n.p. (quotation).

17. Moryson, *Intinerary*, 95, 115, 119–21, 131, 211, 212, 214–15 (quotation); Canny, *Making Ireland British*, 166–69.

18. Moryson, *Itinerary*, 222–31, 234–35.

19. Ibid., 237–39, 248–51, 258–61, 267–74.

20. Nicholas Canny, *Kingdom and Colony: Ireland in the Atlantic World, 1560–1800* (Baltimore: Johns Hopkins University Press, 1988), 34–35, 98–99; Canny, *Making Ireland British*, ch. 1.

21. John Smith, *A True Relation of Such Occurences and Accidents of Noate as Hath Hapned in Virginia*, in *CWCJS* 1: 67 (quotation), 73–75. See also ibid., 57; Smith, *The Proceedings of the English Colonie in Virginia*, in *CWCJS* 1: 248; Smith, *The Generall Historie of Virginia, the Somer Iles, and New England*, in *CWCJS* 2: 152.

22. Frederic Gleach, *Powhatan's World and Colonial Virginia: A Conflict of Cultures* (Lincoln: University of Nebraska Press, 1997), 109–22.

23. The English sent mixed signals to Powhatan in the months following Smith's release. They immediately provided him with gifts of the metal tools and spiritually potent copper and beads he had specified as proper tribute. But they withheld other tribute demanded by Powhatan, notably guns and grindstones. Smith, *Generall Historie*, 151; Smith, *True Relation*, 57.

24. Smith, *A Map of Virginia*, in *CWCJS* 1: 151 (quotation); Smith, *Proceedings*, 226; Lisa Blansett, "John Smith Maps Virginia: Knowledge, Rhetoric, and Politics," in Robert Applebaum and John Sweet, eds., *Envisioning an English Empire: Jamestown and the Making of the North Atlantic World* (Philadelphia: University of Pennsylvania Press, 2005), 68–91.

25. Smith, *Proceedings*, 230–32; Smith, *Generall Historie*, 105–6, 119, 166, 169, 172, 176 (quotation); "Instructions to Sir Thomas Gates," in Philip Barbour, ed., *The Jamestown Voyages under the First Charter, 1606–1609* (Cambridge: Hakluyt Society, 1969), 136, 237; Henry Spelman, "Relation of Virginia," in Edward Arber and A. G. Bradley, eds., *Travels and Works of Captain John Smith, 1580–1631* (Edinburgh: John Grant, 1910), cv–cvi; Smith, *Map*, 149–50, 166.

26. Smith, *Proceedings*, 226–28; Smith, *True Relation*, 51; Smith, *Generall Historie*, 243.

27. *RVC* 3: 17–19 (quotation), 29; William Strachey, *The Historie of Travell into Virginia Britania* (1612), ed. Louis B. Wright and Virginia Freund, Works Issued by the Hakluyt Society, 2nd series, no. 105 (London: Hakluyt Society, 1953), 106–8 (quotation); Smith, *Generall Historie*, 316 (quotation); Smith, *Proceedings*, 224–33 (quotation on 227–28).

28. George Percy, "A Trewe Relacyon," *Tyler's Quarterly* 3 (1921–22), 265–69; Spelman, "Relation," ciii–civ, in Samuel Purchas, *Hakluytus Posthumus; or, Purchas His Pilgrimes . . .* (London: Henry Fetherstone, 1625; repr. Glasgow: J. MacLehose and Sons, 1905–1907), 19: 89, 91–92; Smith, *Generall Historie*, 236, 243–44.

29. Smith, *Generall Historie*, 268; *RVC* 3: 244–47.

30. Sickness had swept through the English settlements that summer, weakening the colonists' ability to withstand an attack despite considerable migration from England in the previous eighteen months. At the same time, a terrible epidemic amongst the Powhatans reminded them of the costs of hosting the English. Moreover, the death of Pocahontas in 1617 had weakened the colonists' ties to Powhatan

(to the extent that those ties depended upon Pocahontas's marriage to John Rolfe). The colony's first-ever representative assembly met that summer and passed several acts betraying their nervousness about Indian relations. *RVC* 3: 152, 161–75, 220, 228, 246; H. R. McIlwaine, ed., *Journals of the House of Burgesses, 1619–1658/59* (Richmond: Colonial Press, 1915), 15 (quotation).

31. *RVC* 3: 244–45; Rountree, *Pocahontas's People*, 64–65, 70.

32. English ships setting out for Virginia from 1619 onward routinely carried "trucking" goods such as beads, copper, and hatchets, and colonists and company officials schemed to bring Italian glassworkers to Virginia to manufacture trade beads on the spot. *RVC* 1: 423, 484, 493; 3: 196, 178–79, 278–79, 299–300, 384, 495.

33. *RVC* 3: 238–39 (quotation); Purchas, *Hakluytus Posthumus*, 19: 146 (quotation).

34. *RVC* 1: 504, 567, 583, 608; 2: 15 (quotation), 104; 3: 488, 515, 526–27, 530.

35. Edward Waterhouse, *A Declaration of the State of the Colony in Virginia* (London: G. Eld. for R. Mylbourne, 1622), 13–20 (quotation on 14).

36. Gleach, *Powhatan's World*, 43–54, 148–60; Smith, *Generall Historie*, 312.

37. Canny, *Elizabethan Conquest*, 161; Waterhouse, *Declaration*, 11, 19, 24 (quotations).

38. Smith, *Generall Historie*, 304–13.

39. Ibid., 307.

40. Ibid., 308–9.

41. Ibid., 309.

42. Ibid., 309–10 (quotation, with emphasis added); *RVC* 3: 654. It is not clear whether Madison brought the letter up from Jamestown or whether it traveled overland from Pamunky to Patawomeck.

43. Smith, *Generall Historie*, 310–12.

44. Ibid., 310–13.

45. Ibid., 313–14.

46. Ibid., 314; *RVC* 3: 697.

47. *RVC* 3: 678–69; 4: 6–7, 9, 10, 12; Smith, *Generall Historie*, 314–15, 318.

48. *RVC* 2: 482; 4: 37, 71, 89, 98–99, 102.

49. *RVC* 4: 61, 89; Smith, *Generall Historie*, 319–21 (quotation on 321).

50. *RVC* 2: 478, 483; 4: 102, 221–23, 234, 250, 261; Robert Bennett to Edward Bennett, 9 June 1623, in "Lord Sackville's Papers Respecting Virginia, 1613–1631," *AHR* 27 (1922), 507.

51. *RVC* 2: 478; 4: 221, 250–51, 292, 399–400, 450–51. Henry Fleet, the boy taken captive in the incident, later revealed that it had taken place at Nacotchtank. Governor Wyatt may not have known this, because Fleet remained in captivity until 1627; see Henry Fleet, "A Brief Journal of a Voyage Made in the Bark Virginia, to Virginia and Other Parts of the Continent of America," in Edward Neill, ed., *The Founders of Maryland as Portrayed in Manuscripts, Provincial Records and Early Documents* (Albany: J. Munsell, 1876), 25; *RVC* 4: 450–51.

52. *RVC* 4: 450–51, 507–8.

53. *RVC* 4: 568–69; H. R. McIlwaine, ed., *Minutes of the Council and General Court*

of Colonial Virginia, 2nd ed. (Richmond: Virginia State Library, 1979), 151, 172, 184, 483–84; Hening, *Statutes* 1: 140–41, 153. As early as December 1622 John Martin had circulated a manuscript on "the manner howe to bringe in the Indians into subjection without makinge an upper exterpation of them together with the reasons." This system of "harshe visitts" and "feede fights" especially served the interests of Virginia's elites, who under the cover of war used the spoils of battle to consolidate even more power and wealth in their hands. *RVC* 3: 704; J. Frederick Fausz and Jon Kukla, "A Letter of Advice to the Governor of Virginia, 1624," *WMQ* 34 (1977), 127; J. Frederick Fausz, "Merging and Emerging Worlds: Anglo-Indian Interest Groups and the Development of the Seventeenth-Century Chesapeake," Lois Green Carr, Philip Morgan, and Jean Russo, eds., *Colonial Chesapeake Society* (Chapel Hill: University of North Carolina Press, 1988), 47–55.

54. *RVC* 4: 37; J. Frederick Fausz, "Authority and Opportunity in the Early Chesapeake: The Bay Environment and the English Connection, 1620–1640," VHS mss 2 F2758 a2. Councilors also used their authority to accumulate land and laborers. They issued land patents to themselves, kept laborers under their thumbs by consistently deciding in favor of masters in disputes with indentured servants, and engrossed still more servants and soil by appointing themselves administrators of deceased colonists' estates. *RVC* 4: 37–38, 81, 231, 234; McIlwaine, *Minutes of the Council,* 151, 483; Edmund S. Morgan, *American Slavery, American Freedom: The Ordeal of Colonial Virginia* (New York: W. W. Norton, 1975), ch. 6; Jon Kukla, "Order and Chaos in Early America: Political and Social Stability in Pre-Restoration Virginia," *AHR* 90 (1985), 283–85.

55. John McCusker and Russell Menard, *The Economy of British America, 1607–1789* (Chapel Hill: University of North Carolina Press, 1985), 121; Kukla, "Order and Chaos," 277. For the link between councilors, captaincy, and the control of labor, compare Fausz, "Authority and Opportunity," tables 2 and 3, with Morgan, *American Slavery,* 119.

Chapter 5. Peltries and "Papists"

1. *RVC* 3: 468–91; Richard Davis, *George Sandys, Poet Adventurer: A Study in Anglo-American Culture in the Seventeenth Century* (New York: Columbia University Press, 1955), 112–17; James Horn, *Adapting to a New World: English Society in the Seventeenth-Century Chesapeake* (Chapel Hill: University of North Carolina Press, 1994), 59; John Krugler, *English and Catholic: The Lords Baltimore in the Seventeenth Century* (Baltimore: Johns Hopkins University Press, 2004), chs. 1–4; and Peter Pope, *Fish into Wine: The Newfoundland Plantation in the Seventeenth Century* (Chapel Hill: University of North Carolina Press, 2004), 4, 41, 51–56.

2. Henry Fleet, "A Brief Journal of a Voyage Made in the Bark Virginia, to Virginia and Other Parts of the Continent of America," in Edward Neill, ed., *The Founders of Maryland as Portrayed in Manuscripts, Provincial Records and Early Documents* (Albany: J. Munsell, 1876), 20–25 (quotation); J. Frederick Fausz, "Merging and Emerging Worlds: Anglo-Indian Interest Groups and the Development of the Seventeenth-Cen-

tury Chesapeake," in Lois Green Carr, Philip Morgan, and Jean Russo, eds., *Colonial Chesapeake Society* (Chapel Hill: University of North Carolina Press, 1988), 60–62; Annie Lash Jester and Marth Woodroof Hiden, eds., *Adventures of Purse and Person: Virginia, 1607–1625* (Princeton: Princeton University Press, 1956), 172–74.

3. Baltimore to Sir Thomas Wentworth, 21 May 1627, in J. Thomas Sharf, *History of Maryland* (Baltimore: J. B. Piet, 1879), vol. 1, 42; *Arch. Md.* 3: 15–17; Neill, *Founders of Maryland*, 49; Pope, *Fish into Wine*, 4–6, 54–56, 124–32; Krugler, *English and Catholic*, 92–118.

4. Fausz, "Merging and Emerging Worlds," 47–68.

5. Anonymous member of the Canada Company, "A briefe delaration what beaver skinnes Captaine David Kirke and his Companie brought from Canada in the yeare 1629," 2 May 1631, PRO CO 1/6, VCRP reel 73, SR 00627; Ian Steele, *Warpaths: Invasions of North America* (New York: Oxford University Press, 1994), 68; Fausz, "Merging and Emerging Worlds," 61–62; Raphael Semmes, "Claiborne vs. Cloberry in the High Court of Admiralty," *MdHM* 26 (1931), 381–404; 27 (1932), 17–28, 99–114, 191–214, 337–52; 28 (1933), 26–43, 172–95, 257–65.

6. Erich Isaac, "Kent Island, Part I: The Period of Settlement," *MdHM* 52 (1957), 93–119; Semmes, "Claiborne vs. Cloberry," *MdHM* 26: 388; 27: 208; 28: 26–43, 173, 177, 179, 182; Governor Leonard Calvert to Lord Baltimore, 25 April 1638, in Clayton Hall, ed., *Narratives of Early Maryland, 1633–1634* (New York: Charles Scribner's Sons, 1910), 153; "Virginia and Maryland, or The Lord Baltimore's printed CASE, uncased and answered" (1655), in ibid., 201; Fausz, "Merging and Emerging Worlds," 62–64.

7. Fleet, "Brief Journal," 20–25 (quotations). On the identity and movements of the Massawomecks, see James Prendergast, *The Massawomeck: Raiders and Traders into the Chesapeake Bay in the Seventeenth Century,* Transactions of the American Philosophical Society, vol. 81, pt. 2 (Philadelphia: American Philosophical Society, 1991).

8. Fleet, "Brief Journal," 26.

9. Ibid., 26–27.

10. Ibid., 26–31.

11. Ibid., 26–32.

12. Ibid., 34–36; Andrew White, "A Briefe Relation of the Voyage Unto Maryland" (1634), in Hall, *Narratives*, 41; "Henry Fleet of Fleet's Bay, Virginia," *Northern Neck Historical Magazine* 12 (1962), 1072.

13. "An Account of the Colony of the Lord Baron of Baltimore" (1633), in Hall, *Narratives*, 8.

14. *Arch. Md.* 1: 42–43 (quotations); Lois Green Carr and Russell Menard, "Lords Baltimore and the Colonization of Maryland," in David Quinn, ed., *Early Maryland in a Wider World* (Detroit: Wayne State University Press, 1982), 180–82.

15. Petition from the Virginia Council to the Board of Trade, 14 March 1634, to the Board of Trade, C.O. 1/39, 119, VCRP reel 73, SR 00627; "Virginia and Maryland," 181–96 (quotation on 189); *Arch. Md.* 3: 17–19, 24–25, 32–33, 39.

16. Leonard Calvert to Sir Richard Lechford, 30 May 1634, in *The Calvert Papers, number three,* Maryland Historical Society Fund Publication no. 35 (Baltimore:

Maryland Historical Society, 1899), 20 (quotation); White, "Briefe Relation," 33–41 (quotation); Captain Thomas Yong to Sir Toby Matthew, July 1634, in Hall, *Narratives*, 54–61.

17. White, "Briefe Relation," 41.

18. Ibid., 41; Yong to Matthew, in Hall, *Narratives*, 55; "A Relation of Maryland," in Hall, *Narratives*, 73; Calvert to Lechford, *Calvert Papers, number three*, 21 (quotation).

19. White, "Briefe Relation," 40–42 (quotations); "Relation of Maryland," 74–75, 89.

20. Calvert to Lechford, *Calvert Papers, number three*, 21–22.

21. Prendergast, *Massawomeck* (quotation on 56); Daniel Richter, *The Ordeal of the Longhouse: The Peoples of the Iroquois League in the Era of European Colonization* (Chapel Hill: University of North Carolina Press, 1992), 50–74; Richard White, *The Middle Ground: Indians, Empires, and Republics in the Great Lakes Region, 1650–1815* (New York: Cambridge University Press, 1991), 1–13.

22. White, "Briefe Relation," 44; *Arch. Md.* 3: 67–68, 73–76; J. Frederick Fausz, "Present at the 'Creation': The Chesapeake World that Greeted the Maryland Colonists," *MdHM* 79 (1984), 16.

23. *Arch. Md.* 3: 30–41; 5: 164–67; Yong to Matthew, in Hall, *Narratives*, 54–61; "Relation of Maryland," 74; Samuel Matthews to Sir John Wolstenholme, 25 May 1635, in *VMHB* 1 (1894), 416–23; Harvey to Sir Francis Windebank, 14 July 1635, in ibid., 425–29; H. R. McIlwaine, ed., *Minutes of the Council and General Court of Colonial Virginia*, 2nd ed. (Richmond: Virginia State Library, 1979), 480, 491 (quotation); The Calvert Papers, MHS mss 174, reel 6, nos. 189, 190; J. Mills Thornton, "The Thrusting Out of Governor Harvey: A Seventeenth-Century Rebellion," 76 (1968), 11–26; Fausz, "Merging and Emerging Worlds," 66–72.

24. *Arch. Md.* 1: 27; 3: 64–66, 70, 76–78, 92–93, 185; 4: 3–4; 5: 155–239; Leonard Calvert to Lord Baltimore, 25 April 1638, in Hall, *Narratives*, 150–59; "The Lord Baltamore's Case" (1653), in ibid., 167–80; "Virginia and Maryland," 187–217; Fausz, "Merging and Emerging Worlds," 72–73; Semmes, "Claiborne vs. Cloberry," *MdHM* 27: 346–51; 28: 260–65.

25. Calvert to Baltimore, 25 April 1638, in Hall, *Narratives*, 151–58 (quotations); *Arch. Md.* 3: 57–59, 62, 65.

26. *Arch. Md.* 4: 5–7; 5: 177, 181, 189, 213–14; "Virginia and Maryland," 190; "David De Vries's Notes," 26, in Albert Myers, ed., *Narratives of Early Pennsylvania, West New Jersey, and Delaware* (New York: Charles Scribner's Sons, 1912), 26; *DRCHSNY* 3: 24; *JR* 33: 134–37; 39: 235; Sharon White, "To Secure a Lasting Peace: A Diachronic Analysis of Seventeenth-Century Susquehannock Political and Economic Strategies" (Ph.D. diss., Pennsylvania State University, 2001), 112–25.

27. Virginia and Maryland continued to license Indian traders, and pelts, roanoke or wampumpeake (belts of beads), and other "trucking goods" routinely crop up in accounts, court cases, and inventories of the period. Roanoke and beaver pelts held their value in exchanges between Englishmen, functioning as currency as well as commodities. For Virginia examples, see Carolyn Jett, *Records of Northumberland*

County, Virginia (Bowie, Md.: Heritage Books, 1994), 3–5; Beverley Fleet, *Virginia Colonial Abstracts*, vol. 2, *Northumberland County Records, 1652–1655* (Baltimore: Genealogical Publishing, 1961), 68, 82, 100, 114, 123; Ruth Sparacio, *Order Book Abstracts of Northumberland County, Virginia, 1652–1657* (McLean, Va.: Antient Press, 1994), 91; Beverley Fleet, *Virginia Colonial Abstracts*, vol. 23 (typescript copy at VHS), 24, 80–81. For Maryland, see Fausz, "Present at the 'Creation,'" 16–18.

28. "Annual Letters of the Jesuits," in Hall, *Narratives*, 119–21, 131, 134; Russell Menard, "Immigrants and Their Increase: The Process of Population Growth in Early Colonial Maryland," in Aubrey Land, Lois Green Carr, and Edward Papenfuse, eds., *Law, Society, and Politics in Early Maryland* (Baltimore: Johns Hopkins University Press, 1977), 95–97; Russell Menard, "British Migration to the Chesapeake Colonies in the Seventeenth Century," in Carr, Morgan, and Russo, *Colonial Chesapeake Society*, 103–4; Lorena Walsh and Russell Menard, "Death in the Chesapeake: Two Life Tables for Men in Early Colonial Maryland," *MdHM* 69 (1974), 211–27.

29. "Annual Letters of the Jesuits," 136, 138; *Arch. Md.* 1: 196–98; 3: 102–8, 116–17, 126, 130–34, 137, 144, 146, 148–50, 161, 163; Beauchamp Plantagenet, "A Description of the Province of New-Albion," in Myers, *Narratives of Early Pennsylvania*, 10, 14; *JR* 31: 99; Timothy Riordan, *The Plundering Time: Maryland and the English Civil War* (Baltimore: Maryland Historical Press, 2004), 34–51, 98–99, 111–15.

30. Hening, *Statutes* 1: 290; *Arch. Md.* 3: 148–50.

31. McIlwaine, *Minutes of the Council*, 502; William Shea, *The Virginia Militia in the Seventeenth Century* (Baton Rouge: Louisiana State University Press, 1983), 62–68; Hening, *Statutes* 1: 285–87, 293, 317–19, 337; Robert Beverley, *The History and Present State of Virginia*, ed. Louis B. Wright (Chapel Hill: University of North Carolina Press, 1947), 61.

32. *Arch. Md.* 3: 148–50 (quotation), 161, 163; "Report of Governor Printz, 1644," in *Narratives of Early Pennsylvania*, 102; Peter Lindeström, *Geographica Americae, with an Account of the Delaware Indians*, trans. and ed. Amandus Johnson (Philadelphia: Swedish Colonial Society, 1935), 241–44.

33. Russell Menard, "Maryland's Time of Troubles: Sources of Political Disorder in Early St. Mary's," *MdHM* 76 (1981), 124–40; James Vardaman, "Lord Baltimore, Parliament, and Cromwell: A Problem of Church and State in Seventeenth-Century England," *Journal of Church and State* 4 (1962), 31–46; Riordan, *Plundering Time*, 86–90.

34. "Lord Baltamore's Case," 202–3; *Arch. Md.* 3: 161, 164–65; 4: 435–36, 455–56, 458–59; McIlwaine, *Minutes of the Council*, 503; Fausz, "Merging and Emerging Worlds," 73–79; Menard, "Maryland's Time of Troubles," 141–58; Riordan, *Plundering Time*, passim.

35. *A Perfect Description of Virginia, being a full and true relation of the present state of the plantation . . . being sent from Virginia, at the request of a gentleman of worthy note, who desired to know the true state of Virginia* (London: Richard Wodenoth, 1649), 8; *Arch. Md.* 3: 281; 4: 176–77.

36. Fausz, "Merging and Emerging Worlds," 79–81; John Krugler, "'With Promise of Liberty in Religion': The Catholic Lords Baltimore and Toleration in Seventeenth-

Century Maryland, 1634–1692," *MdHM* 79 (1984), 30–33; Riordan, *Plundering Time,* chs. 14, 16, 17.

37. *Arch. Md.* 1: 231–32.

38. "Lord Baltamore's Case," 168–80, 198–211, 216–17; *Arch. Md.* 3: 264–72; H. R. McIlwaine, ed., *Journals of the House of Burgesses, 1619–1658/59* (Richmond: Colonial Press, 1915), 79–81; "Speech of Sir Wm. Berkeley, and Declaration of the Assembly, March, 1651," *VMHB* 1 (1894), 75–77; Fausz, "Merging and Emerging Worlds," 81–82.

39. *JR* 37: 97, 105, 111; 39: 191.

40. *JR* 37: 97, 105, 111; *Arch. Md.* 3: 276–78; "Lord Baltamore's Case," 168–80; Richard Bennett et al., to Philip Conner et al., 31 July 1652, MHS mss 2018.

41. *Arch. Md.* 1: 340–41, 351–52; Aubrey Land, *Colonial Maryland: A History* (Millwood, N.Y.: KTO Press, 1981), 51–52.

42. Robert Brugger, *Maryland: A Middle Temperament* (Baltimore: Johns Hopkins University Press, 1988), 20–22; "Annual Letters of the Jesuits," 141–42; *Arch. Md.* 1: 339–56; 3: 320–34.

43. McIlwaine, *Journals of the House of Burgesses, 1619–1658–59,* 85; Edward Bland, *The Discovery of New Brittaine* (London: Thomas Harper for John Stephenson, 1651); Charles Campbell, "An Excursion into the Territory Afterwards Called North Carolina, in 1654," VHS mss 2 C1525 a1; Hening, *Statutes* 1: 374, 376–77; Jett, *Records of Northumberland County, Virginia,* 2–3; Ruth Sparacio, *Order Book Abstracts of Northumberland County, Virginia, 1652–1657* (McLean, Va.: Antient Press, 1994), 91; Sparacio, *Deed & Will Abstracts of Northumberland County, 1655–1658* (McLean, Va.: Antient Press, 1993), 22 October 1657.

44. *Arch. Md.* 1: 332–34.

Chapter 6. *"You Come Too Near"*

1. David W. Stahle et al., "The Lost Colony and Jamestown Droughts," *Science* 280, no. 5363 (24 April 1998), 565; "Annual Letters of the Jesuits," in Clayton Hall, ed., *Narratives of Early Maryland, 1633–1634* (New York: Charles Scribner's Sons, 1910), 126–32, 136; James Merrell, "Cultural Continuity among the Piscataway Indians of Colonial Maryland," *WMQ* 36 (1979), 557; *Arch. Md.* 1: 142–46; 3: 96, 102–8, 110–19, 120–21, 123, 126, 129, 281, 293–94; 4: 176–77.

2. "An Account of the Colony of the Lord Baron of Baltimore" (1633), in Hall, *Narratives,* 6–10; Andrew White, "A Briefe Relation of the Voyage Unto Maryland" (1634), in ibid., 45; Captain Thomas Yong to Sir Toby Matthew, July 1634, in ibid., 60; "A Relation of Maryland," in ibid., 79–83, 96–97.

3. "Account of the Colony," 7–10; "Relation of Maryland," 81, 83.

4. "Relation of Maryland," 76, 93–99.

5. "Virginia and Maryland, or The Lord Baltimore's printed CASE, uncased and answered" (1655), in Hall, *Narratives,* 194; Russell Menard and Lois Green Carr, "The Lords Baltimore and the Colonization of Maryland," in David Quinn, ed., *Early Maryland in a Wider World* (Detroit: Wayne State University Press, 1982), 198; *Arch. Md.* 1: 79, 95, 97–99; Lois Green Carr, Russell Menard, and Lorena Walsh, *Robert Cole's*

World: Agriculture and Society in Early Maryland (Chapel Hill: University of North Carolina Press, 1991), 13, 34–35, 39–43; John McCusker and Russell Menard, *The Economy of British America, 1607–1789* (Chapel Hill: University of North Carolina Press, 1985), 121; Gloria Main, *Tobacco Colony: Life in Early Maryland, 1650–1720* (Princeton: Princeton University Press, 1982), 39, 76.

6. Henry Miller, "An Archaeological Perspective on the Evolution of Diet in the Colonial Chesapeake, 1620–1745," in Lois Green Carr, Philip Morgan, and Jean Russo, eds., *Colonial Chesapeake Society* (Chapel Hill: University of North Carolina Press, 1988), 181–86; Carr, Walsh, and Menard, *Robert Cole's World,* 55–75, 95–97, 217–39. Statutes requiring planters to fence in their corn for protection from marauding livestock also testify to the ubiquity of that crop. See, e.g., *Arch. Md.* 1: 96, 160–61, 344, 413; Hening, *Statutes* 1: 244, 332, 458; 2: 100–101. Literary sources and legal records frequently mention perishable foods such as orchard fruits, dairy, and garden plants, as well as fish, beef, and pork. See *Arch. Md.* 2: 56; 4: 511; 49: 57, 157, 469; 47: 32–24; 65: 507; 69: 139, 316; 70: 87; Thomas Glover, *An Account of Virginia, its situation, temperature, productions, inhabitants, and their manner of planting and ordering tobacco,* Extracted from the Royal Society of London, Philosophical Transactions, vol. 2, no. 126, 20 June 1676 (repr. Oxford: B. H. Blackwell, 1904), 624, 628–29; John Hammond, "Leah and Rachel, Or, The Two Fruitfull Sisters Virginia and Mary-Land" (1656), in Hall, *Narratives,* 201–2.

7. Carr, Walsh, and Menard, *Robert Cole's World,* ch. 3.

8. William Tatham, *An Historical and Practical Essay on the Culture and Commerce of Tobacco* (London, 1800), 17–18, quoted in Carr, Walsh, and Menard, *Robert Cole's World,* 60.

9. Ibid., ch. 3.

10. Ibid. (quotation on 63–64).

11. *Arch. Md.* 49: 197 (quotation); Carr, Walsh, and Menard, *Robert Cole's World,* 95 (quotation) and ch. 3.

12. *Arch. Md.* 1: 295; 3: 260, 10: 192; 41: 223; 15 November 1664, Order Books, Stafford County, reel 7, LV; Certificates to employ an Indian, 26 November 1669, 20 December 1669, 9 May 1670, 11 November 1670, 24 February 1670/01, 20 May 1671, 18 December 1672, 20 February 1672/3, and 1 October 1673, in Order Books, Northumberland County, reel 47, LV; Hammond, "Leah and Rachel," 291.

13. G. Terry Sharrer, "Farming, Disease, and Change in the Chesapeake Ecosystem," in Philip Curtin, Grace Brush, and George Fisher, eds., *Discovering the Chesapeake: The History of an Ecosystem* (Baltimore: Johns Hopkins University Press, 2001), 307, 310–12.

14. Court records abound with information on free-ranging livestock. See (among many, many possible examples) Petition of Elias Bagg, February 1660, Deposition of Mary Redman, 2 February 1660, Deposition of George Dauson, 14 February 1660, and the Deposition of Jane Deeba, 2 April 1661, all in Westmoreland County Deeds, Wills, Etc., 1661–1662, reel 1, LV; Inventory of James Claughton, 20 August 1648 and Inventory of Robert Douglas, 20 March 1655, Northumberland County Record Books, 1652–1658, 1658–1666, 1666–1672, reel 2, LV (an especially rich trove of probated inven-

tories and estate accounts); Carolyn Jett, *Records of Northumberland County, Virginia* (Bowie, Md.: Heritage Books, 1994) (for a flood of earmark registrations, especially in 1651); *Arch. Md.* 1: 408, 418, 450, 486; 4: 48; 8: 362; 10: 48–49, 156, 236; 2: 277–79; 15: 155; 53: 234–37, 630; *A Perfect Description of Virginia, being a full and true relation of the present state of the plantation . . . being sent from Virginia, at the request of a gentleman of worthy note, who desired to know the true state of Virginia* (London: Richard Wodenoth, 1649), 1, 11; Edmund Berkeley and Dorothy Smith Berkeley, eds., *The Reverend John Clayton: A Parson with a Scientific Mind* (Charlottesville: University Press of Virginia, 1965), 54, 79, 87–89; Glover, *Account of Virginia,* 628, 630. See also Virginia DeJohn Anderson, "Animals into the Wilderness: The Development of Livestock Husbandry in the Seventeenth-Century Chesapeake," *WMQ* 59 (2002), esp. 399–400.

15. Though Virginians actually avoided cleared Indian fields of declining fertility, preferring to work fresher soils within a quarter-mile or so of Indian settlements. Stephen Potter and Gregory Waselkov, "'Whereby We Shall Enjoy Their Cultivated Places,'" in Paul Shackel and Barbara Little, eds., *Historical Archaeology of the Chesapeake* (Washington, D.C.: Smithsonian Institution Press, 1994), 27–29. Land claims on lower Aquia Creek can be traced in Nell Nugent, *Cavaliers and Pioneers: Abstracts of Virginia Land Patents and Grants* (Richmond: Virginia State Library, 1992), 218, 290, 293, 298–300, 302, 304, 319, 345, 399–400.

16. Carr, Walsh, and Menard, *Robert Cole's World,* 37; Lorena Walsh, "Land Use, Settlement Patterns, and the Impact of European Agriculture, 1620–1820," in Curtin, Brush, and Fisher, *Discovering the Chesapeake,* 239. Direct evidence of garden plots and fruit trees can most often be found in legal proceedings. See, e.g., *Arch. Md.* 10: 157, 198, 400, 465, 499, 507; 41: 145, 188–89, 297–98; 49: 57–58, 469, 481–82, 517–18.

17. "Relation of Maryland," 77; Deed from Herbert Smith to Michaell Philleps and John Butler, May 1660, Westmoreland County Deeds, Wills, Etc., reel 1, LV; Hammond, "Leah and Rachel," 191, 202; H. R. McIlwaine, ed., *Journals of the House of Burgesses, 1619–1658/59* (Richmond: Colonial Press, 1915), 126; Glover, *Account of Virginia,* 628–29; *Arch. Md.* 70: 87; Carr, Walsh, and Menard, *Robert Cole's World,* ch. 4; James Horn, *Adapting to a New World: English Society in the Seventeenth-Century Chesapeake* (Chapel Hill: University of North Carolina Press, 1994), 302–7; Main, *Tobacco Colony,* 140–66; Cary Carson et al., "Impermanent Architecture in the Southern American Colonies," *Winterthur Portfolio* 16 (1981), 135–96; Henry Miller, *Discovering Maryland's First City: A Summary Report on the 1981–1984 Archaeological Excavations in St. Mary's City,* St. Mary's City Archaeological series, no. 2 (St. Mary's, Md.: Historic St. Mary's City Commission, 1986), 144–45. Robert Keeler's "The Homelot on the Seventeenth-Century Tidewater Frontier" (Ph.D. diss., University of Oregon, 1978), 144–87, includes forty separate diagrams of farmyards from this period, most of them on the Potomac. He also provides a useful census of buildings, fence types, and land uses (including specific fruit trees and field crops) described in Orphan's Court valuations in Maryland (pp. 171–73). Evidence of dogs is scattered, but they are mentioned in a matter-of-fact manner in various legal proceedings, as if their presence was unexceptional. See, e.g., *Arch. Md.* 2: 130, 240; 7: 272; 10: 35, 236, 243, 329, 464; 41: 191; 49:

73, 351, 481–82; 53: 239, 338, 347, 633, 636; 27 July 1692, 30 November 1694, Order Book, Westmoreland County, reel 48, LV.

18. Berkeley and Berkeley, *Reverend John Clayton*, 87; Glover, *Account of Virginia*, 630.

19. Henry Grove Diary, July 1732, VHS mss 5:1 G9193:1.

20. John Nightengale Inventory, 11 May 1660, Deeds, Wills, Etc., 1661–1662, Northumberland County, reel 1, LV. In the fifteen Northumberland County inventories recorded between November 1650 and February 1656, e.g., the ten men who owned livestock possessed a median of eleven cattle and swine combined; a few years later, between January and May 1660, the average (median) decedent owned ten swine and twelve cattle. (These numbers are necessarily approximations, both because of the poor quality of early county records on the Northern Neck and because of the inherent limitations of probated inventories, which were not recorded for all decedents. I've used the most conservative calculations possible, such as counting "[torn] shotes" as only two animals.) Record Books, 1652–1658, Northumberland County, reel 2, LV. Ninety-two percent of the probated inventories taken in Maryland's St. Marys, Charles, and Calvert counties between 1658 and 1677 included cattle, hogs, or both. Carr, Walsh, and Menard, *Robert Cole's World*, 285, n. 14. See also Richard Beale Davis, ed., *William Fitzhugh and His Chesapeake World, 1676–1701* (Chapel Hill: University of North Carolina Press, 1963), 175–76; Glover, *Account of Virginia*, 630; *Arch. Md.* 2: 277–79, 10: 236; 53: 84, 94, 220, 251, 551–53, 206, 238, 321, 371; Berkeley and Berkeley, *Reverend John Clayton*, 88; Main, *Tobacco Colony*, 62; Anderson, "Animals into the Wilderness," 382, 399–400; Keeler, "Homelot," 144, 182, 184–85. On seventeenth-century diets, see Miller, "Archaeological Perspective," 177–90, and Carr, Walsh, and Menard, *Robert Cole's World*, 95–97, 215–18.

21. Governor Charles Calvert to Lord Baltimore, 27 April 1664, in *The Calvert Papers, No. 1*, Maryland Historical Society Fund Publication no. 28 (Baltimore: Maryland Historical Society, 1889), 238–40 (quotation); Berkeley and Berkeley, *Reverend John Clayton*, 79–80, 88; Lorena Walsh, "Community Networks in the Early Chesapeake," in Carr, Morgan, and Russo, *Colonial Chesapeake Society*, 207, 212, 223–24; Walsh, "Land Use," 220–24, 234; Carr, Walsh, and Menard, *Robert Cole's World*, 284, n. 5, 292, n. 54; Edmund Morgan, *American Slavery, American Freedom: The Ordeal of Colonial Virginia* (New York: W. W. Norton, 1975), 219. Big Northern Neck planters such as Gervase Dodson (over 11,000 acres) and the Brent family abound in Nugent, *Cavaliers and Pioneers*.

22. 31 October 1688 and 29 July 1691, Order Books, Westmoreland County, reels 51, 52, LV; Levies of 21 October 1658, 22 November 1659, 15 November 1660 (quotation), 6 September 1665, and 5 November 1668, in Order Books, Northumberland County, reel 47, LV; Levies of December 1686 and November 1689, in Ruth Sparacio and Sam Sparacio, comps., *Deed & Will Abstracts of Stafford County, Virginia, 1686–1689* (McLean, Va.: Antient Press, 1989); Levy of December 1692, in Sparacio and Sparacio, comps., *Deed & Will Abstracts of Stafford County, Virginia, 1689–1693* (McLean, Va.: Antient Press, 1989); Hening, *Statutes* 1: 199, 328, 395, 456; 2: 87, 236, 274, 276; 6: 153; *Arch. Md.* 1: 346, 362–63, 365, 372, 408, 537; 3: 557; 4: 277–78; 53: 55, 274, 523, 619.

23. Hening, *Statutes* 1: 244–45, 332; *Arch. Md.* 1: 96, 344, 413–14, 537; 10: 197; 41: 277, 584; 202: 415; Berkeley and Berkeley, *Reverend John Clayton,* 79; Davis, *William Fitzhugh,* 175–76; Miller, *Discovering Maryland's First City,* 25–33, 49–57; Keeler, "Homelot," 44–74, 84–93, 113–21; 144–86.

24. Donald Worster, "Transformations of the Earth: Toward an Agroecological Perspective in History," *JAH* 76 (1990), 1093–1103.

25. This was common practice in England, where processions might take place every year. A 1662 Virginia statute mandated processions every four years, though this requirement was not always observed before the eighteenth century. In practice, of course, boundaries could be difficult to accurately survey and record, but considerable energy was devoted to determining and maintaining them with as much precision as possible, and Anglo-Americans were, in the seventeenth century, rapidly becoming even more conscious of, and precise about, the identification and maintenance of boundaries. Hening, *Statutes* 2: 101–2; William Seiler, "Land Processioning in Colonial Virginia," *WMQ* 6 (1949), 416–36; Martin Brückner, *The Geographic Revolution in Early America: Maps, Literacy, and National Identity* (Chapel Hill: University of North Carolina Press, 2006), ch. 1.

26. See, e.g., Inventory of John Key, 21 July 1656, Inventory of Ralph Horsley, 1 September 1656, and Inventory of Henry Mosely, 20 September 1656, in Record Books (1652–1658), Northumberland County, reel 2, LV. On the livestock trade, see Richard Ligon, *A True and Exact History of the Island of Barbados* (London: Humphrey Moseley, 1657), 113; Hammond, "Leah and Rachel," 299; *A description of the province of New Albion and a direction for adventurers . . .* (London: James Moxon, 1650), 23, 31; *DRCHSNY* 12: 202; Morgan, *American Slavery,* 192.

27. McCusker and Menard, *Economy of British America,* 121; Lorena Walsh, "Summing the Parts: Implications for Estimating Chesapeake Output and Income Subregionally," *WMQ* 56 (1999), 87.

28. Lois Green Carr and Russell Menard, "Wealth and Welfare in Early Maryland: Evidence from St. Mary's County," *WMQ* 56 (1999), 95–102, 104–5; Carr, Walsh, and Menard, *Robert Cole's World,* chs. 2, 4. Probated inventories and estate accounts from the Northern Neck support Carr, Walsh, and Menard's contention that planters plowed profits back into their farms. Except for the occasional storekeeper, planters of all ranks tended to store their wealth in livestock, bound laborers, farm implements, clothing, guns, small boats, and uncollected debts, rather than in consumer goods or even basic household items such as furniture. See Westmoreland County, Deeds, Wills, Etc., 1661–1662, reel 1, LV: Col. Thos. Speke Inventory, 16 January 1659–60; John Nightengale Inventory, 11 May 1660; Capt. Gabrielle Odyer, 20 January 1659/60, sworn 14 May 1660; Nathaniell Pope, sworn same day; John Hiller Inventory, 29 June 1658; John Knott inventory, 27 May 1660; William Baldridge Inventory, 25 May 1660; Inventory of Walter Brodhurst, 17 April 1661; and Northumberland County Record Books, 1652–1656, reel 2, LV: Inventory of Walter Dowell, 1 November 1650; Inventory of James Claughton, recorded 20 August 1648; Inventory of William Nicholls, 6 May 1651; Inventory of Winton Sharpman, 22 March 1650; Inventory of Robert Honnibourn, 25 November 1651; Inventory of Edward Tempest, 20 January 1652; Inventory

of John Donnit Jr., 20 January 1652; Inventory of John Donnit Jr., 28 January 1652; Inventory of John Doaks, 20 September 1653; Inventory of Robert Sharpe, 30 September 1655; Inventory of Robert Douglas, recorded 20 March 1655; Inventory of Thomas Kingwell, 20 May 1656; Inventory of John Key, 21 July 1656; Inventory of Ralph Horsley, 1 September 1656; Inventory of Henry Mosely, 20 September 1656; Inventory of Thomas Gresham, 27 February 1656.

29. Horn, *Adapting to a New World*, ch. 7; Main, *Tobacco Colony*, ch. 5. A survey of twenty-four inventories in 1652–62 clearly corroborates the work of scholars focusing on the standard of living in southern Maryland and central Tidewater Virginia (see the Westmoreland and Northumberland County inventories cited in ch. 6, n. 28, above).

30. Horn, *Adapting to a New World*, 140–41, 235.

31. Calculated from Lorena Walsh, "Servitude and Opportunity in Charles County, Maryland, 1658–1705," in Aubrey Land, Lois Green Carr, and Edward Papenfuse, *Law, Society, and Politics in Early Maryland* (Baltimore: Johns Hopkins University Press, 1977), 119, table 5.2.

32. David Galenson, *White Servitude in Colonial America: An Economic Analysis* (New York: Cambridge University Press, 1981); Morgan, *American Slavery*; Horn, *Adapting to a New World*, 268–76. On servants in the legal system, see Christine Daniels, "'Liberty to Complaine': Servant Petitions in Maryland, 1692–1797," in Christopher Tomlins and Bruce Mann, eds., *The Many Legalities of Early America* (Chapel Hill: University of North Carolina Press, 2001), 219–49.

33. Colonial accounts of open, park-like forest floors invariably describe woods *before* the dispossession of the Indians; after the conquest there is no further talk of driving carriages between the trees. On erosion rates, soil exhaustion, ragweed pollen, and water quality, see Brush, "Forests before and after the Colonial Encounter," in Curtin, Brush, and Fisher, *Discovering the Chesapeake*, 40–59 (quotation on 40–41). See also William Cronon, "Reading the Palimpsest," in ibid., 363–66; Walsh, "Land Use," 237–40; Henry Miller, "Transforming a 'Splendid and Delightsome Land': Colonists and Ecological Change in the Chesapeake, 1607–1820," *Journal of the Washington Academy of Sciences* (1986), 173–87; and Carville Earle, "The Myth of the Southern Soil Miner: Macrohistory, Agricultural Innovation, and Environmental Change," in Donald Worster, ed., *The Ends of the Earth: Perspectives on Modern Environmental History* (New York: Cambridge University Press, 1988), 175–210.

34. Hening, *Statutes* 1: 274, 323–26, 328–29.

35. Hening, *Statutes* 1: 352–54; Beverley Fleet, ed., *Virginia Colonial Abstracts*, vol. 2 (Baltimore: Genealogical Publishing, 1988), 25; Jett, *Records of Northumberland County*, entry for 15 March 1647; Nugent, *Cavaliers and Pioneers*, 178, 185, 192, 198–99, 201, 205–12. On Mottrom, Claughton, and the clustering of settlement around their lands along the Chicacoan and The Glebe (part of the Chicacoan system), see *Arch. Md.* 3: 76; Fleet, *Virginia Colonial Abstracts*, vol. 2, 41; Inventory of James Claughton, recorded 20 August 1648, Northumberland County Record Books, reel 2, LV; Jett, *Records of Northumberland County*, entries for 24 August 1650 and 17 January 1651/52; Account of John Mottrom's Estate, 22 October 1657, in Ruth Sparacio, *Deed & Will*

Abstracts of Northumberland County, 1655–1658 (McLean, Va.: Antient Press, 1993); Nugent, *Cavaliers and Pioneers,* 185, 205–6, 252; "Mottrom-Wright- Spencer-Ariss- Buckner," *WMQ,* 1st series, 17 (1908–1909), 53, 58.

36. *Arch. Md.* 2: 15 (quotation). See also Hening, *Statutes* 1: 393–94.

37. *Arch. Md.* 53: 231.

38. *Arch. Md.* 15: 237–39; G. Malcolm Lewis, "Maps, Mapmaking, and Map Use by Native North Americans," in David Woodward and G. Malcolm Lewis, eds., *The History of Cartography,* vol. 2, bk. 3, *Cartography in the Traditional African, American, Arctic, Australian, and Pacific Societies* (Chicago: University of Chicago Press, 1998), 51–182 (especially 66–106); Peter Nabokov, "Orientations from Their Side: Dimensions of Native American Cartographic Discourse," in G. Malcolm Lewis, ed., *Cartographic Encounters: Perspectives on Native American Mapmaking and Map Use* (Chicago: University of Chicago Press, 1998), 241–69; Gregory Waselkov, "Indian Maps of the Colonial Southeast," in Peter Wood, Gregory Waselkov, and M. Thomas Hatley, eds., *Powhatan's Mantle: Indians in the Colonial Southeast* (Lincoln: University of Nebraska Press, 1989), 292–343.

39. Edward Price, *Dividing the Land: Early American Beginnings of Our Private Property Mosaic* (Chicago: University of Chicago Press, 1995), 5; Nabokov, "Orientations," 247, 259 (quotations).

40. See, e.g., Ruth Sparacio, *Order Book Abstracts of Northumberland County, Virginia, 1652–1657* (McLean, Va.: Antient Press, 1994), 20 May 1656 and 20 May 1657; Sparacio, *Deed & Will Abstracts of Northumberland County, 1655–1658,* 22 October 1657; Jett, *Records of Northumberland County,* 5, 11, 18; Fleet, *Virginia Colonial Abstracts,* vol. 2, 68; Hening, *Statutes* 1: 415, 525; *Arch. Md.* 10: 192, 220–21; 34: 114–15, 287–88; 60: 34.

41. *Arch. Md.* 1: 362–63; 3: 281 (quotation); 5: 118; 8: 461–62; 10: 52, 158, 484, 495 (quotation), 560; 15: 78, 366, 368–69; Fleet, *Virginia Colonial Abstracts,* vol. 2, 82; Ruth Sparacio, *Order Book Abstracts of Northumberland County, Virginia, 1669–1673* (McLean, Va.: Antient Press, 1995), 26 November 1669, 20 December 1669, 9 May 1670, 11 November 1670, 24 February 1670/1, 20 May 1671, 18 December 1672, 20 February 1672/3, and 1 October 1673.

42. *Arch. Md.* 10: 509; 49: 481–82. See also *Arch. Md.* 2: 80; 10: 158, 192; 8: 341–43.

43. This shift was reflected in the archaeological record. Since sixteenth-century chiefs were fairly successful at regulating the flow of exotic trade goods, few of the people buried at Potomac Creek before 1600 had grave goods bundled with them. Burials dating to the early seventeenth century reveal a slightly more widespread distribution of spiritually powerful goods, but the major shift away from chiefly control of exotic trade goods can first be seen in a burial dating to the 1650s and 1660s, in which the ten deceased were interred with a great many shell beads, half of a shell gorget, and an impressive array of English goods. Stephen R. Potter, "Early English Effects on Virginia Algonquian Exchange and Tribute in the Tidewater Potomac," in Wood, Waselkov, and Hatley, *Powhatan's Mantle,* 160–67.

44. Jett, *Records of Northumberland County,* entry on 10 May 1650, 20 February

1657, and 21 November 1657, Order Books, Northumberland County, reel 57, LV; "Isaac Allerton and the Indians," *WMQ*, 1st series, vol. 8 (1899), 24.

45. *Arch. Md.* 1: 295; 3: 260, 293; Warren Billings, "Some Acts Not in Hening's *Statutes:* The Acts of Assembly, April 1652, November 1652, and July 1653," *VMHB* 83 (1975), 39, 68–69; Hening, *Statutes* 1: 255, 382; Jett, *Records of Northumberland County,* entry for 17 January 1651; Fleet, *Virginia Colonial Abstracts,* vol. 2, 15, 55; 17 January 1651 and 25 November 1652, Order Books, Northumberland County, reel 47, LV.

46. Dodson owned this property, but the Matchotics settled in without incident, likely because the large-scale landowners in this area did not necessarily occupy their property (Dodson's patent alone covered about eight square miles). Order Books, Northumberland County, reel 47, LV, 20 May 1656, 20 February, 20 July and 21 November 1657, 21 May and 22 November 1659 (quotation), and 3 May 1660 (quotation); Nugent, *Cavaliers and Pioneers,* 205, 210–11, 249, 280, 290, 319, 367, 373 (Dodson's patent), 355, 382 ("Appamatucks Creek"), 421–22, 533.

47. On the dispossession of the Chicacoans, Wicocomocos, and Cuttatawomens, see Order Books, Northumberland County, reel 47, LV, 20 January 1655/56, 20 May 1656/57, 20 February 1657, and 20 April, 3 May, 21 May, and 26 June 1660; Nugent, *Cavaliers and Pioneers,* 308, 343; Hening, *Statutes* 1: 515; H. R. McIlwaine, ed., *Minutes of the Council and General Court of Colonial Virginia,* 2nd ed. (Richmond: Virginia State Library, 1979), 1: 505–6.

48. *Arch. Md.* 1: 329–31, 431; 3: 489; 53: 630. On the Wicomico manors, see Walsh, "Community Networks," 202–24.

49. *Arch. Md.* 53: 629–30.

50. *Arch. Md.* 10: 21–22, 81–82, 192–93, 220–21; 3: 293, 489 (quotation); 41: 114–15, 186–88, 230–31; Arthur Karinen, "Maryland Population, 1631–1730: Numerical and Distributional Aspects," *MdHM* 54 (1959), 387–88, 405; Karinen, "Numerical and Distributional Aspects of Maryland Population, 1631–1840" (Ph.D. diss., University of Maryland, College Park, 1958), 149; Nugent, *Cavaliers and Pioneers,* 324; Stahle et al., "Lost Colony and Jamestown Droughts," 565; Stephen Potter, *Commoners, Tribute, and Chiefs: The Development of Algonquian Culture in the Potomac Valley* (Charlottesville: University Press of Virginia, 1993), 198; Helen Rountree, *Pocahontas's People: The Powhatan Indians of Virginia through Four Centuries* (Norman: University of Oklahoma Press, 1990), 95–96.

51. St. Mary's County contained 650 colonists in 1650, and Virginia's Potomac River counties had 742 in 1653. St. Mary's had 2,200 residents in 1675, and Charles County had 1,880 in 1674. Virginia's Potomac counties (Westmoreland, Northumberland, and Stafford) had 3,122 residents in 1674. The Virginia figures are estimates based on the number of "tithables" (males deemed old enough to work plus, after 1662, female slaves and servants of working age) in each county, and converted to total population figures using a modified version of the ratios worked out by Edmund S. Morgan. Morgan's recommended multiplier for 1653 is 1.88 colonists per tithable, and 2.25 for 1674. I instead used multipliers of 1.65 for 1653 and 2.0 for 1674, because (as Morgan notes) the ratio of tithables to residents rose steadily throughout the

seventeenth century as frontier societies developed into long-settled (or more properly "resettled") counties. Estimating a half-generation lag in the proper multiplier for Virginia as a whole (because at that point the Northern Neck was colonized at a later date than the remainder of the province and thus had fewer families and smaller households), I used Morgan's 1640 multiplier to calculate Westmoreland and Northumberland counties' 1653 population, and his 1662 multiplier to calculate the 1674 population for Virginia's side of the Potomac. The resulting numbers were rounded slightly upward, partly in order to avoid giving a false sense of precision, and partly because precision is not necessary to make the point that the population grew by leaps and bounds in this period. Karinen, "Maryland Population," 378, 389, 405; Morgan, *American Slavery*, 395–405, 412–14.

52. Lorena Walsh, "Charles County, Maryland, 1658–1705: A Study of Chesapeake Social and Political Structure" (Ph.D. diss., Michigan State University, 1977), 393; Carr, Walsh, and Menard, *Robert Cole's World*, 37.

Chapter 7. Microbes, Magistrates, and Migrations

1. Timothy Silver, "A Useful Arcadia: European Colonists as Biotic Factors in Chesapeake Forests," in Philip Curtin, Grace Brush, and George Fisher, eds., *Discovering the Chesapeake: The History of an Ecosystem* (Baltimore: Johns Hopkins University Press, 2001); Alfred Crosby, "Ecological Imperialism: The Overseas Migration of Western Europeans as a Biological Phenomenon," in Donald Worster, ed., *The Ends of the Earth: Perspectives on Modern Environmental History* (New York: Cambridge University Press, 1988), 103–17.

2. Virginia's assembly recorded eighty bowmen on the south bank in 1669, well down from the number of bowmen recorded by John Smith in 1608. The population figures here assume a 1:4 ratio of bowmen to villagers (Hening, *Statutes* 2: 274). This ratio may be wrong, and Smith's figures are surely imprecise, but clearly the decline in population was a steep one. For a careful discussion of population estimates in the Potomac Valley, see Stephen Potter, *Commoners, Tribute, and Chiefs: The Development of Algonquian Culture in the Potomac Valley* (Charlottesville: University Press of Virginia, 1993), 20–24.

3. Helen Rountree, *Pocahontas's People: The Powhatan Indians of Virginia through Four Centuries* (Norman: University of Oklahoma Press, 1990), 90, 95–96, 106; Potter, *Commoners, Tribute, and Chiefs*, 194; James Merrell, "Cultural Continuity among the Piscataway Indians of Colonial Maryland" *WMQ* 36 (1979), 565–66.

4. Alfred Crosby, *Germs, Seeds, and Animals: Studies in Ecological History* (New York: M.E. Sharpe, 1994), 57.

5. Notwithstanding some dramatic cases in which epidemics spread well in advance of actual European settlement, they did not spread as easily as some historians have assumed. The assumption may have arisen from several cases of epidemics that actually did spread in advance of European contact. Two of these tragedies took place at times and places that have achieved iconic status; thus they have come to represent the norm in many historians' minds. The Spanish conquest of Mexico in 1517 was

aided by epidemics that weakened the resistance of the Aztecs and their allies even before Cortes led his men and allies to Tenochtitlan, while a devastating epidemic in 1616–18 largely depopulated Plymouth Bay and Massachusetts Bay, shortly before the establishment of colonies there in 1620 and 1630. See Rober McCaa, "Spanish and Nahuatl Views on Smallpox and Demographic Catastrophe in Mexico," *Journal of Interdisciplinary History* 25 (1995), 397–431, and Neal Salisbury, *Manitou and Providence: Indians, Europeans, and the Making of New England, 1500–1643* (New York: Oxford University Press, 1982), 101–9. Those who assume that epidemic diseases predated colonization in the Chesapeake region include Christian Feest, "Virginia Algonquians," in Bruce Trigger, ed., *Handbook of North American Indians*, vol. 15, *Northeast* (Washington, D.C.: Smithsonian Institution, 1978), 254; Rountree, *Pocahontas's People*, 3, 10, 25; James Axtell, "The Rise and Fall of the Powhatan Empire," in *Natives and Newcomers: The Cultural Origins of North America* (New York: Oxford University Press, 2001); and Camilla Townsend, *Pocahontas and the Powhatan Dilemma* (New York: Hill and Wang, 2004), 13.

6. Crosby, *Germs, Seeds, and Animals*, 123 (quotation). For critiques of "virgin soil" assumptions, which posit "no immunity" to newly introduced diseases, see David Jones, *Rationalizing Epidemics: Meanings and Uses of American Indian Mortality since 1600* (Cambridge: Harvard University Press, 2004); Dean Snow and Kim Lamphear, "European Contact and Indian Depopulation in the Northeast: The Timing of the First Epidemics," *Ethnohistory* 35 (1988), 15–33; and Philip Curtin and Douglas Ubelaker, "Human Biology," in Curtin, Brush, and Fisher, *Discovering the Chesapeake*, 137–40.

7. Stephen R. Duncan, Susan Scott, and Christopher J. Duncan, "An Hypothesis for the Periodicity of Smallpox Epidemics," *Journal of Theoretical Biology* 100 (1993), 231–48; and, by the same authors, "Smallpox Epidemics in Cities in Britain," *Journal of Interdisciplinary History* 25 (1994), 255–71; and "The Dynamics of Smallpox epidemics in Britain, 1550–1800, *Demography* 30 (August 1993), 405–24. Smallpox did not readily spread even to the less populous portions of northern Europe: see Peter Skold, "Escape from Catastrophe: The Saami's Experience with Smallpox in Eighteenth- and Nineteenth-Century Sweden," *Social Science History* 21 (1997), 1–25. Measles, too, became endemic in London only after 1700 and thus was unlikely to spread across the Atlantic before then. S. R. Duncan, Susan Scott, and C. J. Duncan, "A Demographic Model of Measles Epidemics," *European Journal of Population* 15 (1999), 185–98.

8. The heavy predominance of males among immigrants kept the proportion of children down. The best figures on the age structure of the population come from the nearby Rappahannock River, where children made up about 10 percent of the population in 1668. Darrett Rutman and Anita Rutman, *A Place in Time: Middlesex County, Virginia, 1650–1750* (New York: W. W. Norton, 1984), 77.

9. Philip Curtin, *The Rise and Fall of the Plantation Complex*, 2nd ed. (New York: Cambridge University press, 1998), ch. 6; John McCusker and Russell Menard, *The Economy of British America, 1607–1789* (Chapel Hill: University of North Carolina Press, 1985), 121, 148–56; David Watts, *The West Indies: Patterns of Development, Cul-*

ture and Environmental Change since 1492 (New York: Cambridge University Press, 1987), ch. 5.

10. The cycle of transmission between *Anopheles* and humans requires precise timing and thus can be sustained only by a bit of luck (from the parasite's perspective) until malaria becomes endemic among humans or some other mammalian host. Even if the cycle takes hold in one locale, it can be slow to spread to a new location, as each species of *Anopheles* prefers a different climate from the others, and none ranges more than two miles in its short life span; all are highly vulnerable to subtle changes in temperature, sunlight, and humidity. Darrett Rutman and Anita Rutman, "Of Agues and Fevers: Malaria in the Early Chesapeake," *WMQ* 33 (1976), 31–60 (quotation on 160); Lorena Walsh, "Charles County, Maryland, 1658–1705: A Study of Chesapeake Social and Political Structure" (Ph.D. diss., Michigan State University, 1977), 43–47. Peter Wood, in *Black Majority: Negroes in Colonial South Carolina from 1670 through the Stono Rebellion* (New York: W. W. Norton, 1974), ch. 3, demonstrates that *vivax* predominated in South Carolina until the 1680s, when the more deadly *falciparum* strain became endemic—a generation after the beginning of substantial English colonization and with the onset of a serious slave trade originating in areas where *falciparum* was common. Jon Kukla argues for the direct transmission of malaria from England by early Jamestown colonists in "Kentish Agues and American Distempers: The Transmission of Malaria from England to Virginia in the Seventeenth Century," *Southern Studies* 25 (1986), 135–47.

11. Rutman and Rutman, "Of Agues and Fevers," 178 (quotation); Walsh, "Charles County," 46–47.

12. Russell Menard, "British Migration to the Chesapeake Colonies in the Seventeenth Century," in Lois Green Carr, Philip Morgan, and Jean Russo, eds., *Colonial Chesapeake Society* (Chapel Hill: University of North Carolina Press, 1988), 104–5.

13. The early 1660s were droughty, but in 1667 forty days of rain spoiled crops, and in late August a hurricane swept in with high winds and a twelve-foot sea surge. Food ran short, and the fall season brought even more sickness than usual. In 1672 bad weather created winter food shortages; drought struck again in 1674; and a series of cold winters in which rivers froze over further stressed the immune systems of Potomac residents. On 1667, see *Strange Newes from Virginia, being a true Relation of a Great Tempest in Virginia* (London: W. Thackeray, 1667); *DRCHSNY* 2: 523; 3: 161; Thomas Glover, *An Account of Virginia, its situation, temperature, productions, inhabitants, and their manner of planting and ordering tobacco,* Extracted from the Royal Society of London, Philosophical Transactions, vol. 2, no. 126, 20 June 1676 (repr. Oxford: B. H. Blackwell, 1904), 635; Hening, *Statutes* 2: 261; *Arch. Md.* 57: 220; Edmund Morgan, *American Slavery, American Freedom: The Ordeal of Colonial Virginia* (New York: W. W. Norton, 1975), 242; Lois Green Carr, Russell Menard, and Lorena Walsh, *Robert Cole's World: Agriculture and Society in Early Maryland* (Chapel Hill: University of North Carolina Press, 1991), 78. Cattle deaths: *EJCV* 1: 534. Drought: David W. Stahle et al., "The Lost Colony and Jamestown Droughts," *Science* 280, no. 5363 (24 April 1998), 565; Richard Beale Davis, ed., *William Fitzhugh and His Chesapeake World, 1676–1701* (Chapel Hill: University of North Carolina Press, 1963), 80; Russell

Menard, "The Tobacco Industry in the Chesapeake Colonies, 1617–1730: An Interpretation," *Research in Economic History* 5 (1980), 136. Ice: *Arch. Md.* 23: 9–11, 27–28, 60; 41: 318, 358; Michael Oberg, ed., *Samuel Wiseman's Book of Record: The Official Account of Bacon's Rebellion in Virginia, 1676–1677* (Lanham, Md.: Lexington Books, 2005), 86; *New York Historical Manuscripts: Dutch, Delaware Papers,* vol. 20–21, trans. Arnold J. F. Van Laer (Baltimore: Genealogical Publishing, 1977), 13.

14. David Jones, "Virgin Soils Revisited," *WMQ* 60 (2003), 703–42; Suzanne Austin Alchon, *A Pest in the Land: New World Epidemics in a Global Perspective* (Albuquerque: University of New Mexico Press, 2003).

15. Walsh, "Charles County," 39–47; Menard, "Tobacco Industry," 127, 135; *Arch. Md.* 20: 256; 49: 94; Durand de Dauphiné, *Voyages of a Frenchman Exiled for his Religion with a Description of Virginia and Maryland in America,* in Gilbert Chinard, ed., *A Huguenot Exile in Virginia* (New York: Press of the Pioneers, 1934), 108; Michael Kammen, "Maryland in 1699: A Letter from the Reverend Hugh Jones," *Journal of Southern History* 29 (1963), 372; and John Duffy, *Epidemics in Colonial America* (Baton Rouge: Louisiana State University Press, 1953), 69–72.

16. "Westmoreland County Records," *WMQ,* 1st series, 15 (1907), 179; John Dorman, ed., *Westmoreland County, Virginia Records, 1658–1661* (Washington: J. F. Dorman, 1970), entry of 20 August 1658; Dorman, ed., *Westmoreland County, Virginia Records, 1661–1664* (Washington: J. F. Dorman, 1972), entry of 14 July 1655. Other patents large and small increasingly hemmed in the Patawomecks: Nell Nugent, *Cavaliers and Pioneers: Abstracts of Virginia Land Patents and Grants* (Richmond: Virginia State Library, 1992), 218, 224, 266, 273, 290, 293, 297–300, 302, 304, 332, 334, 345.

17. Deputy Governor Francis Moryson to Westmoreland County commissioners, 7 August 1661, Westmoreland County Deeds, Wills, &c, reel 1, LV.

18. H. R. McIlwaine, ed., *Journals of the House of Burgesses of Virginia, 1659/60–1693* (Richmond: Colonial Press, 1915), 14–16.

19. Brent had to give Wahanganoche two hundred arms' length of roanoke, and the others one hundred lengths each. Fowke was fined ten thousand pounds of tobacco, and Lord and Mason two thousand pounds. McIlwaine, *Journals of the House of Burgesses of Virginia, 1659/60–1693,* 14–16; Hening, *Statutes* 2: 141, 149.

20. On the events of 1663, see Hening, *Statutes* 2: 193–94, 197, 205; Dorman, *Westmoreland County, Virginia Records, 1661–1664,* 35, 37. On the 1664 killing and its aftermath, see Stafford County (Va.) Court, Extracts from Order Books, 1664–1692, VHS mss 4st135a1, 27 May 1664; Hening, *Statutes* 2: 219–20; H. R. McIlwaine, ed., *Minutes of the Council and General Court of Colonial Virginia,* 2nd ed. (Richmond: Colonial Press, 1924), 488–89; 20 December 1666, Order Books, Northumberland County, reel 47, LV.

21. Carolyn Jett, *Records of Northumberland County, Virginia* (Bowie, Md.: Heritage Books, 1994), 4 (quotation); Indian slaves appeared most frequently in the records of Maryland's Provincial Court. See *Arch. Md.* 41: 82, 186–88, 191, 223 (quotation), 230, 254, 471; 49: 495 (quotation); 66: 226 (quotation).

22. Hening, *Statutes* 1: 323–26, 395, 455–56, 481–82; 2: 15–16, 143, 283 (quotation); Warren Billings, ed., "Some Acts Not in Hening's *Statutes:* The Acts of Assembly, April

1652, November 1652, and July 1653," *VMHB* 83 (1975), 63–65; *Arch. Md.* 1: 346; McIlwaine, *Minutes of the Council,* 488 (quotation); McIlwaine, *Journals of the House of Burgesses of Virginia, 1659/60–1693,* 9 (quotation); "Some References to Indians in Colonial Virginia," *WMQ,* 2nd series, 16 (1936), 591.

23. Rountree, *Pocahontas's People,* 95–96.

24. Morgan, *American Slavery,* 412–13; Hening, *Statutes* 2: 274; Potter, *Commoners, Tribute, and Chiefs,* 20–24.

25. On the possible Tauxenent connection, see Potter, *Commoners, Tribute, and Chiefs,* 197, and Rountree, *Pocahontas's People,* 95. The fate of the Tauxenents is far from clear. In 1622 their werowance took refuge at Patawomeck, telling his hosts that he had been "expulsed" by the Nacotchtanks. After that there is no mention of the Tauxenents, even by fur traders (such as Henry Fleet) who had every reason to reflect on the role the Tauxenents—the farthest upriver group on the Potomac, above even the Nactochtanks—might play in the prospective trade with the Massawomecks. If a functioning Tauxenent polity survived the Nacotchtank expulsion of their werowance in 1622, it was likely scattered again by raiders from the north during the hazardous 1620s, when even the populous, well-fortified, and downriver Piscataways suffered major losses at the hands of the Massawomecks. John Smith, *The Generall Historie of Virginia, the Somer Iles, and New England,* in *CWCJS* 2: 312–13.

26. *Arch. Md.* 1: 322; 60: 62, 225; Dorman, *Westmoreland County, Virginia Records, 1661–1664,* 89; Fleet, *Virginia Colonial Abstracts,* vol. 23, 13, 50 (typescript at the VHS); McIlwaine, *Minutes of the Council,* 237, 245, 488–89; J. Frederick Fausz, "'Engaged in Enterprises Pregnant with Terror': George Washington's Formative Years among the Indians," in Warren Hofstra, ed., *George Washington and the Virginia Backcountry* (Madison, Wis.: Madison House, 1998), 118; T. M., "The Beginning, Progress, and Conclusion of Bacon's Rebellion," in Charles M. Andrews, ed., *Narratives of the Insurrections, 1675–1690* (New York: Charles Scribner's Sons, 1915), 17; John Reps, *Tidewater Towns: City Planning in Colonial Virginia and Maryland* (Williamsburg: Colonial Williamsburg Foundation, 1972), 94, 118; Alice Lippson et al., *Environmental Atlas of the Potomac Estuary* (Baltimore: Johns Hopkins University Press, 1981), Folio Map 1.

27. "Westmoreland County Records," *WMQ,* 1st series, 15 (1907), 179–80; Hening, *Statutes* 2: 193–94; McIlwaine, *Minutes of the Council,* 488; *Arch. Md.* 2: 15, 25, 71–72.

28. Arthur Karinen, "Maryland Population, 1631–1730: Numerical and Distributional Aspects," *MdHM* 54 (1959), 405–6; Lorena Walsh, "Land Use, Settlement Patterns, and the Impact of European Agriculture, 1620–1820," in Curtin, Brush, and Fisher, *Discovering the Chesapeake,* 224–33.

29. *Arch. Md.* 1: 346–53.

30. *Arch. Md.* 3: 360, 402–3, 454, 481–83; Merrell, "Cultural Continuity," 561–62.

31. James Harmon, "The Geographic Conditions of Contact: Native Americans, Colonists, and the Settlement Landscape of Southern Maryland, 1600–1695" (Ph.D. diss., University of Maryland, College Park, 2001), 359; Walsh, "Charles County," 2–5, 393–405. For examples of Indian fields as markers along these tributaries, see *Arch. Md.* 60: 30, 62, 155–56, 225, 289, 486, 599.

32. The following account is derived from the Provincial Court proceedings in *Arch. Md.* 41: 481–91.

33. There is one tantalizing hint that the Langworths had a history of conflict with their Indian neighbors. In 1662 a "Mr. Langworth" joined a party of men that traced a fugitive Indian to the Chopticos' reserve and took him away. The manuscript describing this account has evidently been damaged, but it is clear that something went wrong: "comeing over Wicocomaco River from Capt Fendall's to Mr Robert Slyes howse when they took the Indian Prisoner at Choptico in company with Coll Wm Evans and ... [missing] with several others they there accidentally ... Mr Langworth fell." Was this Mr. Langworth related to Agatha and her children? Did the Langworths conceive a particular dislike of Indians after this incident? Was the captive a Mattawoman? If so, did he or his family conceive a particular dislike of the Langworths? Or did Chotike, Maquamps, the Old Fisherman, and their unnamed accomplice pick out the Langworths for some other reason? *Arch. Md.* 41: 565.

34. *Arch. Md.* 49: 481–82, 491, 512–13.

35. *Arch. Md.* 2: 10–11, 15–17, 20–22. On the Nanjemoy's troubles, see *Arch. Md.* 53: 414–15.

36. *Arch. Md.* 2: 25–27, 131.

37. *Arch. Md.* 5: 34–35; Lippson et al., *Environmental Atlas,* folio maps 4, 7, 8.

38. In 1673 the boundary markers of a tract on the Anacostia River included an oak tree "by the waterside neare an olde Indian Forte," *Arch. Md.* 60: 532.

39. John Smith, *A Map of Virginia,* in *CWCJS* 1: 148; Merrell, "Cultural Continuity," 565.

Chapter 8. *"Away with All These Distractions"*

1. H. R. McIlwaine, ed., *Journals of the House of Burgesses of Virginia, 1659/60–1693* (Richmond: Colonial Press, 1915), 41 (quotation).

2. *JR* 47: 139–43; *Arch. Md.* 1: 400; 3: 402–3, 411–18, 433–35.

3. Stafford County (Va.) Court, Extracts from Order Books, 1664–1692, VHS mss 4st135a1, 27 May 1664 (quotation); *Arch. Md.* 1: 471–72; 3: 498–501 (quotation).

4. *Arch. Md.* 1: 511, 522–26, 539; 3: 501–2 (quotation), 521–22, 549; 5: 34, 65; George Alsop, "A Character of the Province of Maryland," in Clayton Hall, ed., *Narratives of Early Maryland, 1633–1634* (New York: Charles Scribner's Sons, 1910), 365.

5. Ruth Sparacio, *Order Book Abstracts of Northumberland County, Virginia, 1661–1665* (McLean, Va.: Antient Press, 1995), 10 October 1664; Stafford County (Va.) Court, Extracts from Order Books, 1664–1692, VHS mss 4st135a1, 15 November 1664 (quotation).

6. *JR* 52:147, 155, 175; 53: 243, 247, 251, 253; 54: 58; 56: 35–36, 55–57 (quotation); 57: 25; 58: 227. The Susquehannocks stepped up their diplomatic efforts in the south: see *Arch. Md.,* 2: 319; 15: 291–92; and William Talbot, ed., *The Discoveries of John Lederer* (London: Samuel Heyrick, 1672), 11, 26.

7. *JR* 57: 169–71; 59: 251; *Arch. Md.* 2: 378, 425, 428–30.

8. *Arch. Md.* 2: 428–30; Alice Ferguson, "The Susquehannock Fort on Piscataway Creek," *MdHM* 36 (1941), 1–9.

9. *Arch. Md.* 2: 462–63.

10. Virginia DeJohn Anderson, *Creatures of Empire: How Domestic Animals Transformed Early America* (New York: Oxford University Press, 2004), 231 (quotation); "A Narrative of the Rise, Progresse and Cessation of the late Rebellion in Virginia, by his Majesties' Commissioners," in Michael Oberg, ed., *Samuel Wiseman's Book of Record: The Official Account of Bacon's Rebellion in Virginia, 1676–1677* (Lanham, Md.: Lexington Press, 2005), 142–43 (quotation). This account also placed the Susquehannocks at the scene of the initial killings, but other accounts identify only the Doegs at this stage in the conflict.

11. T. M., "The Beginning, Progress, and Conclusion of Bacon's Rebellion," in Charles M. Andrews, ed., *Narratives of the Insurrections, 1675–1690* (New York: Charles Scribner's Sons, 1915), 16.

12. Ibid., 17 (quotations); "Narrative of the Rise, Progresse and Cessation," 142–43.

13. One account has them returning to Virginia to kill Thomas Mathew's son, but Mathew himself makes no mention of this. "Narrative of the Rise, Progresse and Cessation," 143; T. M., "Beginning, Progress, and Conclusion," 16–19; Lyon Tyler, "Washington and his Neighbors," *WMQ* 4 (1895), 86 (quotation); Sir Wm Berkeley to Mr. Ludwell, 1 April 1676, in John Neville, *Bacon's Rebellion: Abstracts of Materials in the Colonial Records Project* (Jamestown: Jamestown Foundation, 1976), 45; Wilcomb Washburn, *The Governor and the Rebel: A History of Bacon's Rebellion in Virginia* (New York: W. W. Norton, 1957), 21–22.

14. Tyler, "Washington and his Neighbors," 86; Barry Kent, *Susquehanna's Indians* (Harrisburg: Pennsylvania Historical and Museum Commission, 1984), 48; *Arch. Md.* 15: 47–49; T. M., "Beginning, Progress, and Conclusion," 18–19.

15. *Arch. Md.* 2: 474–77, 481–83 (quotations); Lyon Tyler, "Col. John Washington: Further Details of His Life from the Records of Westmoreland Co., Virginia," *WMQ*, 1st series, 2 (1893), 39–42 (quotation); T. M., "Beginning, Progress, and Conclusion," 18–19.

16. T. M., "Beginning, Progress, and Conclusion," 19 (quotation); "Narrative of the Rise, Progresse and Cessation," 143–44; "The History of Bacon's and Ingram's Rebellion," in Andrews, *Narratives of the Insurrections,* 47–48 (quotation).

17. T. M., "Beginning, Progress, and Conclusion," 15–16 (quotations), 19–20 (quotation); Hening, *Statutes* 2: 332 (quotation); *Arch. Md.* 15: 57–58 (quotation); Richard Watts to Secretary Williamson, 10 October 1675, in Neville, *Bacon's Rebellion,* 202 (quotations). Archaeologists have found the traces of at least two of these palisades along the Potomac. See Fraser Neiman, *Field Archaeology of the Clifts Plantation Site, Westmoreland County, Virginia* (on file at the Virginia Department of Historic Resources, Richmond), 72, 74–75.

18. "Narrative of the Rise, Progresse and Cessation," 144 (quotations); T. M., "Beginning, Progress, and Conclusion," 19–20 (quotation); Neville, *Bacon's Rebellion,* 45, 203–4; "History of Bacon's and Ingram's Rebellion," 49–50 (quotations); Wilcomb

Washburn, "Governor Berkeley and King Philip's War," *New England Quarterly* 30 (1957), 363–77.

19. Moryson to Sir William Jones, October 1676, in *Samuel Wiseman's Book*, 126–28; Neville, *Bacon's Rebellion*, 45 (quotation); "Narrative of the Rise, Progresse and Cessation," 144–45; Hening, *Statutes* 2: 326–32, 336–38.

20. T. M., "Beginning, Progress, and Conclusion," 20; "History of Bacon's and Ingram's Rebellion," 49; "Narrative of the Rise, Progresse and Cessation," 144–45 (quotations); Beverley, *History*, 74.

21. T. M., "Beginning, Progress, and Conclusion," 20–21; "Bacon's Manifesto," in Oberg, *Samuel Wiseman's Book*, 19–20; Herbert Jeffries, John Berry, and Francis Moryson to Governor and Council, 27 February 1676/77, in ibid., 88–90; "Narrative of the Rise, Progresse and Cessation," 148 (quotations).

22. Washburn, *Governor and the Rebel*, 37–91.

23. "Narrative of the Rise, Progresse and Cessation," 158; "A List of the Names of Those Worthy Persons," in Oberg, *Samuel Wiseman's Book*, 277–84; Tyler, "Col. John Washington," 43–48; T. M., "Beginning, Progress, and Conclusion," 36; *Arch. Md.* 15: 127–32, 137–41.

24. On the Potomac nations' efforts during the war, see *Arch. Md.* 2: 488, 505–6; 15: 56–58, 90–92, 97 126. For the Susquehannocks' postwar diplomacy, see *Arch. Md.* 15: 120–23, 126; Kenneth Scott and Kenn Stryker-Rodda, eds., *New York Historical Manuscripts: Dutch, Delaware Papers*, vol. 20–21, trans. Arnold J. F. Van Laer (Baltimore: Genealogical Publishing, 1977), 104, 112, 173; *DRCHSNY* 12: 553–58, 572; 13: 497–98.

25. T. M., "Beginning, Progress, and Conclusion," 38; *Arch. Md.* 2: 489 (quotation), 401–2; 5: 249–50; 15: 90–92; "Narrative of the Rise, Progresse and Cessation,"159; Oberg, *Samuel Wiseman's Book*, 217; Ruth Sparacio, *Northumberland County, Virginia Order Book, 1674–1677* (McLean, Va.: Antient Press, 1998), 71, 76; Sparacio, *Northumberland County, Virginia Order Book, 1677–1679* (McLean, Va.: Antient Press, 1998), 6–11.

26. Washburn, *Governor and the Rebel*, chs. 7, 8; *Arch. Md.* 15: 369.

27. "Notes and Other Documents Chronicling the Activities and Concerns of the Commissioners," in Oberg, *Samuel Wiseman's Book*, 198 (quotation); *Arch. Md.* 5: 152 (quotations); 15: 137 (quotation).

28. *Arch. Md.* 5: 134–52 (quotations on 132).

29. *Arch. Md.* 5: 152–54, 243–46 (quotations), 251–58; 15: 157.

30. *Arch. Md.* 15: 179–81 (quotations), 183–86, 188–89.

31. *Arch. Md.* 15: 196 (quotation), 212, 217–23 (quotation).

32. *Arch. Md.* 15: 237–43 (quotations). Daniel Richter places the Susquehannocks in Onondaga or Cayuga towns, which fits with the emissary's statement that the Susquehannocks lived in the "two middlemost" Five Nations communities. Richter, *The Ordeal of the Longhouse: The Peoples of the Iroquois League in the Era of European Colonization* (Chapel Hill: University of North Carolina Press, 1992), 136.

33. *Arch. Md.* 5: 270 (quotation), 280–81; Neville, *Bacon's Rebellion*, 168, 203–4, 216; John Banister to Dr. Robert Morison, 6 April 1679, in Joseph Ewan and Nesta Ewan, eds., *John Banister and His Natural History of Virginia, 1678–1692* (Urbana: University of Illinois Press, 1970), 38–40; Lawrence Leder, ed., *The Livingston Indian Records*,

1666–1723 (Gettysburg: Pennsylvania Historical Association, 1956), 48–56; "The On-ondages [*sic*] upon the Propositions," Colonial Papers, misc. reel 609, folder 2, n. 50, LV; Hening, *Statutes* 2: 433–38; *DRCHSNY* 3: 271, 277; Matthew Rhoads, "Assarigoa's Line: Anglo-Iroquois Origins of the Virginia Frontier, 1675–1774" (Ph.D. diss., Syracuse University, 2000), 33–35, 38.

34. *Journals of the House of Burgesses of Virginia, 1659/60–1693*, ed. by H. R. McIlwaine (Richmond: Colonial Press, 1915), 147 (quotation); *Arch. Md.* 15: 269–73 (rumors). On the Potomac nations' worries, see *Arch. Md.* 15: 274–84, 287, 289–92, 299–304, 313–14.

35. *Arch. Md.* 15: 283 (quotation), 329–30 (quotation), 336, 358 (quotation).

36. For examples of the wildly varying accounts of contemporary events that people had to sort through, see *Arch. Md.* 15: 353, 359–63, 373–76, 400, 419–20.

37. *Arch. Md.* 15: 355–56, 364–73, 376–77, 380 (quotation), 384, 386–87, 392–93, 413–16, 419–20.

38. Though false, the allegations appealed to many people precisely because they were so unoriginal; like tales of Papist/savage conspiracies, they artfully synthesized preexisting mythologies, telling people exactly what they were prepared to believe. Barry Coward, *The Stuart Age: England, 1603–1714*, 2nd ed. (New York: Longman, 1994), 326.

39. *Arch. Md.* 5: 311–34 (quotation on 319); 15: 386–93, 399–410.

40. *Arch. Md.* 5: 280–81 348 (quotation), 373–76 (quotation), 400, 417–18; 7: 110–11; 17: 3–4 (quotation).

41. *Arch. Md.* 7: 110–11, 141; 15: 417–18; 17: 3–4 (quotation), 7–8, 12–21.

42. On Baconite stirrings, see Neville, *Bacon's Rebellion,* 100; *Arch. Md.* 5: 351–57, 362, 506–12, 532–35; Warren Billings, ed., *The Papers of Francis Howard, Baron Howard of Effingham, 1643–1695* (Richmond: Virginia State Library, 1989), 228, 320. On attacks from the north, see McIlwaine, *Journals of the House of Burgesses of Virginia, 1659/60–1693,* 159 (quotation), 162, 170, 229, 291–92; *Arch. Md.* 5: 547–52; 7: 260, 269–72 (quotation on 270); Leder, *Livingston Indian Records,* 73, 125, 137–38.

43. *EJCV* 1: 56–57, 496, 499, 503–6; Billings, *Papers of Francis Howard,* 110–11, 122–23, 140–52, 213, 322–23; *DRCHSNY* 4: 417; Leder, *Livingston Indian Records,* 65–66, 73–74, 137–38; McIlwaine, *Journals of the House of Burgesses of Virginia, 1659/60–1693,* 229–30, 234; Hening, *Statutes* 3: 17–22; *Arch. Md.* 5: 539; 7: 260, 265, 269–70, 290–91, 299; 17: 197, 202–15, 364–69, 377, 464–65.

44. Billings, *Papers of Francis Howard,* 152 (quotation), 155 (quotation), 374–75 (quotation), 101; *EJCV* 1: 50–51; *Arch. Md.* 17: 297–98. Lorena Walsh, "Charles County, Maryland, 1658–1705: A Study of Chesapeake Social and Political Structure" (Ph.D. diss., Michigan State University, 1977), 39, noted this spike in the death rate in 1685–1686 in Charles, Calvert, and St. Mary's counties. (See also Walsh, "Charles County," 40–59.)

45. Russell Menard, "The Tobacco Industry in the Chesapeake Colonies, 1617–1730: An Interpretation," *Research in Economic History* 5 (1980), 113–15, 120, 142–53; John McCusker and Russell Menard, *The Economy of British America, 1607–1789* (Chapel Hill: University of North Carolina Press, 1985), 118–23 (quotation on 119), 133–38. Richard

Beale Davis, ed., *William Fitzhugh and His Chesapeake World, 1676–1701* (Chapel Hill: University of North Carolina Press, 1963), 322–23.

46. On competition from Pennsylvania, see *Arch. Md.* 20: 328–29, 280, 392, 394. On the difficulty of purchasing slaves, see Davis, *William Fitzhugh,* 93, 203.

47. Victor Kennedy and Kent Mountford, "Human Influences on Aquatic Resources in the Chesapeake Bay Watershed," in Philip Curtin, Grace Brush, and George Fisher, eds., *Discovering the Chesapeake: The History of an Ecosystem* (Baltimore: Johns Hopkins University Press, 2001), 198; Ruth Sparacio and Sam Sparacio, comps., *Deed & Will Abstracts of Stafford County, Virginia, 1686–1689* (McLean, Va.: Antient Press, 1989), 12 October 1686; Ruth Sparacio and Sam Sparacio, comps., *Order Book Abstracts of Stafford County, Virginia, 1664–1668, 1689–1690* (McLean, Va.: Antient Press, 1987), 13 March 1689/90; John Dorman, *Westmoreland County Order Book, 1690–1698,* pt. 2, *1692–94* (Washington, D.C.: J. F. Dorman, 1963), 4; *Arch. Md.* 13: 568; Robert Beverley, *The History and Present State of Virginia,* ed. Louis B. Wright (Chapel Hill: University of North Carolina Press, 1947), 310; David Jordan, "Maryland Hoggs and Hyde Park Duchesses: A Brief Account of Maryland in 1697," *MdHM* 73 (1978), 91; "Narrative of a Voyage to Maryland, 1705–1706," *AHR* 12 (1907), 335; Walsh, "Charles County," 275–290. For an example of a wealthy planter's diversification strategy, see Davis, *William Fitzhugh,* 175.

48. James Harmon, "The Geographic Conditions of Contact: Native Americans, Colonists, and the Settlement Landscape of Southern Maryland, 1600–1695" (Ph.D. diss., University of Maryland, College Park, 2001), 359–61; Arthur Karinen, "Maryland Population, 1631–1730: Numerical and Distributional Aspects," *MdHM* 54 (1959), 387–90; Edmund Morgan, *American Slavery, American Freedom: The Ordeal of Colonial Virginia* (New York: W. W. Norton, 1975), 411–14; Walsh, "Charles County," 2–5.

49. *JR* 62: 59 (quotation).

50. The two Maryland Indians burned by the Onondagas were referred to as "Gannaouen," and in treaty negotiations in July 1684 Five Nations representatives spoke to Virginia's delegation of "your frinds Indians, called Cochnawaes," or "the Cachnawas, or Virginny Indians," or "your friend Indians called Cachnawys." Billings, *Papers of Francis Howard,* 149.

51. *Arch. Md.* 17: 193; Billings, *Papers of Francis Howard,* 112, 143–44 (quotations); McIlwaine, *Journals of the House of Burgesses of Virginia, 1659/60–1693,* 229 (quotation); Leder, *Livingston Indian Records,* 137–38.

52. *EJCV* 1: 54 (quotations); Ruth Sparacio, comp., *Order Book Abstracts of (Old) Rappahannock County, Virginia, 1683–1685* (McLean, Va.: Antient Press, 1990), 13; McIlwaine, *Journals of the House of Burgesses of Virginia, 1659/60–1693,* 253; Helen Rountree, *Pocahontas's People: The Powhatan Indians of Virginia through Four Centuries* (Norman: University of Oklahoma Press, 1990), 119.

53. *Arch. Md.* 5: 493 (quotation); 8: 53 (quotation).

54. Sparacio and Sparacio, *Deed & Will Abstracts of Stafford County, Virginia, 1686–1689,* 8 February, 16 February, 3 March, and 14 March 1687/88 (quotations).

55. *Arch. Md.* 5: 471–72; 8: 53 (quotation); Sparacio and Sparacio, *Deed & Will Abstracts of Stafford County, Virginia, 1686–1689,* 9 December 1686 and 16 November 1689.

56. Hening, *Statutes* 2: 490–92; Sparacio, *Order Book Abstracts of Northumberland County, Virginia, 1683–1686* (McLean, Va.: Antient Press, 1999), 3, 60; Ruth Sparacio, *Order Book Abstracts of (Old) Rappahannock County, Virginia, 1683–1685* (McLean, Va.: Antient Press, 1990), 72.

57. For an example of an outer chief taking the lead in external relations, see Sparacio and Sparacio, *Deed & Will Abstracts of Stafford County, Virginia, 1686–1689*, 8 February 1687/88. For the succession among the Chopticos, see *Arch. Md.* 8: 53–54. On cultural continuity, see Ewan and Ewan, *John Banister and His Natural History*, 372–86. Banister's observations come mostly from the James River but are generally born out by the archaeological record and small snippets from observers on and near the Potomac. See Durand de Dauphiné, "Voyages of a Frenchman Exiled for his Religion with a Description of Virginia and Maryland in America," in Gilbert Chinard, ed., *A Huguenot Exile in Virginia* (New York: Press of the Pioneers, 1934), 151–53; James Merrell, "Cultural Continuity among the Piscataway Indians of Colonial Maryland," *WMQ* 36 (1979), 548–570. On layoffs of rangers and interpreters, see McIlwaine, *Journals of the House of Burgesses of Virginia, 1659/60–1693*, 310–11; *Arch. Md.* 5:568; 8: 36–37.

Chapter 9. "Frightened Away by Some Threatening Discourses"

1. *Arch. Md.* 8: 70–94 (quotes); Richard Beale Davis, ed., *William Fitzhugh and His Chesapeake World, 1676–1701* (Chapel Hill: University of North Carolina Press, 1963), 287; *EJCV* 1: 104–5 (quotation), 522.

2. *Arch. Md.* 8: 101–7 (quotations), 123 (quotation), 152–62; 13: 233–34, 240. For fuller accounts of these events, see Robert Brugger, *Maryland: A Middle Temperament, 1634–1980* (Baltimore: Johns Hopkins University Press, 1988), 39–40.

3. On colonists' military preparations, see *EJCV* 1: 140–42, 167–68, 182; Ruth Sparacio and Sam Sparacio, comps., *Deed & Will Abstracts of Stafford County, Virginia, 1689–1693* (McLean, Va.: Antient Press, 1989), 16 April 1691; H. R. McIlwaine, ed., *Journals of the House of Burgesses of Virginia, 1659/60–1693* (Richmond: Colonial Press, 1914), 336, 371. On colonists' encroachments on Indian lands, see W. Noel Sainsbury, ed., *Calendar of State Papers, America and West Indies, 1689–1692* (London: Mackie, 1901), 337 (quotation); and James Harmon, "The Geographic Conditions of Contact: Native Americans, Colonists, and the Settlement Landscape of Southern Maryland, 1600–1695" (Ph.D. diss., University of Maryland, College Park, 2001), 359–63.

4. "Order for Ranging," 22 December 1691, in Stafford County (Va.) Court, Extracts from Order Books, 1664–1692, VHS mss 4st135a1 (quotation).

5. *EJCV* 1: 205–7 (quotation), 216; "Order for Ranging" (quotation); Sparacio and Sparacio, *Deed & Will Abstracts of Stafford County, Virginia, 1689–1693*, 9 March 1691/92.

6. *EJCV* 1: 202, 216–17 (quotations), 230–31, 272–73; "Order for Ranging"; "A Journal of our Ranging Given by me David Strahan's Lieutenant of the Rangers of the Potomac," Colonial Papers, misc. reel 610, folder 9, LV; *Arch. Md.* 8: 424, 445; Hening, *Statutes*, 3: 98–101; McIlwaine, *Journals of the House of Burgesses of Virginia, 1659/60–*

1693, 390–91; Sparacio and Sparacio, *Deed & Will Abstracts of Stafford County, Virginia, 1689–1693*, 11 May 1692.

7. *Arch. Md.* 13: 258–60 (quotations).

8. *Arch. Md.* 13: 264–65 (quotations).

9. The gifts included rum, even though the Chopticos had recently asked the government to forbid Englishmen from providing liquor to Indians. *Arch. Md.* 8: 317–23, 328; 13: 268–72.

10. *Arch. Md.* 13: 282–83 (quotation), 310; "A Journal of our Ranging," 17 June and 26 June (quotation); *EJCV* 1: 254 (quotation); Stafford County (Va.) Court, Extracts from Order Books, 1664–1692, VHS mss 4st135a1, 8 June 1692; Ruth Sparacio, *Order Book Abstracts of Stafford County, Virginia, 1692–1693* (McLean, Va.: Antient Press, 1989), 8 June 1692.

11. Richard White, *The Middle Ground: Indians, Empires, and Republics in the Great Lakes Region, 1650–1815* (New York: Cambridge University Press, 1991), 40–49 (quotation on 49); Daniel Richter, *The Ordeal of the Longhouse: The Peoples of the Iroquois League in the Era of European Colonization* (Chapel Hill: University of North Carolina Press, 1992), 145–73; *EJCV* 1: 256; *Arch. Md.* 8: 341–54, 383.

12. *Arch. Md.* 8: 458–70, 478–79, 487–88, 517–19, 524–25.

13. *EJCV* 1: 278–79; *Arch. Md.* 8: 461–62, 517–18 (quotation).

14. John Dorman, *Westmoreland County Order Book, 1690–1698*, pt. 3, *1694–1698* (Washington, D.C.: J. F. Dorman, 1962–1964), 29; *Arch. Md.* 19: 145 (quotation), 151; 20: 191–92 (quotation), 242, 269–70, 274, 327 (quotation).

15. *Arch. Md.* 19: 232–34 (quotation), 251 (quotation); 20: 276 (quotation), 282.

16. *EJCV* 1: 347; *Arch. Md.* 19: 384–85 (quotation), 407–9 (quotation); 20: 424, 436–37, 456–57, 509–10.

17. *Arch. Md.* 19: 382, 441, 445, 447, 484; 20: 412 (quotation).

18. On encroachments against Indians and the promotion of the rum trade, see *Arch. Md.* 19: 384, 408, 566–67 (quotation), 571; 20: 412; 22: 329; 23: 144; 25: 86, 256. On the severe winter of 1696–97, see *Arch. Md.* 19: 516; 20: 557–58; 23: 9–11, 27–28 (quotation), 60, 89–90. Smallpox: *Arch. Md.* 25: 256.

19. *Arch. Md.* 19: 565–69.

20. *Arch. Md.* 19: 566–67 (quotations); 23: 143–45 (quotations).

21. *Arch. Md.* 19: 556–57, 566–68 (quotation); 23: 92–93, 143–45, 266 (quotation).

22. *Arch. Md.* 19: 574; 23: 182–84, 187–88 (quotations). On the negotiations, see *Arch. Md.* 19: 556–74; 23: 92–93, 143–45.

23. *EJCV* 1: 370; *Arch. Md.* 23: 175–77 (quotations), 182–88. Only one defendant was hanged for his role in the attack. Esquire Tom was never captured, Choptico Robin testified for the prosecution, and four defendants were not convicted. Edmund Jennings to House of Burgesses, 23 October 1697, Colonial Papers, misc. reel 610, folder, n. 15, LV.

24. *Arch. Md.* 23: 216–20, 260–61, 325–26 (quotations).

25. *Arch. Md.* 23: 231, 238–47, 294–302; *EJCV* 1: 375–76.

26. The tayac also traveled to Aquia Creek to participate in the interrogation of the men arrested for the Wiggington assaults. *EJCV* 1: 369, 376; *Arch. Md.* 23: 182–86,

325 (quotations); H. R. McIlwaine, ed., *Journals of the House of Burgesses of Virginia, 1695–1696, 1696–1697, 1698, 1699, 1700–1702* (Richmond: Colonial Press, 1913), 105–6, 108–9, 111, 113.

27. *Arch. Md.* 22: 32 (quotation), 80 (quotation), 127 (quotation); 23: 342 (quotation), 383 (quotation). A committee reporting on Indian affairs explicitly linked the new state of affairs to the peace with France. *Arch. Md.* 22: 38.

28. *Arch. Md.* 23: 426–31, 457 (quotation).

29. *CVSP,* 60, 62 (quotation). Even if the prospect of returning had appealed to the Potomac nations, a "violent and raging mortality" that struck both Virginia and Maryland early in 1698 would likely have kept them away. This "epidemicall sickness" struck in January or February, and by late March it had spread throughout the Potomac settlements. Not until July could it be said that "the sickness is pretty well over." Clearly this was not a good time to move back among the English. See Dorman, *Westmoreland County Order Book, 1690–1698,* pt. 3, *1694–1698,* 130, 136–37; *Arch. Md.* 23: 444; 25: 12.

30. Giles Vandercastle and Burr Harrison to Nicholson, 21 April 1699, Colonial Papers, misc. reel 610, folder 12, n. 17, LV (quotations); McIlwaine, *Journals of the House of Burgesses of Virginia, 1695–1696, 1696–1697, 1698, 1699, 1700–1702,* 105–6. On the merger of the two refugee communities in Virginia, see *Arch. Md.* 22: 390. The Piscataways' island, now known as Heater's Island, is visible just below the bridge by which U.S. Route 15 crosses from Virginia to Maryland.

31. As usual, "Seneca" was a generic term for the Five Nations and the Susquehannocks. *EJCV* 1: 369 (quotation); Giles Vandercastle and Burr Harrison to Nicholson, 21 April 1699 (quotation); *CVSP,* 67; *Arch. Md.* 23: 175.

32. *Arch. Md.* 24: 13, 19, 24, 50, 61, 79–81, 86; 25: 83–90, 95, 101–3; *CVSP,* 69–70.

33. *Correspondence between William Penn and James Logan,* Memoirs of the Historical Society of Pennsylvania, vol. 10 (Philadelphia: Historical Society of Pennsylvania, 1872), 1: 43–44; James Merrell, *Into the American Woods: Negotiators on the Pennsylvania Frontier* (New York: W. W. Norton, 1999), 107–10; and Francis Jennings, *The Ambiguous Iroquois Empire: The Covenant Chain Confederation of Indian Tribes with English Colonies from Its beginnings to the Lancaster Treaty of 1744* (New York: W. W. Norton, 1984), 223–40.

34. *CRP* 2: 15–17 (quotations); *Arch. Md.* 24: 145.

Chapter 10. *"I Can Not Live in This Beautiful Land"*

1. *Arch. Md.* 23: 260 (quotation); Michel to Michael Ochs, 20 May 1704, in William Hinke, ed. and trans., "Report of the Journey of Francis Louis Michel, From Berne, Switzerland, to Virginia, October 2, 1701–Dec. 1, 1702," *VMHB* 24 (1917), 295–96 (quotation); *CRP* 2: 403–5; Vincent Todd, ed., *Christoph von Graffenried's Account of the Founding of New Bern* (Raleigh: Edwards & Broughton, 1920), 247 (quotation).

2. Lois Green Carr, *County Government in Maryland, 1689–1709* (New York: Garland Publishing, 1987), 570–77; Fairfax Harrison, *Landmarks of Old Prince William,*

vol. 1 (Richmond: Old Dominion Press, 1924), 143–48; Allan Kulikoff, *Tobacco and Slaves: The Development of Southern Cultures in the Chesapeake, 1680–1800* (Chapel Hill: University of North Carolina Press, 1986), 93–99, 208.

3. Lois Green Carr, "Diversification in the Colonial Chesapeake: Somerset County, Maryland in Comparative Perspective," in Carr, Philip Morgan, and Jean Russo, eds., *Colonial Chesapeake Society* (Chapel Hill: University of North Carolina Press, 1988), 364; Kulikoff, *Tobacco and Slaves*, 78–85; John McCusker and Russell Menard, *The Economy of British America, 1607–1789* (Chapel Hill: University of North Carolina Press, 1985), 118 (quotation), 120–23, 127–30; Lorena Walsh, "Summing the Parts: Implications for Estimating Chesapeake Output and Income Subregionally," *WMQ* 56 (1999), 53–94.

4. Lorena Walsh, "Mercantile Strategies, Credit Networks, and Labor Supply in the Colonial Chesapeake in Trans-Atlantic Perspective," in David Eltis, Frank D. Lewis, and Kenneth L. Sokoloff, eds., *Slavery in the Development of the Americas* (New York: Cambridge University Press, 2004), 89–119.

5. Kulikoff, *Tobacco and Slaves*, 64–68, 82–84, 133, 340–42.

6. Gloria Main, *Tobacco Colony: Life in Early Maryland, 1650–1720* (Princeton: Princeton University Press, 1982), 74–78; Kulikoff, *Tobacco and Slaves*, 99–104.

7. Tate Thompson Brady, "Reports Concerning the History and Locations of Iron Foundries and Furnaces in Virginia and Maryland" (VHS mss 7:3 HD9510 B7298:1); David Curtis Skaggs, "John Semple and the Development of the Potomac Valley, 1750–1773," *VMHB* 92 (1984), 282–87; Ronald Lewis, *Coal, Iron, and Slaves: Industrial Slavery in Maryland and Virginia, 1715–1865* (Westport, Conn.: Greenwood Press, 1979), 20–23, 27.

8. Carr, "Diversification," 342–88; Kulikoff, *Tobacco and Slaves*, 99–104.

9. Arthur Karinen, "Maryland Population, 1631–1730: Numerical and Distributional Aspects," *MdHM* 54 (1959), 406; Karinen, "Numerical and Distributional Aspects of Maryland Population," *MdHM* 60 (1965), 155–58; Kulikoff, *Tobacco and Slaves*, 78–99; McCusker and Menard, *Economy of British America*, 138; Lorena Walsh, "Land Use, Settlement Patterns, and the Impact of European Agriculture, 1620–1820," in Philip Curtin, Grace Brush, and George Fisher, eds., *Discovering the Chesapeake: The History of an Ecosystem* (Baltimore: Johns Hopkins University Press, 2001), 229–34.

10. Only 15 percent of householders who owned land and slaves left the country during that decade. Kulikoff, *Tobacco and Slaves*, 85–93, 263–67.

11. Kulikoff, *Tobacco and Slaves*, ch. 6; Jean Lee, "Land and Labor: Parental Bequest Practices in Charles County, Maryland, 1732–1783," in Carr, Morgan, and Russo, *Colonial Chesapeake Society*, 306–41.

12. The list of garden flowers is from John Mercer, Account Book and Diary, 1725–1768 (VHS mss 5:3 M5345:1), March–June 1766. On gentry houses and gardens, see Richard Bushman, *The Refinement of America: Persons, Houses, Cities* (New York: Knopf, 1992), ch. 4, and Barbara Sarudy, *Gardens and Gardening in the Chesapeake 1700–1805* (Baltimore: Johns Hopkins University Press, 1998).

13. Rhys Isaac, *The Transformation of Virginia, 1740–1790* (Chapel Hill: University

of North Carolina Press, 1983), 43–46, 56–65, 70–74, 98–101; Bushman, *Refinement of America*, pt. 1, and Cary Carson, "Consumption," in Daniel Vickers, ed., *A Companion to Colonial America* (Malden, Mass.: Blackwell Publications, 2003), 334–67.

14. Kulikoff, *Tobacco and Slaves*, 257–75; Bernard Bailyn, "Politics and Social Structure in Virginia," in James Smith, ed., *Seventeenth-Century America: Essays in Colonial History* (Chapel Hill: University of North Carolina Press, 1959), 90–115; David Jordan, "Political Stability and the Emergence of a Native Elite in Maryland," in Thad Tate and David Ammerman, eds., *The Chesapeake in the Seventeenth Century: Essays on Anglo-American Society* (Chapel Hill: University of North Carolina Press, 1979), 243–73; Philip Schwartz, *Twice Condemned: Slaves and the Criminal Laws of Virginia, 1705–1865* (Baton Rouge: Louisiana State University Press, 1988); Charles Royster, *The Fabulous History of the Dismal Swamp Company: A Story of George Washington's Virginia* (New York: Knopf, 1999), ch. 1. Several notable exceptions to the rule that large land grants went to native Tidewater gentry are discussed later in chapter 11 of this volume.

15. Kulikoff, *Tobacco and Slaves*, 262–63, 281–300; Edmund Morgan, *American Slavery, American Freedom: The Ordeal of Colonial Virginia* (New York: W. W. Norton, 1975), chs. 7–8.

16. The most thorough study of sediment cores along the Potomac is Ruth Harris DeFries, "Sedimentation Patterns in the Potomac Estuary since European Settlement: A Palynological Approach" (Ph.D. diss., Johns Hopkins University, 1981), ii–iii, 48–50, 71–78. The best comparisons of pre- and post-1634 sediments comes from three cores she took from the St. Mary's River and Point Lookout (numbers 1, 18, and 19 in her study), but since her data take in the entire colonial period, even the figures given here may exaggerate the increase in ragweed pollen (as we shall see, truly dramatic environmental degradation linked to European colonization dated to the late colonial period). See also Grace Brush, "Forests before and after the Colonial Encounter," in Curtin, Brush, and Fisher, *Discovering the Chesapeake*, 47, 51–52; Brush, "Natural and Anthropogenic Changes in Chesapeake Bay during the Last 1000 Years," *Human and Ecological Risk Assessment* 7 (2001), 1291; and "Effects of Climate Variability and Human Activities on Chesapeake Bay and the Implications for Ecosystem Restoration." U.S.G.S. Fact Sheet FS-00-116 (Reston, Va.: U.S. Geological Survey, 2000). On the possibility of aquatic oxygen depletion, see Thomas Cronin et al., "Historical Trends in Chesapeake Bay Dissolved Oxygen Based on Benthic Formanifera from Sediment Cores," *Estuaries* 23, no. 4 (2000), 488–508; Thomas Cronin and Cheryl Vann, "The Sedimentary Record of Climatic and Anthropogenic Influence on the Patuxent Estuary and Chesapeake Bay Ecosystems," *Estuaries* 26 (2003), 205–6; and "Effects of Climate Variability and Human Activities," 3–4. On the consequences of field clearing and woodcutting, see Timothy Silver, "A Useful Arcadia: European Colonists as Biotic Factors in Chesapeake Forests," in Curtin, Brush, and Fisher, *Discovering the Chesapeake*, 155, 158–59. On fish and wildlife, see Victor Kennedy and Kent Mountford, "Human Influences on Aquatic Resources in the Chesapeake Bay Watershed," in ibid., 196–98; and David Hardin, "Laws of Nature: Environmental Legislation in Colonial Virginia, 1619–1776," *Virginia Geographer* 22 (1990), 54–64.

17. On Martin Chartiere, see Todd, *Christoph von Graffenried's Account*, 247; *CRP* 2: 390, 403–4; Barry Kent, *Susquehanna's Indians* (Harrisburg: Pennsylvania Historical and Museum Commission, 1984), 84–90. On Israel Friend see William Marye, "Patowmeck Above Ye Inhabitants," *MdHM* 30 (1935), 8; Samuel Kercheval, *A History of the Valley of Virginia*, 4th ed. (Strasburg, Va.: Shenandoah Publishing House, 1925), 36; *Arch. Md.* 25: 451; 28: 10–11. For the Cartlidges, see James Merrell, *Into the American Woods: Negotiators on the Pennsylvania Frontier* (New York: W. W. Norton, 1999), 79–83, 115–24; and John Kester, "Charles Polke: Indian Trader of the Potomac, 1703–1753," *MdHM* 90 (1995), 447–66. On Charles Anderson, see *Arch. Md.* 25: 442–43, 450–51. On other traders, see Grace Tracey and John Dern, *Pioneers of Old Monocacy: The Early Settlement of Frederick County, Maryland, 1721–1743* (Baltimore: Genealogical Publishing, 1987), 14–15.

18. Daniel Richter, *The Ordeal of the Longhouse: The Peoples of the Iroquois League in the Era of European Colonization* (Chapel Hill: University of North Carolina Press, 1992), chs. 7–8; José Brandão and William Starna, "The Treaties of 1701: A Triumph of Iroquois Diplomacy," *Ethnohistory* 43 (1996), 209–44.

19. Richard Haan, "Covenant and Consensus: Iroquois and English, 1676–1760," in Daniel Richter and James Merrell, eds., *Beyond the Covenant Chain: The Iroquois and Their Neighbors in Indian North America, 1600–1800* (Syracuse: Syracuse University Press, 1987), 41–57; James Merrell, "'Their Very Bones Shall Fight': The Catawba-Iroquois Wars," in ibid., 117–19; Theda Perdue, "Cherokee Relations with the Iroquois in the Eighteenth Century," in ibid., 137; Douglas Boyce, "'As the Wind Scatters the Smoke': The Tuscaroras in the Eighteenth Century," in ibid., 152–53.

20. *EJCV* 3: 45, 506 (quotation); Cadwallader Colden, "Continuation of Colden's History of the Five Indian Nations, for the Years 1707 through 1720," New York Historical Society, *Collections*, 68 (1935), 363, quoted in Richter, *Ordeal of the Longhouse*, 237–38. See also Lawrence Leder, ed., *The Livingston Indian Records, 1666–1723* (Gettysburg: Pennsylvania Historical Association, 1956), 222; *CRP* 3: 45–46, 78–89.

21. *CRP* 2: 138 (quotation).

22. *PA, Fourth Series* 1: 360–63 (quotation), 366–67 (quotation); *CRP* 3: 92, 97, 99–100; James Merrell, *The Indians' New World: Catawbas and Their Neighbors from European Contact through the Era of Removal* (New York: W. W. Norton, 1989), 118–22; and Kercheval, *History of the Valley*, 35–39. Kercheval, an early nineteenth-century historian, relied heavily on oral traditions. His informants told some wildly improbable stories, but their accounts of clashes between southern and northern Indians are generally consistent with the evidence from other sources.

23. William Byrd, "History of the Dividing Line," in Louis B. Wright, ed., *The Prose Works of William Byrd of Westover* (Cambridge: Harvard University Press, 1966), 257–58; Kercheval, *History of the Valley*, 56. On the size of traveling parties, see also *PA, First Series* 1: 223, 295; *PA, Fourth Series* 1: 437; *CRP*, 3: 309; 4: 630–33; *EJCV* 3: 506; James Patton to William Gooch, 23 December 1742, in Virginia (Colony), Governor, 1727–1740 (William Gooch), Records, 1727–1751, vol. 2, VHS mss 3 V8194 G5907 a; Paul Wallace, *Indian Paths of Pennsylvania* (Harrisburg: Pennsylvania Historical and Museum Commission, 1961), end papers; Warren Hofstra, *The Planting of New Vir-*

ginia: Settlement and Landscape in the Shenandoah Valley (Baltimore: Johns Hopkins University Press, 2004), 17–44.

24. *CRP* 2: 533 (quotation); Todd, *Christoph von Graffenried's Account,* 247 (quotation).

25. Allan Gallay, *The Indian Slave Trade: The Rise of the English Empire in the American South, 1670–1717* (New Haven: Yale University Press, 2002), ch. 10; Richter, *Ordeal of the Longhouse,* 238–39.

26. *CRP* 2: 389; Merrell, *Indians' New World,* 41, 53, 56–57; Gallay, *Indian Slave Trade,* 55–61, 73, 103–4, 174–75, 204–12.

27. On the Tuscaroras, see Kercheval, *History of the Valley,* 56; William Marye, "Patowmeck Above Ye Inhabitants," 123–25. On the Shawnees, see *CRP* 3: 97, 206, 211, 215; *Arch. Md.* 38: 394–95, 442–43, 450–51; Marye, "Patowmeck Above Ye Inhabitants," 4–5, 129–30; and Francis Jennings, *The Ambiguous Iroquois Empire: The Covenant Chain Confederation of Indian Tribes with English Colonies from Its Beginnings to the Lancaster Treaty of 1744* (New York: W. W. Norton, 1984), 264.

28. Gooch to Lords of Trade, 2 June 1713 and 16 November 1713, in Gooch Records, vol. 2 (quotation); John Williams to Samuel Sewall, 13 August 1716, quoted in Richter, *Ordeal of the Longhouse,* 239–40; Merrell, *Indians' New World,* 118–19.

29. *CRP* 3: 89 (quotation).

30. On Virginians getting caught in the crossfire during and after the Tuscarora War, see R. A. Brock, ed., *The Official Letters of Alexander Spotswood,* Collections of the Virginia Historical Society, new series (Richmond: Virginia Historical Society, 1882–85) 1: 132–33, 141–42; 2: 18–20 (quotation on 20); Hening, *Statutes* 4: 9–11. On proposals for buffer communities, see *Arch. Md.* 5: 149 (quotation); Richard Beale Davis, ed., *William Fitzhugh and His Chesapeake World, 1676–1701* (Chapel Hill: University of North Carolina Press, 1963), 250; Hening, *Statutes* 3: 204–6 (quotation); Harrison, *Landmarks,* ch. 13; Warren Hofstra, "'The Extention of His Majesties Dominions': The Virginia Backcountry and the Reconfiguration of Imperial Frontiers," *JAH* 84 (1998), 1281–1312; Brock, *Letters of Spotswood* 1: 40 and 2: 288–97.

31. Brock, *Letters of Spotswood* 1: 143 (quotation); 116, 132–33, 149–52; Todd, *Christoph von Graffenried's Account,* 24–25, 85–91. Michel was in North Carolina during the Tuscarora War and may have reminded Graffenried of this alternative (Gallay, *Indian Slave Trade,* 273).

32. Brock, *Letters of Spotswood* 2: 70 (quotation), 193–96; *EJCV* 3: 371–72; Edward P. Alexander, *The Journal of John Fontaine: An Irish Huguenot Son in Spain and Virginia, 1710–1719* (Charlottesville: University Press of Virginia, 1972), 101–2.

33. H. R. McIlwaine, ed., *Journals of the House of Burgesses of Virginia, 1712–1726* (Richmond: Colonial Press, 1912), 47 (quotation); James Axtell, *The Invasion Within: The Contest of Cultures in Colonial North America* (New York: Oxford University Press, 1985), 192; and Merrell, *Indians' New World,* 58 (quotation), 80. Spotswood also set out to learn more about Virginia's western parts. In August 1716 he joined with a dozen gentlemen, whom he dubbed "Knights of the Golden Horseshoe, together with their servants, fourteen rangers, and four Indians, and struck a westward course from

Germanna over the Blue Ridge to the Shenandoah River." Alexander, *Journal of John Fontaine*, 13–14, 101–9.

34. Leder, *Livingston Indian Records*, 222–23 (quotations); Brock, *Letters of Spotswood* 2: 251–52; *CRP* 3: 21–24; Merrell, *Indians' New World*, 89, 119.

35. "Orders for the inhabitants of the James and Pamunky Rivers to go out as Rangers," 10 June 1717, and Spotswood to Captain Robert Hix, 7 June 1717, in Colonial Papers, reel 611, folder 28, n. 19, LV; Brock, *Letters of Spotswood* 2: 288–89 (quotation); *Arch. Md.* 38: 362–69; *CRP* 3: 92–96, 130–32; Merrell, *Indians' New World*, 97.

36. *CRP* 3: 19–20 (quotations), 66 (quotation), 92–95, 99–100.

37. Spotswood to Captain Robert Hix, 7 June 1717, Colonial Papers, reel 611, folder 28, n. 19, LV (quotation); *CRP* 3: 21–24, 30–31, 45–46, 78–81, 82–89 (quotation on 88), 92–97; Brock, *Letters of Spotswood* 2: 288–89.

38. *DRCHSNY* 5: 657–81 (quotations on 670, 671–72). Maryland sent no representatives to Albany, on the grounds that the 1721 renewal of the Covenant Chain at Annapolis was sufficient. On the cession of land about Conestoga, which turned out to be only a limited grant to Keith alone, see Jennings, *Ambiguous Iroquois Empire*, 293.

Chapter 11. The Trouble with Boundaries

1. Lorena Walsh, "Summing the Parts: Implications for Estimating Chesapeake Output and Income Subregionally," *WMQ* 56 (1999), 62–72; *Arch. Md.* 25: 379–80; Philemon Lloyd to Baltimore, 8 June 1724, Dulany Papers, mss 1265, box 1, MHS (quotation); Fairfax Harrison, *Landmarks of Old Prince William* (Richmond: Old Dominion Press, 1924), 150 (quotation); "Answers to Queries of the Board of Trade, 23 July 1730," in Virginia (Colony), Governor, 1727–1740 (William Gooch), Records, 1727–1751, vol. 1, VHS mss 3 V8194 G5907 a.

2. Stuart Fiedel, John Bedell, and Charles LeeDecker, *Cohongorooto: The Potomac above the Falls; Archaeological Identification and Evaluation Study of C&O Canal National Historical Park*, vol. 1 (Washington, D.C.: Lewis Berger Group, 2005), 78–88; R. Bruce Harley, "Dr. Charles Carroll—Land Speculator," *MdHM* 46 (1951), 93–107; Harrison, *Landmarks*, 147–48; Aubrey Land, *The Dulanys of Maryland: A Biographical Study of Daniel Dulany, the Elder (1685–1753) and Daniel Dulany, the Younger (1722–1797)* (Baltimore: Johns Hopkins University Press, 1955), 40, 56, 59, 63, 99–101; Grace Tracey and John Dern, *Pioneers of Old Monocacy: The Early Settlement of Frederick County, Maryland, 1721–1743* (Baltimore: Genealogical Publishing, 1987), 23–39, 60, 70, 80, 90, 95, 362; Allan Kulikoff, *Tobacco and Slaves: The Development of Southern Cultures in the Chesapeake, 1680–1800* (Chapel Hill: University of North Carolina Press, 1986), 93–95.

3. *CRP* 2: 15–17 (quotation), 244–45 (quotation); *Correspondence between William Penn and James Logan*, Memoirs of the Historical Society of Pennsylvania (Philadelphia: Historical Society of Pennsylvania, 1872), 1: 43–44; *Arch. Md.* 26: 38, 67, 123.

4. *Arch. Md.* 26: 42, 67, 143, 376–77 (quotation); *CRP* 2: 191, 244–45; *Correspondence between Penn and Logan*, 1: 43. Even then a few Piscataways lingered at the island. As

late as 1711 a visitor to the island "made a league with the Canavest Indians." Vincent Todd, ed., *Christoph von Graffenried's Account of the Founding of New Bern* (Raleigh: Edwards & Broughton, 1920), 247.

5. R. A. Brock, ed., *The Official Letters of Alexander Spotswood* (Richmond: Virginia Historical Society, 1882–85), Collections of the Virginia Historical Society, new series, 1: 149–50 (quotation), 168 (quotation); Todd, *Christoph von Graffenried's Account*, 247; "Report of the King's Commissioners Appointed to Settle the Boundaries of the Northern Neck," Gooch Records, vol. 2.

6. *CRP* 3: 148–51.

7. *CRP* 3: 146, 148–52, 156–57 (quotations on 150–52).

8. *Arch. Md.* 25: 379–80, 383–85 (quotations on 379–80).

9. James Merrell, *Into the American Woods: Negotiators on the Pennsylvania Frontier* (New York: W. W. Norton, 1999), 118–21.

10. For examples of seasonal hunting and fishing, see Brock, *Letters of Spotswood*, 1: 141–42; *CRP* 3: 19–20, 45, 121–22, 215; *EJCV* 3: 533–34; *PA, Fourth Series* 1: 366, 368–70; "Narrative of a Voyage to Maryland, 1705–1706," *AHR* 12 (1907), 329–31, 333–34; William Byrd, "History of the Dividing Line," in Louis B. Wright, ed., *The Prose Works of William Byrd of Westover* (Cambridge: Harvard University Press, 1966), 258; William Saunders, ed., *The Colonial Records of North Carolina*, vol. 2 (Raleigh: P. M. Hale, 1886), 224.

11. *CRP* 3: 181–83 (quotations on 181–82).

12. *CRP* 3: 181–85 (quotations on 183, 184); *PA, Fourth Series* 1: 391 (quotation).

13. *CRP* 3: 271–73; *PA, First Series* 1: 240–41; Jane Merritt, *At the Crossroads: Indians and Empires on a Mid-Atlantic Frontier, 1700–1763* (Chapel Hill: University of North Carolina Press, 2003), 41; Francis Jennings, *The Ambiguous Iroquois Empire: The Covenant Chain Confederation of Indian Tribes with English Colonies from Its Beginnings to the Lancaster Treaty of 1744* (New York: W. W. Norton, 1984), 303–5.

14. Gooch to Board of Trade, 28 June 1728, Gooch Records, vol. 1 (quotation); Gooch to Board of Trade, 29 June 1729, in ibid. (quotation); James Thomas, "Account for Expenses at Chenandoah," 1729, in Robert Alonzo Brock Collection, box 227, Huntington Library.

15. *EJCV* 4: 223–24, 229, 232–33, 249–50, 253.

16. *EJCV* 4: 270 (quotation; emphasis added); "A General Map of the Known and Inhabited Parts of Virginia," 1731 (at VHS).

17. Gooch to Board of Trade, 30 July 1730 and 10 July 1731, Gooch Records, vol. 1.

18. Gooch to Board of Trade, 10 July 1731, Gooch Records, vol. 1 (quotation); "Answers to Queries of the Board of Trade, 23 July 1730," in ibid.; Board of Trade to Gooch, 13 September 1732, in ibid. See also Gooch to Board of Trade, 8 February 1732/33, in ibid., and Warren Hofstra, *The Planting of New Virginia: Settlement and Landscape in the Shenandoah Valley* (Baltimore: Johns Hopkins University Press, 2004), 77–81.

19. Gooch to Board of Trade, 26 March 1729, Gooch Records, vol. 1 (quotation); Gooch to Board of Trade, 21 September 1727, 12 February 1728, and 29 June 1729, in ibid. For evidence of an intensifying crossfire, see *EJCV* 3: 125–26; 4: 209; *CRP* 3: 302–4, 309; *PA, First Series* 1: 223, 238–39, 295; and Hofstra, *Planting of New Virginia*, 85.

20. Stuart Brown, *Virginia Baron: The Story of Thomas Sixth Lord Fairfax* (Berryville, Va.: Chesapeake Book Company, 1965), 37–42, 56, 70; Charles Royster, *The Fabulous History of the Dismal Swamp Company: A Story of George Washington's Times* (New York: Knopf, 1999), 18–21; Douglas Southall Freeman, *George Washington, a Biography* (New York: Scribner, 1948), 6: 487–89.

21. *PA, First Series* 1: 295 (quotation); Robert Brugger, *Maryland: A Middle Temperament, 1634–1980* (Baltimore: Johns Hopkins University Press, 1988), 68 (quotation); *Arch. Md.* 11: 10–11 (quotation); 28: 7.

22. Ronald Hoffman with Sally Mason, *Princes of Ireland, Planters of Maryland: A Carroll Saga, 1500–1782* (Chapel Hill: University of North Carolina Press, 2000), 112–13; Tracey and Dern, *Pioneers of Old Monocacy,* 24–29, 33, 45, 115–30, 368–69. See also 34–40, 50, 69–73, 79–81, 84, 89, 94–96, 99, 106–9, 154–56, 185, 222, 228. Other examples are exhaustively cataloged in Tracey and Dern's remarkable reconstruction of early land grants and settlements in western Maryland.

23. Many of these grants are summarized and mapped in Tracey and Dern, *Pioneers of Old Monocacy,* 24, 38, 58 (key to settlement maps), 60, 80, 90, 95, 100, 107, 186, 223, 229, 238, 244, 248, 362 (summary of patents by date). On Maryland grants in the Cumberland Valley, see Paula Stoner Reed, "Building with Stone in the Cumberland Valley: A Study of Regional Environmental, Technical, and Cultural Factors in Stone Construction" (Ph.D. diss., George Washington University, 1988), 90–95. Baltimore also offered two hundred acres of free land to any family that settled "between the Rivers Potomack and Susquehana," in return for modest annual quitrents, but surprisingly few newcomers took up Baltimore's offer; instead they purchased or leased from the large-scale landowners who had already snapped up most of the prime lands along the Monocacy and Potomac. See *Arch. Md.* 28: 25–26; 38: 456; Tracey and Dern, *Pioneers of Old Monocacy,* 156; Aubrey Land, *Colonial Maryland: A History* (Millwood, N.Y.: KTO Press, 1981), 147–49.

24. Robert Mitchell, *Commercialism and Frontier: Perspectives on the Early Shenandoah Valley* (Charlottesville: University Press of Virginia, 1977), 28–29; Hofstra, *Planting of New Virginia,* 91, 94.

25. Hofstra, *Planting of New Virginia,* 33–36, 91, 133; Tracey and Dern, *Pioneers of Old Monocacy,* 69–73; John Kester, "Charles Polke: Indian Trader of the Potomac, 1703–1753," *MdHM* 90 (1995), 449, 454–55, 462, n. 28.

26. *CRP* 3: 459–60; Jennings, *Ambiguous Iroquois Empire,* 303–8, 314–20, 345–46; Merritt, *At the Crossroads,* ch. 1; Merrell, *Into the American Woods,* ch. 4; John Duffy, *Epidemics in Colonial America* (Baton Rouge: Louisiana State University Press, 1953), 78, 191.

27. *EJCV* 4: 270, 288–89, 295, 318–19, 321, 325–26, 336, 347, 375; Hofstra, *Planting of New Virginia,* 9, 26–29, 141, 161.

28. Gooch to Board of Trade, 18 July 1732, Gooch Records, vol. 1; Gooch to Board of Trade, 24 May 1734, in ibid., vol. 2.

29. Royster, *Fabulous History,* 20–21; Brown *Virginia Baron,* 42–43, 46–47; Hofstra, *Planting of New Virginia,* 132.

30. *EJCV* 4: 361–62 (quotation); Gooch to Board of Trade, 19 May 1736 and 8 Janu-

ary 1736/37, Gooch Records, vol. 2; Brown, *Virginia Baron,* 47–49, 61–63, 74. Gooch did have some forewarning through letters from the Board of Trade earlier in 1735, but he apparently did not know the full story until Fairfax's appearance before the Council in November. Gooch to Board of Trade, 21 February 1734/35, and Board of Trade to Gooch, 4 September 1735, Gooch Records, vol. 2.

31. Mitchell, *Commercialism and Frontier,* 36, 61–67, 74–79; Hofstra, *Planting of New Virginia,* 131–42.

32. Fairfax quoted in Hofstra, *Planting of New Virginia,* 132; Hening, *Statutes* 4: 514–23. See also Brown, *Virginia Baron,* 76–77, and Mitchell, *Commercialism and Frontier,* 30.

33. Brown, *Virginia Baron,* 80–82; Gooch to Board, 8 January 1736/37, and Gooch to Board, 21 February 1736/37, Gooch Records, vol. 2 (quotation).

34. Brown, *Virginia Baron,* 80–82; Gooch to Board, 8 January 1736/37, and Gooch to Board, 21 February 1736/37, Gooch Records, vol. 2 (quotation).

35. "Report of the King's Commissioners"; "Report of Fairfax's Commissioners," 8 November 1737, Gooch Records, vol. 2; Benjamin Winslow, "Field Notes of the Survey of the Potomack River from the mouth of Sherrondo to the head Spring," VHS mss 11:3 W7326:1; "Account of the Surveyers of the Northern Neck, 25 April 1737," "Account of the Expenses in Surveying the Boundaries of the Northern Neck, November 1737," and "A List of the Men Employed on the Survey from Sherrando to Chapawamsick," November 1737, in Colonial Papers, reel 611, folder 38, nos. 16, 29, and 30, LV; Brown, *Virginia Baron,* 84.

36. Winslow, "Field Notes"; Gooch to Board, 21 February 1736/37, Gooch Records, vol. 2 (quotation); Brown, *Virginia Baron,* ch. 12.

37. "Report of the King's Commissioners"; "Report of Fairfax's Commissioners"; Fairfax Harrison, "The Northern Neck Maps of 1737–1747," *WMQ,* 2nd series, 4 (1924), 1–15; James Foster, "Potomac River Maps of 1737 by Robert Brooke and Others," *WMQ,* 2nd series, 18 (1938), 406–18.

38. Gooch to Board of Trade, 19 August 1737 and Gooch to Board of Trade, 8 November 1737, Gooch Records, vol. 2; Brown, *Virginia Baron,* 94–98.

39. Mary Elizabeth McDowell Greenlee, Deposition in *Peck v. Borden,* in Kerby Miller, Arnold Schrier, Bruce Boling, and David Doyle, *Irish Immigrants in the Land of Canaan: Letters and Memoirs from Colonial and Revolutionary America, 1675–1815* (New York: Oxford University Press, 2003), 148–54.

40. Mitchell, *Commercialism and Frontier,* 31–36, 38, 52–53, 65–72, 75–76; Hofstra, *Planting of New Virginia,* 39–41, 113.

41. The mapmakers noted the recently abandoned Shawnee fields, and the surveyors' notes show how much they depended upon on Indian traders such as Israel Friend, Charles Polke, and Edmond Cartlidge. Winslow, "Field Notes"; Receipt for Expenses, 28 August 1737, in Colonial Papers, reel 611, folder 38, n. 24, LV; Harrison, "Northern Neck Maps"; Foster, "Potomac River Maps"; Kester, "Charles Polke," 449–50, 455.

42. *EJCV* 4: 327, 330–31; *PA, First Series* 1: 425, 436–38; *CRP* 3: 501–5, 511–12, 564–65, 605–6; *CRP* 3: 606 and 4: 234–35, 447; *CVSP,* 231–32; Samuel Kercheval, *A History of the*

Valley of Virginia, 4th ed. (Strasburg, Va.: Shenandoah Publishing House, 1925), 35–36. For backcountry colonists' perceptions of this increased traffic, see Hofstra, *Planting of New Virginia,* 133 (quotation); Miller, Schrier, Boling, and Doyle, *Irish Immigrants,* 390 (quotation); "Abraham Shriver's Family History," Steiger-Shriver Family Papers, Special Collections Library, Duke University, Durham, North Carolina (quotation).

43. *EJCV* 4: 368, 370, 384, 404, 414, 421–22; *CRP* 4: 203, 245 (quotation); King of the Shawnees to William Gooch, 4 August 1738, in Colonial Papers, reel 611, folder 38, n. 38, LV (quotation); Gooch to Board of Trade, 20 September 1738 (quotation) and Gooch to Board of Trade, 15 February 1738/39, Gooch Records, vol. 2.

44. The Six Nations, Catawbas, and Cherokees finally signed a Virginia- and New York–brokered peace treaty in June 1742, but it did not last through the end of the year. *EJCV* 4: 414, 421–22; Gooch to Board of Trade, Gooch Records, vol. 2 (quotation); *CRP* 4: 203; Edmund Berkeley and Dorothy Smith Berkeley, eds., *The Correspondence of John Bartram, 1734–1777* (Gainesville: University Press of Florida, 1992), 121; Hofstra, *Planting of New Virginia,* 163, 167.

45. *EJCV* 4: 414; H. R. McIlwaine, ed., *Journals of the House of Burgesses, 1727–1734, 1736–1740* (Richmond: Colonial Press, 1910), 320–21, 333, 337–38, 340, 343–44, 349, 386; Hening, *Statutes* 4: 197–204, 323, 395; 5: 24; Hofstra, *Planting of New Virginia,* 164–65.

46. Board of Trade to Gooch, 6 December 1738 (quotation) and Gooch to Board, 15 February 1738/39 (quotation), Gooch Records, vol. 2; Hofstra, *Planting of New Virginia,* 166.

47. Jennings, *Ambiguous Iroquois Empire,* 321–23; Merritt, *At the Crossroads,* 6, 21, 25–41; Merrell, *Into the American Woods,* 168. For an example of a protest from another Indian nation, see *CRP* 3: 234.

48. Jennings, *Ambiguous Iroquois Empire,* ch. 17.

49. *CRP* 4: 80–95; *Arch. Md.* 28: 271–72 (quotation).

Chapter 12. The Backcountry Transformed

1. *Arch. Md.* 28: 262–70 (quotations on 262–63); *CRP* 4: 566–72.

2. *CRP* 4: 570 (quotation), 572 (quotation); *Arch. Md.* 28: 271–74 (quotation).

3. *EJCV* 5: 95 (quotation); Gooch to "My Lord Duke" [Newcastle], 28 July 1742, in Virginia (Colony), Governor, 1727–1740 (William Gooch), Records, 1727–1751, vol. 3, VHS mss 3 V8194 G5907 a; Warren Hofstra, *The Planting of New Virginia: Settlement and Landscape in the Shenandoah Valley* (Baltimore: Johns Hopkins University Press, 2004), 41 (quotation).

4. *CRP* 4: 631, 668 (quotations).

5. James Merrell, *Into the American Woods: Negotiators on the Pennsylvania Frontier* (New York: W. W. Norton, 1999), 167–71; and Hofstra, *Planting of New Virginia,* 17–18, 40–41, 44–48.

6. *EJCV* 5: 114–17; *CRP* 4: 636 (quotation); *DRCHSNY* 6: 241–42. See also Daniel Dulany the Elder to Baltimore, 21 May 1744, Dulany Papers, MHS mss 1265, box 2.

7. *CRP* 4: 636, 643–56, 658, 662–68; *Arch. Md.* 28: 293–95, 298–302; *PA, Fourth Series* 1: 822–24, 826; *EJCV* 5: 120, 130; Gooch to Board, 22 August 1743, Gooch Records, vol.

3; *DRCHSNY* 4: 237 and 6: 235–37, 239–40; Merrell, *Into the American Woods,* 167- 79; Hofstra, *Planting of New Virginia,* 169–72.

8. *A Treaty Held at the Town of Lancaster, in Pennsylvania, by the Honourable the Lieutenant-Governor of the Province, and the Honourable the Commissioners for the Provinces of Virginia and Maryland, With the Indians of the Six Nations, in June, 1744* (Philadelphia: Benjamin Franklin, 1744), 6–22 (quotation on 18).

9. Ibid., 5, 18, 24, 27, 29–34, 37–38.

10. Stuart Brown, *Virginia Baron: The Story of Thomas Sixth Lord Fairfax* (Berryville, Va.: Chesapeake Book Co., 1965), 97–98; Douglas Southall Freeman, *George Washington, a Biography* (New York: Scribner, 1948), 6: 509.

11. Craig's autobiography is ably interpreted and excerpted in Kerby Miller, Arnold Schrier, Bruce Boling, and David Doyle, *Irish Immigrants in the Land of Canaan: Letters and Memoirs from Colonial and Revolutionary America, 1675–1815* (New York: Oxford University Press, 2003), 381–400; for the complete version of Craig's autobiography, see Autobiography of John Craig, 1709–1770, VHS mss 5:1 C8445:1. Irish migration figures are drawn from Marianne Wokeck, *Trade in Strangers: The Beginnings of Mass Migration to North America* (University Park: Pennsylvania State University Press, 1999), 172–73.

12. Miller, Schrier, Boling, and Doyle, *Irish Immigrants,* 385, 388–89.

13. Ibid., 392–93, 395, 398–99; Hofstra, *Planting of New Virginia,* 41, 162. On Ulster Presbyterians' conflicts with the Anglican Church and with each other, see Patrick Griffin, *The People with No Name: Ireland's Ulster Scots, America's Scots Irish, and the Creation of a British Atlantic World, 1689–1764* (Princeton: Princeton University Press, 2001), chs. 2, 5, and S. J. Connolly, "Ulster Presbyterians: Religion, Culture, and Politics, 1660–1850," in H. Tyler Blethen and Curtis Wood, eds. *Ulster and North America: Transatlantic Perspectives on the Scots-Irish* (Tuscaloosa: University of Alabama Press, 1997), 24–30.

14. Miller, Schrier, Boling, and Doyle, *Irish Immigrants,* 394–400. On witchcraft beliefs, see Edward Cowan, "Prophecy and Prophylaxis: A Paradigm for the Scotch-Irish?," in Blethen and Wood, *Ulster and North America,* 15–22.

15. Most migrants went to Eastern Europe. Hans Fenske, "International Migration: Germany in the Eighteenth Century," *Central European History* 13 (1980), 332–47; Mark Häberlein, "German Migrants in Colonial Pennsylvania: Resources, Opportunities, and Experience," *WMQ* 50 (1993), 555–74; Aaron Fogleman, *Hopeful Journeys: German Immigration, Settlement, and Political Culture in Colonial America, 1717–1775* (Philadelphia: University of Pennsylvania Press, 1996), ch. 1; Wokeck, *Trade in Strangers,* 1–16 (quotations).

16. In these wars forces loyal to the new King William rooted out the supporters of James II, who had been ousted in the Glorious Revolution of 1688 and tried to use Ireland as the launching place for his reconquest of England.

17. T. M. Devine, *Scotland's Empire and the Shaping of the Americas, 1600–1815* (Washington, D.C.: Smithsonian Books, 2003), 4–5, 29, 145, 150; Griffin, *People with No Name,* 10–36; Graeme Kirkham, "Ulster Emigration to North America, 1680–1720," in Blethen and Wood, *Ulster and North America,* 89–91; Wokeck, *Trade in Strangers,* 172.

18. A. G. Roeber, "'The Origin of Whatever is Not English Among Us': The Dutch-speaking and the German-Speaking Peoples of Colonial British America," in Bernard Bailyn and Philip Morgan, eds., *Strangers within the Realm: Cultural Margins of the First British Empire* (Chapel Hill: University of North Carolina Press, 1991), 237–57; Wokeck, *Trade in Strangers*, 27–32 and ch. 3; Miller, Schrier, Boling, and Doyle, *Irish Immigrants*, 147–56.

19. Wokeck, *Trade in Strangers*, 44–46, 172. These figures are absolute minimums: Wokeck's figures are very conservative, and responsible scholars can reasonably conclude that she has counted as little as a quarter of the Irish migrants (see Miller, Schrier, Boling, and Doyle, *Irish Immigrants*, appendix 2). Wokeck's figures are nevertheless a good starting point, particularly as her year-by-year figures for new arrivals in Philadelphia and New Castle provide a clear sense of short-term changes in the volume of immigration.

20. Robert Mitchell, *Commercialism and Frontier: Perspectives on the Early Shenandoah Valley* (Charlottesville: University Press of Virginia, 1977), 95–97; Arthur Eli Karinen, "Numerical and Distributional Aspects of Maryland Population, 1631–1840" (Ph.D. diss., University of Maryland, College Park, 1958), 134–36; Miller, Schrier, Boling, and Doyle, *Irish Immigrants*, 146.

21. Elizabeth Kessel, "Germans on the Maryland Frontier: A Social History of Frederick County, Maryland, 1730–1800" (Ph.D. diss., Rice University, 1981); James Lemon, *The Best Poor Man's Country: A Geographical Study of Early Southeastern Pennsylvania* (New York: Johns Hopkins University Press, 1972), 43–50; Carl Bridenbaugh, *Myths and Realities: Societies of the Colonial South* (Baton Rouge: Louisiana State University Press, 1951), ch. 3; Fogleman, *Hopeful Journeys*, 6–8; David Hackett Fischer, *Albion's Seed: Four British Folkways in America* (New York: Oxford University Press, 1989), 633–39.

22. Miller, Schrier, Boling, and Doyle, *Irish Immigrants*, 61–62, 144–45, 154 (quotation), 319, 321–22, 389 (quotation); "Diary of a Journey of Moravians, from Bethlehem, Pennsylvania, to Bethabara in Wachovia, North Carolina, 1753," in Newton Mereness, ed., *Travels in the American Colonies* (New York: Macmillan, 1916), 331–34 (quotations). Scholars have confirmed these impressions by developing an "Index of Dissimilarity" measuring the proportion of the people in two ethnic groups who would have to move to another place in order to achieve an equal distribution for both groups. The index ranges from 0.0 (no segregation) to 1.0 (total segregation). In Maryland the index for Germans versus Scots-Irish and Scots was 0.623, meaning that nearly two-thirds of the people in each group would have had to relocate in order to do away with residential segregation. Fogleman, *Hopeful Journeys*, table 3.2.

23. Wayne Bodle, "Themes and Directions in Middle Colonies Historiography, 1980–1994," *WMQ* 51 (1994), 355–88; Fogleman, *Hopeful Journeys*; Stephen Longenecker, *Shenandoah Religion: Outsiders and the Mainstream, 1716–1865* (Waco: Baylor University Press, 2002); James Rice, "Evangelicals and the Invention of Community in Western Maryland," *MdHM* 101 (2006), 26–54; Sally Schwartz, *A Mixed Multitude: The Struggle for Toleration in Colonial Pennsylvania* (New York: New York University Press, 1987), ch. 1.

24. On ethnic community formation and maintenance, see Roeber, "Origin," 245–81; Renate Wilson, *Pious Traders in Medicine: German Pharmaceutical Networks in Eighteenth-Century North America* (University Park: Pennsylvania State University Press, 2000); Kessel, "Germans on the Maryland Frontier," 203–14, 229, 373–76; Griffin, *People with No Name;* Kenneth Keller, "The Outlook of Rhinelanders on the Virginia Frontier," in Michael Puglisi, ed., *Diversity and Accommodation: Essays on the Cultural Composition of the Virginia Frontier* (Knoxville: University of Tennessee Press, 1997), 108. On middlemen, see "Abraham Shriver's Family History," Steiger-Shriver Family Papers, Special Collections Library, Duke University, Durham, North Carolina (quotation); James Rice, "Crime and Punishment in Frederick County and Maryland, 1748–1837" (Ph.D. diss., University of Maryland, College Park, 1994), 79–82; Hofstra, *Planting of New Virginia*, 33–36, 94–95, 161.

25. Charles Kemper, ed., "Documents Relating to Early Projected Swiss Colonies," 2; William Hinke and Charles Kemper, eds., "Moravian Diaries of Travels Through Virginia," *VMHB* 12 (1904), 143–48; Burwell to Board of Trade, 21 August 1751, Gooch Records, vol. 3; Andrew Burnaby, *Travels Through the Middle Settlements in North-America, In the Years 1759 and 1760,* 3rd ed. (London: T. Payne, 1798; repr. New York: A. Wessels Company, 1798), 56; Robert Mitchell, Warren Hofstra, and Edward Conner, "Reconstructing the Colonial Environment of the Upper Chesapeake Watershed," in Curtin, Brush, and Fisher, *Discovering the Chesapeake,* 167–90; Mitchell, *Commercialism and Frontier,* 19–25, 40–43; and Hofstra, *Planting of New Virginia,* 31–33, 124–31.

26. Burnaby, *Travels,* 55 (quotation); David Hardin, "Laws of Nature: Environmental Legislation in Colonial Virginia, 1619–1776," *Virginia Geographer* 22 (1990), 53–67; *CVSP,* 243; "Examination of Henry Lenard," Colonial Papers, reel 611, folder 43, n. 1, LV; Joshua Fry, Lunsford Lomax, and Peter Hedgman, "Field Notes Taken in Running of the Boundary Line," Autumn 1746, Gooch Records, vol. 3; "Field Notes taken by Thomas Lewis," September 1746–February 1747, Robert Alonzo Brock Collection, folder 27, Huntington Library; Hening, *Statutes* 5: 60–63.

27. Miller, Schrier, Boling, and Doyle, *Irish Immigrants,* 144–45, 317–23; "Diary of a Journey of Moravians," 331–34; Hofstra, *Planting of New Virginia,* 17–22, 31–33, 38, 94–102, 135–42; Mitchell, *Commercialism and Frontier,* 36, 38; Lemon, *Best Poor Man's Country,* ch. 2.

28. Except where otherwise noted, the following account is derived from an analysis of McCullough's journal, in Miller, Schrier, Boling, and Doyle, *Irish Immigrants,* 156–79.

29. On Tidewater agricultural reform, see Rhys Isaac, *Landon Carter's Uneasy Kingdom: Revolution and Rebellion on a Virginia Plantation* (New York: Oxford University Press, 2004), ch. 4.

30. McCullough rarely recorded his own debts and expenditures in his journal; nevertheless it seems probable that Armstrong, Torintine, and others reciprocated when McCullough needed help.

31. The following is an imaginative reconstruction based on the enumeration and passing mentions of fields and buildings in the journal. Though I've followed the hints offered by McCullough, some of the fields (especially those not adjacent to

the farmyard) may well have been arranged in another pattern. In a few cases I've made educated guesses where the journal is silent, substituting knowledge of common practices for concrete evidence of the McCulloughs' practices: e.g., the house may have been built at least partly of stone, as was common in Ulster.

32. McCullough's journal does not indicate what he did with the manure that accumulated in the barn, calfhouse, and sheephouse, but as anyone who has spent time on a farm can attest, it *will* pile up and has to be disposed of somehow. Moreover, the configuration of fields and outbuildings on his farm was well suited to folding and manuring. Manuring and folding were common practices in McCullough's native Ulster and ancestral Scotland, and elsewhere in the southern backcountry. Robert Witherspoon, "Recollections," in H. Roy Merrens, ed., *The Colonial South Carolina Scene: Contemporary Views, 1697–1774* (Columbia: University of South Carolina Press, 1977), 126.

33. My understanding of McCullough's accounts and the "exchange economy" are heavily influenced by Hofstra, *Planting of New Virginia*, 224–35.

34. Mitchell, *Commercialism and Frontier*, 71, 135–43; Hofstra, *Planting of New Virginia*, 196–97, 210–14, 217, 224–35; Carole Shammas, "The Housing Stock of the Early United States: Refinement Meets Migration," *WMQ* 64 (2007), 549–90.

35. Mitchell, *Commercialism and Frontier*, 135–43, 147–49, 181; Hofstra, *Planting of New Virginia*, 206–10, 215–16, 221–22; Kessel, "Germans on the Maryland Frontier," 23–34, 54–55, 59, 76–77, 83–84, 91–92, 99, 101, 109, 114–40, 148–55, 159, 253–65.

36. Robert Brooke Survey Book, 1732–1734, VHS mss 11:3B 7905:1; Mitchell, *Commercialism and Frontier*, 44; Hofstra, *Planting of New Virginia*, 102, 110, 113–16, 138–42; Brown, *Virginia Baron*, 111 (quotation).

37. Brown, *Virginia Baron*, 108–9, 119; Hunter Branson McKay, ed., *Fairfax Land Suit: Transcript of Copy in the British Museum* (unpublished manuscript, Archives Room, Handley Regional Library, Winchester, Va.), 1550 (quotation).

38. Hofstra, 145–46 (quotation); Brown, *Virginia Baron*, 110–12.

39. Dulany to Baltimore, 24 November 1744, The Calvert Papers, MHS mss 174, reel 26, n. 1130; Aubrey Land, *The Dulanys of Maryland: A Biographical Study of Daniel Dulany, the Elder (1685–1753) and Daniel Dulany, the Younger (1722–1797)* (Baltimore: Johns Hopkins University Press, 1955), ch. 11; Land, "A Land Speculator in the Opening of Western Maryland," *MdHM* 48 (1953), 194–203; Kessel, "Germans on the Maryland Frontier," 92–93.

40. Hofstra, *Planting of New Virginia*, 180–95. Staunton, the seat of the upper Shenandoah Valley's Augusta County, developed in a similar fashion on lands donated in 1746 by William Beverley near a mill he had built on Beverley Manor. Mitchell, *Commercialism and Frontier*, 83–84, 144.

Chapter 13. "The Finest Country I Ever Was In"

1. *CRP* 4: 739. For similar reports, see *EJCV* 5: 207 (quotation); Deposition of Thomas Cresap, Maryland Provincial Papers, 1720–1763 (MSA S 53-1), 11; Edmund Berkeley and Dorothy Smith Berkeley, eds., *The Correspondence of John Bartram, 1734–*

1777 (Gainesville: University Press of Florida, 1992), 283; John Carlyle to Dr. George Carlyle, 20 February 1745/6, Carlyle Papers, folder 12, VHS mss 1 C1995 a9–36.

2. James Merrell, *Into the American Woods: Negotiators on the Pennsylvania Frontier* (New York: W. W. Norton, 1999), 179–81; Jane Merritt, *At the Crossroads: Indians and Empires on a Mid-Atlantic Frontier, 1700–1763* (Chapel Hill: University of North Carolina, 2003), 77–79.

3. Peter Mancall, *Valley of Opportunity: Economic Culture along the Upper Susquehanna, 1700–1800* (Ithaca: Cornell University Press, 1991), ch. 3; Merritt, *At the Crossroads,* 77 (quotation); Matthew Ward, *Breaking the Backcountry: The Seven Years' War in Virginia and Pennsylvania, 1754–1765* (Pittsburgh: University of Pittsburgh Press, 2003), 23; Richard White, *The Middle Ground: Indians, Empires and Republics in the Great Lakes Region, 1650–1815* (New York: Cambridge University Press, 1991), 196–202, 219.

4. Francis Jennings, *Empire of Fortune: Crowns, Colonies, and Tribes in the Seven Years War in America* (New York: W. W. Norton, 1988), 14–15, 355–62. A late colonial map of the interior made this explicit: a label noted that "these Lands were granted & partly settled in consequence of a purchase made at Lancaster in the year 1744." "Map of the Interior," ca. 1770, PRO 700 / Maps / Virginia 18, VCRP reel 497.

5. Other large grants were made just to the south and west of the Potomac nation. *EJCV* 5: 133–34, 172–73, 195, 231, 368. See also Charles Royster, *The Fabulous History of the Dismal Swamp Company: A Story of George Washington's Times* (New York: Knopf, 1999), ch. 1.

6. *EJCV* 5: 295–96, 302–3; Gooch to Board of Trade, 6 November 1747 and 16 June 1748, and "Additional Instructions to Our Trusty & Beloved Sir William Gooch," 13 December 1748, in Virginia (Colony), Governor, 1727–1740 (William Gooch), Records, 1727–1751, vol. 3, VHS mss 3 V8194 G5907 a; Royster, *Fabulous History,* 40–43; Jennings, *Empire of Fortune,* ch. 2.

7. Jennings, *Empire of Fortune,* ch. 2; Royster, *Fabulous History,* 42–43; White, *Middle Ground,* ch. 5.

8. William Darlington, ed., *Christopher Gist's Journals with Historical, Geographical and Ethnological Notes* (Pittsburgh: J. R. Weldin & Co., 1893), 78.

9. "The Treaty of Logs Town, 1752," *VMHB* 13 (1905–1906), 160–61; Jennings, *Empire of Fortune,* ch. 3. On the roots of the Delawares' bitterness toward Pennsylvania, see *CRP* 7: 323–25, 677–78, 683, 687–93, and Charles Thomson, *An Enquiry into the Causes of the Alienation of the Delawares and Shawanese Indians from the British Interest* (London: J. Wilkie, 1759).

10. Jennings, *Empire of Fortune,* 65–70.

11. "The Captivity of Charles Stuart, 1755–57," *Mississippi Valley Historical Review* 13 (1926–27), 63–64; John Carlyle to George Carlyle, 15 August 1754, Carlyle Papers, folder 25; Fred Anderson, *Crucible of War: The Seven Years' War and the Fate of Empire in British North America, 1754–1766* (New York: Knopf, 2000), chs. 8, 9.

12. Jennings, *Empire of Fortune,* ch. 7.

13. Ward, *Breaking the Backcountry,* 60–72.

14. Kerby Miller, Arnold Schrier, Bruce Boling, and David Doyle, *Irish Immigrants*

in the Land of Canaan: Letters and Memoirs from Colonial and Revolutionary America, 1675–1815 (New York: Oxford University Press, 2003), 171–78.

15. Parts of the McCulloughs' loom and a device for cleaning raw fibers.

16. Ward, *Breaking the Backcountry*, ch. 5.

17. Anderson, *Crucible of War*, chs. 23, 28; Ward, *Breaking the Backcountry*, 157–78.

18. Merrell, *Into the American Woods*, 242–48; Ward, *Breaking the Backcountry*, 162–65, 177–83 (quotation).

19. Jennings, *Empire of Fortune*, 402–3, 429–34; Ward, *Breaking the Backcountry*, 184; James Smith, *An Account of the Remarkable Occurrences in the Life and Travels of Col. James Smith* (Cincinnati: R. Clarke, 1870), 106–13; Miller, Schrier, Boling, and Doyle, *Irish Immigrants*, 178 (quotation).

20. *EJCV* 5: 279, 295, 460; W. W. Abbot, Dorothy Twohig, and Philander D. Chase, eds., *Papers of George Washington, Colonial Series* (Charlottesville: University Press of Virginia, 1983–), 1: 25, 65–66, 71, 74–75; John Carlyle to George Carlyle, 18 April 1754, Carlyle Papers; Warren Hofstra, *The Planting of New Virginia: Settlement and Landscape in the Shenandoah Valley* (Baltimore: Johns Hopkins University Press, 2004), 192, 232, 237.

21. *Papers of George Washington, Colonial Series* 1: 78, 82, 93–94, 121, 131, 140–43, 150, 153–55, 185–87, 221–22.

22. Robert Brock, ed., *The Official Records of Robert Dinwiddie, Lieutenant-Governor of the Colony of Virginia, 1751–1758* (Richmond: Virginia Historical Society, 1883), 1: 405–7, 413–21, 424–25, 433–36, 447–55 (600,000 lbs. flour), 458–60, 463–64, 479–83, 501–3, 516–17; Stanley Pargellis, ed., *Military Affairs in North America 1748–1765: Selected Documents from the Cumberland Papers in Windsor Castle* (New York: Archon Books, 1936), 59–64, 112–13, 120; Leonard W. Labaree and William B. Wilcox, eds., *The Papers of Benjamin Franklin* (New Haven: Yale University Press, 1959–84), 6: 20–22; *CRP* 6: 415–16; *Arch. Md.* 6: 136–40; Jennings, *Empire of Fortune*, 149–51.

23. John Carlyle to George Carlyle, 15 August 1754, Carlyle Papers, folder 25; Thomas Preisser, "Eighteenth-Century Alexandria, Virginia, before the Revolution, 1749–1776" (Ph.D. diss., William and Mary, 1977), 140–41; Pargellis, *Military Affairs*, 84–85, 93–95; Ward, *Breaking the Backcountry*, 39–40, 61, 75–78, 84, 161–62, 168–69.

24. Ward, *Breaking the Backcountry*, 159–60; Miller, Schrier, Boling, and Doyle, *Irish Immigrants*, 171–78.

25. Hofstra, *Planting of New Virginia*, 245–56.

26. Ibid., 250–59, 264–70, 384, n. 29; Robert Stewart to John Forbes, 7 April 1758, James Abercromby Papers, box 2, folder 123, Huntington Library; Robert Stewart to Sir John St. Clair, 12 April 1758, Abercromby Papers, box 2, folder 146, Huntington Library; S. K. Stevens, Donald H. Kent, and Autumn L. Leonard, eds., *The Papers of Henry Bouquet*, vol. 2, *The Forbes Expedition* (Harrisburg: Pennsylvania Historical and Museum Commission, 1951), 42, 60–62, 95, 104–5, 133, 654; *Arch. Md.* 6: 241.

27. Andrew Burnaby, *Travels Through the Middle Settlements in North-America, In the Years 1759 and 1760*, 3rd ed. (London: T. Payne, 1798; repr. New York: A. Wessels Co., 1904), 55 (quotation); Hofstra, *Planting of New Virginia*, 264–70; Ward, *Breaking the Backcountry*, chs. 7–8.

28. Hofstra, *Planting of New Virginia*, 272–80; Robert Mitchell, *Commercialism and Frontier: Perspectives on the Early Shenandoah Valley* (Charlottesville: University Press of Virginia, 1977), 156–57, 162–67; John J. McCusker and Russell R. Menard, *The Economy of British America, 1607–1789* (Chapel Hill: University of North Carolina Press, 1985), 79, 204–5; Thomas M. Doerflinger, *A Vigorous Spirit of Enterprise: Merchants and Economic Development in Revolutionary Philadelphia* (Chapel Hill: University of North Carolina Press, 1986), 176–77; Carville Earle and Ronald Hoffman, "Staple Crops and Urban Development in the Eighteenth Century South," *Perspectives in American History* 10 (1976), 28–33.

29. Peter Bergstrom, *Markets and Merchants: Economic Diversification in Colonial Virginia, 1700–1775* (New York: Garland Publishing, 1985), 144–46; Preisser, "Eighteenth-Century Alexandria," 121–25, 143–46; Jacob Price, "Economic Function and the Growth of American Port Towns in the Eighteenth Century," *Perspectives in American History* 8 (1974), 151–56; Mitchell, *Commercialism and Frontier*, 172–73, 187–88. Bergstrom's figures are for the South Potomac (Virginia side) and Rappahannock customs districts alone. While they include wheat grown below the fall line, it is evident that most of this increase was driven by backcountry producers (see later in chapter 13). Moreover, these figures do not include the large quantities of backcountry grain shipped out of Philadelphia and Baltimore, southern Maryland, and the James River. The figures from Frederick County are derived from Elizabeth Kessel's research in probated inventories. Kessel, "Germans on the Maryland Frontier: A Social History of Frederick County, Maryland, 1730–1800" (Ph.D. diss., Rice University, 1981), 97–99.

30. Mitchell, *Commercialism and Frontier*, 161–62; Hofstra, *Planting of New Virginia*, 265, 268–69, 303–5. For an excellent example of this trend, see Diary of Thomas Lewis, 1771, VHS mss 1L5896b6.

31. T. M. Devine, *Scotland's Empire and the Shaping of the Americas, 1600–1815* (Washington, D.C.: Smithsonian Books, 2003), 96–131; Marianne Wokeck, *Trade in Strangers: The Beginnings of Mass Migration to North America* (University Park: Pennsylvania State University Press, 1999), chs. 2, 5; Mitchell, *Commercialism and Frontier*, 238; Land, *Dulanys of Maryland*, 252; Hoffman and Mason, *Princes of Ireland*, 118–19.

32. Hofstra, *Planting of New Virginia*, 278–79; Mitchell, *Commercialism and Frontier*, 74–78, 83–84; Paula Reed, "Building with Stone in the Cumberland Valley: A Study of Regional Environmental, Technical and Cultural Factors in Stone Construction" (Ph.D. diss., George Washington University, 1987), 114–38; William Eddis, *Letters from America, Historical and Descriptive; Comprising Occurrences from 1769, to 1777, Inclusive* (London, 1792; repr. Cambridge: Harvard University Press, 1969), 324.

33. *Maryland Gazette*, 23 January 1777.

34. "Tenaments on His Lordship's Manor of Conococheague," in Reed, "Building with Stone," 114–17.

35. Mitchell, *Commercialism and Frontier*, 145, 152–53, 182, 201–9, 216–19; Hofstra, *Planting of New Virginia*, 278–79; Earle and Hoffman, "Staple Crops and Urban Development," 34. On iron furnaces and forges, see Tate Thompson Brady, "Reports Concerning the History and Locations of Iron Foundries and Furnaces in Virginia and Maryland" (VHS mss 7:3 HD9510 B7298:1); David Curtis Skaggs, "John Semple

and the Development of the Potomac Valley, 1750–1773," in *VMHB* 92 (1984), 282–308; Laura Kamoie, *Neabsco and Occoquan: The Tayloe Family Iron Plantations, 1730–1830* (Prince William, Va.: Prince William Historical Commission, 2003); Frances Robb, "Industry in the Potomac River Valley, 1760–1860" (Ph.D. diss., West Virginia University, 1991), ch. 2; Mitchell, *Commercialism and Frontier*, 202–7; and Ronald Lewis, *Coal, Iron, and Slaves: Industrial Slavery in Maryland and Virginia, 1715–1865* (Westport, Conn.: Greenwood Press, 1979), ch. 2.

36. Mitchell, *Commercialism and Frontier*, 195–96 (quotation), 199–200; Hofstra, *Planting of New Virginia*, 261–64, 270–71.

37. Land, *Dulanys of Maryland*, 252; Mitchell, *Commercialism and Frontier*, 83–84, 192, 195–98; Hofstra, *Planting of New Virginia*, 261–64; John Reps, *Tidewater Towns: City Planning in Colonial Virginia and Maryland* (Williamsburg: Colonial Williamsburg Foundation, 1972), 225.

38. Burnaby, *Travels*, 50 (quotation), 55; *Maryland Gazette*, 31 March 1763; Preisser, "Eighteenth-Century Alexandria," ch. 1 and appendices A, D; Reps, *Tidewater Towns*, 202–13; James Munson, "From Empire to Commonwealth: Alexandria, Virginia, 1749–1780" (Ph.D. diss., University of Maryland, College Park, 1984), ch. 6.

39. Preisser, "Eighteenth-Century Alexandria," chs. 2–3 and appendices C, D; Munson, "From Empire to Commonwealth," ch. 7 (quotation); Reps, *Tidewater Towns*, chs. 9–10; Mitchell, *Commercialism and Frontier*, 219–29.

40. Nicholas Cresswell, *The Journal of Nicholas Cresswell, 1774–1777* (New York: Dial Press, 1923), 161 (quotation); Henry Berkeley, "The Port of Dumphries, Prince William Co., Va.," *WMQ*, 2nd series, 4 (1924), 99–116; Pamela Copeland and Richard Macmaster, *The Five George Masons: Patriots and Planters of Virginia and Maryland* (Charlottesville: University Press of Virginia, 1975), 150–53; Doerflinger, *Vigorous Spirit*, 113–15; Preisser, "Eighteenth-Century Alexandria," 164–66; Reps, *Tidewater Towns*, 243–47, 281–95.

41. Cresswell, *Journal*, 204 (quotation); Account Book, 1782–88, Thomas Turner Papers, VHS mss 2 T85815b; Ted Ruddock, ed., *Travels in the Colonies in 1773–1775, Described in the Letters of William Mylne* (Athens: University of Georgia Press, 1993), 72; T. H. Breen, *Tobacco Culture: The Mentality of the Great Tidewater Planters on the Eve of Revolution* (Princeton: Princeton University Press, 1985), 60–69, 180–82; Lois Green Carr and Lorena Walsh, "Economic Diversification and Labor Organization in the Chesapeake, 1650–1820," in Stephen Innes, ed., *Work and Labor in Early America* (Chapel Hill: University of North Carolina Press, 1982), 166–75; Copeland and Macmaster, *Five George Masons*, 66–67, 95–107; Rhys Isaac, *Landon Carter's Uneasy Kingdom: Revolution and Rebellion on a Virginia Plantation* (New York: Oxford University Press, 2004), ch. 4; Kamoie, *Neabsco and Occoquan*, 60 (figure 18); Jean Lee, *The Price of Nationhood: The American Revolution in Charles County* (New York: W. W. Norton, 1994), 30–32; Preisser, "Eighteenth-Century Alexandria," 111–12.

42. Isaac Weld, *Travels Through the States of North America . . . During the Years 1795, 1796, and 1797*, 3rd ed. (London: J. Stockdale, 1799), 137–56 (quotations on 137–38, 142).

43. Cresswell, *Journal*, 15–26, 268 (quotations on 16, 17, 20, 268).

44. Ibid., 26–48, 51–52 (quotations on 26–28, 47–48, 51).

45. Ibid., 48–50, 60–61, 125, 133, 195–99, 266–67 (quotations on 49, 50, 133).

46. Ibid., 49–50.

Coda. Ahone's Legacy

1. Estimates of forest clearances and sedimentation rates are from Grace Brush, "Forests before and after the Colonial Encounter," in Philip Curtin, Grace Brush, and George Fisher, eds., *Discovering the Chesapeake: The History of an Ecosystem* (Baltimore: Johns Hopkins University Press, 2001), 46–47, 57 (quotation on 40–41), and Robert Mitchell, Warren Hofstra, and Edward Conner, "Reconstructing the Colonial Environment of the Upper Chesapeake Watershed," in ibid., 174. Much of this section is synthesized from the essays in this volume. See also Ruth Harris DeFries, "Sedimentation Patterns in the Potomac Estuary since European Settlement: A Palynological Approach" (Ph.D. diss., Johns Hopkins University, 1981); Steven Stoll, *Larding the Lean Earth: Soil and Society in Nineteenth-Century America* (New York: Hill and Wang, 2002); Steven Davison et al., *Chesapeake Waters: Four Centuries of Controversy, Concern, and Legislation,* 2nd ed. (Centreville, Md.: Tidewater Publishers, 1997), 191 (quotation); Howard Ernst, *Chesapeake Bay Blues: Science, Politics, and the Struggle to Save the Bay* (New York: Rowman & Littlefield, 2003), chs. 2, 4, and p. 168, n. 39, n. 41; Tom Horton, *Bay Country* (Baltimore: Johns Hopkins University Press, 1987), 24–29; Debra Willard, Thomas Cronin, and Stacey Verardo, "Late-Holocene Climate and Ecosystem History from Chesapeake Bay Sediment Cores, USA," *Holocene* 13 (2003), 201–14; and Timothy Silver, *A New Face on the Countryside: Indians, Colonists, and Slaves in the South Atlantic Forests, 1500–1800* (New York: Cambridge University Press, 1990), 165–68.

2. Davison et al., *Chesapeake Waters,* 127 (quotation); Gordon Whitney, *From Coastal Wilderness to Fruited Plain: A History of Environmental Change in Temperate North America, 1500 to the Present* (New York: Cambridge University Press, 1994), 209–26; David Curtis Skaggs, "John Semple and the Development of the Potomac Valley, 1750–1773," *VMHB* 92 (1984), 287–88, 293–95; Robert Mitchell, *Commercialism and Frontier: Perspectives on the Early Shenandoah Valley* (Charlottesville: University Press of Virginia, 1977), 202–7; Frances Robb, "Industry in the Potomac River Valley, 1760–1860" (Ph.D. diss., West Virginia University, 1991), ch. 2; Brush, "Forests before and after the Colonial Encounter," in Curtin, Brush, and Fisher, *Discovering the Chesapeake,* 50–58; Joel Achenbach, *The Grand Idea: George Washington's Potomac and the Race to the West* (New York: Simon & Schuster, 2004), 281–87; Gilbert Gude, *Where the Potomac Begins: A History of the North Branch Valley* (Cabin John, Md.: Seven Locks Press, 1984); Robert Brugger, *Maryland: A Middle Temperament, 1634–1980* (Baltimore: Johns Hopkins University Press, 1988), 336–37; W. H. Burton and A. E. Pinkney, "Yellow Perch Larval Survival in the Zekiah Swamp Watershed (Wicomico River, Maryland), Relative to the Potential Effects of a Coal Ash Storage Facility," *Water, Air, and Soil Pollution* 72 (1994), 235–50; "Western Maryland's North Branch Makes an Impressive Recovery," *Washington Post,* 25 September 2005, E3.

3. Charles Royster, *The Fabulous History of the Dismal Swamp Company: A Story of George Washington's Times* (New York: Knopf, 1999).

4. Ibid., 156 (quotation); Joseph Ellis, *His Excellency George Washington* (New York: Knopf, 2004), 53–54.

5. Achenbach, *Grand Idea*, ch. 5.

6. C. M. Harris, "Washington's Gamble, L'Enfant's Dream: Politics, Design, and the Founding of the National Capital," *WMQ* 56 (1999), 542; John Reps, *Washington on View: The Nation's Capital since 1790* (Chapel Hill: University of North Carolina Press, 1991), ch. 1.

7. Harris, "Washington's Gamble"; Sarah Luria, *Capital Speculations: Writing and Building Washington D.C.* (Durham: University of New Hampshire Press, 2006), ch. 1 (quotation on 6).

8. Harris, "Washington's Gamble," 542–43; Luria, *Capital Speculations*, ch. 1; Reps, *Washington on View*, chs. 1–2.

9. Reps, *Washington on View* (quotations on 68, 108). On the history of canals and railroads up the Potomac, see Achenbach, *Grand Idea*, chs. 11–13.

10. Horton, *Bay Country*, passim; "Potomac Basin Facts," Interstate Commission on the Potomac River Basin, www.potomacriver.org (accessed 5 May 2006); Achenbach, *Grand Idea*, 290–91 (quotation).

11. The most visible exception to this is the National Museum of the American Indian, on the National Mall, which opened in 2004. Though national and even hemispheric in its coverage, the museum does acknowledge the Native peoples of the Potomac. Though much less visible, there are two Piscataway-Conoy museums in southern Maryland that are open by appointment. For the most part, however, local historic sites deal with Native people only in passing.

12. David Hackett Fischer and James Kelly, *Bound Away: Virginia and the Westward Movement* (Charlottesville: University Press of Virginia, 2000).

13. T. S. Eliot, *Four Quartets* (New York: Harcourt, Brace and Co., 1943), 39 (quotation).

14. These developments can be followed in the *Potomac River Reporter*, a free newsletter issued by the Interstate Commission on the Potomac River Basin.

15. Gabrielle Tayac, "'So Intermingled with This Earth': A Piscataway Oral History" in *Northeast Indian Quarterly* 5 (Winter 1988), 4–17, (quotations on 4, 7); Tayac, "'To Speak with One Voice': Supratribal American Indian Collective Identity Incorporation among the Piscataway, 1500–1998" (Ph.D. diss., Harvard University, 1999); Christian Feest, "Nanticoke and Neighboring Tribes," in Bruce Trigger, ed., *Handbook of North American Indians*, vol. 15, *Northeast* (Washington, D.C.: Smithsonian Institution, 1978), 245–48; Helen Rountree, *Pocahontas's People: The Powhatan Indians of Virginia through Four Centuries* (Norman: University of Oklahoma Press, 1990), 216; Frank Speck, *The Nanticoke and Conoy Indians: With a review of Linguistic Material from Manuscript and Living Sources* (Wilmington, Del.: Historical Society of Delaware, 1927).

16. W. G. Hoskins, *The Making of the English Landscape* (London: Hodder and Stoughton, 1955), 13.

17. William Strachey, *The Historie of Travell into Virginia Britania* (1612), ed. Louis B. Wright and Virginia Freund, Works Issued by the Hakluyt Society, 2nd series, no. 105 (London: Hakluyt Society, 1953), 102–3.